BETWEEN EUROPE AND ASIA

PITT SERIES IN RUSSIAN AND EAST EUROPEAN STUDIES

Jonathan Harris, Editor

BETWEEN EUROPE & ASIA

The Origins, Theories, and
Legacies of Russian Eurasianism

Edited by

Mark Bassin, Sergey Glebov,
& Marlene Laruelle

University of Pittsburgh Press

The editors would like to express their deep appreciation to the Baltic Sea Foundation (Stockholm), whose financial support helped make this publication possible.

Published by the University of Pittsburgh Press, Pittsburgh, Pa., 15260
Copyright © 2015, University of Pittsburgh Press
Manufactured in the United States of America
Printed on acid-free paper
10 9 8 7 6 5 4 3 2 1

ISBN 13: 978-0-8229-6366-0
ISBN 10: 0-8229-6366-3

Cataloging-in-Publication data is available at the Library of Congress.

CONTENTS

BETWEEN EUROPE AND ASIA

WHAT WAS EURASIANISM
AND WHO MADE IT?

Mark Bassin, Sergey Glebov, & Marlene Laruelle

HISTORIANS have long noted the tortured path of Russia's self-identification vis-à-vis Europe, the West, or modernity on the one hand, and the organization of the domestic political community on the other. At times, the Russian Empire appeared as a European imperium with a civilizing mission in Asia and elsewhere, and at other times it was imagined as an anti-Western force, a bulwark of Romantic visions of spirituality opposed to Western individualism and mechanistic relations.[1] This multifaceted set of oppositions in Russian history—empire versus nation, Europe versus Asia, and modernity versus antimodern utopias—has often intermingled in curious, sometimes fascinating ways, complicating the notion of Russian history in the comparative framework of European modernity. Perhaps nowhere were these complications as visible as in the doctrine and movement of Eurasianism. The focus of this volume is to study Eurasianism from different disciplinary and thematic perspectives.

Scholars have treated Eurasianism as a geographical ideology, a conservative movement akin to German antimodernists in the Weimar period and beyond, as a form of Russian nationalism and as a modernist response to Russia's imperial entanglements. It has also been approached as a scholarly ideology, based on Russian importation and reworking of various European products, from the German idea of the *Landschaftseinheit* or territorial complex to Saussurian linguistics.[2] Individual participants in the Eurasianist movement have received scholarly attention for their contributions to linguistics, history, economics, geography, philosophy, and religious studies. Yet the complexity of the movement and its ideas—elaborated from a variety of vantage points and informed by a range of intellectual lineages and individual circumstances—requires the collective effort of many scholars. This volume seeks to fill the void and elucidate current research on Eurasianism in Russia, Europe, the United States, and Japan from a truly interdisciplinary perspective.

Through this perspective we hope to approach the many connections and entanglements of Eurasianism as a movement and a set of ideas. The main goal of our volume is to go beyond the narratives produced by the Eurasianists themselves and to reconstruct multiple contexts within which the movement and the ideas functioned, to which they responded, and which they generated. In doing so, we also extend our inquiry beyond the history of the movement proper: we hope to trace the origins of Eurasianism in the intellectual and cultural dislocations of imperial Russia, look at the émigré and exile contexts of the production of Eurasianist ideas, and follow Eurasianist influences in time and space, from Japan to the late USSR. In offering this exploration of Eurasianism's externalities, we aspire to contribute to a range of debates on historical issues in Russia and beyond, from diaspora nationalism to the interwar history of global cultural entanglements, and from Russian responses to war and revolution to late Soviet developments.

Eurasianism: People

The Eurasianist doctrine was elaborated by Russian émigrés, refugees from the revolutionary turmoil of 1917 and the following Civil War, when the founders of the movement coalesced in the Bulgarian capital in the summer and fall of 1920.[3] These founders were Prince Nikolai Sergeevich Trubetskoi, a scion of one of Russia's most aristocratic families and later a renowned linguist; Petr Petrovich Suvchinskii, a cultural entrepreneur, connoisseur of music, and publisher; Petr Nikolaevich Savitskii, a young and energetic student of Russia's leading liberal politician and scholar Petr Struve; Georgii Vasil'evich Florovskii, a Church historian and theologian; and Prince Andrei Aleksandrovich Lieven, a poet and eventually an Orthodox priest who descended from the Moscow-based Orthodox branch of the renowned Baltic German noble family. Fresh with experiences of the catastrophic collapse of the imperial state and society, this group engaged in intense discussions of the causes and outcomes of the Russian Civil War and pondered the problem of the Russian Revolution. Eurasianism's first texts in the early 1920s repre-

Mark Bassin, Sergey Glebov, & Marlene Laruelle

sented an immediate result of these discussions, informed, of course, by the range of intellectual fields that each of the Eurasianists represented.[4]

Over the course of the next decade, the group expanded to include individuals both well known and obscure. Prince Dmitrii Petrovich Sviatopolk-Mirsky (known as D. S. Mirsky in the West), a literary critic and lecturer at the London School of Slavonic and East European Studies under Bernard Pares, joined the movement.[5] In 1923 Georgii Vladimirovich Vernadsky (son of the famous Soviet scientist Vladimir Vernadsky and later known in the United States as George Vernadsky, a Yale historian of Russia) began cooperating with the movement. At the same time, Georgii Vasil'evich Florovskii, one of the initial founders, distanced himself from Eurasianism. Lieven, who seems to have played an important role in the early Eurasianist discussions, ceased his participation as well.

Despite Eurasianism's strategic revisioning of Russia's cultural affiliation and its insistence on the importance of Asian and nomadic roots of the Russian state, few non-Russians actually joined the movement. Of these, Erzhen Khara-Davan (Khara-Davaev), a Kalmyk physician evacuated with Wrangel's troops to Yugoslavia, became the most important contributor, writing a book on Chingis Khan.[6] Iakov Bromberg, a Jewish conservative, attempted to offer a Jewish perspective on the reimagining of Eurasia as a future alternative to America, where Jews allegedly lost their Jewishness.[7] However, after emigrating to the United States, Bromberg severed contacts with the Eurasianists and ceased publications in the Eurasianist vein. To be sure, both Suvchinskii and Savitskii cherished their Ukrainian heritage. Both displayed interest in Ukrainian architecture, music, history, and folklore. Savitskii even wrote under the pseudonym of Stepan Lubenskii after his seventeenth-century ancestor Stepan Savitskii, a colonel of the Cossack host of Lubno. Yet, this flirtation with a Ukrainian legacy did not contradict the pan-Russian ideology of Eurasianism: apparently, both Savitskii and Suvchinskii easily combined their loyalty to the "Little Russian" identity of the Russified gentry with a commitment to Russia's imperial state and society.[8]

In 1922, a group of monarchist officers of the former White armies joined the movement. It was led by Baron Aleksandr Vladimirovich Meller-Zakomel'skii, a wealthy émigré, musician, and *homme de la bohème*. Meller later moved on to become the leader of Russian émigré Nazis. The second organizer of that officer group, Petr Semenovich Arapov, a relative of General Wrangel, became a Eurasianist leader on a par with the founders. Arapov was deeply involved in émigré politics, and was likely an agent of the Soviet secret services. His participation in the movement helped to mire Eurasianism in a web of underground activities of the secret services and émigré political organizations. Arapov also helped convert Petr Nikolaevich Malevskii-Malevich, a son of the late imperial Russian ambassador to Japan and a former colonel in Wrangel's army, to the Eurasianist movement.[9]

Malevskii's joining of Eurasianism was important: his contacts in British high society secured the commitment of Henry Norman Spalding, a wealthy philanthropist and theologian, to fund the Eurasianist movement. Unaware of Eurasianism's many contradictions, Spalding believed that the movement could help distract elites among Britain's own colonial populations from Bolshevism and provide them instead with a Christian ideology. Spalding's generous funding fueled Eurasianist publications, meetings, and travel, and provided the material base for the expanding movement. In the course of the 1920s, Spalding's money enabled the Eurasianists to travel, organize conferences and ongoing seminars, publish annual almanacs and numerous books and brochures, and finally, to establish a newspaper, *Eurasia*, in 1928 in the Parisian suburb of Clamart.

Within the movement, several "directions" coexisted, often uneasily. Savitskii and Trubetskoi concerned themselves mostly with the scholarly (and sometimes religious) aspects of teaching. Suvchinskii and Mirsky worked on the literary, artistic, and musical explications of Eurasianism. In 1926 they established a literary journal, *Versty*, which, although not formally part of the Eurasianist publishing empire, pursued a Eurasianist editorial policy. Arapov, Malevskii-Malevich, and Arsenii Aleksandrovich Zaitsev (the latter yet another former officer who joined the movement) focused on Eurasianist politics, converting the émigré youth and Soviet leadership to the principles of Eurasianism. These activities, in particular, mired Eurasianism in a web of connections with the fake monarchist organization, Trest, established by the Soviet secret services to infiltrate the emigration. Some activists of Eurasianism—Arapov and Iurii Aleksandrovich Artamonov in particular—became Soviet agents. The Eurasianist group even included as its member a cadre officer of the State Political Directorate (GPU) Aleksandr Alekseevich Langovoi.

To be sure, these divisions were not clearly drawn. The scholarly and literary participants in the movement never denied the importance of the political work, and officers and agents often took part in the discussions of Eurasianist theory, sometimes, as in the case of Arapov, producing interesting ideas. Equally unclear were the boundaries between the Eurasianists and other intellectuals and activists of the Russian emigration. While the ideological power within the movement—exercised mainly through editorial policies—was in the hands of Trubetskoi, Suvchinskii, Savitskii, and, to a lesser degree, Arapov and Malevskii-Malevich, the movement had numerous adherents and sympathizers who either did not completely follow the policies of the editorial troika or were deemed suspicious by the Eurasianists. For instance, in

Mark Bassin, Sergey Glebov, & Marlene Laruelle

1925 the Eurasianists were joined by Lev Platonovich Karsavin, a medieval-ist scholar, theologian, and philosopher, who helped to elaborate some of the Eurasianist ideas on the revolution, the Orthodox Church, and on "symphonic personality."[10] Karsavin's participation was imposed on the movement by Su-vchinskii (who subsequently married Karsavin's daughter Marianna) and was only grudgingly accepted by Savitskii and Trubetskoi.

George Vernadsky was a protege of Savitskii but his historical studies were dismissed out of hand by Mirsky and Suvchinskii. Petr Mikhailovich Bitsilli, a brilliant historian of the Middle Ages, who published an original and farsighted article on the history of the Old World from the perspective of the East in a Eurasianist collection, was dismissed by Trubetskoi as an untransformed Russian "intelligent" and later ceased cooperation with the movement. The personal connections of the leaders of Eurasianism often drew into the movement very different personalities from a variety of fields: Suv-chinskii's discussions of Eurasianism regularly attracted and excited mu-sicians such as Igor Stravinsky, Vladimir Dukel'skii (Vernon Duke), Artur Lur'e, and, likely, Sergei Prokofiev. Arguably, this influence can be detected in their works.[11] Suvchinskii's relations with and influence on Marina Tsvetaeva and Aleksei Remizov are still underexplored and need further elaboration, but it is clear they were significant. A sizable literature is emerging on the encoun-ter between Trubetskoi and Savitskii on the one hand, and Roman O. Jakob-son on the other, which had important consequences for the emergence of structuralism. Practically unknown are the circumstances under which Pavel Chelishchev, later one of the most exhibited surrealists, was drawn to Eur-asianism and illustrated the early Eurasianist publications. His correspon-dence with Suvchinskii extended over several decades. This is by no means a complete catalogue of Eurasian influence, and thus readers will appreciate that the present volume only scratches the surface of the phenomenal role of Eurasianism and Eurasianists in twentieth-century intellectual history.

Eurasianism's Contexts

Both contemporaries and latter-day scholars have often described Eur-asianism as a "reaction" to the dislocations produced by the First World War, the Russian Revolution, and the Civil War, and the remaking of the Russian imperial state as a socialist federation of nations. Indeed, changes on the map of Europe following the defeat of the Central Powers were reflected in multiple visions, both political and geographic, of the postwar world. Woodrow Wilson and Vladimir Lenin famously agreed on the principle of "self-determination," and however different their understanding of that principle might have been, confirmed the arrival of the nation-state as a norm of the organization of the political space.[12] At the same time, Richard Coudenhove-Kalergi, a Habsburg aristocrat and Czechoslovak citizen, envisioned the United States of Europe as the end goal of his pan-Europa movement.[13] The former Russian Empire was transformed into a heretofore unprecedented agglomeration of cultural and linguistic "nations" held together by a political party subscribing to a utopian communist ideology.[14] This transformation was often predicated on support for cultural and linguistic if not political nationalism of the USSR's many nationalities. The anticolonial movements grew in power and appeal and heralded the arrival of the former colonial peoples on the world-historical scene.

European intellectuals often responded to these profound changes with a sense of cultural pessimism and envisioned the decline of European civilization. In Germany, "Conservative Revolutionaries" such as Arthur Moeller van den Bruck sought a return to some primordial and spiritual values (without, however, giving up on modernity's technological achievements). Oswald Spengler, who was perhaps even closer in spirit to Eurasianism, offered a vision of the decline of the West that became a hallmark of European fin-de-siècle *Kulturpessimismus*. Eurasianist ideology shared the pessimistic assessments of Europe's future but it predicted—rather optimistically—the rise of Eurasia as a potential leader of the colonized peoples of the Orient in their revolt against the declining "vandalistic Kulturtraegerschaft"[15] of Europe.

Eurasia's Many Facets

Eurasianism's many participants and creators brought to the movement a range of interests, ideas, and intellectual lineages. So different were their views that at times one is tempted to dismiss the movement's unity and instead to speak of several Eurasianist streams of thought. Yet some very fundamental premises were shared across multiple divides of the movement and they formed the specific points of departure for the young founders of the movement in 1920–1921.

Among these shared premises was the centrality of the Orthodox faith for the recuperation of Russia after the catastrophe of the revolution. Taking stock of the religious and philosophical efflorescence in fin-de-siècle Russian culture (itself a part of the pan-European rebellion against positivism), the Eurasianist thinkers defined themselves vis-à-vis the great writers and philosophers, such as Nikolai Berdiaev, Petr Struve, Sergei Bulgakov, and others. The latter, in the view of the Eurasianists, failed to bridge the gap between the people and the intelligentsia as well as to produce a viable national ideology. Thus they failed to offer an alternative to the Bolsheviks' "elemental" uprising. The Eurasianists often attributed this failure to a liberal experimentation with Orthodoxy, and the solution was thus seen in a return to a conservatism that remained true to dogmas of the Church and its visions of Christianity. It is important to note that, although the philosophers of the

Mark Bassin, Sergey Glebov, & Marlene Laruelle

prerevolutionary decades saw Orthodoxy as a part of world Christianity, the Eurasianists were not just anti-ecumenical—anti-Western interpretations of Orthodoxy formed the kernel of their ideology.[16]

This focus on Orthodoxy in Eurasianism was interwoven with yet another important theme inherited from the prerevolutionary cultural fermentation. Toward the end of the nineteenth century an "Oriental" theme began to develop in imperial Russia, which came to see Russia's Asian connections as an important, indeed crucial, aspect of national identity.[17] To be sure, this theme was based on at least a century-long flirtation with the ideas of Russia's unique national path in Europe precisely because of its Asian encounters with the steppe peoples. Especially after the French Revolution, when Russia's heretofore extremely successful absolutist Europeanization turned out to be at odds with Europe's most progressive ideas of liberty and citizenship, these notions began to gain followers among the educated public. Nikolai Mikhailovich Karamzin, the founder of Russia's modern historical writing, famously proclaimed that Moscow, whose princes united the Orthodox principalities of the eastern Slavs into a rising state in the fourteenth to sixteenth centuries, owed its greatness to the khans. Alexander Herzen, the great liberal and Romantic thinker and father of Russian socialism, often viewed Russia's Asian connections as a possible resource for a more just society. But after the Crimean War and the Russian colonial acquisition of Central Asia, this interest in the Asian connections of Russia's own past became intertwined with the ideas of Russia's Europeanizing and civilizing mission in the newly acquired territories. Various geopolitical and military entanglements—such as the incorporation of the Amur region in the 1850s, the Russo-Turkish War of 1877–1878, or the construction of the Eastern Chinese Railroad in Manchuria and the ensuing Russo-Japanese War of 1904–1905—have contributed powerfully to the fascination of the Russian elites with their own Orient.[18] Often, as many contributions to this volume demonstrate, this fascination was paralleled by a notion that Russia's imperial projects were somehow better grounded or more benevolent specifically because of its more intimate familiarity with Asia.

However, for the classical Eurasianism of the 1920s, the literary and philosophical variations of this interest in Asia were probably the most significant. The great Russian philosopher Vladimir Solov'ev saw the Orient—especially the "yellow" East of China—as a powerful metaphor for a soulless and mechanistic European civilization. His apocalyptic visions of the end of European civilization involved a clash with the "yellow race." This theme, however important, did not become dominant in late imperial literature. Instead, Alexander Blok, perhaps the most important poet of Russia's Silver Age, reconceptualized the Asian theme in the context of poetic prophesies of the Russian Revolution. For Blok, the end of the philistine bourgeois culture of Europe was in sight, and it was the Russian peasant masses, elemental and Asian, that had the ability to destroy the decaying world of the bourgeois and to unleash a process of rejuvenation of humankind. Blok was a central figure in the emergence of Eurasianist thought: Nikolai Trubetskoi wrote about Blok to Jakobson, and Suvchinskii published Blok's poem *The Twelve* with his own foreword in 1920. When Petr Struve criticized the new movement as "Populist" (*narodnicheskoe*), he meant exactly this belief, shared by the Eurasianists, that the Russian masses had some yet unrevealed elemental potential.[19]

This religious and cultural interpretation of Eurasia was complemented by the notion of a historically constituted cultural, ethnic, and political world. To the Eurasianists, their homeland was heir not to the medieval principalities of Kievan Rus' but to the steppe empire of Chingis Khan and his heirs. The Mongols were important for the Eurasianists for several reasons. First, they were treated as the first unifiers of the Eurasian space, whose conquests and empire building provided Eurasia for the first time with a state tradition embracing the entire "continent." Second, their empire building fit in very well with the idea of Russia's Asian encounters discussed above: their intervention was deemed crucial in saving Russia and its Orthodox identity from the ever-aggressive Catholic West. Finally, but not least important, the Eurasianists believed that the Mongols, by humiliating and destroying the Slavic principalities, had created the conditions for the emergence of a deeply religious culture of Muscovy, in which both the upper and lower strata of the people shared the same totalizing worldview spanning high culture and everyday life. In this, the Mongols appeared to be similar to the Bolsheviks, and the Eurasianists expected a new religious culture to emerge in Russia under the communist yoke.

This notion of a new religious culture ready to emerge in Bolshevik Russia was strangely paired with other kinds of hope pinned on the lost homeland. Thus, for Suvchinskii and Mirsky Soviet Eurasia was a place of the new creativity as opposed to the dying creativity of the uprooted émigrés. In part, their initiative to establish the journal *Versty* was inspired by the desire to publish Soviet authors. The politics of cultural production that these two entrepreneurs pursued was largely based on a turn toward the Soviet Union as the new incarnation of Russia–Eurasia. Contacts with Maxim Gorky were established, and, finally, Mirsky returned to the USSR, where he perished in Stalin's camps. The pro-Soviet turn of Suvchinskii and Mirsky involved other people as well, most notably the circle around the poetess Marina Tsvetaeva and her husband Sergei Efron. It is likely that Efron's work for the Soviet secret services began during his association with Suvchinskii and Mirsky.

On the other hand, the "scholars"—Trubetskoi, Savitskii, and Jakobson, the latter joining the Eurasianist scholarly enterprise but refusing to adhere to the movement's political aspects—saw Eurasia past, present, and future as the locus and main object of a new kind of science. Opposed to the positivist and "atomistic" interpretations of traditional scholarship, the Eurasianist scholars attempted to construe Eurasia's totality through a range of visible phenomena in language, culture, history, geography, and so on. As Patrick Sériot noted, discoveries abounded: a linguistic boundary marking the presence or absence of palatalized consonants or tonality "coincided" with most of the imagined Eurasian "continent" and sharply delineated it from Latin Europe; climatic regularities established a North–South axis instead of the traditional civilizational East–West one, and so on.[20] Trubetskoi elaborated a view of Eurasia as an ethnocultural unity, Savitskii focused on the regularities of landscape and climate, whereas Jakobson produced a curious book on the Eurasian language union (a concept first offered by Trubetskoi in 1923). Following in the footsteps of these scholars, George Vernadsky produced a series of works dealing with Russian history from the perspective of the East. While Vernadsky's work was less imaginative than the brilliant ideas of Bitsilli (who likely pioneered the concept of "world history"), the former remained the only professional Eurasianist historian producing full-length monographs.

Last but not least, the Eurasianist movement offered an unusually early critique of Eurocentrism. Largely pursued by Nikolai Trubetskoi, this critique suggested that European notions of progress and civilization were nothing more than a cynical and self-interested cover for colonialist and aggressive designs maintained through ideological means woven into European scholarship in history, ethnography, philosophy, and so forth. Radically dissociating themselves from what they perceived as colonialist Europe, the Eurasianist thinkers argued that Eurasia itself was a part of the colonial and semicolonial group of countries, along with Turkey, China, India, Iran, and others. Moreover, they recast Eurasia as a potential leader of the colonial world in its upcoming battle against colonialist Europe. Strangely and paradoxically, Eurasianist thinkers linked this association with the colonial world with the neo-Romantic critique of Europe as a standardizing cultural force that eliminates cultural difference through its mechanistic and leveling modernity. Anticolonialist Eurasia was to become a bulwark on the path of this historical force.

Perhaps it was this paradoxical combination of revolutionary radicalism and conservatism that attracted so many diverse people to Eurasianism. The peculiar alliance between the aristocratic, Orthodox, and extremely conservative Trubetskoi and the left-leaning enthusiast of the avant-garde Jakobson was based on a shared distaste for the established cultural hierarchies in the production of knowledge. Trubetskoi detested Europe as a source of revolution and mechanistic progress, and Jakobson detested it as a bulwark of bourgeois conformity.[21] Both agreed on the vision of innovative Eurasia as an alternative, even if they disagreed on some crucial details of the construction of that alternative.

State of the Art

Linked to the collapse of the Soviet Union and the need for a new intellectual framework to understand Eurasian space, research on Eurasianism blossomed in the first half of the 1990s, shedding light on a movement that until then had given rise to few works, with the exception of the precursory research done by Otto Böss,[22] or else it had been evoked in historiographical works on the Mongol yoke,[23] the Russian emigration,[24] or Russian Messianism.[25] The 1990s and 2000s witnessed a revival of works on Eurasianism, from viewpoints mainly linked to political philosophy, the history of ideas, or geopolitics. The Eurasianist movement has been studied as a political philosophy and ideology of the nation,[26] as a geopolitical theory of space,[27] as a reflection on Europe and Russia's colonial situation,[28] as a theory of the conservative revolution,[29] and in its interaction with structuralism and the Prague Linguistic Circle.[30] The biographies of the main Eurasianist founding fathers or Soviet figures such as Vernadsky, Savitskii, and Lev Nikolaevich Gumilev have grown in recent years, partly due to the opening of the Soviet archives.[31] The roots of Eurasianism have also been decrypted by the renewal of research on the Slavophiles, on the so-called pan-Asiatic trend,[32] and on the Scythian and Aryan myths.[33]

The originality of this volume consists in its exploration of hitherto ignored domains of the history of the Eurasian movement. The first two chapters in the collection address the origins of the movement, both in the Slavophile and Orientalist traditions. Chapters 3–5 explain Eurasianist theories and their intellectual novelty. Individual lives of Eurasianist thinkers are the subjects of chapters 6–8, and the final two chapters discuss Eurasianism's filiation in time with the figure of Lev Gumilev, and in space with the Japanese reception of Eurasianist ideas. Using this novel approach, the volume aims to make a new and decisive contribution to furthering knowledge about this intellectual current.

Precis

Our volume begins with the historical background of the Eurasianist movement. Olga Maiorova's contribution studies the roots of Eurasianism in Alexander Herzen, the founder of Russian socialism and populism, and, apparently, one of the first intellectuals to enunciate certain ideas that were much later to become central constructs in the Eurasianist denunciation of the West. Maiorova's contribution offers a better understanding of the long arch of proto-Eurasianist thinking in Russian history and sheds light on both the Slavophile connections of the Eurasianists and their own interest in Herzen (somewhat paradoxical given how much the Eurasianists detested Russia's revolutionary and democratic intelligentsia). Vera Tolz's work explores scholars of the Orient in late imperial Russia and, in a corrective to Edward Said's sweeping generalizations, argues that Russian Oriental scholarship was often critical of "othering" and maintained fruitful and productive intellectual contacts with representatives of the very people it studied. In this, Tolz sees an intellectual climate conducive to the Eurasianist reshaping of Russia's identity vis-à-vis Asia and Europe. As a matter of fact, some leading Eurasianists (such as Savitskii) followed Russian Oriental studies closely and took the contributions of scholars such as Vasilii V. Bartol'd very seriously.

Three contributions to this volume propose general frameworks for the study of Eurasianism. Sergey Glebov's chapter traces the emergence of the Eurasianists' anticolonialist rhetoric in the reception of evolutionism in Russia and suggests that one of the main sources for Eurasianist anticolonialism was prerevolutionary debates on the organization of the Russian Empire's political space. Marlene Laruelle offers an interpretation of Eurasianism as a geographic ideology, rooted in complex processes of spatializing Russian identity, whereas Stefan Wiederkehr proposes viewing the doctrine as a form of Popperian historicism. The Eurasianist understanding of history was as crucial as geography to the temporal orientation of the Eurasianist project. As the Eurasianists attempted to reorient Eurasia spatially (away from Europe) and temporally (by excluding it from the allegedly universal standards of progress and civilization), they articulated a thorough and militant critique of evolutionism and attempted to develop a new holistic philosophy of sciences, based on geography and "personology."

In several studies of classical Eurasianism, contributors to the volume look at different aspects of the Eurasianist doctrine through the life and works of individual participants. Igor Torbakov presents the case of George Vernadsky and his encounters with Eurasianism as a professional historian. Martin Beisswenger explores Petr Savitskii and makes a case for the importance of Savitskii's dissertation, "Metaphysics of Economy," and its roots in fin-de-siècle Russian philosophy, especially that of Sergei Bulgakov. Beisswenger presents a convincing picture of a thinker who linked economics and religion in one holistic teaching, framed in an overall reference to the Eurasianist project. Harsha Ram takes up the underexplored topic of connections between the Eurasianist ideology and Russian modernism and suggests that Roman Jakobson's encounter with Eurasianism, as reflected in his changing views on the futurist poet Velimir Khlebnikov, signified less an attempt to recuperate the destabilizing strategies of late imperial modernism and more an encounter with the new discursive realities of interwar Europe.

In the final chapters of the volume, we take up the cases of Eurasianism's influences over time and space. While Eurasianism's influences beyond Russia still await researchers, Hama Yukiko studies how Japanese intellectuals received and used Eurasianist doctrines in the context of interwar Japanese politics and expansionism. Mark Bassin considers the work of Lev Nikolaevich Gumilev, who remains a crucial figure in the Soviet and post-Soviet reception of Eurasianism, and studies Gumilev's uneven reception by Russian nationalists, at a time when yet another imperial venture was coming to an end.

Together these chapters cover the complexity of the Eurasianist movement and thought and the movement's unusually central location at the intersection of late imperial Russian and Soviet history; reactions to decolonization; studies of literary modernism; and global imperial entanglements. We offer this volume in the hope that it will stimulate further productive discussions of the history of this fascinating phenomenon.

1

A REVOLUTIONARY AND THE EMPIRE

Alexander Herzen and Russian Discourse on Asia

Olga Maiorova

RUSSIAN educated society, a product of Peter the Great's Westernizing reforms, learned to look at the East through European eyes. From the eighteenth century onward, Russian philosophers, poets, and painters borrowed
Western stereotypes of the East, embracing both ends of their evaluative
spectrum—a fascination with the exotic Orient and a condemnation of what
was conventionally labeled as Asiatic despotism, stagnation, and backwardness. Though the European vision of the East was widely accepted by Russians, they could not feel completely comfortable with the Western discourse
of superiority over Asia, knowing that for Europe Russia itself belonged to
the Orient. The eastward expansion of the Romanov Empire also provoked
complex responses to the question of what Asia meant for Russia—responses
that sometimes deviated from Western stereotypes. When imperial explorers,
bureaucrats, and educators came into direct contact with Bashkirs, Kazakhs,
and Turkmen, the standard European notion of the "civilizing mission" began
to strike them as problematic: whereas Russian state institutions, high culture, and modern technologies were undoubtedly seen as superior to those of
Asia, the ordinary Russian people, as many observed, displayed deep affinities with their eastern neighbors and were themselves not "civilized" enough.[1]
As a result, many writers—scholars in particular—had serious reservations

about framing the indigenous peoples of the empire's Asian periphery as a colonial "other."[2]

Despite these challenges, however, the mainstream of Russia's intellectual discourse, as most scholars concur, functioned within the framework of Western Orientalism—with occasional deviations—until the turn of the twentieth century when, under the influence of two late nineteenth-century religious philosophers, Konstantin Leont'ev and especially Vladimir Solov'ev, a more ambivalent vision of the East took shape and found striking expression in literature. The most prominent symbolist and futurist poets (Alexander Blok, Andrei Bely, and Velimir Klebnikov after them) began to cherish Russia's unique, if traumatic, ties with its Asian neighbors as a source of the nation's true identity and future glory, and the fulfillment of its historical mission.[3] This article seeks to show, however, that well-articulated efforts to depart from the Western paradigm can be discerned in Russian intellectual discourse much earlier. It traces this alternative perspective back to the middle of the nineteenth century, when Alexander Herzen, a revolutionary émigré and an overwhelmingly popular political essayist in his day, issued his scathing criticism of European civilization and began to dismantle the conventional East–West binary in order to elaborate a non-European—or rather anti-European—discourse on the Orient and to recast Russian self-definition with regard to Asia.

Though Herzen's effort to reconceptualize the East came at the conclusion of his career, it nonetheless deserves close study, given his profound contribution to the formation of the intelligentsia's mentality.[4] If any one person could be said to have set the agenda for Russian mid-nineteenth-century intellectual discourse, it was Herzen. A great writer and author of a classic autobiography, a key contributor to the philosophical discussions of the 1840s, an early Russian socialist, and passionate advocate of political freedom, Herzen took it as his mission to undermine the regime. In the 1850s and 1860s he flooded all literate Russia—from the Winter Palace to the provincial secondary schools—with subversive writings and periodicals (published in his Free Russian Press operating abroad). As I hope to demonstrate, Herzen's shifting vision of Asia offers an insight into the complex dynamic of Russia's perception of its eastern neighbors—a dynamic that developed in response to the basic ambiguity of the empire–nation nexus in Russia, a country with fluid boundaries between metropolis and colonies and an often murky understanding of how the titular people differed from the subject ones. Herzen contributed substantially to the revision of Eurocentric approaches to both Russia and the East—a revision that would find its most radical implementation much later, in the Eurasianist movement.

Reconsidering the West–East Dichotomy

By the time Herzen emerged on the literary scene, two major modes of depicting the East were already well-established in Russia. From the reign of Catherine the Great well into the nineteenth century, satirists juxtaposed the Russian regime with that of China or Persia in order to attack Russian despotism and reveal the shortcomings of their own country. They were of course familiar with Montesquieu's *Persian Letters* (1721) and with the tradition built on this work by the generations of European writers who painted satirical portraits of their societies by likening them to Asia. As for the second mode of perceiving the Orient, it was also during Catherine's reign—and a direct result of her personal taste—that Moscow and Petersburg aristocrats began to share Enlightenment Europe's passion for the exotic and admiration of the Orient as a picturesque and diverting realm. In the nineteenth century, Russia's fascination with the Orient increased with the beginning of its acquisitions in the Caucasus and, most important, with the ascent of Romantic poetry, which fed this mood by offering a vision of the East as a locus of creative imagination, emotional generosity, wisdom, heroism, and even freedom. It was the Europe-wide Romantic engagement with "primitive cultures" that prompted some Russian writers to go so far as to convert their homeland's links with Asia into an asset for Russia's own identity.[5]

In the 1830s and the 1840s, as the Russian philosophy of history was taking shape, Russia's proximity to the East became grist for speculations about its future. Russian thinkers now perceived its location between Europe and Asia as a manifestation of their nation's unique destiny or tragic fate. It was Petr Chaadaev who opened his first "Philosophical Letter" (written in 1829–1831, and published in 1836) with a spatial metaphor of Russia cast in negative terms: "We are neither of the West nor of the East." Chaadaev designed this maxim to underscore one of his main points: Russia's long centuries of interaction with its eastern neighbors—particularly the pernicious Mongol yoke (of the thirteenth to fifteenth centuries)—had proved fatal to the country's progress and led to its disappearance from world history.[6] Chaadaev's bitter conclusions provoked intellectual responses throughout the nineteenth century.

In refuting his ideas, the Westernizers took Russia's European identity for granted and glorified Peter the Great for transforming Russia into a modern European state. Vissarion Belinsky, the most prominent literary critic of the day, claimed that Peter's reforms made it possible for the nation to revive and evolve, since Peter had restored Russia's natural ties with Europe, which had been forcibly cut off by the Mongol invaders.[7] The Westernizers envisioned Russia more fully joining with Europe in its progressive developments. To emphatically demarcate Russia from Asia, they embraced the Western notion of the Orient as Europe's "other"—a realm of despotism, stagnation, indolence, religious fanaticism, and stifled individuality. Hegel's philosophy of history—to which the Westernizers passionately adhered—informed this vision of the East. Meanwhile the Slavophiles—determined opponents of the Westernizers—fostered anti-European sentiments and defined Russian national identity by tracing its roots to pre-Petrine political institutions, Byzantine Orthodoxy, and Slavic indigenous culture. Despite their paramount disagreements with the Westernizers, the Slavophiles embraced the same conventional assumption of Russia's superiority over the East and carefully avoided identifying their country as part of the Orient. Articulated in the 1840s, the Westernizers' and Slavophiles' views by no means exhausted the range of visions of Russia and renderings of the Russia–Asia nexus, which emerged in later years. Yet the Westernizer–Slavophile controversy played a formative role in shaping the major subsequent paradigms of Russian national self-perception. Almost all thinkers divided along the lines of this dichotomy, although only a handful of them subscribed to the classical versions of these schemes as articulated in the 1840s. Scholars, journalists, bureaucrats, and political figures who were ideologically closer to Westernism tended to consider Russia an agent of European civilization vis-à-vis the Orient and viewed their country's past as that of an outpost of Christianity defending the West from the destructive Asiatic hordes.[8] Those who instead shared some Slavophile assumptions envisioned Russia as a unique nation destined to spread its own civilization and thus naturally to absorb all non-Slavic nationalities of the empire.[9] As profoundly as these constructs differed, they nonetheless concurred in positioning Russia as superior to and different from the Orient, even while acknowledging that Russians had internalized some distinctively Oriental features.[10]

As a confirmed Westernizer, in the beginning of his career Herzen fully accepted the emphatically negative image of the East. For him, as for other Westernizers of the 1840s, it was always the East that epitomized backwardness and stifled individuality. Although Herzen never tired of underscoring the Asian component of Russia's self, in the 1840s he used these affinities with the East, first and foremost, as a satirical weapon. Romantic overtones are obvious in Herzen's writings, but he remained aloof from the attempts at internalizing the East made by Pushkin in his Romantic period and by myriad Romantic poets after him.

Yet, after Herzen emigrated to Western Europe, his entire intellectual agenda and his understanding of the West–East dichotomy underwent profound changes. As for his political views, he moved from hope for the coming victory of socialism in Europe to disappointment at the revolutionary potential of the most developed states—France and England in particular—which in his eyes had previously incarnated "progress." This disillusionment began as he watched the abortive revolutionary wave of 1848 across Europe. In the years to come, Herzen became increasingly frustrated with the West that had survived the crash and lived through the reactionary backlash that followed. Europe, he claimed, had traded liberal values for the pursuit of material wealth and bourgeois comfort. He observed with horror that the French preferred a strong centralized state and interventionist government to a republic. For him, this development not only posed a corrosive threat to society but, most important, revealed Europe's incurable sickness, inherent in its history and institutions. In Herzen's eyes, Western societies did not pass the test of fidelity to the revolutionary ideals they had themselves produced.[11]

As his political views shifted, their theoretical underpinnings also evolved. He moved from faith in the universal "progress" of all humanity—a Westernist belief based on Hegel's philosophy—to questioning the perception of history as a linear advance of all nations toward a single goal. Moreover, by the end of his late period, Herzen expressed deep doubts about the very notion of progress.[12] As a consequence of this shift, the deterioration of Europe (which he never tired of predicting) could be seen in a positive light—no longer the end of the world, it occasioned the birth and triumph of other civilizations. Now Herzen pinned his hopes on the Russians. He declared the peasant commune to be the natural kernel of socialism, an authentic institution of Slavic society that would allow Russia to implement a unique historical mission. Thanks to its inherently self-governing structure, the commune, he believed, had the potential to evolve organically into an institution that would combine social justice and economic success. With its innate predisposition toward socialism, Russia would be able to transform itself and ultimately the rest of the world by developing this new social order. Idealization of the peasant commune colored Herzen's late views with certain elements of the very Slavophilism he had struggled against in the 1840s.

This shift in Herzen's mind-set is well studied, and I do not intend to dwell upon it here. What has thus far eluded scholars, however, is another critically important development that unfolded simultaneously: with his radical reevaluation of the West and the ascent of his belief in Russian socialism, the conventional construct of Asia took on a striking ambiguity in Herzen's writings and he began increasingly, if inconsistently, to question the customary divide between East and West.

From the early 1850s on, Herzen began attributing to Europe—not without dismay, but with his characteristic intellectual intrepidity—the same derogatory features that were conventionally assigned to Asia. France, for instance, traded "all human rights" for the chance to exercise sovereign authority over other peoples. France had thus, in Herzen's opinion, betrayed the principles of liberty and stood ready to become a colonial power of the Oriental type: it could easily settle, he claimed, into "the beautiful, martial channel of Persian life" (*krasivoe voennoe ruslo persidskoi zhizni*). Herzen admitted that France, of course, differed from Asian empires in that it made use of modern technologies—the telegraph, steamships, and railroads. But France did so, he maintained, only to more effectively shackle "other peoples to the fortunes of its centralized despotism."[13] Herzen assigned some Oriental features to England, as well. British contemporary society made all too clear, he observed, how "the oppressive hand of custom stifles development." And because England was driven only by custom and the hunger for personal gain, it "could easily turn into *another China*" (emphasis added).[14] The growing tyranny of bourgeois values and the complete stifling of individuality, Herzen declared, left no room for personal freedom in Europe and served to explain why modern France and England had failed to uphold the ideals of liberty for which they once had struggled. To drive the argument home, he concluded his observations with an implicit comparison of the most developed countries of Europe with "Chinese anthills" and "swarms."[15]

One can find such diatribes against the West scattered throughout Herzen's works during his émigré period. All of the above quotations, however, are taken from one short essay that Herzen published in 1859 in immediate and enthusiastic response to John Stuart Mill's "On Liberty" (1859). Neither a review nor a polemical article, the essay—as it would seem at first glance—was designed with the modest goal of acquainting the Russian public with the ideas of a widely acclaimed English thinker whose views Herzen partially shared.[16] As we will see, however, Herzen's ambition went beyond mere popularization: the essay promotes his own ideological agenda and epitomizes the core ambiguities of Herzen's new perspective on the West–East issue. And this is why he attached such importance to his response to Mill, not only publishing it in periodicals (the article appeared first in an 1859 issue of *The Pole Star*) but also including the entire text in his memoir *My Past and Thoughts*—a maneuver motivated by the desire to capture the broadest possible audience.

One of Mill's central arguments is that "the general tendency of things throughout the world is to render mediocrity the ascendant power among mankind."[17] Though common everywhere, this tendency, Mill's argument goes, is more dangerous in modern Europe than elsewhere: now in Europe, he states, as government control over the individual gradually wanes, the tyranny of popular opinion grows exponentially and the public is "more disposed than at most former periods to prescribe general rules of conduct and endeavor to make every one conform to the approved standard."[18] In Mill's picture of how public opinion works to suppress originality and how popular sovereignty limits individual sovereignty, Herzen recognized a confirmation of his own critique of bourgeois Europe. The Russian émigré was particularly thrilled by Mill's attacks on British society's predisposition to conformity and intolerance of geniuses and eccentrics.

Though the two thinkers partially converged in their judgments, there was a profound contrariety between their overall mental outlooks—a contrariety that Herzen did his best to smooth over. He needed an ally in his criticism of Europe and, as Aileen Kelly astutely observes, the Russian writer deliberately placed his ideas under the protection of Mill as "a European nanny," in order to sound more convincing to Russians who tended to value Western thinkers above their own.[19] A closer examination of both texts shows, however, that Herzen transformed Mill's criticism of Western democracies into a gloomy prophesy of bourgeois Europe's demise, with a pessimistic tone far exceeding that of Mill. While Mill believes that "the yoke of conformity" and the tyranny of mediocrity are not inherent traits of European democracies and can be overcome, Herzen renders them the very essence of Western civilization. Moreover, as Herzen emphasizes, the "ruling class" profits from the present state of things, which in turn poses a profound obstacle to revolutionary movements—herein lies the "tragic inevitability" of Europe's decline.[20] The difference between the two thinkers emerges most sharply when parallels with Asia unfold. Herzen borrowed the phrase "[Europe] will tend to become another China" from Mill,[21] but—paradoxically—used it to call Mill's point into question. In Mill's words, "the whole East" has been backward for a thousand years, because it has "ceased to possess individuality." If in the most civilized countries of Europe "the opinions of masses of merely average men" become "the dominant power," then "the spirit of progress" will be stunted and they will "become another China."[22] While for Mill Europe has not yet become a China and can still rescue itself by allowing each individual to exercise more liberty, Herzen claims that Western countries are already sliding into the "sucking swamp" (*utiagivaiushchii omut*) of indifference and inertia in which China and Persia have long since sunk.[23] While Mill draws the parallel between China and Europe only once in his more than one-hundred-page treatise, Herzen raises it six times in his five-page essay. Herzen's response thus translated the anxious warnings of a British utilitarian into the eschatological scheme of a Russian socialist.

Finally and most importantly, Herzen undermined Mill's vision of the West–East dichotomy. At the beginning of his treatise, Mill proclaims: "We may leave out of consideration those backward states of society in which the race itself may be considered as in its nonage. Despotism is a legitimate mode of government in dealing with barbarians." Mill then points to India as an instance of a backward country. Thus, Mill frames his entire argument in terms of a strict civilizational hierarchy. The principles of liberty that he defends apply only to what Mill calls a "civilized community." For the East (as well as for societies of the past) he finds despotism justifiable.[24] Herzen is clearly uneasy with the conventional divide between "civilized" West and "backward" East and, without explicitly contradicting Mill, he protests against the common practice of describing the deterioration of Europe through comparison with the Orient (this protest is something of a surprise, given that Herzen himself employed the same rhetoric). If you want to understand the decay of Europe, "there's no need to go as far as China," Herzen exclaims bitterly, "just take a look at Holland."[25] Holland, for Herzen, is a country with a heroic past that has stalled completely in its development. It has become remarkable, as he sarcastically observes, only for its placidity and comfort—features that are rapidly rendering it "as pure as porcelain" (*farforovaia chistota*), which for Herzen was synonymous with sterile inertia.[26]

Herzen openly defies Mill's scheme only once, when he quotes his English counterpart's opinion regarding the difference between Europe and Asia. Unlike the East, Mill states, in modern Europe the despotism of custom "does not preclude change, provided all change together. . . . We thus take care that when there is a change, it shall be for change's sake."[27] In Herzen's view, the difference noted by Mill does not speak in Europe's favor: the "senseless changes" in the West are worse than "Asiatic repose" because the former only conceals the futility that the latter reveals.[28] After such an assertion there remains but a single step to come to the defense of Asia. And Herzen takes this step at the conclusion of his essay, when he suddenly expresses indignation at the contempt customarily directed at the East: "to tell the truth, I do not know . . . how it is that China and Persia may be insulted with impunity."[29]

But this rhetorical gesture seems to undermine Herzen's own narrative because throughout his essay Herzen himself measures Europe's decline by comparing it to China and Persia. This paradox betrays Herzen's ambiguous attitude toward the dominant European discourse about the East. He, after all, represented a country that the West disparaged almost as much, even though Russia viewed itself as belonging to Europe. Thus, in contrast to Mill, Herzen begins to question the European discourse of superiority, but at the same time does not fully exclude such idioms from his own writing. This reflects the problematic position in which he found himself. On the one hand, he was living in Europe, felt its pain as his own, and was fully at home with its intellectual currents. On the other hand, deeply disillusioned by the failure of the bourgeois democracies of Europe, he now forcefully opposed the prospect of Russia following the path of development England and France had taken. It is in this context that he became increasingly frustrated with the West's derogatory assumptions about the rest of the world.

In terms of the theoretical underpinning of his emerging skepticism regarding the West–East binary, Herzen replaced Hegel's teleology of history with a notion of evolutionary process and an organicist concept of history: societies, like animal species, grow, flourish, decline, and decay. All civilizations—Eastern and Western alike—can exhibit the same patterns of organic development. Being subject to the same process equalizes them and makes the present hierarchy of civilizations reversible. As we have seen, Herzen believed that modern Europe was in a state of decomposition comparable to oriental stagnation.[30] In terms of historical scheme, his efforts to rethink the conventional West–East dichotomy required profound revisions of the grand narrative of Russian history. Herzen proposed that, in the course of Russia's development, the role of the Asian peoples might not have been entirely negative. To prove this thesis, he shifted his focus from China and Persia—customary emblems of the Orient—to Russia's own East and embarked on a reevaluation of the entire trajectory of Russian history.

The "Barbarian" Dimension of Russian Socialism

As early as *From the Other Shore* (1847–1850)—a collection of essays written in response to the 1848 catastrophes—he draws a parallel between the degradation of contemporary Europe and the twilight of the Roman Empire. In the first centuries of the Common Era, savage Teutonic tribes conquered the cultured and educated but depraved Romans—and at that point the stream of history carved a new channel. Young and energetic barbarians took the fate of Europe in their hands, while at the same time the Christians, who only recently had been hiding in the catacombs, offered Europe a new mission.[31] Now, Herzen prophesies, a similar profound transformation awaits a weakened Europe. Sensitive people, he claims, already can "hear" the approach of "the new Christians marching to build, the new barbarians marching to destroy."[32] In his revolutionary scheme, "barbarians" signifies non-European peoples—and the role of Christianity passes to socialism.

Herzen believed that it could be—even must be—Russia, or more precisely "its mighty and still enigmatic people" who would alter the course of history.[33] Lest it be thought that this rescue invasion into Europe might come from America, Herzen firmly rejects any such speculation. In his view, the United States is simply the "last, well-produced edition" of old Europe "in a crude English translation," which means, for him, that America suffers from the same inherent diseases of inertia and stagnation.[34] In the Russian people, on the contrary, he emphasizes the "freshness of youth and natural inclination towards socialist institutions."[35] Not surprisingly, during his long émigré years Herzen proudly refers to himself personally and to Russians in general as barbarians and Scythians. He thus redeploys the theme of Russian backwardness—always viewed as a source of shame—using it to cast barbarism as a boon.

But how were the Russians to preserve their barbarism while living in a Westernized empire? And how was it possible that in such a state the village commune would stand fast and guarantee Russia's turn to socialism? Had Herzen answered these questions by saying that Peter's reforms affected only the upper social strata and barely reached the depths of the masses, he would merely have been reiterating Slavophile belief in the pure *narod* that shielded itself from the corrupting influence of the state. Instead, Herzen advanced a radically new thesis. In his article "Russia and Poland," written in the same year that his essay on Mill appeared (1859), Herzen emphasizes a fundamental discontinuity in Russia's development: "The break in our history caused by Peter deprived us of our past," and left Russians with nothing but memories of how the mighty state violated individual rights. "Our recollections," he adds caustically, "go no farther than the manor house where we are whipped and the barracks where we are beaten." Herzen thus created a mythology of emptiness—and it is precisely this mythology that helps him to refashion Russians as barbarians charged with a profound historical mission. Because "we" have been deprived of the past and of historical memory, Russians are more dynamic, mobile, and younger than Europeans. For barbarians, "history lies ahead," and Herzen joyfully exclaims: "What good fortune that [the Russian Empire] is such a monstrous state!"[36] If for English liberals (including John Mill), the British Empire was a powerful engine of progress that modernized its subjugated societies,[37] for Herzen the Romanov Empire is the instrument of oppression, deprivation, and retardation of the development of all its peoples, Russians included. In his eyes, Russia is a mighty reserve of barbarous energy that, once reconfigured, will have the power to remake the world.

To strengthen this point Herzen focused on the Mongol Yoke. If Peter tore Russia away from its past, the Mongols tore it away from Europe. This assessment of the Mongols' influence on Russia—a central axiom of the Russian historical narrative so dramatically presented by Chaadaev and Belinsky—traditionally featured the Mongol yoke as Russia's principal historical trauma. Herzen, in his disillusionment with Europe, vigorously reassesses this cliché. "Is it not the greatest good fortune that we drew closer to Europe so late [that is, only with Peter's reforms—O. M.]?" he exclaims. After all, if Russia had not been conquered by the Mongols but had instead been thoroughly Westernized, it would now be perishing on the "sinking ship" of Europe.[38] Herzen then goes on to make his most stunning declaration: he welcomes the Mongol conquest—and indeed the whole panoply of Russians' painful military encounters with Asiatic peoples. He bluntly states: "We may yet come to bless the 'Chud and Turanian elements' that inhibited our development in ancient times."[39] Given that Chud was a conventional name for the Finno-Ugric peoples, as was Turanian for the Turkic ones, Herzen here transforms the image of a pernicious Asia, cursed by many generations of Russian intellectuals, into a protective shield that saved his homeland from the West and hence from an untimely death. The Russian people, of course, have paid for this isolation from the West with arrested development and a sea of blood (Herzen never denied these outcomes), but this was the only way for Russians, Herzen proclaims, to preserve their youthful energy.[40]

This rendering of the role of the Mongol yoke in Russian history was an attempt to look through a new lens at the entire spectrum of interactions between Russia and Asia. As we have seen, Herzen maintains that the Asian nomads' raids into Russia, which would seem to have had only negative consequences, in fact set the Russian people on a course toward fulfilling their purgative mission in Europe. The accomplishment of this mission would, in turn, mark the beginning of Russian history, which, he wrote, had essentially not yet begun. Herzen incorporates the savagery of the Russians into the narrative of the revolution and boldly couples the notion of barbarism with the expected triumph of socialism, the necessity of the latter justifying the former. As Herzen develops his notion of barbarism, he increasingly insists on linking together the Russian people and their Asiatic neighbors (and often former conquerors). Thus he began to place these combined masses—the Russian and non-Russian peoples of the Romanov Empire—on a low rung of the civilizational ladder, thereby suggesting that together they represented a historical force that would transform the world.

Russia's culturally and ethnically mixed character always figured prominently in nineteenth-century intellectual discourse, but it was usually assumed that the Slavic substratum in this mixture would dominate and absorb the other ethnic influences.[41] Herzen, by contrast, was proudly identifying Russia as a land of "Turanian barbarians."

To understand the provocative nature of this identification of Russia with the Turanians and to grasp Herzen's objective in employing this construct, it is important to bear in mind that in the 1850s–1860s identifying Russia with Asia was an instrument of anti-Russian propaganda used by the leaders of the Polish independence movement. Popular among the Polish revolutionary émigrés from the Romanov Empire was Franciszek Duchiński's theory that Russians belonged not to the Slavic but the Turanian race.[42] Duchiński propounded these ideas not only in his ethnographic and linguistic studies but also in public lectures he gave regularly in France and Switzerland. A wide assortment of Russians indignantly repudiated this theory.[43] Herzen, on the contrary, readily acknowledged what most of his compatriots regarded as a racial insult. It was entirely justifiable, he agreed with the Poles, to consider

Russia a "deficiently Slavic land"—deficient in terms of its dearth of Slavic traits. This recognition constituted an important step in the formation of Herzen's understanding of the relationship between Russians and Asians. If in his previous writing it was the break with the past, the absence of historical memory, and the nation's backwardness that had fused Russians together with the Asian peoples of the empire into a barbarous mass, now Herzen recognizes that ethnic ties also cemented all these rationalities together.

In nineteenth-century Russia, the Mongol yoke was considered not only the nation's main historical trauma but also the source of a pernicious legacy that left an imprint of Oriental despotism on the Russian political system. Many writers drew on and perpetuated this stereotype. Designed to criticize the imperial regime, parallels between the Russian tsars and Mongol khans figured prominently in Herzen's own works. Yet as Herzen discovered the positive potential of barbarism, he shifted his focus from the state to the nation. Or, to put it differently, he shifted his focus from the state's institutions, infected with Oriental despotism and hampering the nation's progress, to its puissant young people—the masses of mixed origins, capable of changing the course of history. In his depiction of these masses, Herzen treated the Russians as the equals of all the subjugated nationalities of the empire. Our "proximity to and kinship with the Chud and Turanian tribes have served to foster humble recognition of them as equals—Jew and Finn, Tartar and Kalmyk; do we not equally serve as the caryatid supporting the Winter Palace; what right have we to look down upon them from the heights of Western civilization?"[44] For Herzen the Russians, who are oppressed by the regime no less than the other peoples of the empire, do not represent the colonizer. They are themselves colonized. This conclusion determined Herzen's vision of the empire's future.

The fall of the Romanov Empire seemed more probable to him as the imperial colossus appeared less stable following Russia's defeat in the Crimean War and the rise of separatism within the empire (particularly the intensification of the Polish independence movement). But his expectations of the regime's demise by no means implied that Herzen advocated the disintegration of imperial space. When the Romanov Empire collapses, he predicted, "the gigantic masonry and the foundation will remain."[45] By "gigantic masonry" and "foundation" he meant not the state institutions (these were destined to perish, according to his revolutionary prophecy), but the immeasurable space populated by the constituents of the empire. The imperial period of Russian history, he declared, "created enormous empty forms without content that are still waiting for something."[46] He not only did not call for the destruction of these "forms," he began to defend the right and ability of the Russian people to continue building on the already-constructed foundation. After all, Herzen maintained, the Russians are "as self-confident in matters of state-building" (*gosudarstvennaia samouverennost'*) as are the French and English, with the added advantage that the Russian people, unlike their European counterparts, are still young, energetic, and brave. Why then, he asks, should these young people abstain from enjoying the benefits of what has been already built?[47]

In this vision of the empire's future Herzen uses a rhetoric of national pride that never appears in his critique of the Romanov Empire. The empire stretching "from the Baltic to the Pacific" is now labeled by Herzen a "*purely Russian* [*chisto russkaia*] empire, far more Russian than the government" (Herzen's emphasis).[48] Taken out of context, his apology for empire is strikingly similar to the language of Mikhail Katkov and other conservatives who defended the integrity of the empire during Alexander II's reform era. In the 1860s they also distinguished between "*russkaia imperiia*" (that is, the empire that reflects the nature of the Russian people) and "*rossiiskaia imperiia*" (the Westernized supranational state that stifles Russians and other subjugated peoples alike). Beneath this surface similarity, however, there was a fundamental difference. The Hegelian Katkov envisaged a multiethnic empire forged into a single political nation by the state. Regarding the bureaucracy as the key instrument for the homogenization of the empire, he advocated the dominance of Russian culture within it and projected that Russia would gradually come to resemble a nation-state on the Western model. Herzen, in contrast, declared all of the peoples of the empire to be equal and did not regard the nation-state as an ideal toward which they should strive. By "purely Russian empire" Herzen seemed to imply—though, unfortunately, he did not further elaborate the point—a unique formation distinct from Western states.

Here we are confronted with a paradox: a fierce enemy of the Romanov Empire is defending the notion of a "purely Russian empire" and believes that it—or a significant part of it—can survive the collapse of the monarchical state. This paradox reflects the essential ambiguity of the empire–nation nexus in Russia, a country in which it is difficult to draw a precise boundary between the metropolis and the colonies. In responding to this challenge Herzen proposes a state based on a Russo-Turanian symbiosis. Although he never fully elaborated on how Russians had converged with the Asiatic peoples of the empire, he believed that, over the course of many centuries, these peoples were molded by the same pressures into a unified barbarian mass lacking a past and open to the future. Thus, one can credit Herzen with one of the first—if not the first—well-articulated constructs to propose Russians' ties with their eastern neighbors as a source of the nation's true identity, of the unique nature of its empire, and of the fulfillment of its historical mission.

The historical, political, and philosophical views espoused by the founders of Eurasianism (Nikolai Trubetskoi, Roman Jacobson, and Petr Savitskii) did not represent such a sharp break from the previous theories as they claimed.[49] Nor was their approach to the Russia–Asia encounter, or their vision of the Russian Empire, without precursors in nineteenth-century intellectual discourse. Herzen—the Eurasianists' predecessor as eternal émigré—also faced the need to reposition Russia with regard to the East and, like the Eurasianists, he did so at a time when his entire system of values had come into question and he found his belief in Western socialism shattered. Like the Eurasianists after him, Herzen also imagined a renewed Russian Empire as a new totality that would address the challenges of his time.[50] Given Herzen's overwhelming popularity among the intelligentsia, it is plausible to assume that his attempt to reconceptualize the East had intellectual repercussions and can be used to explain some of the twists in Russian discourse on Asia. Of course, Russians continued to perpetuate Western cultural stereotypes regarding Asia, even long after Herzen wrote the pieces discussed above—and long after the 1870s and 1880s, when some of his ideas were further elaborated by Konstantin Leont'ev, whom the Eurasianists credited as their predecessor. Still, as Herzen's construct suggests, nineteenth-century efforts to break the mold of European discourse on the Orient were bolder than has often been assumed. These efforts were not articulated as systematically and forcefully as they were in the writings of the Eurasianists, but their intellectual expression was nonetheless more pervasive than is commonly acknowledged.

THE EURASIANS AND LIBERAL SCHOLARSHIP OF THE LATE IMPERIAL PERIOD

Continuity and Change across the 1917 Divide

Vera Tolz

MAJOR intellectual projects, such as the Eurasian movement's attempt to (re)conceptualize Russia's role in the world and critically assess the position of Europe vis-à-vis other cultures, can be properly understood only within the broader cultural, political, and social context in which they are articulated. A proper definition and appreciation of such a context allows us to fully grasp continuities and changes in intellectual history and to establish the origins of important ideological shifts. By looking at the history of ideas within a longer time span we can see more clearly the intellectual (and, at times, related political) paths taken and not taken, thus avoiding teleological traps in writing historical narratives. The context in which the theories of Classical Eurasians originated is commonly understood to be that of the aftermath of the Great War, the 1917 Russian revolutions, and these thinkers' personal experiences of emigration.[1] Although they acknowledge that the Eurasians built their theories on the ideas of certain Russian and European thinkers, contemporary scholars tend to emphasize the novelty and, in many ways, unprecedented nature of the ideology of the Eurasian movement for the Russian intellectual tradition. In particular, the Eurasians' broad assault on the Eurocentric worldview as well as their suggestions about how to preserve a multiethnic state on the territory of the defunct Russian Empire in the age of nationalism have been widely regarded as manifestations of the Eurasians' decisive break with the Russian intellectual tradition of the imperial period.[2] Challenging this dominant perception, this chapter will question the degree of originality of the Eurasian ideology and the extent of its departure from the Russian and pan-European intellectual currents of the late nineteenth century and the fin de siècle. The chapter thus contributes to the growing body of scholarship of Russia that is increasingly questioning the perception of 1917 as the time of all-embracing ideological change.[3]

There is no doubt that two of the factors that played an important role in shaping the ideas of the ideologists of the Eurasian movement were the cataclysmic events of the Great War and the revolution, and the complex personal experience of living outside one's homeland. Yet this chapter proposes that the genealogy of the Eurasian theories should be sought from within a broader temporal and cultural framework, namely, that the movement should be understood as a particularly radical manifestation of the ideas associated with the period that scholars have recently called "the second Oriental Renaissance" in Europe. The latter dates back to the 1870s–1880s, when against the backdrop of far-reaching political and social changes in European societies, engendered by the upheavals of industrialization and urbanization, a range of influential thinkers began openly to challenge accepted norms, values, and identities. In this period, contrary to Edward Said's interpretation of Europe's engagement with its "Oriental" Other,[4] non-European cultures started to be widely seen as offering positive alternative models of development in areas ranging from the economy to the arts.[5] In Europe during this period—one of the most intense in terms of intellectual and artistic ferment—criticism of the Eurocentric nature of dominant historical narratives was voiced, and established hierarchies of "advanced" and "backward" societies, of the East–West dichotomy and of "the presumption that the West alone had agency" were questioned.[6]

These fin-de-siècle searches for alternatives to the historical narratives, scientific modes of inquiry, and artistic traditions, dominant during most of the nineteenth century, were particularly intense in Russia. Given the specific situation of the Russian Empire, on the periphery of Europe, where pan-European social and economic upheavals at the turn of the twentieth century played out in particularly traumatic ways, it is not so surprising that the emerging critique of Eurocentric biases and Europeans' ambitions to measure all societies according to the (West) European yardstick was expressed particularly boldly. This chapter investigates the Eurasians' indebtedness to this broader pan-European intellectual trend by comparing the ideas of the Eurasians with the arguments articulated, often before the Eurasians had appeared on the intellectual scene, by a particular group of Russian scholars, specializing in studying the Orient and art history.

In her pathbreaking studies of German Orientalism, Suzanne Marchand made a claim about the importance of German and Austrian Orientology, archaeology, and art history in shaping wider intellectual trends in Europe when she argued that without the radical reconceptualization of the origins and development of European culture in this scholarship between the 1880s and 1914, "Spengler's *Decline of the West* [published in 1918 and 1923—V. T.] would be . . . unthinkable."[7] In the developments described by Marchand, which included a growing critique among certain groups of scholars of Eurocentric biases in academic research and these scholars' acknowledgment of the influence of the Orient on early Christianity, European history, and the formation of European cultures, Russian scholars played an active and, at times, pioneering role.[8] I would argue that Marchand's contention about the connection between German academic scholarship and Spengler's view of the decline of Western civilization can be applied to the case of the Russian scholarship discussed here and the Eurasians. Furthermore, similarly to Germany, where a link can be established between the often liberal pursuits of its Orientology of the fin de siècle and racial scholarship of the Nazi period, in Russia, the ways in which some intellectual trends of the late imperial period were reinterpreted in the 1920s underscore the complexity of the relationship between pre-1917 liberalism and the illiberal ideologists of the Soviet era.

The Schools of Nikodim Kondakov and Viktor Rozen

It was in the 1870s and 1880s, against the backdrop of significant political and social changes and as a result of developments internal to scholarship such as new archaeological and textual discoveries about the nonbiblical cultures of the ancient East, that major revisionist trends in the humanities became evident in Europe. These trends were facilitating a broad shift in European culture from the hitherto little-challenged "Western self-satisfaction" to a tentative critique of Eurocentrism. As the nineteenth century drew to a close, scholars began to question prevailing dominant stereotypes, prejudices, and platitudes, including the perception of "European civilization" as unique, necessarily superior, and largely rooted in classical antiquity.[9]

In the context of Russia, this new revisionist agenda was actively promoted by two closely intertwined academic schools of great importance to the development of the country's cultural life. These were the "new schools" of art history and Orientology (*vostokovedenie*), which were formed in the 1880s and 1890s and founded by Nikodim Kondakov (1844–1925) and Viktor Rozen (1849–1908), respectively. In the words of the contemporary Byzantologist Robert Nelson, Kondakov was "the real founder" of Byzantine art history.[10]

Most significantly from the point of view of our topic, his history of Byzantine art emphasized the importance of Oriental influences on the development of early European art forms, focusing on the multiplicity of these forms and the transnational rather than national nature of their formation. Kondakov also questioned established cultural hierarchies by singling out the role of nomadic peoples of the Eurasian steppe in transmitting major cultural innovations between different communities East and West.[11] As we will see below, in the 1880s, Kondakov proceeded to define "Russian culture," its origins and development, in ways that would have a strong influence on perceptions of Russia among intellectuals, literati, and artists during the Silver Age and the 1920s.[12]

The Eurasians were directly influenced by Kondakov. Petr Savitskii maintained close personal ties with this leading art historian; Georgii Vernadskii (known in the West as George Vernadsky) saw himself as working in Kondakov's tradition.[13] Kondakov spent the last three years of his life in Prague building around himself a circle of younger intellectuals, which included the Eurasians Savistskii, Vernadsky, Nikolai P. Toll, and Tatiana Rodzianko as active participants. Upon Kondakov's death in 1925 they founded the Seminarium Kondakovianum, which in 1931 was transformed into the Archaeological Institute named after N. P. Kondakov.[14]

In turn, a typical product of the Russian imperial state, Rozen was a baron from its Baltic provinces who wrote only in German when he entered St. Petersburg University in 1866. It is there that he turned into a statist Russian nationalist, promoting the view that scholarship should serve the interests of the nation to which a particular scholar belonged. Rozen's loyalty was, above all, to the Russian nation, which he perceived, as did Kondakov, to be multiethnic in nature, and in the throes of cultural unification within its state borders.[15] A leading Russian Arabist, elected as a member of the Imperial Academy of Sciences in 1890, and between 1893 and 1908 the dean of the Oriental Faculty at St. Petersburg University, Rozen played an instrumental role in both the internationalization of Russian Orientology (i.e., its recognition as a major player on the scene of European Orientalism) and its simultaneous nationalization (which in Rozen's interpretation required Russian scholars to have a special interest in studying Russia's own non-European communities).[16] Similarly to Kondakov, Rozen's agenda encouraged a focus on what he called the nodes (*uzly*) of cultural, political, and economic interaction between peoples of the East and West and the promotion of a view of "Russian culture" as a space where the "East" and the "West" met.[17]

In the first decades of the twentieth century, some of Rozen's disciples offered a critique of the Eurocentric biases found in contemporary scholarship. It was a critique that surpassed the interrogation of Eurocentrism that was taking place in other European academic centers. Rozen's disciples also emphasized the constructed nature of the categories of "East" and "West" and dwelled on the relationship between European culture and colonialism.[18] One of the leading representatives of the Rozen school, the specialist on Islam and Central Asia, Vasilii Bartol'd (1869–1930) corresponded with Savitskii who, in his obituary of Bartol'd, discussed, at times exaggerating, the similarity between Bartol'd's views and those of the Eurasians.[19] Three other disciples of Rozen, whose ideas are relevant to our assessment of the extent of the originality of the Eurasian theories, were the linguist and archaeologist of the Caucasus, Nikolai Marr (1864–1934), and the specialists in Buddhism, Sergei Ol'denburg (1863–1934), and Fedor Shcherbatskoi (1866–1942).

These scholars either exercised a direct influence on the Eurasians or, particularly in the 1920s, developed similar ideas in parallel to the Eurasians. Their arguments can be compared in five areas: their definitions of Russian and Eurasian cultures; their critique of Eurocentrism and of the hierarchical view of cultures; their reinterpretations of Russian history "from the Eastern perspective"; their view of the relationship between European knowledge and colonial power; and their attempts to resolve the contradiction between empire and modern nationalism.

Culture and the Unity of the Russian Empire

The scholarly agendas of the above-mentioned Russian scholars and the Eurasians were to a significant extent informed by the same two broad issues of major importance for many Russian intellectuals at the time. The first was the role of Russia in the historical arena, which was first fully articulated by the Slavophiles in the early nineteenth century in response to Petr Chaadaev's provocative criticism of Russia in his first "Philosophical Letter."[20] In an essay assessing Kondakov's work four years after his death in 1925, the émigré Russian scholar, Evgenii Anichkov, observed that, although Kondakov was not a Slavophile himself, his research agenda was underpinned by attempts to find an answer to the same question that was first posed by a leader of the Slavophiles, Aleksei Khomiakov, about "the place of the Slavs in world history."[21] The second issue was the relationship between empire and nation in the context of Russia. Kondakov, Rozen, and their disciples lived at a time when the reality of imperial diversity was already increasingly hard to reconcile with the homogenizing and equalizing ideas of emerging national movements. In the period following the 1917 revolutions, during which the Eurasian movement took shape, these two issues, even if now slightly reformulated, further gained in significance.

In their attempts to resolve the challenges that modern nationalism posed to the imperial nature of the Russian and then Soviet state, the Eurasians postulated the existence of a Eurasian cultural unity that was the major unifying force of "Russia-Eurasia." For them, the peoples of Eurasia were united "not by race, but by a common historical fate (*obshchnost'iu istoricheskoi sud'by*), common work in the creation of one and the same culture (*sozdaniem odnoi i toi zhe kul'tury*) or one and the same state."[22] In the imagination of the Eurasians this culture was not limited to specifically ethnic Russian or Slavic roots.

In their search for elements of the Russian intellectual tradition that have inspired the Eurasians' cultural visions, contemporary scholars have singled out the influence on the Eurasians of the pan-Slavists Nikolai Danilevskii and Vladimir Lamanskii, specifically their theories of "cultural-historical types" and of Russia as a separate geographical world, notions first made public in 1869. Also recognized as having shaped the ideas of the Eurasians are German and Austrian ethnologists' questioning of the validity of the categories of backward and civilized along with their ethnological interest in morphological similarities of cultural areas that transcend ethnonational boundaries (*Kulturkreise* theory).[23]

Yet one crucial source inspiring the Eurasian holistic definition of culture interpreted as a product of the interaction of various nationalities on the territory of Eurasia is usually overlooked. The first person so consistently to emphasize the multiethnic origins of "Russian culture" and this culture's unifying role for the empire was Kondakov.[24] In turn, Rozen and his disciples focused on the role of "Eastern" peoples in the creation of this culture. Advancing a theory of special "cultural historical types" and juxtaposing "Romano-Germanic" with "Slavic types," Danilevskii attempted to incorporate the eastern borderlands into the Russian national space by virtue of the migration of Russian settlers to the east.[25] Kondakov and Rozen went further than Danilevskii, arguing that these areas achieved integration through partaking in joint cultural activities and the creation of a common state. Accordingly, they articulated an argument that would become essential in developing the concept of Eurasia in the 1920s.

Kondakov's seminal multivolume work, *Russian Antiquities* (*Russkie drevnosti*) published between 1889 and 1899, forcefully outlined his definition of "Russian culture" as the common work of the various nationalities of the Russian Empire. It also emphasized the influences of Oriental cultures on Russian artistic styles. The first volume began with the following definition of "Russian culture": "In the course of two and a half thousand years many tribes and nationalities had been living and settling within the borders of our fatherland, as history remembers. And the more varied the ethnic composition (*plemennoi sostav*) of the population has been, and the longer it has taken to transform [these diverse people] into one state with a single nation (*odno gosudarstvo s edinym narodom*), the greater the contribution of [these nationalities] has been to the treasury of Russian antiquities."[26]

Kondakov went on to explain that the specifically Russian architectural style was created by merging together the styles of churches in the North of Russia, Kiev, Novgorod, and Moscow with those of the historic buildings of Georgia and Crimea. Russian artistic style had been influenced by that of the ancient Greek colonies on the Black Sea coast as well as by Byzantine and Persian traditions that penetrated Russia through the Caucasus, Central Asia, and the shores of the Danube. The book noted that the trade in cultural artifacts between the peoples populating the territory of the future Kievan Rus' and the Persian Empire had flourished long before any relationship between the Eastern Slavs and the Varangians (i.e., representatives of the West) was established. In addition to this trade, the movement of people from the "depth of Central Asia and Siberia to the shores of the Danube" transported "oriental cultural forms" (*formy vostochnoi kul'tury*) to the West.[27] Kondakov's *Russkie drevnosti* had an influence well beyond academia, insofar as the book was read by wide circles of artists and literati of the early twentieth century.[28] Savitskii's description of Eurasian culture, articulated in 1921, as a "joint creation" and a common heritage of the people of Eurasia" was an almost verbatim repetition of the definition of Russian culture offered by Kondakov in 1889, of which Savitskii was aware.[29]

Rozen, in turn, subscribed to the definition of "Russian culture," which was similar to that of Kondakov, and encouraged his disciples to focus on instances of the creation of new syncretic cultural forms through mutual influences among various nationalities on the territory of the Russian Empire.[30] Kondakov pointed to the role of the steppe nomads in absorbing and dispersing the results of the creativity of the settled cultures across the territory of the future Russian state. This was further studied by members of the Rozen school, Bartol'd in particular. Thus they anticipated and influenced the Eurasians' concern with the nomads' role in Eurasia.

The Eurasians acknowledged their debt to Kondakov and Rozen's disciple Bartol'd in this area. Vernadsky, for instance, emphasized the importance Kondakov attached to the role of nomadic communities, particularly those of Central Asia, in the development of Byzantine, Russian, and European art, thus seeking support for the Eurasian position on this issue in the works of his famous teacher.[31] In turn, in support of his own view on the nomads' role in the creation of "Eurasian civilization," Savitskii referred specifically to Kondakov and Bartol'd.[32] Indeed, Savitskii drew on the names of these widely respected scholars and exaggerated Bartol'd's Eurasian credentials in order to defend the Eurasians against widespread criticism of their ideas among Russian émigrés.[33]

The Critique of Eurocentrism

Central to the Eurasian views was a sustained critique of Eurocentrism, the rejection of the Europeans' claim about the universality of their culture and of the hierarchical view of peoples and cultures based on the assumption of Europe's superiority. This critique was already systematically elaborated in Trubetskoi's *Europe and Mankind* (*Evropa i chelovechestvo*), which had appeared in 1920, a year before the publication of the Eurasians' manifesto *Exodus to the East* (*Iskhod k Vostoku*). Scholars have argued that Trubetskoi's work appeared within the context of hostility toward Eurocentricism, engendered by the Great War (e.g., in the works of Spengler and Hermann Graf Keyserling), and of the questioning of the universality of European values by European and Russian ethnographers and anthropologists in the first decades of the twentieth century.[34] In fact, in many areas of European scholarship that went well beyond ethnography, the criticism of Eurocentrism had been so prominent since the 1880s that the very attack on the Eurocentric worldview by the Eurasians was not original at all. The novelty lay in the passion with which the Eurasians rejected Europe's claim about the universality of its culture.

As Marchand had convincingly shown, between the 1880s and 1914, in works widely read by intellectuals and politicians in Europe, German and Austrian scholars had already mounted a "frontal assault" on Eurocentric histories.[35] As early as the 1880s, the eminent Austrian Arabist Alfred von Kremer (1828–1889) expressed hope that the discoveries made at the time by Orientologists would overcome the tendency to perceive as universal ideals that, in fact, amounted "to the prejudices . . . professed exclusively by a small faction of humanity (i.e., Europeans)."[36]

Rozen regarded Kremer as one of his mentors, and thus, criticism of Eurocentrism became a key premise on which Rozen built his own school. Both Kondakov and Rozen began to question the hierarchical view of cultures. Kondakov presented the role of "the Orient," including nomadic communities of Central Asia that were widely perceived as backward, as a major force, alongside ancient Greece and Rome, in the development of European art. Rozen argued that the cultures of the Syrians, Armenians, and other hitherto little noticed people were as important to the formation of early Christians as were the cultures of the Jews and the Greeks.[37] Of Rozen's disciples, Marr was at the forefront of rejecting the categories of civilized and backward peoples, postulating in 1916 the greatness of small minority groups in the Caucasus precisely because their cultures were repositories of the non-European cultural heritage of the region.[38] For instance, by the middle of the second decade of the twentieth century, Marr provocatively claimed that the Abkhaz of

Transcaucasia, who did not have their own literary tradition in the vernacular, had a language that "stands at the highest stage of development among human languages." He went on to argue that the folklore of smaller minority groups of the Caucasus without literacy in their vernacular languages offered a "more solid and rich source" for the study of "living antiquity," "indigenous" pre-Christian and pre-Islamic traditions in the Caucasus, than the literatures of people with established literary traditions.[39]

As was the case with German and Austrian Orientology and art history, these fields of scholarship in Russia encouraged a rethinking of the very categories of East and West, Europe and Asia, which would later find reflection in Eurasian theories. In the first two decades of the twentieth century, Orientologists of the Rozen school revealed the constructed nature of these categories, rejected the existence of a boundary between Europe and Asia, and exposed the East–West dichotomy as a figment of European popular imagination. In this area, Bartol'd played a particularly important role. In the aftermath of Russia's defeat in the war with Japan, which had a major influence on how Russia's educated public perceived "the East," Bartol'd began teaching a course at St. Petersburg University on the history of the study of the Orient in Europe and Russia. Published in book form in 1911,[40] this innovative study showed that the categories of "East" and "West," "Europe" and "Asia" were political, geographical, and cultural constructs whose boundaries had been shifted according to the arguments that those evoking them aimed to advance. Using a wide range of primary sources, the scholar described the definitions of "the Orient" and "Europe" as having first been articulated by the Greeks and the Romans, traced the belief in the inferiority of the Orient to Roman times, and showed how perceptions of these categories had transformed in the Middle Ages. He finally concluded that contemporary perceptions of the East–West divide were fully formed only during the Enlightenment period.[41]

The denial of any objective boundary between Europe/the West and Russia, on the one hand, and the Muslim world, on the other, together with a belief that the East was an integral part of Russia, permeated Bartol'd's work. He argued, for instance that:

> The Near East, with the inclusion of Egypt, which is usually meant in
> Western Europe when [people] speak about the "East," in reality, despite
> frequent military clashes constitutes one cultural-historical whole with
> Europe. Together they constitute the "West" in relation to more eastern cul-
> tural states such as India and China. From the very beginning the culture
> of the Near East and Southeastern Europe shared the same origins in the
> ancient culture of Egypt and Babylon; later on, political and cultural supe-
> riority shifted back and forth between the Europeans and the peoples of the

Near East, but throughout those times the role of the West (broadly defined) remained the same in relation to the countries of the Far East.[42]

In turn, Shcherbatskoi, an eminent Buddhologist, and his disciples, whose works were also widely read by members of the broader public,[43] rejected the existence of any boundary dividing Europe/the West from the Buddhist cultures of the Far East and East Asia. Thus, Shcherbatskoi's student Otton Rozenberg (1888–1919) pointed out that the categories of "East" and "West" had no meaning without each other and posed the question of "whether, in relation to Buddhism, it is correct to speak about the East." His answer was in the negative; he postulated that it was impossible to identify where "this so-called gap that separates us from the Far East lies."[44]

A close focus on the constructed nature of the key categories in the contemporary European imagination enabled Bartol'd to conduct further research that traced how centers of particularly intensive cultural activity and their resulting political predominance had shifted historically between different regions of "Europe" and "Asia." That research prompted Bartol'd to draw his conclusion about the temporary nature of contemporary West European cultural domination.[45] In his obituary of Bartol'd, Savitskii acknowledged that Bartol'd's views predated those of the Eurasians.[46] Savitskii singled out Bartol'd's theory of "the migrations of cultural centers" as particularly significant for the Eurasians, even though at the time of writing his own article on "The Migration of Culture" (*Migratsiia kul'tury*), which appeared in 1921, Savitskii did not yet seem to have known Bartol'd's work.[47] In his obituary of Bartol'd, Savitskii also noted that Bartol'd's ideas in this area anticipated Vernadsky's theory of the periodic migration of centers of intensive cultural activity.[48]

Revising a Dominant Narrative of Russian History

The broad assumption that "Russian culture" was a result of East–West interaction and symbiosis encouraged both Russian scholars and Eurasians to reinterpret some of the key episodes in Russian history. The reinterpretation of Russia's historical relationship with Asia and, in particular, of the role of the Mongols for Rus'/Russia, tends to be presented as the Eurasians' novel contribution to the study of Russian history.[49] Although nineteenth-century historians such as Nikolai Karamzin and Mikhail (Mykola) Kostomarov acknowledged that the Mongol invasion to some extent facilitated the consolidation of the Russian state around Moscow, in the dominant national narrative of Russian history as articulated by Sergei Solov'ev (1820–1879) and Vasilii Kliuchevskii (1841–1911) the role of the Mongols appeared to be overwhelmingly negative and its significance was downplayed. The "Tatar-Mongol yoke" of the thirteenth to fifteenth centuries was presented as responsible for the cultural backwardness of Russia in comparison with Western Europe. At the same time, it was seen as an "accidental episode" that had little influence on the European nature of Russia's cultural identity. In this narrative, Rus' acted as a shield guarding Europe against the Mongol menace.[50]

This account was rejected in Trubetskoi's *The Legacy of Genghis Khan (A Perspective on Russian History Not from the West but from the East)* (*Nasledie Chingizkhana* [*Vzgliad na russkuiu istoriiu ne s Zapada, a s Vostoka*]) (1925) and by Vernadsky, who emphasized the major and often positive role of the Mongols in the history of Russia.[51] Rather than being particularly original, the historical schemas of Trubetskoi and Vernadsky only continued what Bartol'd had begun in the 1890s. In his dissertation, "Turkestan in the Era of the Mongol Invasion" (*Turkestan v epokhu mongol'skogo nashestviia*) (1900), Bartol'd had already started, in his own words, to fight against the "appalling images," both popular and in scholarly works, of the Mongols, rejecting the view that they brought nothing but destruction to the societies they conquered.[52] In fact, the scholar believed, they brought political stability to Rus' and all other conquered societies. In his *History of the Study of the East* (*Istoriia izucheniia Vostoka*) and other works Bartol'd reinterpreted the Mongol invasion of Rus' as a period that was beneficial rather than detrimental to Russia not only politically but also culturally. He concluded: "In contrast to the widespread view, even the influence of European culture on Rus' in the Mongol period was much greater than in the Kievan period."[53] Rather than seeing the Mongol invasion as an episode that led to the subsequent cultural backwardness of Rus'/Russia, Bartol'd argued that, in fact, the period simply revealed the existing backwardness of Rus' because Rus' was not fully able to use the Mongol invasion to enrich its own culture with knowledge from and about the East.[54]

The Eurasians themselves acknowledged Bartol'd's preeminence in revising the dominant narrative of Russian history. In his first proto-Eurasian interpretation of the Mongols' role, published in 1914, Vernadsky directly referred to Bartol'd. He both used Bartol'd's interpretation and disagreed with him over the assessment of the backwardness of medieval Rus'.[55] Using the subtitle of Trubetskoi's essay, Savitskii pointed out that it was Bartol'd who had been the first to offer a "perspective on Russian history not from the West but from the East" (*vzgliad na russkuiu istoriiu ne s Zapada, a s Vostoka*). Savitskii added that Bartol'd's works "in their comprehensiveness can compete with similar attempts made recently [by the Eurasian writers], and in terms of timing, they predate them."[56]

The Relationship between European Culture and Colonialism

Whereas some of the issues that preoccupied Russian scholars and the Eurasians at the turn of the twentieth century are today only of historical interest, the relationship between European culture and colonialism still informs the intellectual agendas of many contemporary scholars. Anticipating the arguments of current postcolonial scholars, in the context of the First World War, the Revolution, the Civil War, and the Wilsonian discourse of national self-determination, in his *Europe and Mankind*, Trubetskoi forcefully argued that European culture, with its ambition to serve as a yardstick against which other societies could be classified as backward, was an effective tool of European imperialism, whose influence was invariably destructive for colonized societies. This argument is often viewed as "radically new and original" for its time.[57] For instance, David Moore claimed that Trubetskoi's work constituted "the world's first . . . critique of world-spanning Eurocentrism."[58] Moore went on to note the similarity between Trubetskoi's views and those of the Third World intellectuals of the 1950s and the 1960s, who influenced Edward Said's critique of European Orientalism.[59] Most contemporary postcolonial scholars in the West do not know about Trubetskoi's work and they tend to credit scholars such as the U. S. anthropologist Bernard Cohn and Said for first noticing the existence of a direct link between European culture and colonial domination.[60]

As Marchand aptly noted in this connection, after analyzing the work of German Orientologists of the late nineteenth and early twentieth centuries: "It is the conceit of too many modern historians that they are the first ones to have discovered the evils of Eurocentrism."[61] Intellectual developments in early twentieth-century Russia further confirm Marchand's observation. It is too often assumed without further investigation that in the nineteenth and early twentieth centuries European scholars were oblivious to the existing relationship between European culture and Europe's political power.[62] This is, however, far from being the case. In reality, "knowledge is power" (*znanie— sila* in Russian) was the main slogan of nineteenth-century European scholarship.[63] Accordingly, the Eurasians' interest in the relationship between European culture and colonialism should be placed in the wider Russian and pan-European context of the turn of the twentieth century.

In fact, by the time Trubetskoi's book appeared, most scholars fully subscribed to the view that culture and scholarly knowledge were what gave the Europeans the greatest power to dominate the rest of the world.[64] The difference between imperial scholars of the past, on the one hand, and the Eurasians and contemporary postcolonial critics, on the other, lies, therefore, not in the identification of the connection between culture and power, but in the moral evaluation of this connection. Whereas Trubetskoi and the postcolonial critics condemned European culture for being a tool of colonial policies, the majority of imperial scholars tended to note with pride the extent to which culture, and particularly scholarship, contributed to Europe's establishment of imperial control over the rest of the world. For instance, during his dissertation defense, Bartol'd did not hesitate to argue that "Eastern people will believe in the superiority of our culture when they become convinced that we know them better than they know themselves."[65] Such a position did not prevent some imperial scholars from occasionally criticizing the influence of the imposition of European models on non-European societies. For instance, by 1916 Marr had moved beyond condemning specific examples of European imperialism and had drawn some general conclusions about the destructive nature of the influence of "the European civilization" on non-European societies. He used as an example smaller minority groups in the Caucasus, and presented them as having preserved, up to the present day, elements of a culture that had been greater than and given rise to "European civilization," a culture that incoming "Aryan-European tribes" had undermined and subjugated even as they benefited from it.[66] Yet even Marr's critique in 1916 of manifestations of European imperialism did not match the level of passion and detail with which Trubetskoi made his arguments.

Prior to the appearance of Trubetskoi's book, the most detailed discussion in Russia of the link between European culture and political power had been offered in Bartol'd's *History of the Study of the East*. In this publication and in a number of subsequent works, Bartol'd systematically argued that there existed a clear "link between Orientalist knowledge and [Russia's] ability to exercise influence over it [the Orient], that is, between the development of Russian Oriental Studies and the fulfillment of Russia's political and cultural aims in the East."[67] His *History of the Study of the East* was permeated with his explicitly stated conviction that it was European epistemological supremacy, whose origins he dated to the late sixteenth century, that had facilitated Europe's imperial conquest and domination of "the East." A new type of economic and political relationship between Europe and the East further developed in the nineteenth century "under the influence of [the] general success of European culture," Bartol'd observed.[68] As was the case for Trubetskoi and contemporary postcolonial critics of European imperialism, for Bartol'd military and technological advantages were simply a by-product of the European way of knowing the world scientifically.[69] While having virtually the same views on the centrality of European culture for Europe's imperial expansion and domination, Bartol'd, on the one hand, and Trubetskoi and Said, on the other, gave almost opposite evaluative assessments of the consequences of the power–knowledge relationship, insofar as Bartol'd never condemned modern European imperialism as such.

It would be in the 1920s and the early 1930s, in the context of the Bolsheviks' strong anticolonial rhetoric, that two other scholars of the Rozen school, Marr and Ol'denburg, would start to systematically condemn European culture, and Orientology specifically, as a tool of colonialism. Their arguments developed in parallel to those of the Eurasians.[70] Yet there is evidence that the two groups knew more about each other's works than is usually assumed: it appears that in December 1927 Marr gave a lecture at a closed meeting of the Eurasians in Paris.[71]

At the same time, in a critical period in terms of his own career and the situation of the Academy of Sciences vis-à-vis the Soviet regime, Ol'denburg published a series of articles, elaborating in a particularly radical way his earlier concerns about the European tendency of viewing the Orient from a position of unchallenged superiority. In these publications, which appeared between 1927 and 1932, Ol'denburg argued that the way in which the Europeans from the time of ancient Greeks to the present imagined "the Orient"—as backward and stagnant—directly facilitated European imperialism.[72] In Ol'denburg's words, "The entire history of the relationship between East and West, from the Greeks in antiquity through the time of the Crusaders, in the Middle Ages and extending up to the modern and contemporary era" was marked by "attempts [on the part of the West] to enslave the East, . . . rendering the East voiceless" (*besslovesnyi*).[73] This goal "naturally" was "reflected in the scholarship of the East," influenced by the perception of the profound difference between the East and the West. "In the history of juxtaposing the East and the West, imperialistic tendencies always played a key role." In the past this was the imperialism of Alexander the Great, in contemporary times "European colonialism."[74] Ol'denburg then offered a sustained critique of modern Oriental Studies in Europe as a tool of European colonial policies.[75] Similar to the Eurasian theories, Ol'denburg's sweeping conclusions had their roots in the pan-European tradition of the turn of the twentieth century. As I have argued elsewhere, in 1963 Ol'denburg's arguments were repeated by Anouar Abdel-Malek, a Marxist sociologist from Egypt, whose essay "Orientalism in Crisis" was acknowledged by Said as an important source for his own arguments.[76]

Of course, there could not be a complete similarity between the theoretical approaches of contemporary scholars and works that were written in the early twentieth century. Yet the ideas formulated by scholars such as Ol'denburg and the Eurasians pose the question of the extent of originality not only of Eurasian theories but also of contemporary postcolonial studies. This instructive example of the circulation of ideas tells us a great deal about the relationship between the production of knowledge and the political and social contexts within which knowledge producers operate. We should not subscribe to the simplistic view that all knowledge is generated in response to political demands because much research has little to do with immediate societal goals and political developments. Yet historical circumstances sometimes compel intellectually ambitious scholars and thinkers to frame their questions by projecting onto the past the immediate concerns of their own societies. The collapse of the Russian Empire in the course of the Great War and the emergence of anti-imperial movements in Russia's borderlands had helped to sharpen the existing concerns about European colonialism among Russian Empire savers, whether they were the Bolsheviks, the Eurasians, or the Orientologists. In these circumstances specific to Russia, its scholars and thinkers of the early twentieth century began to pose particularly radical questions about the relationship between imperial power and European culture. These questions would only become similarly topical for their Western counterparts following the disintegration of the West European overseas empires in the wake of the Second World War. Let us now turn to the practical alternatives the Eurasians offered to the dominant imperial and colonial relationships that they so sharply criticized.

Solving the Contradiction between Empire and Nation

In their attempts to identify ways of preserving a multiethnic state on the territory of the former Russian Empire at the time of the disintegration of European land-based empires, the Eurasians, particularly Trubetskoi and Konstantin Chkheidze, suggested that all the nationalities of Eurasia should foster multiple identities and develop an interconnected and complementary hierarchy of loyalties.[77] The Eurasians argued that the peoples of Eurasia should possess a simultaneous sense of belonging to their own culturally defined national groups and to the overarching Pan-Eurasian nation. In Trubetskoi's words, "[t]he nationalism of the peoples should have a corresponding foundation: Pan-Eurasian nationalism should arise as a broadening of the nationalism of each people of Eurasia, as a merging of these individual nationalisms into a whole."[78] Challenging widespread perceptions of ethnocultural hierarchies, the Eurasians postulated the equality of all the nationalities of Eurasia, yet they still insisted that the Russians, because of their population size and historical significance, had a special status.[79] The nationalism of various nationalities, which the Eurasians regarded as compatible with and complementary to the pan-Eurasian unity, was cultural. They feared political nationalism with a separatist agenda, which they thought was noticeable among the Ukrainians, for example.[80] Yet again, the Eurasians formulated this position in a dialogue with other Russian intellectuals and politicians who had pondered over this issue since the late nineteenth century.

Contemporary scholars have noted that the Eurasians' proposals for preserving the unity of the former Russian Empire and resolving the contradiction between the imperial structure and the forces of modern nationalism were a reaction to the Soviet project of fostering complementary loyalties among peoples of the new Soviet state to their local ethnocultural communities as well as to the communist state as a whole. The Eurasians borrowed certain ideas from the Bolshevik approach to managing multiethnicity and simultaneously criticized it. The Eurasians were also responding to various federalist projects for the organization of the nationalities of the former Russian Empire proposed by non-Russian émigré intellectuals.[81] Finally, it has been noted by contemporary scholars that the Eurasians began to dwell on the relationship between empire and nation prior to the 1917 revolution, being interested in Petr Struve's well-known concept of Russia as a nation-state empire in the making, which singled out Russian culture as the main binding force in the imperial state.[82]

In addition to acknowledging some of the wider intellectual and political context in which Eurasian ideas were formulated, contemporary scholars also see the Eurasian concept of pan-Eurasian nationalism—which presupposed the complementarity of local ethnocultural nationalisms and the overarching Eurasian national identity—as containing strong original elements that were foreign to the prerevolutionary thinking on the nationality question.[83] Recent research on late imperial Russia tends to emphasize its development toward the colonial empire model with something resembling a "Russian national core" and the treatment of the eastern borderlands as colonial possessions.[84] Even Struve's idea rested on the little-questioned assumption of the superiority of ethnic Russian culture over cultures of the empire's non-Russian minorities. While not denying the originality of some aspects of the concept of the pan-Eurasian nationalism as well as the existence of the above-described trend in the development of the Russian Empire in the last decades of its existence, we will now focus on another important intellectual tradition of the late imperial period that has noticeable similarities to both Soviet policies on nationalities and the Eurasian project. The Orientologists of the Rozen school were representatives of this tradition from the end of the nineteenth century onward.

Arguments about the need to foster people's complementary loyalties and about a close relationship between local and overarching state-framed identities, which the Eurasians articulated so clearly, actually began to be voiced in the nineteenth century. The best-known example is the proposition of the missionary Nikolai Il'minskii (1822–1891) that the first step toward the conversion to Orthodox Christianity of non-Russian minority groups in the Volga region was to make these minorities more conscious and proud of their own distinct ethnocultural specificities.[85] However, in striking contrast to the later ideas of the Eurasians, Il'minskii's understanding of people's identities, including Russian national identity, was a traditional religious one.[86] It was also based on a highly hierarchical view of cultures, with its unquestioned sense of the superiority of Orthodoxy and European culture.

At the same time, in the 1870s, another set of arguments was articulated in favor of strengthening the empire through the complementarity of local and pan-state identities, now imagined as broadly cultural and civic rather than religious. These new ideas were first voiced in relation to the Russian population. At the turn of the twentieth century, they were extrapolated to the eastern minorities.[87]

These new ideas were associated with the emergence of the "small native homeland" (*malaia rodina*) movement, whose advocates were concerned about how to make a pan-national loyalty, a feeling of common overarching identity, take root in Russia despite its huge size and diversity.[88] Originally articulated most vocally by intellectuals in Siberia and the provinces of European Russia in relation to the Russian-speaking population rather than the minorities, the concept was based on the assumption that in order to foster a sense of national loyalty to the entire state-framed community, one should first develop a thorough knowledge of and love for the history and cultural tradition of one's place of birth and permanent residence. One could relate to the entire Russian fatherland (*otechestvo*) only through a strong affiliation with one specific locality ("small native homeland"), it was argued. Russia was so large that it was impossible to know all of it well and to love it as a whole, equally, in abstract terms. The belief was that instead of a conflict between a strong local identity and an overarching pan-Russian one, there was a complementary fusion of the two identities.

As Yuri Slezkine noted, the place of non-Russian eastern minorities in the vision of the best known representatives of the "small native homeland" movement, the Siberian regionalists, was ambiguous. On the one hand, non-Russian minorities represented Siberia's indigenous roots, but on the other, they were the manifestation of Siberia's backwardness.[89] The leader of the Siberian regionalists and a champion of the rights of Siberia's indigenous population, Nikolai Iadrintsev, nevertheless spoke about the minorities as "inferior races," and stated that mixing with them had a negative effect on the physical, intellectual, and moral qualities of Russian settlers. He therefore proposed the increased immigration of good quality Russian settlers to Siberia.[90] But Iadrintsev's was not the only way of viewing the situation of the eastern minorities through the prism of the ideology of the "native homeland movement." In his 1899 speech to mark his appointment to a post in Armenian Studies at St. Petersburg University, Marr applied the ideas of the "native homeland" movement to the non-Russian subjects of the empire in the same way that they had been applied to Russian settlers by Siberian regionalists. Marr observed: "As for the Armenians and the Georgians, in particular, the state has all the more reason to regard Armenian and Georgian studies as an excellent tool, because it is clear that they develop and strengthen enlightened love and respect for the native homeland (*rodina*). Who can deny the fact, which is axiomatic to me, that one who is indifferent to the plight of one's own region cannot deeply embrace a more abstract and complex feeling for the fatherland (*otechestvo*)."[91]

Other Orientologists of the Rozen school shared Marr's view and argued that the growth of "ethnocultural awareness" of non-Russian minorities would not prevent them from strengthening their pan-Russian loyalty but, on the contrary, would be conducive to this. The latter, rather than being ethnic Russian, was supposed to be state-framed and rooted in the sense of sharing a common historical fate and partaking in the creation of a common culture as defined by Kondakov and Rozen.[92] The scholars took upon themselves the role of facilitating such a development, in particular, by fostering the emergence of local intelligentsias with a strong sense of interconnected loyalties among small minority groups in Siberia and the Caucasus.[93] As with other empire savers, including the Eurasians, these scholars were champions of the ethnocultural nationalisms of minorities with "weak" cultural identities but they feared political nationalism with a separatist potential.[94]

These prerevolutionary perceptions influenced the Bolshevik nationalities policies,[95] and because future Eurasians had begun to think, prior to the revolution, about how to preserve the unity of Russia, there is little doubt that they knew the arguments articulated in the late imperial period about the alleged conduciveness of local ethnocultural nationalisms to the formation of an overarching pan-Russian identity. So, the 1917 revolutions appear not to be such a major divide in the thinking about the management of Russia's multiethnicity in the era of nationalism as is often perceived, even if the actual policies of the Bolshevik government toward nationalities constituted a major break with the way in which their tsarist predecessors dealt with the issue.

When properly placed within the broader pan-European context of the period spanning the last decades of the nineteenth century and also when compared to contemporary postcolonial scholarship, the Eurasian ideology—inflected by a radical anti-Westernism and conceptualizing Russia as separate from Europe—appears to be as much a manifestation of Europe's own intellectual trend as it is a reflection of Russia's specific circumstances. It was also not only in Russia that the above-described intellectual revisionism of the fin de siècle, which was aimed at promoting cultural inclusivity, mutated into antiliberal visions based on an ever greater vilification of the nation's "Other." Whereas in Russia the fin-de-siècle fascination with the Orient and the questioning of Eurocentrism led to the articulation of a binary opposition between Russia and the West/Europe, in Germany the ambiguous heritage of its revisionist Orientology made it possible to use some of its findings and assumptions in support of the racist ideology of the Third Reich.[96]

An understanding of the Eurasian movement as part of a pan-European intellectual trend originating in the last decades of the nineteenth century also helps us assess the significance of the 1917 revolution as a turning point in Russian history. The evidence presented in this chapter points to a substantial continuity in the intellectual pursuits across this divide, thus demonstrating that certain post-1917 trends and developments cannot be properly understood without appreciating their origins in the prerevolutionary period. And yet, the outlined similarities notwithstanding, there were also differences between those intellectuals, such as Kondakov and members of the Rozen school, whose broader visions were formed in the late nineteenth and early twentieth centuries, on the one hand, and the Eurasians of the 1920s, on the other.[97]

Not surprisingly, the difference between the two groups was manifested particularly clearly in their attitudes toward Europe. This difference allows us to see that, although still responding to many of the issues whose origins can be traced to the turn of the twentieth century, the Eurasians also reflected the beginning of a new period. After all, the contexts in which the ideas of the imperial scholars and the Eurasians were formed were fundamentally different. For the imperial scholars it was a period of the greatest optimism in the aftermath of the Reforms of the 1860s about Russia's ability to follow the West European path of political development, even if the understanding of what "Europe" meant was becoming much more complex and ambiguous than before. For the Eurasians it was a period of widespread disillusionment with "European civilization" and of the collapse of hopes about Russia's ability to follow West European political models. Not insignificantly, the academics discussed in this chapter were secure and comfortable with their identity as European scholars. The Eurasians were émigrés struggling to find a place in their host societies.

In the immediate aftermath of the February Revolution, Marr defined Russia as "a historically formed part of the special cultural world, neither West European nor East Asiatic."[98] If one removes the "West" from the adjective West European, Marr's definition would almost coincide with the definitions given to "Russia-Eurasia" by the Eurasians. The fact that Marr juxtaposed Russia not with Europe but with Western Europe is, however, significant and it marks a difference between the Eurasians and the scholars of the Kondakov and Rozen schools. Marr's definition of Russia was informed by the assumption of East European intellectuals, dating back to the eighteenth century, that Europe and its Western core were not one and the same. This assumption was articulated at the time when West European elites constructed the concept of "Eastern Europe" as an intermediate world between culture and barbarism.[99] By separating Europe and Western Europe, East European intellectuals fought the "Orientalization" of their societies by West Europeans.[100] To some extent, the insistence of Bartol'd and other Orientologists on the constructed and regularly changing nature of the boundaries between Europe and Asia and the categories of East and West reflected their attempt to assert Russia's European identity while at the same time acknowledging its difference from Western Europe.

The Eurasians agreed with the Orientologists that there was no objectively identifiable boundary between Russia and Asia, but they postulated the existence of an impenetrable border between "Russia-Eurasia" and Europe. The difference between the views of the scholars discussed here and those of the Classical Eurasians was well reflected in Trubetskoi's reaction to Peter Bitsilli's article, "The 'East' and the 'West' in the History of the Old World," which appeared in one of the Eurasianist publications.[101] A historian whose main patron in emigration was Kondakov,[102] Bitsilli reiterated Kondakov's ideas about the importance of Persian influences on early European art and of Byzantine art on the culture of the Renaissance. Following the research initiated by Rozen and his disciples, Bitsilli dwelled on the role of "Eastern" thinkers in the formation of Christianity, and following Kondakov and the Orientologists, he discussed the role of the nomads in dispersing various cultural forms across the Old World. Furthermore, following Bartol'd and other Orientologists, Bitsilli insisted that the concepts of "East" and "West" did not reflect any objective reality.[103] A boundary between Europe and Eurasia, which was central to the worldview of the Eurasians, was not part of the picture drawn by Bitsilli. His ideas were thus a mere reiteration of the arguments of the scholars of the Kondakov and Rozen schools. It is instructive that Trubetskoi found them neither sufficiently original nor sufficiently Eurasian.[104]

In line with their idea of the existence of the impenetrable boundary between Europe and Eurasia, the Eurasians unequivocally condemned Europe's influences on non-European peoples as "takeovers" destructive for native cultural traditions.[105] This position was at odds with the way in which cultural influences were perceived by the scholars discussed here. Most members of the Kondakov and Rozen schools, particularly Bartol'd, regarded cultural influences, including European influences on "Eastern" societies, as mostly positive or value-neutral forces that stimulated new creative developments. Of Rozen's disciples it seems that only Marr, with his childhood experience of being a "native" under European colonialism, eventually departed from his teacher's optimistic vision of "cultural interactions." In the last prerevolutionary decade Marr began to argue that internal impulses rather than external ones such as migration should be used to explain major cultural and linguistic shifts; he also started to describe ancient Greek and other European influences in the Caucasus as largely detrimental to local cultures. In the 1920s Marr's views further radicalized and became more isolationist.[106] In this vilification of (Western) Europe, Marr differed from most of Rozen's disciples, and in the 1920s he came closer to the Eurasians than any of them.[107]

After 1917 some of Kondakov's and Rozen's disciples maintained views different from those of the Eurasians on crucial issues such as Russia's relationship with Europe or the nature of cultural encounters between peoples. This suggests that we should avoid articulating teleological accounts of the origins of illiberal ideologies and policies of the Soviet era in the pursuit of liberal Russian scholarship of the fin de siècle and we should avoid drawing causal connections between the latter and the former.[108] On the contrary, any complex intellectual tradition such as the one associated with Europe's "Second Oriental Renaissance" is bound to give rise to a range of different interpretations, some of which can run counter to this tradition's original fundamental premises.[109]

N. S. TRUBETSKOI'S *EUROPE AND MANKIND* AND EURASIANIST ANTIEVOLUTIONISM

One Unknown Source

Sergey Glebov

THE Eurasianist movement burst onto the Russian émigré scene in the wake of tragic and dramatic events, each of which had a worldwide significance. The First World War, the Russian Revolution, the Civil War, and the emergence of the Bolshevik regime were all enormously important for the articulation of the Eurasianist vision for the space of the former Russian Empire. Russia's disintegration as an empire following the war and revolution, the Bolsheviks' international isolation, and their grand project of building an anticolonialist and socialist empire have largely obscured for historians the extent to which Eurasianism was intellectually a part of the ongoing discussion about the organization of the political space of the Russian Empire in the second half of the nineteenth century. It was in the context of that conversation that the Eurasianist movement offered a new imagery of the political and cultural community in the former Russian Empire.[1]

Among the main themes of this imagery were a rejection of centrifugal nationalisms, a vision of a totalizing unity of the Eurasian space, and a strong critique of "European" ideas of civilizational competence and hierarchies, while Eurasia was reinvented as a colonized country, a potential leader of the uprising of the colonized against the colonizers.[2] Many of these ideas strikingly resembled critiques of colonialism as a form of knowledge articulated in the second half of the twentieth century, including Edward Said's famous *Orientalism*.[3] Paradoxically, the Eurasianist "postcolonial" argument was not emancipatory but pursued several goals: to sustain the unity of the imperial space, to disarm local nationalisms, and, perhaps more important, to articulate a non-European subjectivity of the Russian imperial space. This subjectivity hinged not so much on "Eurasia" as a geographical space but on a profound reorientation of the Eurasian space temporally. Russia-Eurasia, when it "left the European space," also abandoned the evolutionary map of world cultures and a universal vision of history.

In this chapter, I offer a discussion of the Eurasianist critique of European colonialism and associated forms of knowledge, such as evolutionism. By analyzing both published sources and archival references, I argue that the Eurasianist rebellion against colonialism should be read in the context of the Russian reception of evolutionist ideas in sociology, in particular in the writings of Maksim Maksimovich Kovalevskii, a scholar whose ideas were both universalist (he believed in the universal laws of societal development) and particularist (he defended a program of the internal division of imperial Russian society into a "civilized European" core and an "ethnic and backward" periphery). N. S. Trubetskoi's treatise *Europe and Mankind* was a response, albeit a belated one, to Kovalevskii's ideas.

The key Eurasianist thinker who was responsible for the movement's anticolonialist and relativist edge was Prince Nikolai Sergeevich Trubetskoi (1890–1938). A scion of one of the empire's most aristocratic families (the Trubetskoi princes were connected to the centers of power through a myriad of marital and familial ties built over several centuries), Trubetskoi had a protected and happy childhood. Somewhat unusually for the Russian titled aristocracy, the Trubetskois became an academic dynasty. N. S. Trubetskoi's father, Prince Sergei Nikolaevich Trubetskoi (1860–1905), was a famous philosopher and historian of Christianity, and a close friend of Vladimir Solov'ev. A professor at Moscow University, S. N. Trubetskoi became the school's first elected rector during the turbulent events of the 1905 Revolution. Less than a month later, after numerous, largely unsuccessful attempts to strike a balance between his liberal views and his commitment to public order, S. N. Trubetskoi collapsed during a meeting at the Ministry of People's Enlightenment and died. By that time, Trubetskoi, only fifteen years old, had developed a strong interest in ethnography and had even published short articles in the academic journal *Etnograficheskoe obozrenie* and established correspondence with some of Russia's leading ethnographers. Trubetskoi's biographers like to cite the following episode: V. G. Tan-Bogoraz, a revolutionary exile turned ethnographer of Siberian peoples, who had received a letter from Trubetskoi seeking advice on Paleoasiatic languages, decided to pay a visit to his scholarly colleague. However, he left Trubetskoi's house in anger at the aristocrats who had poked fun at him, when, following his request to see "Prince Nikolai Sergeevich," he was greeted by a teenager.[4] Lavishly educated by private tutors and at the famous Fifth Moscow Gymnasium (where Boris Pasternak and Vladimir Mayakovsky were also students), in 1908 Trubetskoi entered Moscow University, where he had initially studied West European literature but moved to linguistics and ethnography. He recalled later that his decision was inspired by the belief that linguistics was the most scientific of all humanities and should therefore provide a method for research in humanities. As Anatoly Liberman noted, this was a "radical statement for the year of 1909," and it certainly forecast the importance of the discipline in the twentieth century.[5] In 1910–1911 Trubetskoi switched completely to comparative linguistics.[6] This shift coincided with a range of developments in Russian linguistics that had an influence on young Trubetskoi. The Dialectological Commission initiated research on the dialects of the Russian language (including Ukrainian and Belorussian, which were then considered dialects of Russian), and on the eve of the First World War published the first results of this research.[7] At Moscow University the Linguistic Circle, in which Roman Jakobson and Trubetskoi took an active part, started its deliberations.[8] Jakobson recalled that at the time Trubetskoi "in vain sought a discussion with contemporary philosophers and psychologists at Moscow University, namely, a discussion on the most pressing issues of people's psychology, historiosophy, and methodology of the humanities. Both of us clearly remembered how we had taken turns in seeing each other off to our houses on foot after the meetings of the Commission for Popular Philology or the Moscow Dialectological Commission and vividly discussed the theoretical foundations of nationalism."[9]

Thinking about nationalism and its foundations, Trubetskoi attended lectures by the linguist V. K. Porzhezinski, historians R. G. Vipper and M. M. Pokrovskii, and others. In the course of the 1910s he also participated in the activities of the Ethnographic Section of the Society of Lovers of Natural Sciences, Anthropology, and Ethnography. At this time, Trubetskoi closely cooperated with Vsevolod Fedorovich Miller, a scholar of Iranian languages (Ossetian, in particular), a researcher of Russian folklore, and founder of the journal *Etnograficheskoe obozrenie* (Ethnographic Review), which published several articles by Trubetskoi from 1906 to 1914.[10] At Miller's dacha in the North Caucasus, near Kislovodsk, Trubetskoi spent summer months doing fieldwork on Caucasian languages and mythology.

At the university, Trubetskoi became a student of the so-called Moscow Linguistic School, which featured A. A. Shakhmatov and V. K. Porzhezinski as its leading scholars and produced a phenomenal group of linguists prominent in the twentieth century: Nikolai Durnovo, Roman Jakobson, Nikolai Iakovlev, and Petr Bogatyrev. Of this group, many would be associated with the Prague Linguistic Circle in the 1920s. Others, such as Iakovlev, would be prominent in the process of creating alphabets and standardizing languages for Russian nationalities as the Bolshevik state embarked upon the policies of *korenizatsiia* in the early 1920s.[11]

In 1913 Trubetskoi passed his university examinations and began work to prepare for magisterial exams. He spent the academic year of 1913–1914 in Germany, and returned to Moscow on the eve of the Great War in the summer of 1914. In the spring of 1916 Trubetskoi passed his magisterial examinations in the form of two public lectures and became an assistant professor (*privat-dotsent*) at Moscow University. His first teaching assignment was Sanskrit.

The period that began in the fall of 1917 must have been truly dramatic for the young scholar. He took sick leave from the university in late autumn 1917 as the Bolsheviks assumed power in the capitals, and moved to the South of Russia along with thousands of other members of the educated classes. He went to Kislovodsk in the Caucasus, then to Baku, and then to Rostov-on-Don. From time to time, he taught at the new schools and universities established by different regimes in the imperial borderlands. In December 1919, Trubetskoi was evacuated from Rostov-on-Don to Yalta in Crimea, and chose almost immediately to leave for Istanbul (in February 1920, almost a year before the evacuation of the last White armies from Crimea). Staying in the war-stricken south of Russia underscored the collapse of the Russian Empire for Trubetskoi. In a letter to Roman Jakobson he recalled, "during my wanderings in the Caucasus I once came to Baku in March 1918, exactly during the 'Muslim uprising against the Soviet power,' or, more precisely, during this short period of time when the Armenians were slaughtering the Tatars."[12] Interethnic conflicts in the Caucasus, similar to the March Days in Baku in 1918, which Trubetskoi witnessed, undoubtedly colored his perceptions of the nationalist movements in the former empire.[13]

From Istanbul, Trubetskoi contacted Bulgarian scholars whom he met in his father's house. The Trubetskoi name carried a lot of weight and he was invited to come to teach at the University of Sofia in Bulgaria, and thus began an illustrious academic career in Europe, which led to his assumption of a position as professor of Slavic languages at the University of Vienna in 1922. Trubetskoi remained in Vienna until his death in 1938, and it was in Vienna that he composed his works laying out the foundations of structural phonology, which established his reputation as one of the twentieth century's greatest linguists.

It was in Sofia in 1920 that Trubetskoi met other leaders of the Eurasian-ist movement and published his brochure *Europe and Mankind*, with the Russian-Bulgarian Publishing House, the main outlet for early Eurasianist publications. The book came out well before the first Eurasianist collection. Curiously, Trubetskoi chose to write his book without specific references to the Russian experience, focusing instead on a generalized critique of the Euro-centric worldview. As Trubetskoi put it in the introduction to his book, "my ideas concern not just the Russians but all other peoples who more or less accepted the European culture without being Romano-Germans by origin."[14]

Trubetskoi's starting point in *Europe and Mankind* was the problem of cosmopolitanism. The author claimed that a European can take one of two possible positions with respect to the national question: a cosmopolitan or a chauvinistic one. For most Europeans these two positions appear as oppo-sites, fundamentally different from each other. However, a closer look at the problem reveals that they are not, in fact, in opposition to each other. A chau-vinist "proceeds from an a priori notion that his own nation is the best in the world." A cosmopolitan, on the other hand, "denies all distinctions between nationalities. If such distinctions exist, they need to be destroyed. Civilized humanity must be whole and must have a single and universal culture. Un-civilized peoples must accept that culture and, having entered the family of civilized nations, must accompany them on the path of world progress." In this representation of the two opposites they, indeed, "appear as strikingly different from each other. In the first case one postulates the supremacy of one ethnographic and anthropological unit, whereas in the second it is pos-tulated for the culture of supra-ethnographic humanity." The trick, however, is in "what content the European cosmopolitans ascribe to such concepts as "civilization" and "civilized humankind." Under "civilization they understand the same culture that was created in the common work of the Roman and Germanic peoples of Europe, and under 'civilized peoples' they understand the same Romans and Germans, followed by other peoples who accepted European culture." Because European cosmopolitans thus propagate the cul-ture of a "specific ethnographic and anthropological unit, the same unit whose supremacy the chauvinist dreams of, there is no principal difference between chauvinism and cosmopolitanism."[15]

From this point Trubetskoi concluded that "European culture is not the culture of humankind. It is a product of history of a very definite ethnic group. Germanic and Celtic tribes, influenced in varying degrees by the Roman cul-ture and thoroughly intermixed, created a certain common way of life from the elements of their national and Roman culture." Trubetskoi believed that "these common elements were so significant that the feeling of Romano-Germanic unity always subconsciously lived in these peoples." When these peoples turned to the sources of their culture, "cosmopolitan ideas of antiquity became the foundation of education in Europe. Planted on the favorable soil of the subconscious feeling of Romano-Germanic unity, these foundations generated the theoretical fundament of so-called European cosmopolitanism, which ought to be called openly 'common Romano-Germanic chauvinism.'"[16]

Trubetskoi believed that the psychological foundations of European cosmopolitanism were to be found in egocentrism, which again makes cosmopolitanism indistinguishable from chauvinism. "Few Europeans," Trubetskoi argued, "can move beyond so-called cosmopolitanism, that is, Romano-Germanic chauvinism. We do not know whatsoever any such Europeans, who would have accepted the cultures of so-called savages as equal to the Romano-Germanic culture. It appears that such Europeans simply do not exist." Because at the basis of cosmopolitanism, "this religion of the common humankind, we find an anticultural principle of egocentrism, . . . an earnest Romano-German ought to refute both chauvinism and cosmopolitanism."[17]

How, then, should representatives of non–Romano-Germanic peoples relate to the notion of European cosmopolitan culture? Trubetskoi bemoaned the fact that "among the Slavs, Arabs, Turks, Indians, Chinese, and Japanese there are already a lot of cosmopolites." "A Russian *intelligent* [i.e., a member of the intelligentsia] rejects angrily any thought that he could be a tool of German nationalist Junkers, whereas he is not scared of submission to the common Romano-Germanic chauvinists." The solution to this paradox is to be found in the "hypnosis of words." The Romano-Germans were so sure that "only they were human beings that they called themselves 'humanity' and their own culture 'the all-human civilization,' and their own chauvinism 'cosmopolitanism.'"[18]

Thus, the commitment of non–Romano-Germans to "European civilization" was the result of an "optical illusion." The non-European educated classes need to open their eyes and "change their attitude to the culture of their own peoples." They can only decide on the value of Europeanization if they consider the following questions: Can it be objectively proven that the culture of Romano-Germans is more perfect than any other culture in existence now or in the past? Is it possible for a people to completely embrace a culture created by another people without the anthropological mixing of both peoples? Is joining European culture (to the extent that it is possible) good or bad? If these questions are answered negatively, Europeanization needs to be refuted and new questions need to be posed: Is general Europeanization unavoidable? How does one fight the unwelcome consequences of Europeanization?[19]

To respond to the first question, Trubetskoi addressed the problem of evolutionary development, which in his view was "permeated by egocentrism":

"Evolutionary ladder," "stages of development" are deeply egocentric concepts. In the foundation of these concepts is the idea that the development of humankind proceeds along the path of so-called world progress, and this path is thought to be a certain straight line. Humankind was allegedly proceeding along this line, but certain peoples stopped at different points on this line and they continue to stay at these points, whereas other peoples have gotten farther along the line. . . . Correspondingly we can observe . . . the entire human evolution, for at each particular point on the path already trodden by humanity, a particular people remains even now. . . . Contemporary humanity, in its entirety, represents a kind of cinematogram of evolution unfolded and cut into pieces, and cultures of various peoples differ from each other exactly as the different phases of common evolution, as different stages of the common path of world progress.[20]

For Trubetskoi, if one accepts this vision of human civilization, one still cannot determine where the end and the beginning of the evolution are. One can only determine the beginning and the end in some irrational, suprascientific way. Remaining objective, we can only group cultures according to the presence of common or similar traits in these cultures. But in this case we do not get a "ladder," but a "rainbow," and we still do not know the exact sequence of colors in that rainbow. The Europeans determined their own position at the top of the evolutionary progress due to their own "egocentric" psychology, which suggested that Europe was the beginning and the end of evolutionary development: "Instead of remaining objective . . . the Europeans simply took themselves and their own culture to be the crown of human evolution."[21]

However, as Trubetskoi maintained, "objectively speaking, this entire "ladder of progress" just groups peoples and cultures according to how much they resemble Europeans." The historical argument, which asserted that Europeans were also savages in the distant past, did not withstand criticism, Trubetskoi thought. The fact that the Europeans as savages were maximally different from their current stage of development does not suggest that the evolutionary universal principles work. The concept of "savage culture" is negative and is deprived of any meaningful content, insofar as today's European scholars apply it to both their own distant path and to cultures of the Eskimo and Africans, and it is obvious that these cultures have nothing in common. To call them "savage" in this context is just to assert that they are maximally different from modern European civilization. And when European scholars argue that "savage" cultures are "stagnant," they fall victim to an optical distortion. At any given moment in history, a culture different from the European civilization remains; and a European scholar who is seeking signs of commonality will not find any dynamics in "savage" cultures, because they will always remain maximally different from contemporary Europe. History in these cultures does not exist for the Europeans, but for the representatives of these cultures it is a dynamic process full of meaningful events. This notion of the evolution of humankind as "objective" did not withstand the trial of logic: "The moment of judgment, which makes a ladder of stages of perfection from this classification, is not objective and is founded on purely subjective egocentric psychology."[22]

Similarly, Trubetskoi refuted the argument that compared representatives of "backward" cultures to European children. In his opinion, this comparison was also based on a misunderstanding. According to Trubetskoi, each person's psyche consists of features that are hereditary and acquired. Because we have only hereditary features in common with peoples who are culturally distant from us, we only recognize them when we encounter them, whereas the acquired features, as shaped by a foreign culture, remain invisible to us. After all, Trubetskoi argued, the so-called savages also often view Europeans as "child-like." The idea of the "elementary nature of the savage's psyche is based on an optical illusion." Trubetskoi considered another popular argument in favor of the supremacy of European civilization—the often claimed European superiority in military matters and Europe's victories over the "savages." He thought that the "rudeness and naiveté of this argument ought to be clear to every objectively thinking person. This argument clearly shows the extent to which the veneration of brute force, which makes up an essential feature of the national character of those tribes that created the European civilization, is still alive in the consciousness of every descendant of ancient Gauls and Germans. Gallic 'vae victis!' and Germanic vandalism systematized and deepened by the traditions of Roman soldiery appear here in all of their clarity, even if covered by the masque of scientific objectivity." Even European scholarship has to admit that historically the "less developed" nomads often emerged victorious over the "civilized" settled populations. Hence, "no positive conclusion can be derived from the mere fact of the European victory over the savages."[23]

Trubetskoi also criticized the popular arguments in favor of Europe's supremacy. Europeans often argue that their intellectual advantage over the "savages" is evident because the intellectual "luggage" of a European is vaster. Trubetskoi suggested that "a good savage, who possesses all the qualities that his tribe values in a person—keeps in his mind an enormous storage of various kinds of knowledge." This knowledge is not chaotic, it is systematized, but it is also fundamentally different from the knowledge a European might perceive as valuable. Hence, "the intellectual luggage of the savage and the European ought to be recognized as incomparable, and the question regarding the supremacy of one or another left as insolvable." Similarly, Trubetskoi refuted the notion that European culture is allegedly more complex than the cultures of non-Europeans. The "savages" follow codes of behavior common to the whole collective, whereas in Europe only the upper classes have "good manners." The "savages" often have more complex ways of decorating their bodies than Europeans. Similarly, whereas in Europe "the monogamous family officially exists under the protection of law, it is accompanied by the most unbound sexual liberty, theoretically condemned by state and society but in practice tolerated. Compare this to the detailed and thought-through institution of group marriage among the Australian aborigines, where sexual life is placed in the strictest framework and, although individual marriage is absent, all measures are taken to care for the children and to prevent incest."[24]

All historical arguments that Europeans put forward to support their alleged "supremacy" are based on logical inconsistencies:

> What is considered the latest rage of civilization in Europe or the top of progress not yet achieved, if encountered among the savages is then declared to be a feature of extreme backwardness. Futurist paintings drawn by Europeans are treated as products of the most refined aesthetic taste, but similar products by "savages" are viewed as naive attempts, the first dawns of primordial art. Socialism, communism, and anarchism are all "bright ideals of the coming and highest progress" but only when they are proselytized by a modern European. When these "ideals" turn out to have been realized in the everyday life of "savages," they are immediately described as revelations of primeval wilderness.[25]

Trubetskoi concluded that there can be no "objective proofs of European supremacy over the savages, and there can be none simply because in comparing different cultures Europeans know only one measure: what looks like ours is better and more perfect than what differs from ours." Hence, the "ladder of civilization . . . needs to be destroyed. If its top is not higher than its foundation, then it is obvious that it is also not higher than those stages that are between the top and the foundation."[26]

For Trubetskoi, the power of the notion of European supremacy rested on European control of modern disciplinary knowledge, which was permeated by "egocentric" European chauvinism. In a startling passage that linked European imperialism and colonialism with knowledge, Trubetskoi demanded:

> The moment of evaluative judgment [has to] be purged once and forever from ethnography and the history of culture as well as from all evolutionary disciplines in general, for evaluative judgment is always based on egocentrism. There are no superior and inferior [cultures]. There are only

similar and different ones. To declare that those similar to ours are superior and those different from ours are inferior is arbitrary, nonscholarly, naïve, and, finally, simply unintelligent. European evolutionary disciplines, in particular ethnography, anthropology, and the history of culture can become real scientific disciplines only when they have overcome this deeply rooted superstition and expunged its consequences from their very methods and conclusions. Until this is done, they remain in the best case a means to fool people and to justify in the eyes of the Romano-Germans and their accomplices the imperialist colonial policies and the vandalistic *Kulturtraegershaft* of "the great powers of Europe and America."[27]

Echoing a century-long concern of Russian intellectuals about the imitative nature of their own culture, Trubetskoi also considered the possibility that one people could accept the culture of another. To analyze this problem, he turned to the ideas of the French sociologist, Gabriel de Tarde. Tarde's sociological works focused on the problem of the diffusion of cultural values. He argued that the entire process of the production of culture can be broken down into several fundamental processes. First, a new cultural value is created by combining the existing elements with some innovation in what Tarde called "invention." New "inventions" are then spread through the process of "propagation," entering into competition with the existing cultural norms and values in what Tarde described as "duel logique." Since both "invention" and "propagation" involve already existing cultural norms, Tarde proposed that the overall framework for understanding cultural change should be described through the notion of "laws of imitation."[28] Trubetskoi described Tarde as "an outstanding European sociologist of the past century who, unfortunately, was comparatively little known and wrongly evaluated in Europe." Trubetskoi thought that Tarde "came closer to the truth than most in his general views of the nature of social processes and methods of sociology." Still, "his passion for generalizations and his striving . . . to give a view of the entire evolution of 'humankind' ruined this erudite scholar." Trubetskoi believed the roots of Tarde's misconceptions were in "European egocentric prejudices," which prevented him from "taking a point of view of the equal value and qualitative incomparability of peoples and cultures, and from thinking of 'humanity' as other than a single whole, the separate parts of which are located on the evolutionary ladder."[29]

Given that during the process of imitation both tradition and heritage play a role, Trubetskoi argued that the culture of people who are imitating the culture of another will never be equal to the culture that is being imitated. Whereas new cultural values are propagated by schools, the army, factories, and other such institutions, the family will remain the source of cultural values inherent in people attempting imitation. As a result, the overall "cultural direction" of people attempting the imitation will be a mixture and never a complete identity with the culture being imitated.

The distinction between "assimilation" (*priobshchenie*) and "mixture" (*smeshenie*) was a crucial one for Trubetskoi. He was determined to argue against Europeanization as a harmful process, but he was not opposed to a mixture or "synthesis" of cultures. After all, the Eurasianist project attempted to endow the geographical space of Eurasia with a cultural content of cultural and ethnographic mix, and the notion of any cultural mix as harmful would have undermined that project. As an example, Trubetskoi turned to the legacy of the Roman Empire and argued that "the culture of Romanized provinces had always been mixed. After all, even the so-called Roman culture itself, which was more or less implanted in all provinces of the empire was a motley mix of heterogeneous elements of the most diverse cultures of the Greco-Roman world. As a result, we have not an assimilation of different peoples by the culture created by one people but rather eclecticism, a synthesis of several cultures."[30]

For Trubetskoi, complete Europeanization was undoubtedly harmful in that it led to a loss of subjectivity of Europeanized peoples. Whereas "the Romano-German in the realm of culture accepts as valuable only that which makes an element of his own contemporary culture . . . a Europeanized people . . . does not assume the place of a European but evaluates itself and its own culture from the point of view of Romano-Germans." As a result, Europeanized peoples are placed at a disadvantage in the process of production of cultural values: they have "to be guided not by their own but by an alien, Romano-Germanic national psychology, and they must, without a blink, accept all that is created and considered valuable by true Romano-Germans." This phenomenon makes "the process of absorption and propagation of imported cultural values very difficult."[31]

Europeanization, according to Trubetskoi, is also harmful because it tends to generate ruptures in the national body. In those peoples that had accepted an alien culture, "each generation lives by its own separate culture, and the difference between "fathers and sons" will always be stronger here than in those peoples that have their own national culture." Due to different paces of Europeanization by different social groups, "at any given moment of time different parts of the Europeanized people, its classes, estates, professions could represent different stages of absorption of the Romano-Germanic culture, different types of combinations in different proportions of the elements of the national and foreign cultures." In a clear reference to the notion of rupture in Russian imperial society between the Europeanized elites and the Eurasian masses, Trubetskoi's thinking was that "all these different classes do not represent parts of one national body but are separate cultural units, as if they were separate peoples with their own traditions and cultures, customs, concepts and languages." These differences caused by Europeaniza-tion "generate the spread of class struggle and complicate transition from one class to another."[32]

These negative aspects of Europeanization translated into the perennial backwardness of a Europeanized people. Put at a disadvantage and forced into a competitive comparison with Romano-Germans, Europeanized peoples had to compete while at the same time dealing with ruptures in the national body and difficulties in generating authentic cultural output. As Trubetskoi argued, the degree of Europeanization did not matter: any people entering a relationship with the Romano-Germanic culture of Europe "enters into the sphere of necessary cultural exchange with Romano-Germans, which makes its 'backwardness' a fateful law. . . . A Europeanized people becomes an ob-ject of 'jumping evolution': having no chance to go along with the Romano-Germans and becoming more and more backward in comparison to them, a Europeanized people from time to time makes an attempt to catch up, mak-ing more or less protracted jumps. . . . It has to jump over an entire row of historical stages and to create immediately, 'ex abrupto,' what in Romano-Germanic culture was an outcome of consequent historical changes." Although these "historical jumps give the temporary illusion of achieving a 'common European level of civilization,' . . . this jumping evolution spends even more national energies, whereas the people's energies are overspent by the very fact of Europeanization." Trubetskoi concluded that the "overall consequences of Europeanization are so heavy and terrible that it has to be considered evil."[33]

But if European cosmopolitan culture was a deception and Europeaniza-tion was not the spread of a universal civilization but a traumatic encounter with a predatory colonialist power, how could a conscious representative of a non-European people counter it? "What," Trubetskoi asked, "if this fight is impossible and universal Europeanization is a necessary worldwide law?" He believed that a general uprising by the colonized peoples against the Romano-Germans was not very likely. Instead, Trubetskoi suggested that the non-Europeans should free themselves from the hypnosis that makes them believe in the universal nature of European cultural norms. He recognized that "the solution I offer has no historical precedents; however, this does not make it impossible." The solution was to be found in the realm of culture and "psychology of the intelligentsia of Europeanized peoples." Members of this intelligentsia "used to be agents of the Romano-Germans. Having recognized that Europeanization is absolute evil and cosmopolitanism is a barefaced deception, they will stop helping the Romano-Germans and the triumphal spread of 'civilization' should stop."[34]

Trubetskoi envisioned a global, totalizing cultural struggle, in which the intelligentsias of non-European peoples would act together and in alliance: "Even for a moment we should not be distracted from the core problem, we should not be distracted by particularist nationalisms and partial solutions such as pan-Slavism and other 'pan-isms.' These particularities only cloud the essence of the problem. We need to always firmly remember that the juxtaposition of Slavs and Germans or Turanians and Aryans will not provide a solution to the problem, and that there is just one real opposition: the Romano-Germans versus the other peoples of the world, Europe versus Mankind."[35]

Scholars have long debated the origins of Trubetskoi's ideas and the particular circumstances in which *Europe and Mankind* was written. Nicholas Riasanovsky considered Trubetskoi's ideas "an early and extreme anti-colonial *pronunciamento* by a European intellectual" and described them as "a striking example of a tract for the times and an outstanding Russian contribution to the debate on the colonial problem."[36] Roman Jakobson, ever a scholarly revolutionary and a tireless propagator of Trubetskoi's legacy, somewhat cumbersomely explained Trubetskoi's radicalism in *Europe and Mankind* by the pathos of scholarly innovation: "The negative position of this platform (which was further developed by the author's ideology) essentially corresponds to the pathos of fundamental revision of the foundations of traditional linguistics, a revision that Trubetskoi had feverishly elaborated since 1917 despite all the external troubles."[37]

One obvious source of Trubetskoi's assault on European universalism was the pan-Slavist thinker Nikolai Danilevskii, whose term "Romano-Germans" and conception of clearly delimited civilizations or cultural types Trubetskoi borrowed.[38] Again, obvious parallels to Oswald Spengler's *The Decline of the West* were suggested by Trubetskoi himself, who maintained that Spengler's work "had some common ideological points with 'Europe and Mankind,' and considered inviting him to write a foreword to the German translation of the book."[39] Although German scholars suggested parallels between early Eurasianist writings and the German "Conservative Revolution," Trubetskoi himself generally rejected any interpretation that put his ideas in the context of the German debate on *Zivilisation* and *Kultur*.[40] While European cultural pessimists focused on the distinction between *Zivilisation* and *Kultur*, the Eurasianists did not see the distinction as particularly important.[41] As Trubetskoi argued in his postscript to the German translation of *Europe and Mankind*:

> Many of my critics believe that the "fault" of my system is caused by the lack of distinction between the concepts of "civilization" and "culture," which are

used in my book as if interchangeably, and that my system would collapse if the distinction were properly maintained. However, this is not more than an illusion, which can be resolved under more careful consideration. Anyone, who takes care to think through my points will understand that from the point of view of those problems that I treat, the distinction is irrelevant and that the mutual replacement of these concepts in my thought is absolutely appropriate.[42]

From Trubetskoi's point of view, this distinction was important in dealing with the internal problems of Europe. Even if he shared in the critique of the rise of "Zivilisation" in Europe, it is the universalist claims of European culture that he found most disturbing.

Given how little evidence Trubetskoi left about the genealogy of his ideas and how few citations are present in the text of *Europe and Mankind*, how are we to interpret this radically relativist and anticolonial text? Should we treat it in the context of the transformation of the Russian Empire into an anticolonialist empire by the Bolsheviks? Or, alternatively, should we see it as a reaction, albeit a rather unique one, to the collapse of the European order in the Great War and Revolution? To answer these questions, we have to return to the scant evidence that Trubetskoi himself left us.

In the introduction to *Europe and Mankind*, Trubetskoi explained that he had arrived at the ideas expressed in the book over ten years earlier. He suggested that the delay in publication was due to the lack of understanding of his ideas that he encountered in personal conversations: "most people simply did not understand my thoughts. And they did not understand them not because I expressed them poorly but because for most European educated people these ideas were almost organically unacceptable as contradictory to some indestructible psychological foundations, upon which the European way of thinking rests."[43]

Trubetskoi also suggested that in recent years some fundamental shift in the thinking of educated classes had taken place. He attributed this shift to "the Great War, and especially to the 'peace,' that followed it, which we still have to put within quotes, which shattered faith in 'civilized humanity' and opened the eyes of many."[44] He echoed this point in a letter to Roman Jakobson, explaining that "it looks like a shift in the consciousness of the intelligentsia is about to arrive, it may well sweep off all the old directions and will create new ones, on entirely new foundations. All this is too indefinite at this point but undoubtedly 'something is coming, something is being prepared,' and in these conditions it is necessary to arouse thought, to shake it out of slumber, to awaken it, to move it from the dead point, to tease it with unacceptable paradoxes, to stubbornly reveal what people attempt to hide from themselves."[45]

However, when Jakobson, to whom Trubetskoi had sent the book, explained it as a reaction to the war and revolution, Trubetskoi responded with a more or less detailed history of the ideas expressed in it. According to Trubetskoi, he had conceived these ideas in 1909–1910, and was planning to write a trilogy under the common title "Justification of Nationalism." The first part, which was supposed to be dedicated to Kopernik, was to be titled "On Egocentrism." The second part of the trilogy was supposed to be titled "On True and False Nationalism," and was to be dedicated to the memory of Socrates; the third and final part was to focus on "The Russian Elements" and was to be dedicated to the memory of Russian peasant rebels Stepan Razin or Emelian Pugachev. Trubetskoi explained that he dropped the dedication to Kopernik as pretentious and replaced the title with the "brighter" "Europe and Mankind." Trubetskoi told Jakobson that "the purpose of the book is purely negative. . . . Its sole purpose is to destroy certain idols and, having placed the reader in front of empty pedestals, make him think in search of a solution."[46] The second and third parts of the planned trilogy actually appeared in Eurasianist publications.[47]

If we take seriously Trubetskoi's suggestion that he had conceived of the ideas expressed in *Europe and Mankind* "a decade earlier," we might want to explore what he was preoccupied with in 1909–1910. We know that in these years he was studying Ossetian folklore and spending summers in the Caucasus, near Kislovodsk, at the estate of academician Vsevolod Fedorovich Miller, one of Russia's leading scholars of Iranian languages. By that time, Trubetskoi had already published reviews of works on Caucasian folklore in scholarly journals and immersed himself in the literature on the Caucasus.[48] His interest in the Caucasus was bound to turn his attention to the works of Maksim Maksimovich Kovalevskii (1851–1916), Russia's leading sociologist, who was a close associate and collaborator of V. F. Miller.

Kovalevskii was Russia's leading social evolutionist and a self-proclaimed student of Sir Henry Sumner Maine.[49] Kovalevskii believed in the possibility of using a comparative method in order to uncover universal evolutionary processes in human societies. Not unlike Maine, who studied the institutions of colonial India to better understand Europe's own past and establish cultural and civilizational hierarchies, Kovalevskii explored the origins of family and property in the material of medieval European and contemporary Russian societies.[50] Importantly, Kovalevskii emerged as one of Russia's leading scholars of ethnic diversity. He argued that it was the task of Russian ethnographic scholarship, privileged with access to the empire's extraordinary diversity, to supply European scholarship with data and thus participate in the worldwide "mapping of mankind."[51] His massive study of legal traditions in the Caucasus was an attempt to process such data on the basis of evolutionary theory.[52]

Although Kovalevskii spent many years of his life in Europe and often wrote in French, his influence in late imperial Russian scholarship should not be underestimated. Most of his works were immediately published in Russian translation and he corresponded with Russian scholars and reviewed their works. Perhaps more importantly, in the atmosphere of political change and mobilization in the Russian Revolution of 1905, Kovalevskii, who was also an important player in liberal politics, defended a particular vision of how Russian imperial diversity had to be structured. The demands of progress and liberal reform, in his view, required the separation of the legal order of the Russian Empire into "the metropolitan sphere of political freedom and equality versus the sphere of a particularistic colonial legal order."[53] This separation was warranted by the alleged backwardness of "inorodtsy,"[54] whose level of cultural development was below what is required by modern political institutions: "let us imagine a Caucasian mountaineer who discusses some articles of the Criminal Code, although he is convinced that blood should be wiped away only by blood or compensated with cows and sheep."[55] As Marina Mogilner has demonstrated, such visions of the imperial space were challenged even by liberal Russian anthropologists, who often refused to ascribe political hierarchies to cultural differences.[56]

Kovalevskii's role in shaping the Eurasianist discourse of anti-evolutionism appears to have been more direct and we can count him as an "antisource" in the emergence of the Eurasianist critique of evolutionism, Eurocentrism and Europe's cultural colonialism. Some of the evidence for this role is indirect, suggesting the possibility that Trubetskoi was aware of Kovalevskii's work and reacted to it. One such instance is Trubetskoi's interest in the work of Gabriele de Tarde, whose Russian translations appeared in the early 1900s with introductions by Kovalevskii. V. F. Miller, Trubetskoi's host in the Caucasus in 1909–1910, had been Kovalevskii's collaborator on the Caucasian expedition of 1883 and we can presume that Kovalevskii's evolutionary views were discussed by Miller and Trubetskoi.

But the conclusive evidence of Trubetskoi's a posteriori reaction to Kovalevskii's evolutionism comes from the archive. In 1927, Trubetskoi sent P. N. Savitskii his comments on N. N. Alekseev's brochure, "On the Paths toward Future Russia (Soviet Order and Its Political Opportunities)." In the comments, Trubetskoi criticized Alekseev's celebration of the unification of criminal law in the USSR by invoking Kovalevskii's argument about the inability of the mountaineers of the Caucasus to follow Russian law (and hence, about the need to divide the empire into a metropole and colonial periphery):

It was exactly in the North Caucasus that they used to refer to criminal law to substantiate the need for regional differentiation of legislation: the mountaineers' notions of some crimes are so different from the Russian criminal code that the decisions of the Russian courts always appeared unjust to them. It is not much different in Turkestan. If the contemporary Soviet government argues for the unification of criminal law, this is in significant measure because regional differences of legal consciousness mostly rest on so-called backwardness (that is to say, on the difference of native psychology from the Romano-German one) or on "religious prejudices." For us, of course, this cannot be a valid argument.[57]

As Marc Raeff perceptively noted, in the eighteenth century European thinkers were faced with a significant challenge. On the one hand, universalist concepts of the Enlightenment suggested that human beings ultimately possessed the same abilities and potentials. On the other hand, in the wake of the age of exploration, European scholars became increasingly aware of the stunning human diversity of the world. This controversy was reconciled by replacing the spatial arrangement of human diversity with a temporal one: various peoples that were perceived as different from the Europeans were thought to be passing through a stage of development Europe had long since passed.[58] By the middle of the nineteenth century evolutionism had begun to function as an "alibi for empire," in the words of Karuna Mantena.[59] The notion that human societies are all located at a particular point on the ladder of stages of development was often used to substantiate specific and particularistic forms of colonial rule—and indirect rule, shared sovereignty, and regimes of exceptions were deemed more suitable for the "underdeveloped" or "savages." This notion also came to substantiate the idea of a specifically modern "civilizing mission": European empires no longer played the role of converting "heathens" to Christianity but primarily of "helping savages" to reach the modern stage of civilization.

To be sure, evolutionism was not a coherent body of ideas, and many of those who subscribed to a vision of society that progressed from one stage to another could only be called "evolutionists" with a degree of approximation.[60] Still, by the late nineteenth century there existed a powerful consensus of very diverse thinkers about the temporal dimension of civilization and the place of particular cultures on the more or less universal ladder of progress from lower and simpler forms to more complex and developed.

Trubetskoi's assault on evolutionism places the Eurasianist movement in its proper context of imagining how a multiethnic imperial state and society could be reorganized in the modern age. Those who articulated ideas about future organization of the imperial space in the prerevolutionary period were primarily liberals. Between various projects for national and cultural autonomy and the more radical visions of the above-mentioned Kovalevskii and Struve (who also saw the future imperial space as structured along the lines of a civilized core and an underdeveloped colonial periphery), liberals firmly dominated the field of imagining the imperial future. On the other hand, their visions often clashed with more nationalist, even racist plans to establish homogeneous, nationally bounded communities after the empire's fall.

The Bolshevik takeover in 1917 and especially the evacuation of Wrangel troops from Crimea in the fall of 1920 (about the time when *Europe and Mankind* was written) made it abundantly clear that the liberals, so successful and articulate in waking up the revolutionary forces of late imperial Russia, had ultimately failed to take control of them. For many, the victory of the Bolsheviks was the liberals' failure, and their visions of political community had to undergo a revision. Perhaps even more important, the Bolsheviks, whom the Eurasianists aspired to replace as ideological leaders of Russia's transformation, were committed evolutionists (arguably even more so than the liberals).

While evolutionism seemed to fit nicely into the ideological repertoire of West European empires, in the Russian case it was challenged for several reasons. First, Russians themselves were not at the top of any evolutionary ladder according to the evolutionist wisdom of the day. In the grand history of civilization imagined with the help of evolutionism, Russia occupied a curious place between the realm of European civilization and various "savage" or "underdeveloped" parts of the world. During the reign of Peter the Great, a famous projeteur and adviser to the tsar, Heinrich Fick, stated in his memorandum on the education of Russian youth (which allegedly inspired the tsar to establish the academy): "it is to be noted that all European peoples laid the foundation of the happy condition in which they now find themselves through Academies and schools; in particular it is known that 300 years ago in England, Denmark, and Sweden there was semi-barbarity, people were hardly aware of studies and moral scholarship." For Fick, this state of affairs was supported by the Papacy, which was looking to maintain its grip over the superstitious peoples. "The Germans," Fick continued, "were considered by the Romans to be as wild as savages in America are considered today. And now we find the German nation liberated from the Papacy to be more learned and civilized (*polirter*) than those who are still under its yoke." And this, Fick believed, may well be the fate of the Russians: "Now it is well known that for a hundred years already the former glorious rulers in Russia have gone through great labor to introduce good laws and regulations (*gute Gesetze und Ordnungen ein zu fuehren*), except that this labor could not bear the desired fruit to the people because the education of the youth could not be pursued because travel, studies of foreign languages, and books were forbidden."[61] As the Russian nobility absorbed European ideas, throughout the entire post-Petrine period, the Russian Empire was inevitably an aspiring European state but always behind an imagined European standard. This notion was also perennially challenged by Russian thinkers, who had developed a range of "postcolonial" ideas.[62]

As a result, in Russia, evolutionism was often employed to fight visions of a special path of development, such as Slavophile ideas. These visions often focused on the institution of the peasant commune, allegedly a unique Russian phenomenon. The above-mentioned Maksim Kovalevskii explored the medieval history of England, Germany, and France to prove that communal forms of rural life were present in the past of these societies. Hence, according to Kovalevskii, Russia was not a non-European civilization but a member of the European family, except with the belated development of representative institutions and parliamentary politics.[63]

Evolutionism thus placed Russia in the position of student or follower of the more advanced European societies. At the same time, domestically, evolutionist ideas established hierarchies between different ethnic groups. The Russian Empire was not an organic whole but a motley array of peoples of widely varying degrees of "progress" and "civilization," and they allegedly required a corresponding form of political organization. But what seemed relatively easy in the case of the British Empire—separation between the "developed" metropole and the colonial periphery—ran into problems of geography and politics in Russia. When the Russian Empire collapsed along social, ethnic, and confessional lines in the turmoil of the revolution and the Civil War, and the peoples of the borderlands presented their demands for independence or autonomy, evolutionist ideas appeared dangerous to the Eurasianists as they undermined the call for the unity of the Eurasian space on the one hand, and established Russia's inferiority vis-à-vis Europe on the other.

Trubetskoi's rebellion against evolutionism, innovative as it was in terms of articulating it in anticolonialist terms, relied on a long tradition of the Russian reception of evolutionary ideas. Although most Russian scholars in biological fields accepted Darwin's conception and sought to add new experimental data or theoretical refinements to it, a few powerful voices challenged Darwin's conception of the accidental nature of evolutionary change.[64] One of Europe's greatest pre-Darwinist biologists and a towering figure in the Russian scientific establishment of the nineteenth century, Karl von Baer, accepted the main postulates of evolutionary theory but passionately defended the purposeful and teleological nature of biological change. Unlike Darwin, who perceived the world from a mechanistic point of view, von Baer understood nature from the vantage point of *Naturphilosophie* and the metaphysical principles of classical German philosophy.

Following in von Baer's footsteps, Nikolai Iakovlevich Danilevskii (who had served as von Baer's scholarly aide-de-camp during the Astrakhan expedition of 1853–1857) subjected Darwin's work to a critical reading and argued in favor of a teleological and "regular" understanding of evolutionary change.[65] Perhaps more significantly, Danilevskii combined this teleological critique of Darwin's theories with a fervent assault on the perceived hierarchy in the production of knowledge and insisted that Russian scholarship should cease its uncritical acceptance of European ideas. Danilevskii's anti-Darwinism was also combined with a pan-Slavic ideological project and a diversitarian view of history.

Although the Eurasianist thinkers had not been aware of the works of Lev Semenovich Berg, an extraordinarily erudite geographer, historian, and limnologist, until 1926, they immediately recognized the affinity once they read his magnum opus dedicated to the concept of "nomogenesis or evolution on the basis of regularity."[66] In a letter to Petr Suvchinskii dated March 5, 1926, Trubetskoi wrote: "Savitskii told me of two interesting books that were published in Russia. . . . The first is *Nomogenesis* by Berg. . . . It is especially interesting because Berg proclaims himself a follower of Danilevskii and in his theses he develops propositions that are close to ours (in particular to my ideas developed in *Europe and Mankind* and *The Tower of Babel*)."[67]

In this context, Trubetskoi's critique appears to have been at least in part rooted in a rejection of the "internal evolutionism" of Kovalevskii and other liberal thinkers who defended the separation of the Russian Empire into a "civilized" core metropole and "backward" ethnic periphery. While the Eurasianist project was to defend the unity of Russia-Eurasia and endow it with ethnographic, cultural, and geographical content, "internal evolutionism" threatened to rupture the national body of Russia-Eurasia. The Eurasianist thinkers took their critique of late imperial developments and reformulated them in the conditions of postrevolutionary emigration, similar to the way that they carried their rejection of the beginnings of Russia's modern bourgeois culture on the eve of the revolution into the illiberal juncture of interwar exile.

CONCEIVING THE TERRITORY

Eurasianism as a Geographical Ideology

Marlene Laruelle

IN a polemical text written at the end of the 1920s, Prince Yuri Shirinski-Shikhmatov accused the Eurasianists of endorsing "maximalist nationalism" and criticized the fact that, for them, "it is not a spiritual trait but a material, geographical element that predestines the path of Russia."[1] What, then, is this ever so significant "material" element in Eurasianist discourse—a discourse that was after all fashioned by Orthodox religious philosophy, by multiple historical references to the steppe world, by debates with the literary émigré circles, and by intellectual proximity to the linguistic structuralism of the Prague Circle?[2] This "material" element is territory. In Eurasianist theory, the geographical milieu and culture are in reciprocal interaction. The community of destiny of the Eurasian peoples is intrinsically linked to the territorial specificities of Eurasia as a unique continent and closed world: identity is enshrined in the data of physical geography. Russia allegedly has a "transparent" geographical structure,[3] which reveals its identity characteristics to those able to decipher them. The vocation of Eurasia is thus held to transcend all terrestrial solidarities and to be inscribed in the element of the telluric.

This chapter aims to explore how Eurasianism conceives of territory and argues that one can interpret it as a geographical ideology. To understand Eurasia in terms of its spatial relations was the core intellectual activity of the movement's geographer and economist, Petr Savitskii. As Martin Beisswenger shows in his chapter, Savitskii presented the Orthodox Church as the foundation for his new economic ideas and tried to endorse a synthetic and universalist type of thinking. For Eurasianism, the stake of scientific work is to unveil what is hidden and what preexists every investigation. The movement adheres to a systemic principle, according to which Eurasia is necessarily a structural totality, explicable through its own internal elements and not in terms of its interaction with the outside. Savitskii based himself on the theories of Vladimir Vernadsky (1863–1945), the famous Russian scientist who developed the notion of the noosphere and the tendency of continents to self-organization, that is, the notion that each cultural world is supposedly moved by an internal centripetal dynamic. In underscoring the relationship between the exact sciences, philosophy, and an explanation of Russia, the Eurasianist movement also refers to Dmitri Mendeleev (1834–1907), whom it praises as "the founder not only of new chemistry but also of a new science of Russia (*rossievedenie*)."[4] Savitskii's pioneering work combined these different intellectual traditions by interrogating the idea of a structural geography intrinsically linked to the very nature of Eurasia, leading him to claim that "Russian geographical science is a scientific world apart."[5]

Eurasia as a Systemic, Regular, and Hermetic Totality

Similar to George Vernadsky's or Nikolai Trubetskoi's defense of an iconoclast version of Russian historiography, Savitskii took on the task of deconstructing the classic geographical representations of Russia, interpreted as a two-part space divided by a border allegedly represented by the Urals.[6] For the Eurasianist movement, Eurasian culture can be neither European nor Asian; it is a peculiar space, which affirms simultaneously its internal unity and its difference from the rest of the world. "Russia's culture is neither a European nor an Asian culture, nor is it the sum or mechanical combination of elements of one or the other."[7] Several critics of the Eurasianists reproach this founding ambiguity: neither Europe nor Asia, or Europe and Asia simultaneously? Not all the Eurasianists have, however, sought to define Eurasia as a third continent at any price. For Vernadsky, for instance, Eurasia is constituted "by the oriental part of Europe and the northern part of Asia."[8] It is thus understood as the meeting of two continents, which means that its unity must be demonstrated in the field of history or of culture, not in that of geography.

For Savitskii, Eurasian unity is not to be sought in the existence of one and the same geographical territory, definable by a single feature. Very much to the contrary, unity is established by the systematic character precisely of its diversity, by the regularity, or law-like conformity (*zakonomernost'*, based on the German model of *Gesetzmässigkeit*), in which different natural features intersect. In the Eurasianist perception, Europe and Asia are both geographical mosaics made up of numerous regions shaped as small blocks. This supposedly illustrates geographically their cultural parceling as compared with the massive and continental unity of Eurasian culture. Savitskii tried to systematize this Eurasian character using tables. As he explained, "The system-map [is] a magnificent image of the nomogenesis or of evolution on the basis of law-like regularity."[9]

According to the Eurasianists, Eurasian unity can be proved by a comparative analysis of different criteria (temperatures, flora, fauna, soils, linguistic and cultural traits, etc.) that, because they coincide, attest to its existence as structure. Eurasia, for Savitskii, is thus defined by four botanical and pedological horizontal ribbon-like strips, running from north to south on an east –west axis: the tundra (along the Arctic Ocean shores), the taiga (a line Altai-Tyumen-Kazan-Kiev-Carpathians), the steppe (at the south of the forest border), and the desert (Aralo-Altaic and Mongolian). Savitskii does not attribute an equal role to each strip in the construction of Eurasia. The steppe, for him, constitutes the geopolitical "flesh" of Russia, its primary element, and major explanatory principle. "Eurasia as a geographical world is defined as being in the north of the Tibeto-Iranian mountains and as having as its foundation the region of the desertic steppes that extend in an uninterrupted stretch from the Chinese Wall to Galicia."[10] These strips themselves intersect transversally by means of three plains: the one linking the White Sea to the Caucasus, the Siberian Plain, and the Turkestan Plain. By means of their orographical system, Savitskii tried to demonstrate the unity of the three plains and therefore to deny implicitly any continuity between the European and Russian plains. "It can be said that the East European Plain, which the Eurasianists called the 'Caucasus-White Sea,' is, by its geographical nature, much closer to the plains of Western Siberia and Turkestan than to those of Western Europe."[11]

From this meeting between strips and plains, between a latitudinal and a longitudinal principle, is born the Eurasian world, defined by Savitskii as "a world of systems of periodic and symmetrical zones."[12] The botanical zones of Eurasia are in fact alleged to comprise a specific system in which all the givens intersect mutually. He claims, for example, that a symmetry exists between the evolution of north–south temperatures and the humidity from west to east. "Nowhere on our planet can one observe—in going from the south to north—a more consistent substitution of botanical and pedological types, than by traveling through the plains of Russia-Eurasia."[13] In addition, the Eurasian rivers flow from the north to the south or from the south to the north, but none in a horizontal manner: only the steppe and the three other pedological strips can ensure travel on the east–west axis. The great rivers, the Yenisei, the Ob, and the Lena serve as natural paths unifying steppe and forest and enabling the transition from one strip to another. It is also claimed that a correspondence exists between natural phenomena and sociocultural phenomena. Savitskii noted, for example, a coincidence between the map of Russia's dialectal isoglosses (imaginary lines separating two geographical zones that are distinguished by a single linguistic trait) and that of the Russian climate's isotherms, as well as the existence of a border between the Ukrainian and Great Russian dialects, on the one hand, and the breeding of pigs and cattle, on the other,[14] two elements that, according to him, make it possible to geographically differentiate Eurasia from Europe.

The proof of Eurasia's existence can thus be obtained by creating coincidences between data pertaining to diverse disciplines.[15] According to Savitskii, Eurasia is marked by the "unchanging relief of botanical and pedological zones unfolding, [and is] influenced by the fundamental rules of the north–south and center–periphery axes."[16] The main *law*—in the sense of regularity—explaining Eurasia as a specific continent is therefore precisely this constant potential parallel between north–south and center–periphery. "In Russia-Eurasia the progression from the south toward the north, in relation to the continental massif as a whole, is par excellence a progression from the 'center' toward the 'periphery.'"[17]

However, the notions of center and periphery raise problems for the Eurasianists because they implicitly undermine the equality claimed for all the territories of Eurasia. The Eurasian geographical and historical linchpin is the steppe, itself glorified as a world without center, in perpetual movement. The steppe is the historical theater and geographical scene of the two waves of population movement comprising the history of Eurasia. One of these moved from east to west during the first centuries of our era (the great migrations), and the second, more recent one, from Europe toward the shores of the Bering Strait (the Russian expansion). The limits of this twofold population movement and the positive reevaluation of the great migrations, traditionally discredited in Russian historiography, are thus claimed to highlight the steppe as Eurasia's center. Thus there is an ambiguity between the will to define Eurasia by its law-like regularity and its absence of a center on the one hand, and the staging of the identity of the steppe world on the other.

Eurasianism in fact tends to substitute space for time, or at the very least to subordinate the latter to the former, claiming that history is only a subdivision of geography. This phenomenon is expressed by George Vernadsky in his very first publication in 1914:

> What is already in the past for the Muscovite Rus', according to Moscow's distance, can still be present in Siberia. Here is expressed the law of the

correspondence between time and space as a factor of the historical process. A social phenomenon undergoes analogical changes that bridge space and time. A social phenomenon for one and the same space develops according to time. For one and the same moment of time a social phenomenon differs according to its geographical location. . . . The further we see, the more we see rigid circles behind us, the repercussions of what was once in the center and has been well and truly dead for a long time.[18]

Different historical times are thus to be found present simultaneously within Eurasian space, which cannot therefore be placed unambiguously on a linear temporal scale. Eurasia is conceived as the largest continuous space on the planet under the control of a single political power and it has the unique property that the farther out one looks, the further one goes back in time. Vernadsky went so far as to specify this time–space relation: the distance of one thousand versts is tantamount to a trip back in time of one hundred years. Eurasia thus comes to form an object of astronomical science in such a way that Eurasian experience applies to the rest of the universe. As such, there exists not only an asynchrony between center and periphery, which actually live in different eras, but also a spatial and measurable materialization of Russia's own various periods.

After having defined Russia in terms of the law-like regularity of the intersection of its various geographical features, the question of borders arises. Conventionally, Eurasia conforms to the territory of the Russian Empire and/or of the Soviet Union, but the Eurasianists add to this certain territories and subtract others from it. For them, the main point is to demonstrate the existence of two categories of borders, hermetic and porous. The relation to Europe aims to be hermetic, and that to Asia, porous.

The border with Europe is close and did not change in history, because it is an epistemological and identity border between two different civilizations. On the contrary, the frontier with Asia is open and potentially subject to modification, embodied by the territorial extension of the Russian Empire. This conceptualization of borders as having dual natures belongs to a particular historical context. In the interwar period, the trauma of the diverse treaties used to dismember the defunct Habsburg and Ottoman empires shaped the feeling that some borders, conceived as natural and historically justified, are "true," whereas "false" borders are drawn up by the political forces of the moment and therefore are potentially reversible. The Eurasianists echoed this common discourse on the veracity of borders by sticking to the notion that some are porous, whereas others are hermetic.[19]

The existence of two types of borders around Eurasia implies various forms of physical discontinuity between it and the spaces around it. The western borders are the most clearly defined and the most impermeable because the Eurasian identity has to preserve itself from so-called Romano-Germanic imperialism.[20] They are therefore said to be as visible in geography (changes in climate, dialects, and breeding tradition), as they are in culture (rationality and individualism versus mysticism and collectivism) or religion (with the transition from the Latin rites of Christianity to the Greek ritual–Uniatism and Orthodoxy), or even in epistemology (fragmented sciences versus a holistic approach). Thus, Galicia, Volynia, and Podolia are considered legitimate parts of Eurasia, whereas Crimea and the Caucasus are peripheral zones. Though the Eurasianists regret the loss of Orthodox Bessarabia during the First World War, they lay claim neither to Catholic Poland nor Protestant Finland, which are considered to be European, and whose loss reinforced the Eurasian destiny of Russia. In contrast to their Slavophile predecessors, the Eurasianists are not very attracted by the rest of the Slavic world, and only some of Trubetskoi's texts imply a form of Orthodox solidarity with the Balkan world.

While the division between Europe and Eurasia is presented as obvious, the borders with Asia are drawn more tentatively. In Savitskii's geography, the Far East is classified as Asian and not as Eurasian because it constitutes the symmetrical counterpart of the Baltic countries (northwest versus southeast), which are themselves considered as part of Europe. This position, however, is not supported unanimously within the movement, insofar as the founding of Vladivostok in 1860 is also celebrated as proof of Russia's vocation in the Pacific Ocean. Vernadsky, for his part, criticized Russia's loss of California in the 1840s and the sale of Alaska to the United States in 1867: if Russia had been able to stretch over three continents, Siberia would have been the geographical and political center between the Old and New Russian worlds.[21] Indeed, he claimed that the conquest of Alaska was a creative achievement of the Russian nation, the product of its spiritual and geographical development. For this reason, this territory ought not to be considered as some sort of expendable property of the Russian state, but rather as having a stake in its identity. Other ambiguities toward Siberia can be noted. While each geographical strip is supposed to have its own culture, the assimilation of which to the others helped create the Eurasian entity, there is no reference in the Eurasianist narrative to the cultures of the tundra. Siberian space therefore illustrates certain of the paradoxes of Eurasianism, which was unable to make its historical, linguistic, and geographical discourses coincide. The tundra and the Far East seem excluded from Eurasia, whereas the idea of an empire spread over three continents fires the movement's imagination.

Eurasia's southern border remains the vaguest and the more permeable: Where does Eurasia stop and where does Asia begin? The highlighting of the Mongolian legacy necessitates, for example, expanding beyond Soviet borders.

For the Eurasianists, Mongolia, independent since 1911, quite naturally belongs to Eurasia, since it is situated in the steppe and stands out as the homeland of Chingis Khan. In his correspondence with Lev Gumilev (1912–1992), Savitskii even said he had been convinced of Tibet's belonging to Eurasia since the 1920s but had not mentioned the region in his publications of the interwar years.[22] The question also arises for the Uyghur world, which Savitskii considered to be the most extreme example of continentalism (measured by distance from the seas) and therefore a symbol of Eurasian antimaritime identity. Within the Soviet space, sedentary Central Asia definitely figures in the definition of Eurasia as representing the desert zone, but the mountain regions of Central Asia such as the Kyrgyz Tian-Shan or the Tajik Pamir are a priori excluded from Eurasian territory and relegated to Asia. The Transcaucasian region is also practically ignored.

In separating Eurasia from Asia, the criteria of physical geography almost cease to be evoked, making way for cultural arguments. Eurasianists define Asia by its three subspaces, Chinese or Confucian-Buddhist, Indian or Buddho-Brahmanist, and Iranian or Islamo-Mazdaist. Each area of civilization is therefore assimilated to a religious culture. In this manner the Chinese world and the Indian world come to form the extreme alterities of Eurasia, although the relation to China has been subject to lively debates with the Eurasianist sympathizers based in Harbin, Manchuria. Some of them, such as novelist Vsevolod Ivanov, a former student of Nikolai Losskii in Moscow and a journalist attached to Aleksandr Kolchak's armies in Siberia during the Civil War, who eventually emigrated to China, claimed on the contrary that the Eurasian principle would find its realization in the fusion of Russia and China.[23]

Convergence of the Sciences and Geosophy

The Eurasianists' obsession with territory and border makes sense when put into its philosophical context, that of geosophy as the "queen of sciences" and the symbol of the convergence of sciences Eurasianists have been calling for. The movement has a paradoxical relation to science, seeking simultaneously to derive inspiration from it, while at the same time criticizing its supposedly European character. Science is perceived as forming a key part of Europe's quest to master human and natural reality and to deny the divine part of phenomena. According to Eurasianists, "Science is not capable of delimiting life itself; it must wait for new facts, without which the circle of known development is not complete."[24] Some like Savitskii nevertheless displayed a strong scientific drive founded on the model of the natural sciences: they hoped to prove that knowledge can help to prognosticate the future. As Savitskii explained to Lev Gumilev, "the Eurasianist method is precisely a method for the deduction of facts with a predictive value."[25] The discovery of general laws is thus supposed to make it possible to divine or at least to master the future. Eurasianism sees itself as a hermeneutics that interprets phenomena as transcendent signs. This is why it is critical of Western science, the science of the "how," whereas it lays claim to a scientific legitimacy founded on the discovery of the "why."

But Eurasianism encounters difficulties when it comes to formulating its epistemological position. It is critical of naturalism yet proposes a complex neonaturalist perspective, fascinated by laws and the regularities of nature. It refuses the atomism and mechanicism of Comptian positivism, without however criticizing positivism as a philosophy. For Eurasianism as well, facts exist prior to the gaze that one casts on them. It conceives the human sciences on the model of the natural sciences, yet also puts forward argumentation that is often close to metaphysics. It develops a social science, which takes as its subject society construed more or less as a predetermined organism. Eurasianism therefore partakes of a form of antiscientist critique prevalent at the beginning of the twentieth century, while simultaneously being marked by German Romantic thinking. It does not champion a positive evaluation of the individual, the particular, chance, or freedom, but believes in a natural totality. Thus, if the Eurasianists reject the idea that similar phenomena are genetically bound, it is by no means in the name of the freedom of humankind but in that of a neo-Platonic view of the world in which totalities are manifest. Patrick Sériot has shown how, in linguistics, the Prague Circle had an approach toward structuralism that was not Saussurian but founded on a history of concepts different from that of the West. It was a structuralism of totalities and naturality, and not the epistemological universe of Roland Barthes or Claude Lévi-Strauss.[26]

Eurasianism is thus a systemic form of thinking that calls for the constitution of new disciplines but, above all, for the rediscovery of a lost unity. The future of the sciences is thought to be located in synthesis and convergence. According to Eurasianists, "Life demands a new synthesis, a new system of the sciences. . . . We need a new vision of the scientific world, that is to say, the unification of disciplines that are divided in an anarchic manner, their spiritualization in a new scientific ideology."[27] Eurasianism thus fully participates in Romantic organicism, the last grand attempt to avoid the dissociation between knowledge and meaning, between science and religion.[28] According to Savitskii, only a metascience, a new philosophical system would enable humans to overcome the apparent chaos of the world. The need for total science corresponds to this desire to understand the world in its totality. Savitskii said, "To move closer, within the limits of modest human possibilities, to a global comprehension of the world, we have to bring the various sciences into contact with one another."[29] Simply putting things into a system does not suffice, for it still remains to demonstrate their organic unity. According to Trubetskoi, "In this way, instead of an encyclopedia, i.e., an anarchic conglomerate of non-coordinated scientific, philosophical, political and aesthetic ideas, it is necessary to create a coherent and harmonious system of ideas."[30]

The unity of sciences on which the Eurasianists pin their hopes is intrinsically dependent on the emergence of a new discipline that would give meaning to humankind, which they called personology. Since the nineteenth century, Russian philosophy has dissociated the individual, construed outside of a totality, from the person (*lichnost'*), which is realized only in symphony (*sobornost'*) with a collective organic entity.[31] The Eurasianists believe in the supremacy of the national collectivity over the individual. As Trubetskoi explained:

> It is important that the scholars who undertake research are conscious of the fact that their inquiry is only part of a general study and that the common object of this study is the collective person in his physical environment. . . . Alongside purely descriptive studies there have to be interpretative studies of the factual material, alongside of history a historiosophy, alongside of ethnography an ethnosophy, alongside of geography a geosophy, and so on. On the basis of these interpretative works a "theory of the concrete person" has to be formed, establishing the internal link between the different characteristics of this person and defining his specific traits.[32]

For the Eurasianists, the sciences are not neutral, they are in the service of a project and a program: "Alongside of these theoretical investigations some applied studies are needed to establish which political, economic, and so on, conditions are the most propitious to life and to the evolution of the person."[33] Sciences are applied because they entertain an ambiguous relation to the state and to the nation, and when they are separated from the spiritual life of the totality, they become abstract and sterile. Thus, although the theories advanced by the Eurasianists aim to have a universal value, they only provide examples and an application for Eurasia. The idea, in other words, is not separable from its material form, nor culture from its geographical space. The same holds for the sciences, which possess a specific national identity and their own methodological conceptions. Trubetskoi in particular was convinced of the existence of national sciences. The Romano-Germanic science is expressed by positivism and the idea of progress, whereas Eurasian science represents a more complex and totalizing approach, characterized by the notion of idiosyncrasy and the specific logic of each system. Eurasianism thus presents itself as an organic system of ideas, constituting a whole, closed world. It cannot admit relativism and can only express itself in the mode of a discourse of truth. "Eurasianism is a complete system and is sufficient in itself; it has its own logic of development and its own historical consistency and for this it cannot be submitted to external temptations and actions."[34] Its closure is in fact a sine qua non condition of its *nationality*.[35]

The epistemological response to the scientism of the West, perceived as something foreign, is therefore doubled with a cultural response, and the rejection of philosophical principles is accompanied with a discourse about the existence of national sciences. Fitted with such conceptions, the Eurasianists seek to demonstrate the existence of sciences peculiar to Eurasia. They claim, "The unique geographical and historical individuality of Russia-Eurasia as a specific world vouches for the ability of Russia to be able to bring a new speech into all the domains of study of our planet: this individuality contributes to the establishment of a whole series of questions. The particular and the concrete open the path to the universal and the global."[36] This demonstration makes it possible both to legitimate the existence of Eurasia as a specific cultural area and to explain it. Eurasianist sciences study an object that they create themselves, but claiming it exists a priori to all investigation. The task of science is thus not to verify whether Eurasia exists but to confirm its organic totality.

Among the new sciences and methods specific to Eurasia, the Eurasianists insist especially on geosophy, which allegedly constitutes a specifically Russian science distinct from those developed by their West European counterparts. They are thus part of a long tradition initiated by the father of Slavophilism, Aleksei Khomiakov (1804–1860), as well as by Dmitri Mendeleev, Afanasii Shchapov (1831–1876), Vassili Dokuchaev (1846–1903), and the geographer Vladimir Lamanskii (1833–1914).[37] For Savitskii, Russia cannot be solely a passive object of geography; it conceives—and therefore transforms—its own geography. Geographical unity subsumes the unity of civilization and vice versa. He affirms, "The traits of Eurasia's isolation and unity referred to have not only a geographical signification but also a historical one, lending to a Russian historiosophy."[38] The soil itself is thus held to explain the hidden meaning of events and destinies, revealing Russia to itself because its structure is transparent. According to Savitskii, "The constitution and the analysis of such [geographical and psychological] parallelisms prove to be the main object of geosophy in its application to Russia-Eurasia."[39] Eurasian territory is thus a living participant in history, a person embodying the unity between historical human life and that of nature and the cosmos.

Among German geopoliticians such as Friedrich Ratzel (1844–1904) or, later, Karl Haushofer (1869–1946), biogeography is associated with human geography. The state is envisioned as a living organism tied to the soil and symbolizing the interaction between the natural and human worlds. The notion of "ecological niche" exists for nonorganic and organic worlds as it does for human societies. The Eurasianists claim this same interaction between a state and its geography insofar as "the correspondence between the borders of a specific cultural world and a specific geographical region cannot be random."[40] There exist, however, notable differences between the German anthropogeographers and the Eurasianists, for whereas with the former the spirit of the people is uniquely a product of the geographical framework, with the latter there is no direct causality but a reciprocal symbiosis. Eurasianism refutes all reasoning of a biological type, refusing to explain the link between language, people, and territory by a relation of genetic causality. It prefers the more subtle idea of an explanation by teleology: there allegedly exists a predeterminism of the internal laws, a development of common "tendencies" within Eurasian space, which would tend to direct geography as much as politics and history toward the same end. The dependency of historical phenomena on geographical conditions is therefore far from being unilateral. The territory influences events and humans, modifying them and giving them meaning, but above all, it unifies elements of diverse, and even opposed, origin among themselves. Though the geographical milieu imposes some character traits, this is not through biology or genetics. The continuity is horizontal and spatial, not vertical or temporal, and the affinities are acquired and not innate. The Eurasianists take up in their own way the comments that Leo Berg (1876–1950) put forward on the theory of convergences: links of culture exist that give the same characteristics to two species without genetic relation simply because they are adjacent to one another and live in the same environment.[41]

The subtle geographical determinism of Eurasianism therefore does not aim to turn humans into a product of geography and biology but to demonstrate the existence of affinities between the soil and human beings as well as between different national collectivities. Effectively, the territory creates a community of destiny. As Trubetskoi writes, "This link [between the collective person and territory] has to be considered as functional, without having to ask whether the person chose the physical environment that suited him or whether, on the contrary, it was the environment that exerted an influence on the person by adapting him to it."[42] From here comes the importance of the concept of the developmental space, or the topogenesis (*mestorazvitie*)[43] of human societies. As this concept was first formulated, Savitskii did not hesitate to link it to the natural sciences as far as geographical space, minerals, and soils are concerned. However, this developmental space, close to the vocabulary of naturalism, arises from the reciprocal and equal influence of natural and sociohistorical milieus. "The sociohistorical milieu and its territory must, for us, link into a united whole, a geographical individual, or a *Landschaft*."[44] Eurasianism therefore remains nuanced in its apparent geographical determinism insofar as humans also create their territory, modify the natural givens, and give them meaning. As Savitskii wrote to Gumilev, "I think that peoples have chosen, and continue to choose, their topogenesis for their formation and transformation (e.g., the Russians 'chose' the grand Taiga from Onega to the Okhotsk Sea for their transformation into the largest people of the world) more than they are created by it."[45]

The geographical determinism of Eurasianism is therefore not mechanical, as German anthropogeography often is; instead, it seeks to conceptualize the "tendencies" common to the people and its territory. Through the idea of topogenesis, Savitskii hoped to demonstrate the mystical bond linking territory, religion, and culture. His notion reveals a teleological conception of human–nature relations, a romantic apprehension of the nature–culture totality. Born of this encounter between history and territory is a geographical being that the Eurasianists present as a living organism, a unitary person. Topogenesis also marks the territorialization of the destiny of Eurasian peoples. There exist different types of topogenesis, which fit into one another: if Eurasia is the topogenesis of reference, small topogeneses, playing a specific role at certain moments in Russian history and each constituting a world in itself, form the largest unity. This idea of the link justifying the totality was reworked by Trubetskoi and Jacobson in their ethnographical and linguistic texts on Eurasia. Eurasian unity allows affiliations with multiple communities and with mutually compatible "individuations"—thus one can be at once Buryat, Russian (*rossiiskii*), and Eurasian. As Trubetskoi stated, "It is not an obliteration of the individual features of each part that creates the unity of the whole, but the continuity of the rainbow network itself."[46]

Territory as the Site of Expression and Realization of the State

The geographical unity of Eurasia subsumes a practical unity, in the sense that the philosophical tendencies of the territory must correspond to similar political and economic choices. In this spirit, Eurasianism is fully inscribed in the German tradition of geopolitics as it appeared at the end of the nineteenth century.[47] By explaining that some factors are invariable—subject neither to historical time nor to political will, geopolitics puts Eurocentric historicism into question and proposes a geographical reading of struggles between powers. The Eurasianists also use this geopolitical argument for the purpose of an epistemological rejection of Europe and its understanding of the world. International relations must no longer be understood historically because this would allow for European preeminence; it must be understood geographically, thus making it possible to legitimize the expansionism of young nations and the imperial structuring of Eurasia.

The Eurasianists are part of a civilizationist mode that followed the publication, in 1918, of *Der Untergang des Abendlandes* by Oswald Spengler (1880–1936), who put forth a cyclical theory of the rise and decline of civilizations, but preceded Arnold J. Toynbee (1889–1975), whose twelve-volume analysis of the rise and fall of civilizations, *A Study of History*, was published between the 1930s and the 1960s. Like Spengler, Savitskii himself noted the displacement of the centers of civilization in the course of the global historical process. After having established a cartography of temperature averages, he theorized the relation between climate and civilization, announcing that the cultural centers of the old continent were moving toward ever colder regions.[48] The third millennium, he claimed, will experience an annual temperature of zero degrees Celsius, which meant that the center of civilization during this period can only be coming from a "cold" region, namely, Eurasia. This global geographical displacement of the center holds even within Eurasia itself. The Eurasianists insisted on the regular evolution of Eurasia's political centers. While Dmitri Mendeleev forecasted that the center of Russia's population was moving from west to east, the capitals of the country seem to be headed from the southeast toward the northwest (Chingis Khan's empire in the steppes, Tamerlane's empire in Central Asia, Muscovy, and Saint Petersburg).[49] After the collapse of the Russian Empire and the catharsis of the Bolshevik revolution, Eurasianists envision a pendulum movement that will herald anew Eurasia's political center to the east. They can thereby only be happy about the change of capital effectuated by the Bolsheviks, leading the political center of Russia back more to the southeast, from Saint Petersburg to Moscow.

Eurasianism shares with German and Anglo-Saxon geopoliticians the idea that the land–sea binary expresses two differing political concepts. Though Eurasianist discourses do not employ the terms of tellurocracy and thalassocracy, they nevertheless associate the maritime sphere with parliamentary democracies and the continental one with more autocratic regimes. This duality of the world seems to reappear in Savitskii's thought with the existence of two models of empire. One of these is continental and is marked by the importance of ideas and civilizational patterns, on the model of the Roman/Byzantine Empire. The other is a maritime one and is marked by the predominance of economic or trade relations as well as by the leveling of the cultures that it dominates, on the British model. Only the continental model, which applies to Russia, is deemed to be a healthy imperialism capable of creating a supranational culture and serving the progress of humanity. This imperialism comprises a particular type of macro-state that enlarges its national culture beyond its geoethnic borders. This differentiation between imperialism (positive and Eurasian) and colonialism (negative and European) was reproduced by a number of Eurasianist ethnographical and historiographical discourses.

The Eurasianists therefore encourage Russia to abstain from all maritime ambitions, for the idea that power comes with the control of the seas belongs to the identity imperialism of Europe. Though Russia has had a glorious maritime history, its seas are nonetheless enclosed by ice. The counterpart of the western oceanic adventure is therefore realized in the conquest of the desert, for only the steppe is capable of making the junction between the different areas of civilizations. According to the formula originally borrowed from Sir Halford Mackinder (1861–1947), the Eurasianists declare that "whoever dominates the steppes will easily become the political unifier of all Eurasia."[50] Savitskii thus strove to turn Eurasia's continentality into an asset, proposing that the new Russia adopt the slogan of a continent-state as much as a continent-ocean. He stated Russian theoreticians "have not understood that in such a quest for an exit onto the sea, the ocean . . . lies not before but behind them, is not an ocean-sea but a continent-ocean. . . . The economic future of Russia does not reside in a simplistic copy of the oceanic politics of the others, which for many is inappropriate, but in the full consciousness of its continentality and its predisposition to it."[51] Countries with a maritime economy suffer less from distance in global commerce, whereas Eurasia, a country of extreme continentalism, is compelled to develop a trade specific to its hinterland. According to him, "By its geographical situation, Russia is destined to call into new life the regions that, situated in the center of the Asian continent, appear to be disinherited in regard to the oceanic economy."[52]

For the Eurasianists, Russia cannot permit itself to participate in the global market and to be interdependent with other national economies. Rather, its essential nature impels it toward autarky. This latter point is founded on the study of discontinuities between the European and Eurasian worlds, and on the complementarity of the Eurasian soils and their climates. According to Savitskii, Eurasia has economies of forest (the taiga), agriculture (the chernozem or black soil), livestock breeding (the surrounding areas of the Caspian and the Kazakh steppes), cotton (Turkestan), the extraction industries (Ukraine, the Urals, and Kazakhstan), and many industrial zones. This economic complementarity therefore confirms the structural aspect of the Eurasian totality. For Trubetskoi, an autarchic economy makes sense only for a state that represents a world in itself, one that is not part of a larger ensemble and does not have any colonies in the Western sense of the term. The idea of autarky is, then, what constitutes the specificity of Russia, unique in its combining of territorial continuity and a community of destiny.[53] The United States of the time constitutes, paradoxically, a model for the Eurasianists with its strong economic nationalism, its Monroe Doctrine unifying the north and the south of the continent, its continental consciousness, and its nonmembership in the League of Nations. For V. P. Nikitin, one of the Eurasianist doctrinaires close to Savitskii, "Eurasian continentalism is a greatness comparable to American continentalism, but at the same time it differs strongly from it by its internal meaning."[54]

In the agricultural sector, for example, Russia's originality shows itself in relation to the steppe, transforming a space of transhumance into an agricultural zone. Savitskii defined three possible models: a Europeanized agriculture in Russia's western regions, an extensive agriculture in the black soil regions and the steppes, and spaces left aside for transhumance in the eastern parts of the country. Eurasia thus reproduces in itself—in an agricultural form—the three continents of the old world, with its "authentic" identity naturally being constituted in the median space of the extensive. Russians are not only a peasant and laboring people, but also a livestock-breeding, forest, and merchant people, and even a nomadic one, which mediates between different geographical strips and represents the set of economic modes and cultures existing in Eurasia. Once again, geographical and economic givens are revealed to be the bearers of an identity value.

The geographical and economic autarky of the Eurasian territory subordinates the political autarky of the state. As Trubetskoi explained in a very straightforward way: "The territory of a veritably ideocratic state has to coincide with a separated autarkic world."[55] In Eurasianist discourse, the state is not a political mechanism, a technocratic management of society, but a historical-cultural organism, that is, a subject of history whose mission is to develop its geographical individuality. As a symphonic individual, it is predestined by the philosophy that animates it to develop the identity potentialities of its territory. For Savitskii, "The economy in Russia-Eurasia sets into perspective the development of a specific intracontinental world. There exists a determinate link between the economic and political missions. The first can only be realized in the conditions of a balanced political order, . . . of the Pax Rossica."[56] The Soviet state and its system of planning therefore gives life to the vast Eurasian expanses, strengthening Eurasia's natural unity. Only the state is in fact deemed capable of regulating the differences, unifying the parts with the totality, revealing their complementarity and their common rhythm. "It should be remarked that a state economy and statism are traditional for Russia-Eurasia. Statism constitutes the red thread running through the entire history of Eurasian spaces, and this is so for all entities that have appeared from the Empire of Chingis Khan via Muscovite Russia and the imperial period up until the USSR. The difference resides only in the degrees and scale of activity."[57]

Eurasianism's economic, autarkic, and statist choices as well as its geopolitical stances of endorsing a continental voluntarism, constitute only a practical means and do not represent an end in itself. These decisions attempt to highlight or reinforce the structural unity of Eurasia as well as to confirm the existence of this third continent as a natural individuality endowed with metaphysical meaning. The Eurasian world is thus valorized both as state and continent: the link between these two terms is carried out by means of the imperial structure, which alone is able to give the reality of a statehood to a continent. In addition, if Eurasia is a "natural" space, then it cannot accept any sort of amputation, which is regarded as a sort of violence against nature. As Savitskii stated, "The nature of the Eurasian world is very unfavorable to all types of separatism, political, cultural, or economic,"[58] a political message that could not have been clearer at a time, in the 1920s, when the debates on Ukrainian and Belorussian autonomy raged among the émigrés as well as in the Soviet Union.

The Eurasianist approach to geography and geosophy constitutes probably the most interesting and challenging attempt to demonstrate Eurasian unity, going further in terms of philosophical principles than just debating Eurasia's historical community of destiny or its geopolitical mission to counter Europe/the West. The geographical unity of Eurasia takes as its foundation a paradoxical scientistic and metaphysical conception of the territory, as illustrated by the terms of geosophy, topogenesis, and law-like regularity, all of which work to promote Eurasia as a living organism. Eurasianist scientific discourse is thus ontologically tied to the ideology of Eurasia itself because, according to Petr Suvchinskii, "ideology must become methodology."[59]

This geographical unity constitutes only the first piece of the Eurasianist puzzle, however, and is meaningful only when seen alongside the philosophical discourse of the movement. The spatial closure of Eurasia is necessary for the construction of its political utopia of ideocracy and for the Eurasian peoples to become aware of their inevitable community of destiny. As Savitskii described it, "Russia-Eurasia is, in many of its characteristics, a closed circle, a complete continent, a world in itself."[60]

EURASIANISM AS A FORM OF
POPPERIAN HISTORICISM?

Stefan Wiederkehr

ONE of the major concerns of the Eurasianists was to revise the fundamental principles underlying scientific inquiry.[1] This project was not an end in itself, for they believed that the function of science was not only to provide explanations but also to guide action. In this spirit, they did not restrict themselves to developing innovative methods to investigate the past and the present. In their attempt to conceive a philosophy of history, they instead extended their historical analyses to include predictions of the future course of world history. They claimed that these predictions were based on valid scientific methods, and thus believed that this gave them the right or even the duty to promote the alleged course of world history. To this extent, Eurasianism shares two main characteristics with what Karl Popper has termed "historicism."

The aim of this chapter is to evaluate Popper's concept of "historicism" as a tool to interpreting and understanding Eurasianism. My intention is not to question the results of previous research (most notably Michael Hagemeister's groundbreaking study) that has explained Eurasian "activism" in terms of the reception of Nikolai Fedorov's *Philosophy of the Common Task* (*Filosofiia obshchego dela*). In fact, Fedorov's philosophy of action and his idea that humankind will spiritually unite by fulfilling a common task played an important role in the split of the Eurasian movement at the end of the 1920s.[2] Rather than concentrate on the question of philosophical influences on the Eurasianists, I intend to analyze the structure of their philosophical argument and the fundamental principles underlying their theory of action.

This chapter is divided into two main parts. The first part gives a definition of Popperian "historicism" and applies it to Eurasian ideology in general. In the second part, more specific problems are discussed, focusing on the question as to how far the Eurasian theory of ideocratic government and economic planning as well as Eurasian messianism can be interpreted as being "historicist."

"Historicism" According to Popper

Popper defined historicism as "an approach to the social sciences which assumes that *historical prediction* is their principal aim, and that this aim is attainable by discovering the 'rhythms' or the 'patterns,' the 'laws' or the 'trends' that underlie the evolution of history."[3] Vehemently rejecting this approach, he passionately argued in *The Poverty of Historicism* that "the belief in historical destiny is sheer superstition, and that there can be no prediction of the course of human history by scientific or any other rational methods."[4] What he called the "central mistake" of historicists was their faith in absolute trends and laws, "which carry us irresistibly in a certain direction into the future."[5] According to Popper, historicists believe that they can only interpret history and are unable to change predetermined development. Historicism does not, however, imply fatalism, nor does it paralyze its proponents. On the contrary, historicists display a clear tendency toward "activism" based on the desire to accelerate impending social change toward the allegedly predetermined telos of history. From this perspective, "social midwifery is the only perfectly reasonable activity . . . the only activity that can be based upon scientific foresight."[6]

In another polemical work Popper argues that the function of historicism is to relieve the individual of the burden of responsibility for his or her actions. Vigorously objecting to this, Popper stressed that reason and conscience make it impossible for any individual to shift the "supreme responsibility for [his or her] actions" to a higher authority.[7]

A third element that is typical for "historicism" is a holistic worldview. According to Popper, historicists are proponents of an organic theory of society. They interpret social groups by analogy with living organisms passing through life cycles from birth to death, being "wholes" and therefore having clear-cut borders to other social groups and definite internal structures assigning a specific place and function to each of its members.[8]

Patterns, Rhythms, Laws

The first collection of Eurasianist essays *Iskhod k Vostoku* (Exodus to the East) contains an article that describes the alleged historical laws concerning the "Migration of Culture," that is, the shift of the leading cultural centers.[9] Its author, Petr N. Savitskii, argued that he found empirical evidence that the cultural center of the Old World had historically shifted northward into regions with lower average temperatures, the "velocity" being five degrees Celsius per millennium.[10] Extrapolating this trend, he predicted that in the third millennium Eurasia and North America would be culturally dominant:[11] "Projecting into the future the tendency of geographical and cultural shifts described above leads, apparently, to the supposition that the principal centers of world culture—which throughout the last centuries has been represented by Western Europe—will move to Russia-Eurasia and to North America."[12]

The idea of *translatio studii* is a recurring motif in the writings of the Eurasianists.[13] Previous studies have shown the importance of Nikolai Danilevskii's theory of cultural-historical types and Konstantin Leont'ev's morphological vision of culture for the emergence of Eurasianism.[14] It is no surprise that the Eurasianists, within this framework, predicted the decline of Europe and the cultural blossoming of Eurasia. This can be illustrated by a fragment from *Iskhod k Vostoku*: "A new culturo-geographical world, one that up to this point has not played a guiding role, has entered the arena of world history. . . . Is the Goddess of Culture, whose tent for so many centuries has been pitched among the valleys and hills of the European West, not heading for the East?"[15]

Numerous studies have interpreted Eurasianism in the wider context of European *Kulturpessimismus* after the First World War. Previous research has connected it with Oswald Spengler's idea of a "morphology of cultures," in particular.[16] The Eurasianists themselves commented on various occasions on their connection with Spengler. On the one hand, Trubetskoi hoped for some time that Spengler, whom he considered to have a similar ideology, would write the preface to the German translation of *Evropa i chelovechestvo*.[17] On the other hand, the Eurasianists would insist that they had worked out their theories independently from Western models.[18] In fact, they did not focus on the "Decline of the West," but on the birth of a new epoch in world history. They interpreted the catastrophic events of the First World War, the Russian revolutions, and the Russian Civil War as the painful beginning of a new era and compared it to the Barbarian invasions of Late Antiquity.[19] They saw a religious dimension in the tribulations of revolution and emigration,[20] and they expected the latter to act as a sort of atonement and purge their past sins.[21] In the introduction to *Iskhod k Vostoku*, they presented this point in the following way:

The essays that make up the present volume were put together in an atmosphere of a consciousness of catastrophe. We perceive the segment of time within which our lives pass, beginning with the coming of the war, as a pivotal, and not merely a transitional time. In what happened and in what is happening we see not just shock, but crisis, and in the future we anticipate a profound change in the customary countenance of the world. In the catastrophic nature of what is happening we see a sign of the ripening, quickening resettlement and regeneration of culture. . . . We honor the past and the present of West European culture, but it is not in this culture that we see the future. . . . We do know that the world cataclysm, separating one epoch of world history from the next, has already begun. We do not doubt that the replacement of the West European world will come from the East.[22]

Lev P. Karsavin developed this historicist idea further. According to him, the Russian Revolution not only had a fixed place and meaning in world history, but itself also followed a scheme of predetermined phases.[23] In general, the Eurasianists reinforced and perpetuated old Slavophile stereotypes,[24] especially in the way they characterized the old and the new epochs as well as in the way they anchored these epochs in the West and the East.[25]

The Eurasianists were proponents of a synthetic conception of science.[26] Within this programmatic framework, they contrived what they called "personology" (*personologiia*) as a means to systematically combine different disciplines with each other in order to erect a "system of sciences."[27] Following the tradition of neo-Platonism and German *Naturphilosophie*, the Eurasianists conceived symmetry as the universal principle of order. On this basis, they deduced the existence of Eurasia—in their sense—from the symmetry of geographic and linguistic phenomena within the alleged third continent between Europe and Asia. For them, the coincidence of geographic isolines, isoglosses, and cultural borders could not be accidental; instead it manifested a hidden, deeper reality.[28] That is why Savitskii declared that the revelation of this hidden order of the world was the "scientific task of Eurasianism":

> The comparison of the data from general and economic geography with the
> data from the history of economics, ethnography, archaeology, and linguis-
> tics has hardly begun, despite the fact that it could offer an entirely new
> *synthetic* image of Russia-Eurasia. . . . What has to be found is a focus that
> allows us to understand various different phenomena from the perspective
> of one single regularity. . . . [In Russia-Eurasia], the phenomena of soil life,
> botany, and climate correlate more completely than in any other geographic
> world. In the case of Eurasia, this correlation is not some abstract presump-
> tion. It is rather *numerically evident* and expressed in a periodical and

rhythmic system (*periodicheskaia ritmika*). It is absolutely necessary to add historical, economic, archaeological, and linguistic phenomena to this rhythmic system. This is a step toward the establishment of a periodical system of being (*periodicheskaia sistema sushchego*).[29]

In a later text he put it even more radically: "The basis for the Eurasian worldview is the *idea of the periodical system of being*. By this term the Eurasianists try to denote the *regularity and rhythm* that constitute the order of the world. History and nature both provide clear proof regarding the nature of this phenomenon. . . . The periodical system of [geographic] zones in Russia-Eurasia corresponds to the periodical and rhythmic system of its history."[30] From this point of view, the researcher's only task is to find preexisting phenomena and to connect them correctly, in order to reveal the existence of Eurasia as an organic whole: "[Coordinated research on Eurasia provides] an approximation to a synthetic worldview by understanding a variety of phenomena in terms of uniform categories. . . . The specificity of the Eurasian methodological approach to Russia lies in the idea that the facts of every discipline are arranged according to this specific and unique system. What is revealed in this way is the inner structure of phenomena and the uniformity that connects them."[31]

This quote, however, indicates that the Eurasianists did not take into account a fundamental distinction of the modern theory of science. As Patrick Sériot has pointed out, they did not make a distinction between the real object and the scientific object of knowledge, which is constructed by the researcher. In contrast to the poststructuralists, they still believed in real objects beyond discourses and the mind of the researcher.[32]

The real object that the Eurasianists believed they would simply be able to uncover by means of personology was the "cultural personality" of Eurasia: "The main object of the descriptive sciences is the multinational personality, which together with its physical environment (the territory) the Eurasianists call Eurasia. This personality has to be studied such that . . . every scientific specialist . . . focuses his attention on it and that the efforts of all specialists are coordinated. This calls for a collaborative effort, aimed at producing a scientific and philosophical synthesis . . . which determines the meaning and the direction of the collaboration in general and of every special study as well."[33]

Thus, the proof of the existence of Eurasia as an organic whole becomes circular. The Eurasianists called for a coordinated focus of all scientific disciplines on one allegedly preexisting object, which, however, was only created as a scientific object by this coordinated research. The fact that the Eurasianists did not realize this was probably the most serious weakness of their epistemological approach.

Activism

The Eurasianists assigned their ideology—which was based on the belief in historical rhythms, symmetries, and laws—the function of directing and legitimizing action. The very first Eurasian text, Trubetskoi's *Evropa i chelovechestvo*, already called for action: "Many people are currently preoccupied with the 'reevaluation of values.' My ideas, for those who will accept them, will serve as one indicator of the direction in which this reevaluation should proceed. Certainly the theoretical and practical work which will follow the acceptance of my theses must be a collaborative work. . . . Many minds are needed to develop an idea into a system and to put it into practice. I call upon all those who share my convictions to join in this effort."[34]

Later, in 1925, Savitskii put it as follows in the first systematic manifesto of Eurasianism: "Eurasianism is not only a system of historiosophical and other theoretical doctrines. Its aim is to connect thought and action. Together with a system of theoretical insights, this also leads to the affirmation of a certain methodology of action."[35]

At the end of his treatise on personology, Trubetskoi again stressed that science must lead to action: "All theoretical and applied studies . . . have to be coordinated and, thus, constitute a uniform *system of sciences*. This, however, cannot be an exhaustive description of the tasks of Eurasianism as a *system of ideology (sistema mirosozertsaniia)*. . . . A harmonious and coherent *system of ideas* has to be established. What has to correspond to this system of ideas is a *system of practical actions*."[36]

Similarly, Savitskii called for activism in science, that is, to accelerate impending change by coordinated scientific work: "It is typical of scientific life in our time that representatives of various disciplines work on one single object, united in an organized and planned manner. The Eurasianists achieve such a union in their own scientific practice. . . . On the one hand Eurasianism reflects our epoch, on the other it also aims to *influence it*."[37]

The allegedly predetermined telos of history, toward which the Eurasianists' actions were directed, was the national and political unity of Eurasia:

> The destinies of the Eurasian peoples have become interwoven with one
> another, tied together in a massive tangle that can no longer be unraveled.
> The separation of any one people from this unity can be accomplished only
> by an act of contrived violence against nature, which will necessarily result
> in suffering. This does not apply to the ethnic groups forming the basis of
> pan-Slavism, pan-Turanianism, and pan-Islamism. None of them is united
> to such a degree by a common historical destiny. Not one of these "pan-isms"
> is pragmatically as valuable as is pan-Eurasian nationalism. That national-

ism is not only *pragmatically valuable*; it is nothing less than a vital necessity, for only the awakening of Russia-Eurasia's self-awareness as a single, multiethnic Eurasian nation will provide it with the ethnic substratum of statehood without which it will eventually fall to pieces, causing unheard-of suffering for all its parts. For pan-Eurasian nationalism to function effectively as a unifying factor for the Eurasian state, it is necessary to *re-educate* the self-awareness of the peoples of Eurasia.[38]

In contrast to most other bearers of nationalism, Trubetskoi did not even try to hide the fact that Eurasianism was an ideology conceived to serve the ends of nation building:

For the separate parts of the former Russian Empire to continue as parts of a single state there must exist a single substratum of statehood. . . . A stable and permanent unification is . . . feasible only on the basis of an ethnic (national) substratum. . . . *The national substratum of the state formerly known as the Russian Empire and now known as the USSR can only be the totality of peoples inhabiting that state, taken as a peculiar multiethnic nation and as such possessed of its own nationalism. We call that nation Eurasian, its territory Eurasia, and its nationalism Eurasianism.*[39]

As a political program, Eurasianism was aimed at the restoration of one single state and the domination of the Russian people on the territory of the former Russian Empire. In this sense, of course, Eurasianism called for action. At the same time, however, Eurasianism was much more than a simple political program of a certain political party. The Eurasianists' strategy was far more sophisticated. They consciously attempted to realize their political goals by formulating scientific theories and offering patterns of thinking. They were convinced that if their historicist theories and patterns of thinking were accepted, they would necessarily lead to conclusions and actions that corresponded to their own Eurasianist vision. In the second part of this chapter, the heuristic value of the concept "historicism" will therefore be tested by applying it to selected aspects of Eurasian ideology.

Ideocracy

"Ideocracy" (*ideokratiia*) was a key concept in Eurasian ideology. In the Eurasianists' definition, ideocracy meant the absolute rule of ideology in every aspect of life. As early as 1923, Savitskii argued that the Eurasianists should accept the "citizenship of the idea" (*poddanstvo idei*) instead of their lost Russian Imperial citizenship, and sacrifice themselves accordingly in order to put this "guiding idea" (*ideia-pravitel'nitsa*) into practice.[40] In the same year, Iakov Sadovskii argued that "all aims of the state . . . can be achieved technically much more perfectly—indeed perhaps can only be achieved at all—if the state is ruled by a cultivated, conscious minority dedicated to an idea."[41] This minority, which they also called the "ruling echelon" (*praviashchii otbor*) should unite to form the only party and rule the state in the name and interest of the people. In their eyes, it was the function of the state to enforce the rule of ideology: "The Eurasianists consider the practical organization of life and the world to be their main task. They believe that the most effective means of organization is the state. . . . The Eurasian state system is defined as *ideocracy*."[42]

Therefore, the role of the ideocratic state differs fundamentally from the role of the democratic state: "What corresponds to ideocracy is state-maximalism . . . that is, the active and leading participation of the state in economic and cultural life. In this respect, ideocracy fundamentally differs from democracy and its state-minimalism."[43]

In a later text, Trubetskoi juxtaposed the democratic state and the ideocratic state as follows: "The democratic state has no convictions of its own (because its rulers come from various parties) and therefore cannot direct the culture and the economy. For this reason, it tries to interfere as little as possible with both ('freedom of trade,' 'freedom of the press,' 'freedom of art,' etc.). . . . Contrariwise, the ideocratic state has its own convictions and its own governing idea (whose bearer is the ruling echelon united in a single ideological state organization), and it must itself organize and control all aspects of life."[44]

According to the Eurasianists, individuals had duties toward the state's aims, which the latter should enforce.[45] This did not, however, involve any use of physical violence. As the Eurasianists held that their ideas were true, they believed that they would be able to convince the people by arguments and education. They simply denied the possibility of conflict between the people's will and the free will of an individual member of the people because, in their eyes, Eurasianism embodied the people's will: "Ideocracy will not be violence, as the supporters of Western democracy think . . . but a most rational organization of public life. Moreover, state power will by its existence . . . embody the historical idea of a given people and thus most perfectly express this people's will."[46]

Thus, the Eurasian doctrine of ideocratic government reflects an organic theory of society and also bases the rulers' action on an understanding of the laws of historical evolution. These are both core ideas of historicism.

The "Force of the Organizing Idea" in Economics

The Eurasianists were fascinated by the "force of the organizing idea" in economic life and therefore became fervent supporters of a planned economy in the 1930s.[47] In his introduction to *Novaia epokha*, Vladimir A. Peil' put it like this: "From suffering and pain emerges a *new epoch* of construction (*stroitel'stvo*) and harmony. . . . Those with clear reason and broad minds feel the coming of *regularity* in economy, society, and state. The new epoch brings to an end the traditional chaos that results from the lack of planning. . . . It is necessary to have a *general plan* inspired by the leading ideological core, foresight, and the proper alignment of forces and means. It is necessary *to assign the economy to its proper place.*"[48] Sofiia Bokhan, one of the few women in the Eurasian movement, criticized Western capitalism in the same collection of essays. In contrast, she admired Soviet economic planning: "Chaos and unjustifiable lack of planning . . . rule in the West. In the USSR, statewide economic *planning* has come into being. . . . [This is] one of the greatest achievements of the Russian Revolution."[49]

In the eyes of the Eurasianists, Eurasia also constituted an economic whole.[50] What they interpreted as proof of Eurasia's autarky was the fact that Soviet Russia's industry grew at a tremendous pace during a time when the rest of the world was suffering from the Great Depression.[51] In 1932, Savitskii made it clear that the economic program emerged from the Eurasian fundamentals: "Sooner or later, under one slogan or another, Russia will become a self-sufficient world. . . . Eurasianism can claim the role of the organizing idea that determines the organization of this world. . . . It is precisely in the Eurasian system that Russia's autarky is fully legitimized from within; precisely in this system, it is essential and indispensable. Autarky emanates from the doctrine of Russia-Eurasia as a special type of a 'symphonic personality,' it corresponds completely to the Eurasian thesis of Russia as a unique geographic, historical, ethnographical, and linguistic world."[52]

As a consequence of their growing fascination with planning, the Eurasianists did not question the Soviet planned economy as a whole, but rather criticized its unilateral focus on industry.[53] While the Eurasianists were always critics of capitalism as a product of European civilization,[54] there is evidence that the rise of economic planning in their thinking was a direct reaction to developments in the Soviet Union, especially to the First Five-Year Plan. In their attempt to appropriate this idea, the Eurasianists also adopted the discursive style of Soviet propaganda: "The Eurasian state is a state of the working people (*gosudarstvo trudiashchikhsia*), a state of social justice and truth. Consecrated by its religious origins, the workers' state (*trudovoe gosudarstvo*) is the common task (*obshchee delo*) inherent to Russian consciousness at all times."[55]

The last quote shows that the Eurasianists oriented themselves toward the past and the future at the same time. This fact places them in closer proximity to fascism and the German "Conservative Revolution" than to Bolshevism.[56] For example, in 1933 Bokhan claimed an indestructible connection between revolution, tradition, and the use of scientific methods:

[These outlines of] the synthesis that characterizes the *new epoch* correspond to the system of Eurasian ideas, which has been worked out in detail.
This system covers all aspects of life and represents a distinctive combination of intuitive knowledge of the rhythm of history with insights from
pure scientific work. . . . It is the task of the Eurasianists to complete the
Revolution, to realize its last stage leading directly to its *telos beyond history (sverkh"istoricheskaia tsel')*. Providing a synthesis of Russian *tradition*
and the Russian *Revolution*, and laying a sound foundation for the Eurasian
symphonic, multinational culture, Eurasianism stands for a new epoch in
the history of mankind.[57]

This is undoubtedly another piece of evidence proving that Eurasian
thinking had a historicist structure. In the Eurasian writings from the 1930s,
we can find an increasing number of examples expressing a heroic emotional
style, which was also typical for fascism. This can be seen in the following observation: "Many individuals and the peoples of Eurasia have made enormous
sacrifices for the common task. The future asks for even greater efforts, but
we *must not let go*. There must be no retreat! . . . The heroic youth of the new
epoch does not surrender for a mouthful of philistine happiness. . . . We must
work for the spiritual victory, for the idea and the plan; we must fight to the
very end."[58] The heroism and self-sacrifice in the name of higher historical
goals (instead of action driven by individual reason and responsibility) apparent in this quote are typical for historicism.

Messianism

One key function of Eurasianism was to offer a common ideology of integration that would be shared equally by all the peoples of the former Russian
Empire. As has been shown elsewhere, the Eurasianists tried to safeguard
Russia as a multinational state at a time when the Ottoman and Habsburg
empires were collapsing.[59] They also offered a political and economic model for
this territory. However, another central aspect of Eurasianism remains to be
mentioned. As an ideology of isolation at its core, Eurasianism nevertheless
claimed a global mission in one respect: in the eyes of the Eurasianists, Russia
had to be the leader of the emerging anticolonial movement. If this strategy
had succeeded, discussions about Russia as an anachronistic colonial empire
could have been effectively stifled and potential separatist movements would
have been delegitimized.

In 1922 Trubetskoi maintained that the "Romano-Germans" (i.e., the
West European peoples) tried to solve "The Russian Problem" by imposing
their rule on Russia so that it would suffer the same fate as Africa. According
to Trubetskoi, the Bolsheviks' resistance could only be temporary.[60] Not even

world revolution could reduce the threat of a foreign yoke in Russia, for in a socialist world Russia would be a peripheral state, too: "World revolution will not bring change in any essential way to the gloomy prospects confronting Russia. Without it, Russia will become a colony of the bourgeois Romano-Germanic countries, and with it a colony of Communist Europe. But a colony she will be in either case. The page of history on which 'Russia, a Great European Power' is inscribed will have been turned once and for all. . . . In the future, Russia will be a colony similar to India, Egypt, and Morocco."[61]

Trubetskoi interpreted anticolonialism as a global uprising against European (cultural) imperialism, thereby developing further the argument from *Evropa i chelovechestvo* that the rest of the world had to be united in opposition to Europe.[62] Russia had a long tradition of independent statehood and should therefore, according to Trubetskoi, be the leading force in the struggle with the colonial powers.[63] The Eurasianists did not conceive this as a political decision. In their eyes, it was determined by nature: "The Eurasianists hold that the orientation of Russian foreign policy toward Asia is the only natural orientation for Russia."[64]

Fighting the spirit of world revolution, the Eurasianists' thinking sometimes came very close to that of their ideological enemies, the Bolsheviks. This was, however, inextricably intertwined with older traditions of Russian messianism,[65] as can be illustrated by a quote from Karsavin, who as a religious philosopher followed the tradition of Vladimir Solov'ev's doctrine of All-Unity (*vseedinstvo*): "It is possible to create an all-human culture, but *only* by creating one's own national and multinational one. Sometimes, events in one culture have decisive influences on the development of mankind. Such an event is the Russian Revolution, which uncovers the *universal* meaning of the Russian-Eurasian problem and reveals Russia's *historical mission*. The fates of the reawakening Asian cultures are now as much intertwined with the fate of Russia as is the way out of the individualistic crisis through which European culture is now passing, on its way out or—to its death."[66]

In 1929, an anonymous manifesto in *Evraziiskii sbornik* assigned Russia-Eurasia a "messianic task" in the struggle with Western thinking.[67] Nikolai N. Alekseev pursued this line of argumentation in the next decade: "Eurasianism has not only a national, but also a universal (*vselenskaia*) task. The Russian nation (*narod*) has to overcome in itself and by itself the Western race, which has spread its culture all over the world. By its universality, Eurasianism differs from fascism, national socialism, and other movements that turn out to be national socialist, because they do not face any universal tasks."[68]

Savitskii had already clearly stated in 1923 what he considered to be Russia's universal task: "Russia has to liberate the world from the slavery imposed upon it by the recent Romano-Germanic models. This liberation is first of all a spiritual problem."[69]

Because of its messianic character, Eurasianism can be considered part of the Slavophile tradition in the broad sense of the term. As was the case with Danilevskii a century ago, the Eurasianists as well saw themselves on the threshold of a new era that was to become the last age of world history. According to the Eurasianists, the coming epoch was not just the next one in a series, but the synthesis of the highest achievements of human civilization: "The Eurasianists devote themselves completely to practice. The 'practical practice,' however, is for them only a stage and a path to final liberation and salvation. They combine hard efforts in worldly matters, that is, matters the meaning of which the West has expressed during the past centuries, with the lively and mighty preservation of the eternal values of the Eastern spirit. In this way they prepare the future—Eurasian—historical synthesis."[70]

This idea of dialectics and final synthesis to be spread by Eurasia throughout the whole world is strongly developed in the writings of two minor Eurasian authors, Ivan V. Stepanov and Georgii N. Polkovnikov.[71] It is also the key issue in the anonymous booklet *Evraziistvo i kommunizm*. Sharply criticizing capitalism and rhetorically converging with Soviet propaganda, this booklet seems to have been addressed to the Bolsheviks. The authors' obvious intent was to present communism as the antithesis to capitalism and the resolution of this contradiction in the synthesis of Eurasianism: "The time has come when historical dialectics take their most important step: from the thesis of capitalism and the antithesis of communism to the synthesis of Eurasianism."[72]

This booklet reaches its climax in the final sentence: "It is only the program of the Eurasianists that will secure for our country the great historical role that has been entrusted to it by the will of history."[73] This is Popperian historicism in its purest form.

The Eurasianists did not restrict themselves to an analysis of the past or to a description of the world. According to them, history has an end and there are laws governing historical evolution. The Eurasianists believed that they had uncovered the laws that determine the past as well as the future. They further believed that, knowing these laws, they had a duty to speed up the course of history toward its telos. Thus, Eurasianism was also a philosophy of action directed toward the future. Previous research has correctly linked this aspect of Eurasianism, its activist heroism and its messianism, to influences of Fedorovian philosophy. This chapter has argued that it is also important to appreciate it as "historicism" in the sense that Karl Popper has given the term.

Using the concept of "historicism" as an analytical tool offers an additional explanation as to why, toward the end of the 1920s and especially in the 1930s, some Eurasianists approached Marxism, whereas others sympathized with the German "Conservative Revolution" and with fascism. What these currents have in common is, in fact, their "historicist" character in Popper's sense. It is likely that a common style of thinking and the similar structure of arguments outweighed the decisive differences in ideological content that existed between these currents. The Eurasianists proved to be receptive to illiberal ideologies from both left and right because these ideologies shared the Eurasianists' activist spirit of historicism.

METAPHYSICS OF THE ECONOMY

The Religious and Economic Foundations of P. N. Savitskii's Eurasianism

Martin Beisswenger

AMONG the leaders and ideologists of the Eurasianist movement Petr Nikolaevich Savitskii has attracted particular scholarly attention. No doubt, this attention is partly the result of his eventful biography. Born in the Ukrainian city of Chernigov in 1895, Savitskii experienced the First World War, the Russian Revolution, and the Civil War, and subsequently emigrated from Russia. In 1921 he moved to Czechoslovakia, where he lived under German occupation during the Second World War. He was arrested by Soviet forces in 1945 and spent ten years in Stalin's Gulag. In 1956 he returned to Prague, where he died in 1968. At the same time, however, the broad interest in Savitskii's person is also the result of the originality of his ideas, in particular of his attempt to answer once and for all the fateful question of Russia's identity by claiming that Russia was neither Europe nor Asia, but a self-contained continent apart—Eurasia.[1]

Unfortunately, the secondary literature on Savitskii has hitherto focused primarily on his writings on Russian geography.[2] In order to acknowledge a few of his many other intellectual interests, some scholars have characterized his ideas as "economic-geography," "geosophy," or "geopolitics."[3] In fact, however, the sphere of Savitskii's interests was truly universal. As this chapter will argue, Savitskii's ideas were essentially a quest for synthetic and universal thinking, a quest primarily based on economic and religious principles. Initially Savitskii's ideas were entirely secular. In the early 1920s, however, his thinking was fused with a strong religious element and he attempted to create a new and comprehensive political economy subordinated to the teachings of the Orthodox Church. This new political economy, Savitskii was convinced, would not only be more holistic than West European economic teachings but would also fit the particular conditions of "Eurasia." It would promote Russia's harmonious economic modernization, yet, at the same time, allow the preservation of the country's religious potential. It would enable Russia to accomplish its spiritual mission, the resurrection of the "East." Thus, political economy provided Savitskii with the theoretical tools to conceptualize his ideas and made possible his Eurasianism—as a coherent system of political, cultural, scientific, and religious thought.

Savitskii's economic ideas, in particular those of his master's thesis "Metaphysics of the Economy," stood firmly in the epistemological discourse of late nineteenth- and early twentieth-century Russian thought, characterized by neoidealist attempts to reaffirm the relative autonomy of the "metaphysical" sphere of philosophy against the exclusively empirical claims of materialist positivism.[4] Like the authors of the almanacs *Problems of Idealism* (1902) and *Signposts* (1909), Savitskii affirmed the role of "metaphysical" principles in science and searched for a new spiritual foundation of reality. In this respect, Savitskii was a typical representative of the so-called Russian Silver Age, a heterogeneous anti-materialist cultural, political and religious revival that shaped the intellectual life of early twentieth-century Russia.[5] At the same time, however, Savitskii was also a prominent participant in a larger, pan-European "revolt against positivism," a trend that rejected a simplistic materialist worldview in favor of more complicated models of man and society.[6]

Savitskii's religious and economic understanding of Eurasia and his call for the country's economic modernization sharply distinguished his Eurasianism from the views of many other Eurasianists. As we shall see, Savitskii's particular economic views became the subject of contention among leading Eurasianists. This fact suggests, as the present chapter also argues, that the Eurasianist movement in general was conceptually more heterogeneous than commonly assumed.

Young Savitskii and the Economic Modernization of Russia

Savitskii's synthetic thinking emerged gradually from the early 1910s until the mid-1920s. Growing up in Chernigov, he was interested in economic theory and practice. Very likely this interest was stimulated both by his family's involvement in the affairs of the local *zemstvo* administration and by the country's rapid industrialization at the turn of the century.[7]

Already then Savitskii never saw economic questions isolated from other issues. For instance, he promoted the modernization of the local economy with the help the of the region's artistic traditions. Moreover, Savitskii's quest for universal knowledge and its practical application revealed itself when, soon after his graduation from high school, he self-consciously demanded curricular changes. The teaching of natural sciences, he argued, should be balanced with that of the humanities. Historical education must give more than a mere listing of the facts of political history; these need to be complemented with the history of culture, and the history of social and economic life, art, and everyday life. Only then could schools produce those "conscious and firm activists in the sphere of the social and economic construction" whom the country desperately needed.[8]

After Savitskii became a student at the St. Petersburg Polytechnic Institute in 1913, under the influence of his teacher P. B. Struve, his economic ideas acquired a more explicitly political twist. Following Struve, who in his 1908 programmatic essay "Great Russia" had openly embraced Russian nationalism and imperialism in the Black Sea region, regarding them as important values for a future democratic and economically strong Russia,[9] Savitskii called for the Russian Empire's continuous imperial mission in the East. There it could create "an organic imperial entity," resembling the Hellenistic monarchies of the East and the Roman Empire, because "Russian culture is able to become strong enough to reinvigorate the cultural life of these people, who had left such wonderful traces of their bygone culture."[10] Russia's "organic" imperialism, the result of its empire's "continental" rather than "colonial" character, was far superior to that of Germany and Britain.

Russia's imperialism, Savitskii claimed, avoided its imperial rivals' almost exclusively economically motivated imperialism. It allowed for a mutual cultural interaction between the "imperializing" and "imperialized," and created a new supranational culture with "equal economic strength and equal rights of all people."[11] In order to realize its imperial future in the East, Savitskii was convinced, Russia needed a balanced agricultural-industrial economy.

And for that reason any assessment of Russia's productive forces needed to consider the country as a whole, including its Asian territories. "Russian industry," Savitskii assumed, "can find the riches of natural resources for its development not in the European plain but in the mountains of Asia."[12]

Already in his earliest writings, thus, Savitskii examined aspects of Russia's economic development that later would constitute essential components of his Eurasianist works, such as the economic integrity of the country and its imperial mission. It was not until 1917, however, that his economic thought acquired an explicitly metaphysical component. In his master's thesis "Metaphysics of the Economy and Its Experimental Cognition" (1917–1920),

Savitskii argued that political economy was a complex discipline, standing somewhere between the "exact" sciences and the humanities, in particular philosophy and art.[13]

Although this study was largely based on Bulgakov's *Philosophy of the Economy* (1912) and Struve's *Economy and Price* (1913), Savitskii attempted to transcend them and thus to build the new economic theory merely anticipated by his mentors.[14] The main goal of Bulgakov's *Philosophy of the Economy* was to counteract positivism and materialism and to bridge the gap between the Kantian "thinking subject" and the "external world," the *Ding an sich*. Bulgakov introduced the concept of "labor" as the central element of human agency and the means to overcome this division. According to Bulgakov, by engaging in "labor" the "laboring subject" interacts with the divinely inspired sphere of "Sophia" and thus partakes in divine creation.[15] Savitskii acknowledged the metaphysical dimension of labor, but criticized Bulgakov for not precisely demarcating the empirical and metaphysical economic spheres. Savitskii advanced a more narrowly focused definition of the economic sphere than Bulgakov: "The economic world is the world of [material] objects that can be acquired by human beings. This world is characterized by a certain correlativity but it is opposed by the absoluteness of beings, which are self-sufficient, can neither be sold nor bought, and are sociologically not interchangeable."[16]

Whereas Bulgakov had approached the economy from a metaphysical, "sophic" perspective, Struve had criticized traditional economics from an empirical standpoint. Unlike Bulgakov's metaphysical speculations, Struve's argumentation was concrete and historical, focusing on Marx's concept of "value." In his *Economy and Price* Struve sought empirically to demonstrate that prices are not determined by their labor content, as Marx would have it; instead the empirical prices themselves had always defined the value of goods.[17] Unlike orthodox Marxists, Struve acknowledged that the economic sphere contained metaphysical components and thus conceptually his ideas did not contradict those of Bulgakov or, later, those of Savitskii. Unlike them, however, Struve was not interested in exploring metaphysical aspects of economic activity beyond the acknowledgment that they did exist. On the contrary, Struve's main goal was to safeguard the empirical sphere of political economy against metaphysical "contamination," Marxist or otherwise.[18] Although Savitskii did not explicitly criticize Struve, he did not agree with his teacher's rigorous empiricism. He observed ironically that if even an empiricist like Struve had reluctantly acknowledged the metaphysical element in economics, there was no question that the metaphysical sphere in the economy in fact existed.[19]

Neither Struve nor Bulgakov, taken alone, could satisfy Savitskii's thirst for synthesis. It goes without saying that Marxism did not satisfy Savitskii either. Unlike Struve and Bulgakov, who had been youthful adherents of Marxism, Savitskii never sympathized with Marxist ideas. Strangely, for Savitskii central Marxist precepts proved the necessity of implicit metaphysical assumptions in political economy.[20] One typical example of such a metaphysical assumption was Marx's "labor theory of value," where "value" is defined as a "congelation of labor."[21]

This definition, Savitskii argued, was clearly an abstract a priori statement, plainly lacking any "substantiation, taken from the empirical reality." "Labor, as a 'substance,' as the 'reason' of value, can only be its 'ultimate,' but never its empirical 'reason.'" To be sure, Savitskii explained, such claims were not necessarily faulty, but they should be taken for what they actually were, that is, a priori assertions not empirical statements.[22]

The presence of metaphysical assumptions a priori in Marxism was thus, in Savitskii's opinion, a crucial piece of evidence in support of his thesis that political economy was a synthetic all-encompassing discipline, truly combining the empirical and metaphysical. He defined its place in the continuum of academic disciplines as between the empirical natural sciences on the one end and pure metaphysics on the other. Political economy encompassed and adapted for its purposes all other academic disciplines. Political economy, Savitskii claimed, "can be characterized as a cognitive method with a complex composition." It was at the same time "metaphysical," "deductive," and "inductive." From such a synthesis of the empirical and the metaphysical both sides could only gain; they did not contradict each other, but, on the contrary, were mutually beneficial, fertilizing and inspiring each other.[23]

Savitskii's enthusiasm for his discipline was the result of his personal searching for integral and universal knowledge, and of his interest in natural sciences, art, philosophy, and politics. There is little doubt that he was talking about himself, when he emphatically exclaimed that "[a] researcher who loves an abstract-logical way of thinking usually devotes his attention to mathematical investigations—someone who likes to think 'geographically' devotes himself to geography. To the economy, however, he can devote himself and receive satisfaction someone whose heroine is the Beautiful Lady of Abstract Thinking, [and] someone who is under the spell of 'geographic pathos.'"[24] Economic thought ideally satisfied Savitskii's spiritual need, his passionate quest to solve the "ultimate" questions of life. In a passage that doubtlessly expressed Savitskii's very own personal attitude toward the purpose of his research, he confessed: "Human reason aspires to find the 'cause of causes,' some single source and center of economic phenomena; the human mind seeks the explanation of those goals, which the Supreme Reason has insinuated in the creation of the economy: [human reason] aspires not only to cognize but also to 'evaluate' the present empirical world and to determine if the human being himself can set forth some 'universally applicable' goals."[25]

Thus, "Metaphysics" was perhaps Savitskii's most personal work of scholarship. It came from his deepest intellectual convictions and cognitive aspirations. It summarized his earlier interests in art and economy and set the tone for his widespread activities throughout the 1920s and beyond. "Metaphysics" made it clear for him that it was in principle possible to gain synthetic knowledge, to combine the empirical and metaphysical, to interact with one's environment and still to serve a higher purpose.

The "Blessed Economy" of Eurasia

Although Savitskii was baptized as a child, until 1921 there are few indications that religious principles determined his scholarly work or philosophical outlook. By late 1921, however, after the dramatic events of the Russian Revolution and Civil War, this had changed in a way that strongly suggests that he must have experienced a religious awakening. It is quite possible that this awakening was initiated by Savitskii's encounter in Sofia in early 1921 with four other Russian émigré intellectuals: the musicologist P. P. Suvchinskii, the linguist N. S. Trubetskoi, the theologian G. V. Florovskii, and the future priest A. A. Liven. Suvchinskii later characterized this meeting a "miracle."[26] This group formed the nucleus of what over the next year would emerge as the Eurasianist movement and, in particular after the publication of its first almanac *Exodus to the East* in August 1921, gained broad publicity among Russian émigré circles.[27]

In any case, in a November 1921 letter to a friend Savitskii made his religious fervor explicit when—already an ardent Eurasianist—he declared that he had chosen the Russian Orthodox Church as the foundation for his new economic ideas. Compared to other religions, Savitskii explained, Orthodox Christianity was an active religion with extraordinary relevance for the contemporary human soul. Having himself thus experienced the power of faith, Savitskii invited his friend to join him in his newly discovered spirituality. After all, only together and united within the Church, Savitskii claimed, was it possible to rebuild Russia.[28]

Savitskii's religious passion now provided the basis for his economic thought. It explicitly motivated his rejection of Marxism, materialism, and positivism. Savitskii's new economic theory would avoid the rational one-sidedness and deification of goods characteristic of European economic materialism. It would be the perfect synthesis: "practical mysticism, idealist practicality." Capitalism needed to be "infused with a soul." The era of capitalism, together with the achievements of science and technical progress, had to be given higher meaning and to be transformed into an "era of faith."[29] The economic reconstruction and resurrection of Russia, Savitskii was convinced, were possible only under the banners of Russian Orthodoxy and with the help of a "blessed economy," as Savitskii now called his alternative political economy. To this noble cause he was willing to devote himself and all his power.[30]

Just as the "blessed economy" was not an end in itself but inevitably served a higher metaphysical purpose, so too the economic reconstruction and resurrection of Russia were not ends in themselves. Savitskii was convinced that the new political economy would turn the reconstruction of Russia into a salutary event, into a first step toward the Transfiguration of the whole world. "Russia's current spiritual task is precisely the creation of a new chemical combination, a combination of practicality and mysticism. If it can do so, Russia will outgrow the world."[31] Savitskii boldly declared that the economic reconstruction of Russia-Eurasia was transcending the merely material and empirical sphere: it represented a kind of religious deed, the accomplishment and realization of a divine commandment: "We will build the earthly city, as God grants us space and materials, and we have to build it, but in our souls we will carry the Heavenly City."[32]

Savitskii turned to the New Testament as a valuable source of economic guidance. In late 1921, for instance, he carefully combed the Gospels for examples of economic activities, in parables and otherwise, and compiled them into a comprehensive survey.[33] He was firmly convinced that the teachings of the Gospels "comprehensively cover the entire spectrum of contemporary earthly necessities." Religious knowledge, Savitskii explained, did not contradict other forms of knowledge. On the contrary, acquiring economic knowledge was mandated by God, who had lifted the burden of economic necessity only from saints. To all others, Savitskii explained, to those

> who are far from being perfect, to us, as God's serfs, was given the parable of the talents. Economic activity is blessed by all possible images, by the ideas of the parables of the Gospels. In them the Heavenly Father is depicted as a good master: "For the kingdom of heaven is like unto a man that is a householder" [Matthew 20: 1–15]. . . . Doesn't that mean that it is a rightful and blessed thing to be a master? . . . The same is true for knowledge. Because how can we have the right to demand miracles, if the whole universe, as it is now revealed by science is a permanent miracle?[34]

In addition to the Gospels, Savitskii claimed, there were other religious sources of divinely inspired knowledge about the economy. His own views on economic values, for example, had greatly benefited from the writings of the Fathers of the Church, who had produced "a comprehensive system of economic teachings, the most comprehensive of all those known," besides the classical school of political economy.[35]

According to Savitskii, atheist scientists can never comprehend in full the astounding construction of the universe, because their perception is limited and one-sided only. A scientist, economist, or politician believing in God and his creation will look at the world with different eyes; his way of cognition will be more comprehensive and on a higher level; he will, so to speak, receive a surplus value in whatever he is doing in his field of specialization.[36]

The religious mode of cognition, the application of the "blessed metaphysics" to the empirical and scientific cognition of the world, Savitskii implied, made it essential for human beings to make use of all technological and scientific achievements. From a religious perspective, he claimed, it is not only legitimate to employ modern technology, but imperative to do so, because it is "a means to the realization of the Covenant, made by the Creator with the human race: 'And God said, Let us make man in our image, after our likeness: and let them have dominion over the fish of the sea, and over the fowl of the air, and over the cattle, and over all the earth, and over every creeping thing that creepeth upon the earth' [Genesis 1: 28]." To realize and uphold this "metaphysical" Covenant, human beings have to make use of the benefits provided by empirical science.[37]

Throughout the first half of the 1920s Savitskii continued to develop his project of a new Orthodox political economy. His ultimate goal was the creation of a coherent system of thought that by 1925 he called "masterocracy," yet another label for what had earlier been his "blessed economy." In his essay "The Master and the Economy," Savitskii focused on the central element of this intended system: the "master," a holistic subject, firmly rooted in the economic sphere, yet able to reach out into other spheres as well.[38]

Perhaps Savitskii's fascination with the Gospels and with the figure of the "master" had been stimulated by his evacuation from Crimea to Constantinople and thus to Asia Minor in November 1920. There, at Narli in the "Holy Land of the Apostles,"[39] in the immediate vicinity of the "Second Rome," his parents had acquired a small farmstead. Savitskii's description of the agricultural work there and of the organization of the enterprise reflected the "blessed economies" of the Gospels. Indeed, Narli appears as the perfect reproduction of the ideal economic enterprise, a "blessed economy." The estate comprised twelve *desiatinas* of irrigated vineyard and six *desiatinas* of vegetable garden, four thousand *desiatinas* of mountainous pasture with five hundred goats and six cows.[40] The whole enterprise, although formally a cooperative, was firmly guided by Savitskii's father, who in this capacity was indeed a prototypical "master."

Although, in Savitskii's view, the "master" was the ideal type of human being engaged in economic activities, regrettably, contemporary European economic doctrine did not know this concept and thus overlooked the economy's most important principle. Instead European economic theory focused on the "entrepreneur," an economic actor merely interested in the technical aspects of the economy and in gaining the highest possible net profit. Not so the "master." Besides purely economic aspects, Savitskii claimed, the master's relationship to his activity was determined by a "striving for preservation, consolidation, and widening of the fullness of functioning and fullness of development" of the "living and tangible whole," of "human beings and things," seen as a "spiritual system." In this respect, maximizing income was only one economic goal among others.[41] The concept of the "good master," Savitskii maintained, was neither merely a myth nor an aesthetic fiction. It was an economic reality, going back to the evangelical image of the "Good Master," that is, to figures depicted in the Gospels, the protagonists of numerous parables.

To be a "good master" meant several things in Savitskii's interpretation. First, the master had to know that the basis for his economy was the human being engaged in it. He had a special, caring relationship toward the people working for him in his economy. For them he was even willing to suffer material sacrifices because he knew that only on the basis of devoted personnel could his enterprise develop and flourish. He provided for the material well-being of his employees but also promoted good personal relations with them. In larger economic enterprises, where personal relations were difficult to establish, the master's charisma and his assistants could replace his personal presence. The same caring attitude would be exercised toward the equipment under his supervision—such as machines, animals, buildings, the soil, and so on. Not unlike his divine counterpart, the worldly "master" transcended material economic self-interest. His strivings necessarily included a more general interest in the well-being of his neighbor, and in the harmonious well-being of the whole world. In sharp contrast to the entrepreneur, the "master" pursued a holistic approach to the economy, just as God cared about his creation. The unrestrained quest for maximum profit, Savitskii cautioned, endangered the economic interests of future generations; it raised the danger of "overstraining" human resources. Not so the "masterly economy," which provided for economic "sustainability." The master would preserve capitalism as a "technical principle," but reject the "capitalist spirit."[42]

On a more theoretical level, Savitskii's "masterly" approach to the economy was an attempt to "bridge" the gap between the two spheres of "relative" and "absolute" values, to reconcile the "empirical" and the "metaphysical." A "masterly" attitude to the economy, Savitskii explained, often emerged from religious convictions and was permeated by a strong impulse toward the Absolute. "There were and are masters, who actively, to the limits of their ability, strove to emulate the Supreme Master of the world, toward Whom, in His Existence and in His masterly evaluation of the world, they had turned their searching eyes."[43] In other words, economic activities, as Savitskii (and before him Bulgakov) understood them, ultimately turned into deeds of faith. "Masterocracy," as Savitskii envisioned it, was thus more than mere economic theory. Ultimately, it would generate a new society, providing something that neither capitalism nor socialism were able to achieve: the consolidation of the person in the economy.

"Masterocracy," Savitskii was confident, could provide a third way between capitalism and socialism. Only in a "masterocracy" could human beings realize themselves as persons. Only "masterocracy" could "connect the economic personality with God, consolidate a God-confessing instead of a godless personality. Its tie with the Absolute determines the personality of the 'masterocracy' not as an atomized, but as 'conciliar' principle."[44] Although, in Savitskii's opinion, the Russian-Eurasian tradition appeared particularly well suited to develop the concept of the "masterocracy," as a universal principle it was potentially available to the whole world.[45]

Religion, Economy, and Savitskii's Eurasianism

Despite its potentially universal implications Savitskii's religiously inspired political economy was first and foremost to serve the Russian-Eurasian cause. In this respect it represents the central component of his Eurasianism—the spiritually guided economic modernization of Russia-Eurasia to which he devoted his best-known Eurasianist publications. In his *Geographic Particularities of Russia*, for instance, no doubt Savitskii's magnum opus, he revealed the country's specific Eurasian character from a geographic point of view, on the basis of a complex examination of vegetation and soil. Establishing a regular, flag-shaped outline of Eurasia's vegetation zones, Savitskii intended not only to facilitate the comprehension of the country's geographic specifics but also, and more important, to promote its economic development. In fact, this study was deliberately designed as only the first step of a comprehensive examination of Eurasia's natural resources. It was intended merely as the introduction to a second volume on agriculture, where "the phenomena and zones, determined by characteristics of vegetation and soil will be compared with and related to analogous phenomena and zones according to agricultural characteristics."[46]

Unfortunately, this second volume, particularly important for Savitskii's argument about Russia-Eurasia's extraordinary economic potential, was never realized. Instead Savitskii focused on the industry, in a sense the third step of his "masterly" examination of Eurasia. In his *Place of Development of Russian Industry*, Savitskii enthusiastically surveyed the geographical distribution of Russia-Eurasia's abundant mineral resources. He concluded that "only through the orientation toward the East, only through transforming

Russia into a genuinely *Eurasian entity* can the development of Russia's heavy industry be accomplished."[47] In other words, only through a comprehensive and systematic examination of Russia-Eurasia's geography, natural environment, and mineral resources could Russia accomplish its Eurasian mission, the economic modernization and resurrection of the East, the synthesis of economy, science, and religion.

Russia-Eurasia's mission in the East, Savitskii was convinced, was more than just technical modernization. It was the perfect synthesis of science and faith, nature and spirit. It would create a new Garden of Eden. "Everyone, who has seen the Near and Middle East," Savitskii claimed in 1921, "knows that these areas are 'cultural graveyards,' in a sense hundreds of times more real than is true of Western Europe." These countries desperately needed Russia's support to awaken from their passivity. Because postrevolutionary Russia was in a state of heightened activity and was spiritually closely connected with the East, Savitskii predicted that "Russia can become a factor in the renaissance of these countries. . . . Retaining to a certain degree its potential as a European people, Russia in its historic role will become the leader of the Asian peoples." Savitskii foresaw the economic rebirth of the most exotic places in present-day Afghanistan, China, Kyrghizia, and other Central Asian countries and their beneficial influence on the new Russian culture of the future:

> Oases located in the depth of the continent: Balkh and Mazar i Sharif, Kashgar and Yarkand, Tufan, and Kuldzha . . . Now endless necropolises give evidence of past life, of times, when these countries, located in the heart of the continent, were centers of world trade, stretching from one edge of the continent to the other. In the economic sense, Russia is called to *rehabilitate the continent*. Turned into a forgotten and superfluous desert by the contemporary epoch of "oceanic" economy, [the continent] will again be watered by fountains of living water; once again caravans will move through its depths, roads will traverse it; but this time not only trains of camels but railway trains.[48]

Absorbing the vibrant religiosity of the East, where in contrast to present-day Russia and Europe, the "era of faith" had never been replaced by an "era of science," Russia-Eurasia would be able to produce a harmonious synthesis of both. With this achievement, Savitskii was convinced, Eurasia would set an example for the rest of the world, it would become the location of a great spiritual synthesis of particular Western and Eastern qualities: the East will contribute faith and religion, whereas Russia will contribute the "European" values of knowledge and economic skills, qualities the country had acquired through its participation in a process of Europeanization.[49]

Savitskii's heroic vision forecast the emergence of a land of plenty, a blessed and sacred landscape, a Eurasian Paradise on Earth, the economic reconstruction of Eurasia.[50] This utopian vision, although most prominently proclaimed in the early 1920s, remained a central component of Savitskii's thinking for the rest of his life.

To a certain extent Savitskii's ideas were shared by some of his fellow Eurasianists, for example his fascination with the "East" or, more important, his idea that individual phenomena could never be entirely understood if they were examined in isolation—the direct consequence of his holistic economic theory. For the study of Eurasia's geography this meant that "every geographical description, regardless of how particular it might be, allowed one to see the entire space in all directions of the described section, as if through a 'magical crystal.'" Such a description and new form of vision would allow scholars "to see the concrete and detailed in the *totality* of its phenomena." Only if the whole and the particular were seen together, Savitskii declared, was it possible to determine the relationship between the particular and the whole. The concept of "Eurasia," for instance, made it possible "to comprehend the most diverse phenomena from the point of view of *one* regularity." Thus, this concept reduced complexity and promoted scientific progress by allowing scholars to detect the "connections between phenomena," to uncover the deep structure of history, and to provide a "holistic understanding of the world."[51]

Savitskii's concept of the structural interrelationship of the whole and its parts is the perfect example of what more recently (with reference to linguistic structuralism) has been called the "systemic principle." This principle emphasizes "the interconnectedness of all elements within a system and the impossibility of defining the features of any element without considering its relation to other elements and its position in the system as a whole."[52] It was probably no coincidence that Savitskii summarized his ideas in the very same city and at the very same time that Prague School structuralism emerged.[53] He was introduced to the group through his fellow Eurasianists Roman Jakobson and Nikolai Trubetskoi and participated both in the school's conferences and its publications. It is quite probable that central principles of Jakobson's structuralism were influenced by Savitskii's ideas. For example, Jakobson's influential 1929 essay "On the Contemporary Preconditions for Russian Slavic Studies" clearly echoed Savitskii's ideas. In this essay Jakobson established a Russian "structuralist" tradition and characterized Russian science as being dominated by an emphasis on regularities and correlations. This science decisively rejected positivism, which was seen merely as the result of mechanical influences from abroad.[54]

Despite obvious formal parallels, in their ultimate significance Savitskii's structuralist ideas differed from those of Jakobson and Trubetskoi. For them structuralism was primarily a new and promising scholarly approach. For Savitskii, however, structuralism was aimed toward the sphere of the divine, toward the solution of ultimate questions. It aspired to explain the universe in its totality as a "system of systems."[55] Empirical science, Savitskii was convinced, had explicitly gnostic qualities. "From a religious point of view," he declared, "empirical science is the revelation of the picture of God's world. And in proportion to the achievements of knowledge this picture is becoming more and more perfect and complete, more and more clearly revealing the Wisdom of the Creator."[56]

Savitskii among the Eurasianists

Although many of Savitskii's Eurasianist ideas were shared by other members of the movement, some of them were ignored or even rejected. Characteristically, for example, Savitskii had to publish his *Geographic Particularities*, soon to become one of the most popular Eurasianist publications, at his own expense. In fall 1926 he was denied funding by the movement's treasurer, P. N. Malevskii-Malevich, who wanted to devote the available financial means to the propaganda of Eurasianist ideas among Russian émigré veterans rather than to the publication of a sophisticated scholarly work. Only after the book's apparent success in early 1927 were Savitskii's expenses reimbursed.[57]

Moreover, the reaction of Savitskii's fellow Eurasianists to his central concept of the "master" was predominantly critical. Only Trubetskoi ultimately considered Savitskii's programmatic article "The Master and the Economy" somewhat useful. Suvchinskii bitterly complained about Savitskii to Trubetskoi. Suvchinskii found in the article too many remnants of Savitskii's classical economic education with Struve and not enough combative Eurasianism: "I cannot say that I wholly liked [the article]. We argued about it a lot, and [Savitskii] revised numerous passages. There are 'Struvisms,' and there is also 'economic sentimentality.' The 'good master' is most likely a proper category, but every now and then [Savitskii]'s account turns into a 'landscape' from the Venetian school."[58]

Already after the publication of the Eurasianist almanac containing Savitskii's article, Trubetskoi judged it in a somewhat more conciliatory fashion: "Despite all its shortcomings 'Masterocracy' is a valuable contribution nevertheless." Yet his wife, Vera Trubetskaia, more critical and still unconvinced, added: "And in my opinion the 'Master etc.' doesn't lead anywhere, and those essentially valuable ideas are presented in such a way that they turn people away from 'Masterocracy' for good!"[59] In answer to Trubetskoi's letter, Suvchinskii and P. S. Arapov, another leading Eurasianist, expressed their full solidarity with Vera Trubetskaia: "[We] fully agree with her opinion concerning the 'masterocracy.' Terribly sugary and pretentious. Besides that, the 'consistent individualism' quite heavily sticks to one's teeth."[60]

Savitskii's views on political economy as he had them developed and announced in early 1925 in the form of a "masterocracy" remained a permanent source for intra-Eurasianist conflict for years to come. For instance, in late 1928, just a few months before Eurasianism would experience its most serious crisis, Suvchinskii again took issue with Savitskii's economic ideas, in particular with his rejection of purely materialist, Marxist explanations of economic conditions. To be sure, by this point personal antipathies between the leading Eurasianists, in particular between Suvchinskii and Savitskii, had virtually paralyzed the Eurasianist movement. Ideological contradictions, however, played a no less important role in the movement's ultimate "schism."[61] By now Suvchinskii had developed a particular interest in the social question and a fascination with Marxism. No wonder that he was shocked when Savitskii sent to him for publication in the upcoming issue of the *Eurasianist Chronicle* several essays that dealt with the economic development of the Soviet Union from a nonmaterialist perspective.

Most of all Suvchinskii was enraged by an analytic essay by the economist and statistician D. N. Ivantsov, Savitskii's colleague at the Russian Agricultural Cooperative Institute in Prague, who argued against the common perception of the labor movement as a mere "offspring of material needs." Suvchinskii resolutely rejected any attempts to replace Eurasianism's "pathos of social justice" by any kind of "doubtful scientism." "It turns out," Suvchinskii complained, "that (according to Ivantsov and probably also to [Savitskii]), the whole trouble is that the workers are prevented from following their 'economic instinct!'"

First of all, Suvchinskii claimed, what else if not material needs prevent workers from exercising their "instinct." Second, poverty was a "fully real and self-sufficient category." In its assessment of reality, Suvchinskii argued, communism was right: "In the present it is impossible to accept capitalism in the name of economic scientism (?!), or to deny the obvious necessity to find new ethical and morally healthy forms of social life. To the devil with 'science' if it can defend only the Stinnes, Rašíns, Cotys [i.e., capitalists like the German Hugo Stinnes, the Czech Alois Rašín, the French François Coty] and other scum." In order to have an effect on communists and workers, Suvchinskii insisted, the Eurasianists had to address them in language and with ideas they actually understood. And all of a sudden, here again was Savitskii with his appeal to "common sense" and to "Struvianist vulgarities."[62]

Those "vulgarities" that so enraged Suvchinskii, we may assume, were once again Savitskii's ideas for a careful, yet effective modernization of the economy, his call for the workers to become conscious of themselves and their spiritual goals, to engage in meaningful, sustainable economic activities, and thus, ultimately, to become "masters."

The critical reaction of several leading members of the Eurasianist movement to Savitskii's economic ideas is highly indicative of the movement's intellectual heterogeneity. Each of the Eurasianist thinkers contributed a certain set of ideas to the movement as a whole. Some of these ideas overlapped with the ideas of other Eurasianists. Others, however, were not shared or were even rejected by some Eurasianist thinkers, yet remained of essential significance for their authors and even found support among non-Eurasianists. In this respect Savitskii's religious-economic concept of the "master" is a particularly revealing case in point. This concept was the result of Savitskii's profound and lifelong interest in economic and religious issues. It symbolized the possibility of a synthetic approach to the economy that would integrate both its metaphysical and empirical aspects. No wonder, Savitskii was unable to abandon it, even if his persistence ultimately contributed to the split of the Eurasianist movement.

Whereas some Eurasianists, such as Suvchinskii and Arapov, passionately objected to Savitskii's "masterocracy," other Russian émigré scholars recognized in this concept traditional ideas of a Christian socialism or the well-known West European economic principle of the "homo oecomomicus," albeit hidden under a "thick and smoky curtain" of Savitskii's idiosyncratic terminology.[63] Indeed, Savitskii's "master" can also be interpreted within the long tradition of Christian stewardship.[64]

In fact, many of Savitskii's ideas and models were not as unique as he might have claimed. Some of his ideas clearly echo similar attempts to redefine and spiritualize political economy undertaken by contemporary European scholars. In particular Savitskii's effort to interrelate economic activity and religious principles and his use of the phrase "capitalist spirit" strongly suggest Savitskii's familiarity with the German sociologist Max Weber's famous study on the influence of a Protestant work ethic on the development of capitalism.[65] Although there is no clear evidence that Savitskii actually knew Weber's study, he was familiar with Weber's work on the economy of the ancient world and his examination of the *oikos* (household), in a sense the smallest unit of the master's economic activity. Furthermore, as part of his exam preparation in 1922 Savitskii had studied Ernst Troeltsch's lecture *Religion and Economy* and thus must have known how economic models can be related to religious foundations.[66] Finally, Savitskii's construction of the "master" as a positive alternative to the profit-seeking "entrepreneur" strikingly echoes

Werner Sombart's juxtaposition of the positive figure of the "entrepreneur" and the negative type of the "bourgeois," without, however, sharing Sombart's racism.[67]

Savitskii's familiarity and engagement with the European intellectual tradition of his time strongly suggest that his importance by far transcends the rather narrow limits of being merely a Eurasianist geographer. In fact, he was an ambitious and gifted economist who dreamed of Russia-Eurasia's economic modernization that would preserve the country's cultural and religious identity. At the same time, however, like many other prominent early twentieth-century thinkers, he also attempted to overcome some of the central contradictions of modernity and reconcile science and religion, knowledge and faith.

BECOMING EURASIAN

The Intellectual Odyssey of
Georgii Vladimirovich Vernadsky

Igor Torbakov

> There is only one Russia, "Eurasian" Russia, or Eurasia.
> —GEORGE VERNADSKY, *A HISTORY OF RUSSIA*

IT is very difficult for outsiders, Czeslaw Milosz famously noted, to understand the intractable national problems of Eastern Europe. In his beautifully written *Native Realm*, Milosz, himself a typical East European, according to his own self-description, paints a nuanced and colorful picture of the mind-boggling mosaic of the numerous peoples, religions, and cultures cohabitating in the East European marchlands that were incorporated in the Russian Empire. In his childhood years in Wilno (now Vilnius), Milosz recalled, "Practically every person I met was different, not because of his own special self, but as a representative of some group, class, or nation. One lived in the twentieth century, another in the nineteenth, a third in the fourteenth."[1] To be sure, the interplay between all those sociocultural groups on the one hand, and the different relations that each one had with the central government on the other made the issue of local loyalties and identities extremely complex. But, as Milosz points out, the Romanov Empire's disintegration and the rise of a number of national states in its former borderlands did not make matters any easier. In fact, he writes, the shift from the often loose imperial allegiance to a more rigid nation-based identity led to the most dramatic developments: sometimes it "severed even the closest ties and set brother against brother.

One was forced to make a choice, the more emotional for being based on unclear data, yet, like every decision, demanding proper motives."[2]

The chaotic exit from the imperial order in 1917–1920 could not fail to trigger a quest, both inside and outside "historical Russia," for new paradigms that would problematize the relations between center and periphery, cultural (and political) liberation and subjection. Intensive and heated debates created an intellectual atmosphere concerned with the problems of cultural relativity and emancipation. Out of this very atmosphere Mikhail Bakhtin's theory of polyphony or heteroglossia emerged in literary criticism that, some scholars argue, can be perceived as a latent theory of nation and nationalism.[3] Within the Russian émigré milieu in Europe in the 1920s–1930s, the notion of polyphony, similar to Bakhtin's, was upheld by the Eurasianists who were struggling with how to harmonize the "voice" of the imperial center with those of the multiple subimperial communities.[4]

Significantly, over the past decade, the body of scholarly literature on "classical" Eurasianism has been steadily growing.[5] The broadest reason for this interest is obvious. Following the collapse of the Soviet Union and the emergence of the new geopolitical landscape in what has tellingly come to be designated as Eurasia, both scholars and general public alike have experienced crises of identity—not unlike those that tormented the Eurasianists themselves in the wake of the unraveling of the Russian Empire—and are still grappling with how best to analyze the new reality. A 2004 essay by the historian Mark von Hagen is both a manifestation of those crises and a helpful attempt to show the way out of them. Remarkably, not only did von Hagen invoke the iconoclastic spirit of classical Eurasianists, he also advanced Eurasia as the antiparadigm for the post-Soviet era.[6]

The study of Eurasianism, however, has produced mixed results so far. As one contemporary student of this fascinating school of thought observes, "As a body of doctrine, Eurasianism has been much more frequently summarized than critically examined."[7] The Eurasianism-related archival materials, in particular the voluminous correspondence among the participants of the movement, still need to be studied. Moreover, interest in Eurasianism has traditionally been skewed toward the geopolitical (the "Exodus to the East"), the sociopolitical (Eurasianism's authoritarian leanings toward "ideocracy"), and, to a lesser extent, the historiosophic. Since 2000, some useful studies of Eurasianist theory of culture have appeared.[8] But the Eurasianists' attempts at rethinking empire and nation and at crafting a new historical narrative in which Russia's multiethnic character would find a more thorough treatment were not sufficiently explored.[9]

This brings me to the figure of Georgii (George) Vernadsky, who is rightly regarded as Eurasianism's principal historian. There is, it would appear, a virtual flourishing of Vernadsky studies in today's Russia. Most of the works of the émigré historian have been reprinted in his historical homeland and there is a seemingly endless stream of monographs and articles on his life and scholarship.[10] Surprisingly, as the eminent Harvard historian Richard Pipes has remarked, since its emancipation from communism a kind of cult of Vernadsky has emerged in Russia.[11] This atmosphere of adulation has also prompted the senior Russian historian Nikolai Bolkhovitinov, Vernadsky's most recent biographer, to comment that, while in Soviet times G. V. Vernadsky was a popular "whipping boy," mercilessly criticized for his non-Marxist understanding of the historical process, in postcommunist Russia, he has become the object of almost "limitless praise."[12]

But despite the impressive range of scholarly research on Vernadsky, the question persists: How well do we understand his intellectual legacy—in particular, the links between his own national identity (identities?), his choice of the Eurasianist paradigm, and his historical scholarship?

George Vernadsky is generally regarded as a historian of Russia.[13] At first blush, this seems quite understandable: his multivolume magnum opus is titled *A History of Russia*, and his last big study, published posthumously, was *Russian Historiography*. Yet this traditional perception of the scholar obscures the fact that Vernadsky's ambition was to write not the history of Russia as a nation-state but the history of Russia-Eurasia—the vast territory, virtually a world unto itself, inhabited, to borrow his Eurasianist friend Petr Savitskii's words, by an "assembly of peoples" (*sobor narodov*). Thus Vernadsky tried to create a master narrative that would incorporate the histories of all major peoples living on the Eurasian plains—both the eastern nomads ("the peoples of the steppe") and the western neighbors of the Great Russians, first of all the Ukrainians. In doing this, he naturally drew heavily upon Russian imperial historiography in whose tradition he was steeped in Moscow and St. Petersburg universities. But Vernadsky also introduced a new vision of Russian history obviously inspired by his Eurasianism. In 1933, in a letter to his father, Vladimir Ivanovich Vernadsky, he described his work on *An Essay on the History of Eurasia*: "In the general concept of Russian history I try to devote much more attention than has been given previously to Western Rus' and Ukraine."[14] In the same vein, in his study of Russian historiography one finds the scholarly portraits of the leading Ukrainian historians of the nineteenth and twentieth centuries, such as Mykola Kostomarov, Mykhailo Drahomanov, Volodymyr Antonovych, and Dmytro Bahalii.

Furthermore, Vernadsky appeared to view the history of Ukraine as a legitimate subject per se. He authored an English-language biography of Hetman Bohdan Hmelnytsky and wrote an introduction and did editorial work for a translation of Mykhailo Hrushevsky's one-volume history of Ukraine. Ver-

nadsky seemed to be especially fascinated by the personality of Mykhailo Drahomanov. In the mid-1930s he urged a fellow émigré Aleksandra Gol'shtein, a
family friend and long time acquaintance of Drahomanov, to write a memoir
about him.[15] Later Gol'shtein sent him a manuscript of her reminiscences,
along with her copious correspondence with Drahomanov.[16]

Among Vernadsky's works preserved in his archive are two typescripts
underscoring his professional interest in the history of Ukraine—"The Kievan
and Cossack Periods in Ukrainian History" and "Prince Trubetskoi and the
Ukrainian Question."[17] This archival collection also contains two folders of
materials titled "The Ukrainian Question before and during the Second World
War." It would be only proper to add that as early as 1941, in an interview
with an English-language Ukrainian publication, Vernadsky spoke in favor
of plans to establish a Ukrainian research institute in the United States that
would publish a Ukrainian-language journal.[18]

Given all this, a strong case can be made for revisiting George Vernadsky's
understanding of what he himself called a "Russian history." Particularly
intriguing is the exploration of how Vernadsky's Eurasianism relates both to
his own struggles with identity issues and to his thinking on empire, nation,
Russian and Ukrainian history.

Thus, in this article I propose to place Vernadsky's research on Russian
and Ukrainian history within the context of his biography and Eurasianist
worldview. My central argument is that George Vernadsky's post-1917 historical scholarship was influenced by one powerful motive—namely, his personal search for national identity, a search that was obviously made more
complicated by his exile. Internal contradictions and the resultant tensions
between Ukrainian origin and imperial weltanschauung, between his ardent
love of "historical Russia" and his wretched status as an émigré deprived of
his beloved homeland by the victorious Bolshevik regime, made grappling
with the issue of identity emotionally agonizing for Vernadsky, but also fruitful in terms of producing new and unorthodox solutions.[19]

Like other Eurasianists, Vernadsky understood that after the 1917 Revolution it was simply impossible to turn the former Russian Empire into a
classic nation-state. The early Soviet practices that were aimed at managing
multiethnicity only confirmed his view. At the same time, Vernadsky, in keep-
ing with the Eurasianist intellectual tradition, put an immense value on the
preservation of the unique geopolitical and geocultural space that this school
of thought called "Russia-Eurasia." The need to reconceptualize the notion of
nation and the way national history should be written was thus inevitable.
I argue that Eurasianism was precisely the intellectual framework within
which to achieve this goal.

Two key Eurasianist ideas were instrumental in shaping Vernadsky's historical vision. The first was the concept of Eurasian nationalism advanced by Prince Nikolai Trubetskoi, who contended that the nationalism of each people of Eurasia should be combined with pan-Eurasian nationalism. Being a precursor to the theory of multiple identities, this concept not only helped resolve the problem of Vernadsky's personal soul-searching but also appeared to show the way to preserving the precious unity of "historical Russia." The other fundamental idea, set forth by Petr Savitskii, was the image of Eurasia as a natural "developmental space" (*mestorazvitie*) for the host of various ethnic groups residing in its vast expanses. Eurasia, being a highly cohesive geographic world, had molded those groups into a unique "assembly of nationalities and religions," and, in turn, was itself being reshaped in the process of those peoples' economic and cultural activity. Eurasianists asserted that the political unity of the Russian Empire was the result of the efforts of not only the Great Russians but of many peoples of Eurasia. That vision had prompted Vernadsky to steer away from the traditions of Russian imperial historiography that tended to write the history of Russia as that of a nation-state. In contrast, Vernadsky was among the first to try to craft a historical narrative of Russia as a *Nationalitatenstaat*. The Eurasianist conceptual limitations, however, prevented him from writing a truly comprehensive history of Russia as a multiethnic *empire*.

Biographical Context

Given all the current interest in classical Eurasianism, what is really surprising is the dearth of explanation of what exactly prompted George Vernadsky (and, for that matter, all other leading members of the movement) to adopt such an unorthodox outlook on the Russian historical process. Some researchers (for instance, Nikolai Bolkhovitinov) simply state the fact of Vernadsky's association with the Eurasianist movement without bothering to investigate the underlying reasons for this affiliation.[20] Other scholars (such as Natalia Alevras) try to prove that Vernadsky was somehow predestined to become a Eurasianist, given his prerevolutionary scholarly interests in Russia's eastward expansion and colonization of Siberia.[21] Alevras refers to the early, pre-1917 works by George Vernadsky and Petr Savitskii,[22] calling them the "proto-Eurasianist" essays that prefigured the authors' postrevolutionary embracing of Eurasianist historiosophy.[23]

There are also scholars who, while acknowledging the tremendous importance of Vernadsky's choice of Eurasianist paradigm for his subsequent historiographic development, claim that we will probably never know the true reasons that were behind his Eurasianist affiliation. "Only detailed biographical information about individual Eurasianists can illuminate the distinct characteristics of those original minds which led them to non-normative beliefs," wrote Charles Halperin, Vernadsky's American biographer. "For Vernadsky," he added, "and perhaps for all the Eurasian epigones, such information is lacking."[24] Indeed, Halperin is right in noting that Vernadsky "was not a self-revealing man and did not dwell in his memoirs upon this momentous intellectual event"—that is, his joining the Eurasianist movement in mid-1920s. But this lack of direct evidence should nevertheless not prevent a researcher from attempting to reconstruct George Vernadsky's intellectual evolution in the aftermath of the 1914–1921 "Russian catastrophe." My starting point here will be an analysis of all available information that might shed light on Vernadsky's struggle with the problem of his own national identity following the collapse of the Russian Empire, the Whites' defeat in the Civil War, and his flight into European exile.

In his seminal article, "The Emergence of Eurasianism," Nicholas Riasanovsky noted that it is probably not accidental that the main Eurasianist theorists had Ukrainian roots.[25] He did not elaborate on this valuable intuition and it was largely neglected in the subsequent scholarly literature.[26] Indeed, it does not seem a mere coincidence that three of the four founding members of the movement—Petr Savitskii,[27] Petr Suvchinskii[28] and Georgii Florovskii[29]—originated in Ukraine and/or spent some time there in their childhood and youth. Prince Nikolai Trubetskoi,[30] Eurasianism's fourth founding father, was the descendant of Gedymin, the Grand Prince of Lithuania, and his keen interest in all things Ukrainian was, in Vernadsky's description, a manifestation of an ancestral instinct.[31] And George Vernadsky himself (who joined the movement somewhat later), although he was born and grew up in Moscow, could boast of a long and illustrious Ukrainian pedigree. This "Ukrainian connection" appears to be crucially important indeed. On the one hand, the attachment to Ukraine and its culture would distinguish Vernadsky and other key Eurasianists (particularly Savitskii) from the bulk of their fellow Russian émigrés who continued dreaming of Russia's resurrection as a "unified state"—"one and indivisible"—and were bent on denying the Ukrainians even a modicum of a distinct identity that might make them look somewhat different from the Russians and result in some sort of Ukrainian autonomy.[32]

On the other hand, Vernadsky and his fellow Eurasianists held that the Russian-Ukrainian unity forged throughout several centuries of intensive interaction within one state produced tremendously beneficial results for both East Slavic peoples. Most important among them was the high culture of the late imperial epoch that was, in Vernadsky's view, both Russian and Ukrainian—a magnificent product of the two peoples' fruitful collaboration. This dual loyalty—Ukrainian *Landespatriotismus* and appreciation of the imperial high culture that flourished under the conditions of political unity of "historic Russia"—created an internal tension that had to be reconciled. This reconciliation appears to have involved the reconceptualization of empire and nation within the Eurasianist philosophical framework.

The Vernadskys' Ukrainian roots are very well documented, including by George Vernadsky himself. Shortly before his death in 1973 Vernadsky started publishing his memoirs: several chapters were serialized in *Novyi zhurnal*.[33] A fascinating manuscript in the Vernadsky archival collection titled "The Story of the Vernadsky Family as Related by My Father" is particularly interesting in that both Vernadskys, father and son, had made an attempt to reconstruct their Ukrainian lineage and trace the ties that connected Vernadskys with other illustrious old Ukrainian families such as the Korolenkos and Konstantinoviches.[34] Extremely valuable information on the Vernadskys' Ukrainian roots and interests can also be gleaned from Vladimir Vernadsky's diaries.[35]

But of course place of origin or ethnic roots do not necessarily define one's national identity and loyalty. More important, most scholars within the humanities disciplines today hold that national identity is "not a fixed category, but a fluctuating process, in the course of which one or more identities can evolve side by side in the same person, in greater or lesser tension with each other . . . [N]ational identity can be multiple or compound . . . an individual can be both Scottish and British, or Ukrainian and Russian. The two (or more) national identities are not just superimposed on one another, but may complement each other, since the defining features of each nation differ from case to case."[36] In this sense, the Vernadskys case is particularly instructive in that it shows how complex, contradictory, and vague the issue of national identity and political loyalty was in Imperial Russia's twilight years.

Most contemporary historians seem to agree that, since the 1860s, when the slow but steady rise of Ukrainian ethnic nationalism prompted the imperial regime in St. Petersburg to come up with its own "nationalizing project," and until the Russian Empire's collapse in 1917, Ukraine represented an administrative territory where a whole gamut of loyalties and identities existed simultaneously.[37] To be sure, the bulk of Ukraine's population, the local peasants, had not yet been affected by this new nationalist discourse; for the most part, they remained in the premodern stage until approximately the late 1910s, defining themselves just as "locals," good Orthodox and loyal subjects of the tsar. Ukraine's "nationalist front" was represented by a tiny group of activists, mostly members of local intelligentsia, who consciously called themselves *Ukrainians*—in contrast to *malorosy* (Little Russians), an official appellation of the region's population that did recognize certain insignificant regional differences but generally presupposed the unity of *malorosy* and *velikorosy* (Great Russians)—and advanced the idea that Ukrainian people are a full-blown nation, linguistically and culturally distinct from the *veli-korosy*. For its part, the imperial establishment, which was very wary until the mid-nineteenth century—as any authority presiding over the multinational empire would be—of pursuing nationalizing policy, decided that the time had come to confront the challenge posed by what it labeled "Ukrainian separatism." Thus it launched a set of measures that some scholars characterize as a "greater Russian nation project"—a policy that ideally was supposed to lead to the formation of the Russian Empire's core nation comprising all three East Slavic peoples—the Great Russians, Little Russians, and Belarusians.[38]

Now, this nationalizing activism on the part of St. Petersburg authorities with its incoherent and poorly executed policies of Russification and persecution of the nationalist-minded members of the Ukrainian intelligentsia made the picture of local identities and loyalties even more complex.[39] Depending on how they perceived the imperial government's policies, we can discern—apart from the mostly passive and premodern peasantry and those members of local society who retained a prenationalist, dynastic type of loyalty—at least four other social types that existed in the prerevolutionary Ukraine. First, the Ukrainian nationalists, quite naturally, opposed Russification and rejected the idea of a single Russian nation. (This attitude, however, did not prejudge the vision of a further political relationship with the Russians: some Ukrainian nationalists advocated complete separation, whereas others were ready to settle for a federation.) Second, those people in Ukraine (of whatever ethnic origin), who believed they were Russians, wholeheartedly supported the authorities' attempt to forge a "greater Russian nation."

Third, there were ethnic Ukrainians who persisted in proudly calling themselves *malorosy* and who perceived themselves as constituting an inseparable Russian triad together with the Great Russians and Belarusians. They were supportive of the government's efforts to form the empire's "core nation" and castigated the Ukrainian nationalists for their perceived desire to break the "historic" East Slavic unity. Finally, there were people, mostly ethnic Ukrainians, who would, in fact, have a hybrid or dual identity. They would describe themselves as "both Ukrainian and Russian" or as "Ukrainians belonging to the world of Russian [high] culture."

This group, arguably the smallest in comparison with the other three, found itself in the most difficult situation as its relations with the Ukrainian nationalists on the one hand and the Russian nationalists on the other were equally strained. Its members were appalled by the crude Russification measures and the stubborn reluctance of the imperial government to recognize Ukrainians as a nation in their own right, possessing their own language and culture. But they also found the Ukrainian nationalists' drive toward political separation as counterproductive and believed that Ukraine would be much better served if it stayed united in one powerful state with Russia, sharing in the magnificent riches that the late imperial culture had produced.

As the Russian Empire's days drew to a close and the struggle over the "Ukrainian question" became more acute, this group found itself between a rock and a hard place, being forced by the circumstances to make a political choice and define what their ultimate loyalties and identities were. For the members of this group who held dual "Ukrainian-Russian" identity, this was a kind of choice they would prefer to avoid making. All of the evidence we have suggests that the Vernadskys likely belonged to this small group of ethnic Ukrainians who had dual "Russian-Ukrainian identity."[40]

There were some interesting nuances, though. The paths that led Vladimir and George Vernadsky to this dual "Ukrainian-Russian" identity differed markedly. There is a general consensus among scholars that from very early on Vladimir Vernadsky (who, although born in St. Petersburg, did live as a young boy with his parents in Ukraine—in the city of Kharkiv) was conscious of his Ukrainian origin.[41] He maintained a keen interest in Ukrainian affairs after he moved to St. Petersburg and Moscow,[42] and during the decade preceding the Russian Revolution participated in all of the important debates on the "Ukrainian question" in his dual capacity of prominent academic and influential politician.[43] But with George Vernadsky the situation may be much trickier. It is only now that the evidence found in his personal papers allows us to reconstruct the long and winding odyssey in the course of which he developed what appears to be a dual "Russian-Ukrainian" identity.

It would seem that throughout his life in Russia—the period between 1887, the year he was born in Moscow, and November 1920, when he fled together with the remnants of Baron Petr Wrangel's army to Constantinople —George Vernadsky thought of himself as Russian. Fascinating evidence to this effect is provided by none other than his father. In 1920, Vladimir Vernadsky wrote in a letter to his Parisian friend Aleksandra Gol'shtein: "I am tremendously happy with my kids . . . [But] the children, though they are good friends, turned out to be quite different. My son is Orthodox and Russian, lacking any Ukrainian sympathies whatsoever, while my daughter is Ukrainian and in this sense she is spiritually closer to me."[44] George Vernadsky himself was quite explicit when, in an unpublished passage of his memoirs, he described his trip in the summer of 1908 to the Slavic Congress in Prague and his encounters with Ukrainian students there. As one of the three delegates elected to the congress from the Moscow student body, George met student representatives of other Slavic peoples, including Ukrainians, at a gathering presided over by professor Tomáš Garrigue Masaryk. The Ukrainians, Vernadsky pointedly notes, "treated us Russians in a particularly unfriendly way."[45]

The collapse of the Russian ancien régime followed by a string of political upheavals that irretrievably buried "historic Russia" could not fail to deeply shake George Vernadsky and affect his perceptions of personal identity. Between November 1920 and February 1922, George Vernadsky and his wife Nina were literally struggling for survival, leading the difficult life of refugees in the eastern periphery of postwar Europe. The painful sense of being "stateless persons" undoubtedly exacerbated their angst and deepened their identity crisis. "We will likely never return to Russia—we are already a cut-off piece [*my otrezannyi lomot'*]," Nina Vernadsky wrote in her diary. "We had left Russia because we could not accept [the rule of the Communist] Internationale but now we lost nationality ourselves."[46]

From Constantinople the Vernadskys moved in 1921 to Athens and then, in 1922, to Prague where the Masaryk government had just launched the so-called Russian initiative (*Ruská akce*), having provided funds to support a number of Russian scholarly and educational institutions in Czechoslovakia.[47] It is also in Prague that George reunited with his parents after almost two years since they had parted, in a most dramatic way, in Crimea on the eve of the Bolshevik seizure of the peninsula. (In May 1922, the Soviet government allowed Vladimir Vernadsky to go abroad to take a teaching position at the Sorbonne. As soon as they were issued foreign passports, he, accompanied by his wife and daughter, traveled to Paris via Prague.)

I would argue that this family reunion—particularly, the reestablishment of ties with his father that would never be broken again until the latter's death in 1945—played a crucial role in the transformation of George Vernadsky's personal identity. Reflections on Russia's—and his own—trials and tribulations following the 1917 Revolution, coupled with Vladimir Vernadsky's powerful influence, appear to have reshaped George's perception of self, steering him away from an exclusively Russian identity and toward a mixed "Russian-Ukrainian" one.

Archival documents provide evidence illustrating this fascinating process. While Vladimir Vernadsky stayed in Paris in 1922–1925, father and son appear to have used the opportunity of personal meetings to discuss, among other things, matters pertaining to family history and the Ukrainian connection.[48]

George Vernadsky's interest in the issue appears to have grown constantly because he frequently returned to it in his diaries and notes in the 1930s. For example, one of the entries in George's diary for 1932 (the year he had a chance to see his father again—incidentally, in Prague, the city they chose as a meeting point because one was coming from the United States and the other from St. Petersburg [Leningrad]), begins with the following passage: "These last days, both Dad and Mom were telling a lot about the lives of their parents and families. All this is precious and very interesting. It's a pity that previously I knew so little and paid little attention, but now I want to learn every single detail." Then he adds: "In general, everyone has to know the history of his family and kin, and I—a historian—even more so. . . . And I knew so little."[49]

A document that George finished compiling in 1936—but was based, as he himself specifies, on the conversations he had with his father in Paris in August 1923—gives us a good idea of what George Vernadsky learned about his Ukrainian ancestors and their political attitudes. Here's a noteworthy description of George's grandfather, Ivan Vasilyevich Vernadsky, who at one time was an economics professor at Kyiv University. Ivan Vernadsky, writes George in this genealogical memo, "knew Ukrainian very well and loved this language. He was on friendly terms with Shevchenko, Kulish, Kostomarov [the leading members of the Ukrainian movement in the mid-nineteenth century] and his pro-Ukrainian sympathies had likely increased partially under their influence." George also notes that Ivan, even when he was a young boy, criticized his father for the failure to learn Ukrainian. Later, George adds, Ivan Vasilyevich passed on his Ukrainophile sentiments to his son Vladimir, George's father.

George ends the description of his grandfather with a short but telling outline of his historical-political views: "Ivan Vasilyevich believed that [Hetman] Mazepa was one of the last fighters for Ukraine's independence. And he had a negative view of Peter the Great because of his [ruthless] Ukrainian policy."[50] Among many additions and corrections that Vladimir Vernadsky personally introduced into this genealogical text, one is particularly remarkable. Its heading, in Vladimir's own handwriting, reads: "About our family as Ukrainians, *not* Russians." "Both my father and mother," he specifically stressed, "very acutely felt their distinctiveness from the Russians. [They] knew from legends and books the history of Ukraine. [I] heard a lot [about it] in my childhood."[51]

Boosted by the renewed close association with his father, whom he greatly revered, George Vernadsky's reevaluation of his identity appeared to be going apace, as Vladimir Vernadsky, in his diary entry of September 5, 1924, referred to the "Ukrainian tendencies of [my] son."[52] That those tendencies persisted and probably even grew stronger over time we know from George Vernadsky himself. In January 1940, in a letter to an editor of the Ukrainian émigré publication in America, he wrote (in Ukrainian!): "[I] regard myself as *both Ukrainian and Russian* and also believe that the strength of Russian and Ukrainian peoples lies in cooperation and not in separation of one from the other."[53] These were precisely the words that his father could have used to describe his own identities and loyalties.

It would be safe to conclude, then, that throughout the 1920s the positions of George and Vladimir Vernadsky on the "Ukrainian question" were coming closer together until they became basically identical. The stance that they both shared can be summed up in the following points:

1. Both the Great Russians (*velikorosy*) and the Ukrainians are closely related but still distinct peoples in their own right, each having its own language and culture.

2. At the same time, their close association throughout the ages, their common endeavors and shared sacrifices gave rise to the great imperial state—the global power with a world-class culture that can be truly called a pan-Russian (*obshcherusskii*) culture because it is the result of the close collaboration of both the Great Russian and Ukrainian peoples.

3. Russian-Ukrainian unity can rest only on mutual understanding and respect, including the appreciation of national (cultural and linguistic) peculiarities.

4. Both the attempts to suppress national distinctiveness and the desire to politically separate one people from the other are equally lethal for the unity of the pan-Russian state and the wholeness of pan-Russian culture.

5. Thus, the worst enemies of Russian-Ukrainian unity are (a) the radical Russian nationalists, who deny the very existence of the Ukrainian people and hold that the "Ukrainian question" is a mere instrument in the perfidious geopolitical designs of Russia's European neighbors, and (b) the Ukrainian separatists, who, by seeking to tear Ukraine away from Russia, doom Ukrainian culture to wretched provincialism and Ukrainians to a parochial existence.[54]

It seems plausible that, having shaped the perspective outlined above, George Vernadsky would find the previous approaches to Russian history—as well as the previous interpretations of what "Russia" and "Russian" mean—inadequate. What type of loyalty do these terms describe—imperial, political, or cultural? Do the history of Russia and the history of the Russian Empire study the same subject? If not, how do they correlate?

To answer those questions, a thorough reconceptualization of the Russian historical process was needed. But what would be the proper analytic framework for such a rethinking? Incidentally, since February 1922 George Vernadsky was living in Prague—the Central European city that during the first postwar decade was turning into the principal center of the Eurasianist movement.[55] It would not take too long for Vernadsky, who was looking for a new paradigm to better understand Russia's past and present, to realize that Eurasianism was exactly the framework that appeared to fit the bill.

The Eurasianist Framework

In a letter of March 7, 1921, to his friend, the linguist, Roman Jakobson, Prince Nikolai Sergeevich Trubetskoi, the indisputable intellectual leader of the emerging Eurasianist movement, famously asserted that most of the basic ideas that he expressed in his fascinating *Europe and Mankind*— and that underlie much of what he wrote on historical-cultural issues in the 1920s–1930s—were formulated at least a decade before, around 1909–1910.[56] But there is little doubt that several crucial factors born of the global turmoil of 1914–1918 gave rise to classical Eurasianism as we know it. These were the disintegration of the Russian Empire, the unprecedented upsurge of "borderland nationalisms," the victory of the Bolsheviks in the atrocious civil war and the beginning of the implementation of the Soviet nationality policy, the West's reaction to the "Russian catastrophe," and the Entente Powers' plans for restructuring the defeated continental empires. And, last but not least, it was the very fact that all of the major Eurasianist theorists were émigrés— people deprived by the harsh circumstances of their homeland and living in an alien, and often not very friendly, environment. According to one witty commentary, the Eurasianists had lost Mother Russia and also failed to find a Mother Europe: "When Europe proved an alien world, there followed a fundamental re-examination of the self—what was Russian in a Russian."[57] The urge to sort out the profound identity crisis was thus one of the most potent driving forces of Eurasianism. As one perceptive observer, the Russian philosopher, V. V. Zenkovsky (himself an émigré who left Russia at the end of 1919), had noted quite awhile ago, "Not ideology, but psychology, is essential and influential in Eurasianism."[58]

To fully comprehend the inner logic of the Eurasianists' reconceptualization of empire and nation, we, then, have to place and analyze their writings within four intersecting contexts: (1) Russia's prerevolutionary imperial policies, (2) Soviet practices, (3) heated debates within the Russian émigré community in Europe, and (4) a discussion of nationalism in what the Eurasianists called, not without a degree of contempt, the "Romano-Germanic world."

Because most key Eurasianists originated in Ukraine, they were likely well aware of the uneasy relationship between empire and nationalism even before the First World War brought about, along with unspeakable destruction, a previously unheard of mobilization of ethnicity.[59] Their personal experiences in the tumultuous years spanning the Russian Revolution and Civil War left them with no illusions as to the destructive potential of ethnic nationalism and the grave danger that "borderland separatism" poses for the integrity of "historic Russia." For example, Nikolai Trubetskoi and Petr Savitskii, the second founding father of the Eurasianist doctrine, described in private correspondence with friends what they had to live through during Russia's second "Time of Troubles." In a letter, mailed from Istanbul on February 4, 1920, to his superior, Konstantin Gul'kevich, the Russian diplomat posted in Norway, Savitskii vividly portrayed the situation he witnessed in war-torn Ukraine:

> I saw the regime of the Central Rada; during three months by the force
> of word and the force of arms together with my officer friends I had been
> defending my Chernigov estate from the Bolshevik gangs; I was liberated
> from this siege by the Germans and was witness to their seven months' long
> regime; as a subaltern I fought in the ranks of the Russian Corps, which
> defended Kiev from Petliura and I lived through the fall of the city; together
> with my father I fled—or left, who can tell?—the city of Kiev; I saw and
> associated with the French in Odessa and waited long enough to see the
> "glorious" end of *l'occupation française*. From March 1919 to August I was
> in Ekaterinodar; from August to November I was floundering in the whirl-
> winds of the Russian "White *Sovdepia*," the Russian South, which was just
> liberated from the Bolsheviks. I spent several weeks at the front line and
> I lived in the cities and villages of Kharkov and Poltava. Then I moved to
> Rostov.[60]

For his part, Trubetskoi witnessed this period of turmoil at the empire's other borderland—in the Caucasus. At the time of the October 1917 Bolshevik coup he was in Kislovodsk; then he moved to Tiflis (Tbilisi) and finally to Baku. Two a half years later (in December 1920) he wrote to Jakobson from Sofia: "During my wanderings in the Caucasus I came to Baku in March 1918, just in time of the 'rebellion of the Muslims against Soviet Power,' or, to be more exact, during that short time when the Armenians were slaughtering Tatars. I was alone there, had no means of subsistence, caught typhus, and after the hospitalization got a permit to leave with great difficulty. I did not have a single acquaintance there."[61]

No wonder, then, that Nicholas Riasanovsky came to the conclusion that the Eurasianists had a "catastrophic view of history."[62] What is even more important for the purposes of our discussion, however, is that the Eurasianists' experiences, which among other things revealed the fragility of their homeland and its borders, during the years of the Great War and its truly catastrophic aftermath in Russia compelled them to address head-on the tangled relationship between empire and nation. This was done, mostly by Trubetskoi and Savitskii, in essays that they penned during the first half of the 1920s, beginning with Trubetskoi's tract *Europe and Mankind* and Savitskii's review of this book which is rightly regarded as Eurasianism's foundational text.[63] That the problems of nationalism from the very beginning lay at the heart of the Eurasianists' intellectual preoccupations is evident from Trubetskoi's letter to Jakobson mailed in March 1921. Trubetskoi told his friend that *Europe and Mankind* was in fact initially conceived as the first part of a trilogy that was going to be titled "A Justification of Nationalism." At the core of this study there should have been a discussion of true and false nationalism. "Our Russian 'nationalism' of the pre-revolutionary period," asserted Trubetskoi, was definitely false. "The true nationalism is yet to be created," he concluded.[64]

The intellectual task that the Eurasianist theorists set for themselves can be roughly formulated as follows: how to remap (reimagine) the "Russian imperial space" to escape the seemingly unavoidable contradiction brought about by modernity—the one between empire and nationalism. Since the Eurasianists' ultimate goal was of course to prevent the political fragmentation of this "Russian imperial space" at all costs, some students of the movement perceptively note that the Eurasianist strategy was to seek the preservation of the empire through its negation.[65]

Three main considerations appear to have influenced their thinking. First, the Eurasianists sought to repudiate the legacy of tsarist Russia's nationality policy. However contradictory and incoherent the nationality policy of late Imperial Russia might have been,[66] recent research demonstrates that there was a slow but steady trend to revamp the traditionalist dynastic empire and refashion it according to the modernist Western template whereby the state would pursue national policies in certain regions of the realm and colonial/imperial policies in the other regions.[67] In the last decades of imperial rule there were debates on the need to single out something resembling a "national core" within the Russian Empire and to clearly define the territories in the Caucasus and Central Asia as colonial possessions. "The direction in which the late imperial Russian state's practices were moving was very similar to 'overseas' colonial empires such as Britain and France," argues Peter Blitstein. "Russia was looking more and more like a colonial 'empire of a nation.'"[68] Remarkably, Trubetskoi sharply criticized tsarist imperial policy in the Caucasus, especially the brutal subjugation of the mountainous peoples. In a letter to Petr Savitskii, Trubetskoi derided this policy as "colonial," adding, "I believe that for Eurasianists the tendency to idealize Russian great-power spirit and Russian nationalism is especially dangerous, and it should be suppressed by all means."[69] To be sure, for the Eurasianists, such "aping" of the "pernicious West" was anathema—not only because nationalism was a Western concept but also because they sensed that any attempt to define a

Russian-based "national core"—no matter which criteria for determining the "Russianness" were employed—would undermine their cherished image of the cultural, political, and economic integrity of the imperial space.

Second, the Eurasianists were definitely wary of liberal Wilsonianism that sought to bring notions of sovereignty based on national self-determination to the East and South European borderlands of the collapsed continental empires.[70] The meddling of the victorious Entente Powers into "Russian" affairs in 1918–1920, including the decision to recognize several "secessionist territories" of the former Russian Empire as sovereign states, were still very vividly remembered by the Eurasianist thinkers.[71] The latter understood full well the challenges presented by Wilsonian ideas and policies. On the one hand, they now had to rethink the "Russian space" in such a way that it could not be classified as yet another unwieldy continental empire ready to be partitioned into national states. On the other hand, as they were aware that "nation" was increasingly becoming the "name of the game" in the contemporary world, the Eurasianists sensed the need to refashion the multiethnic imperial space so that it could be represented as some peculiar "super-nation," a "multiethnic nation," or, to use their metaphoric manner of expression, a "symphonic personality."

Finally, the Eurasianists could not fail to reflect on the rival project of rethinking empire and nation—namely, the Bolshevik project. The latter of course was not just pure theorizing; instead, it represented the set of concrete policies that were being implemented right before the Eurasianists' eyes. Ironically, the Soviet government, which by the end of 1920 had restored its control over most territories of the former Russian Empire, was itself eager to preempt the calls for decolonization and thus sought to appease "borderland nationalisms."[72] In 1920, the Bolsheviks convened in Baku the First Congress of the Peoples of the East—a gathering that forcefully upheld the ideas of national liberation and anti-imperialism.

At the same time, the Bolshevik ideologues—not unlike the Eurasianists —sought to strongly emphasize the "organic," almost indestructible, tie between Russia and its Asian possessions.

In 1919, some two years before the first Eurasianist symposium saw the light of day (!), G. V. Chicherin, the Bolshevik commissar for foreign affairs, wrote:

Indeed, *the history of Russia and of two-thirds of Asia practically forms one indivisible whole.* In the course of historical events two centers of state power emerged alternatively in this part of the world: the center of Mongol-nomad power, and the center of Great Russian, agriculture-based power. . . . The Tatar Khans were the immediate predecessors of and . . . to a large extent models for the Moscow tsars. . . . The nineteenth-century expansion of Russia into Central Asia was the completion of the *process of unification into one state*—first under the khans, then under the tsars —*of the continuous plain* that extends over this part of the world.[73]

But for the Eurasianists, the Soviet practices of "territorializing ethnicity," whereby in several cases "nations" would be artificially created, assigned a clearly delineated "homeland," and given a specific status within the complex hierarchy of the "Soviet peoples," were much worse than the most brazen imperial policy. Instead of disarming the nationalists, the Eurasianists argued, the Bolsheviks were encouraging them and in so doing they were undermining the indivisibility of the former imperial space.[74]

In their treatment of the "empire vs. nation" problem, the Eurasianists were striving to build a theoretical model that would somehow manage to reconcile their desire to preserve the integrity of the former imperial space with the full recognition of the multiethnic character of the populations residing in these lands. This left the Eurasianist thinkers with precious few options. The imperial model seemed to be discredited both because it was rejected by the peoples of the former Russian Empire and, more important, because it was associated with European colonial practices. The classical national-state model appeared to be too narrow a framework for such a vast territory with ethnically diverse populations. The only way out, the Eurasianists argued, would be to refashion the former Russian Empire as a sui generis supranational entity. Thus Russia would become "Eurasia."

Two Eurasianist concepts are particularly relevant here. The first one, advanced by the geographer Petr Savitskii, was the vision of Eurasia—whose borders, incidentally, roughly coincide with those of the Russian Empire before 1917—as a highly cohesive landmass. The integrity of this vast geo-massif, Savitskii argued, is an objective fact of physical geography because it is based on the region's specific natural "structure": the correlation between the horizontally shaped ecological zones and vertically shaped river systems.[75] "Eurasia is indivisible," Savitskii asserted. Being a "special geographical world," it serves as a natural *mestorazvitie* (developmental space, or topogenesis) for the numerous peoples residing in Eurasia.[76] The Eurasianists held that an organic connection exists between a geographical territory, the peoples (ethnic groups) that reside in that territory, and the character of cultural development. Environment and culture constantly interact, experiencing mutual influences and tensions. So *mestorazvitie*, a key Eurasianist category, was coined specifically to embody this complex process of interaction between various types of natural and sociohistorical milieus. "For us," asserted Savitskii, "a sociohistorical milieu and its territory should merge into a single unified whole—into a geographical individual or a landscape."[77] The Eurasianists argued that this "geographical individual," because it was supposedly born of an intimate interaction between culture/history and territory, was in fact a live organism—a "symphonic personality."

Clearly, by inventing the concept of *mestorazvitie*, Savitskii meant to put a respectable scientific façade on what sounded rather like a mystical connection between Eurasia as a geographical entity and the culture of its diverse peoples. Incidentally, in his letter to Jakobson of July 28, 1921, Trubetskoi conceded that in the Eurasianists' views there was a "strong dose of mysticism —a trait characteristic of all of us."[78] As one student of Eurasianism wittingly notes, the term *mestorazvitie* was likely introduced to compensate for the repressed word "empire."[79]

The other crucial concept—the idea of Eurasian nationalism—was advanced by Nikolai Trubetskoi. Trubetskoi, a brilliant linguist and ethnographer, took the Eurasianist reconceptualization of nation one step further and suggested—in an almost Gellnerian manner—that a "peculiar" Eurasian nation might, in fact, be created. He developed his arguments most fully in the short essay titled "Pan-Eurasian Nationalism."[80] The revolution and the collapse of the Russian Empire, asserted Trubetskoi, radically changed the position of the Russians within the former imperial space. The borderland peoples have attained new broad rights that they would never give up voluntarily, whereas the Russians appeared to have forever lost their role as the "master race" within the realm. At the same time, the political upheaval that followed the revolution and imperial implosion caused only a temporary fragmentation of the Eurasian space, and its unity was quickly restored—a fact that, according to Trubetskoi, should serve as yet another proof that "Eurasia constitutes a geographical, economic and historical whole." Here, however, is a dilemma: "There is no return to the situation in which Russians were the sole owner of the state territory, and, clearly, no other people can play such a role." Trubetskoi boldly resolves this conundrum in a famous passage. "Consequently," he asserted, "the national substratum of the state formerly known as the Russian Empire and now known as the USSR can only be the totality of peoples inhabiting that state, taken as a peculiar multiethnic nation and as such possessed of its own nationalism. We call that nation Eurasian, its territory Eurasia, and its nationalism Eurasianism."[81]

To prevent the rise of political nationalism (separatism) within the borderland peoples, Trubetskoi suggested that all ethnic groups residing in Eurasia should develop a hierarchy of loyalties that would be interconnected and complementary. Every individual people in Eurasia should combine its own local nationalism with the overarching Eurasian nationalism. By the same token, "all citizens of the Eurasian state" should be conscious of and take pride in the fact that they simultaneously belong both to a given people and the Eurasian nation.

Trubetskoi conceded, though, that this "Eurasian nation" was still a work in progress as the understanding of the common destiny of the Eurasian peoples had yet to become a "significant part of their consciousness." As an astute analyst of nationalism, Trubetskoi fully appreciated the need to "re-educate national self-awareness with a view toward establishing the symphonic (choral) unity of the multiethnic nation of Eurasia."[82] In this sense, historical scholarship was of course an absolutely indispensable instrument. Furthermore, the Eurasianists were aware that they were engaged in a kind of "race against time," because the intellectuals from the borderland nations were busy advancing their own, "nationalist," narratives meant to challenge the discourse that highlighted "Eurasian unity."[83] The need to intellectually rebuff the "separatists" was a constant motif in the Eurasianist correspondence. "I somehow cannot reconcile myself with an idea of self-determination that includes the right of complete secession—either of Ukraine, or the Caucasus, or Turkestan, etc.," wrote Vasily Petrovich Nikitin, a renowned Middle East specialist and active contributor to Eurasianist publications in the 1920s, in a letter to George Vernadsky. "The reading of the separatists' journals—[and their assertions like] 'we don't have anything in common with Russia,' 'we belong to the Mediterranean culture'—drive me up the wall. All this is utterly ridiculous. Should we really throw our entire historiography into a waste basket? Had it or had it not its own logic? Isn't this logic valid also today?"[84]

An elaboration of a Eurasianist interpretation of Russian history that would uphold the idea of the historical unity of Eurasia was thus in order. "It is necessary to re-examine a number of disciplines from the point of view of the unity of the multiethnic Eurasian nation, and to construct new scientific systems to replace old and antiquated ones," Trubetskoi forcefully argued. "In particular, *one needs a new history of the Eurasian peoples including the history of the Russians*."[85]

George Vernadsky and the History of Russia-Eurasia

In the mid-1920s, the Eurasianist theorists were looking for a good Russian historian, a true specialist (*spets* was the word they liked to use—the same shorthand that had wide currency in the Soviet Union) who would complete the crafting of the concept of Eurasia by adding a historical dimension to the geographical-cultural construct. At the same time, George Vernadsky, a trained historian of Russia, was looking for a new theoretical framework to help him reconceptualize Russian history. The paths of the theorists and the historian finally crossed in Prague.

On April 28, 1926, Nikolai Trubetskoi argued in a letter to a Eurasianist colleague, Petr Suvchinskii, a gifted musicologist and intellectual living in Paris, that the Eurasianist doctrine had been developed well enough to serve as a foundation for serious specialized work in concrete fields, particularly in history. "Our geographical-historiosophic schemes," noted Trubetskoi, "are polished to such an extent that, were a historian to mount them, he would automatically roll, as if on the rails, precisely in the direction we need him to proceed." In this same letter he shared with Suvchinskii his impressions from a recent visit to Prague and, among other things, mentioned that "one of the most interesting and rewarding moments" was his meeting with George Vernadsky. "He is working fully in accordance with our schemes but at the same time retains all the seriousness of a good *spets* as well as his ability to carry out original and independent research," Trubetskoi noted approvingly. He expressed the hope that Vernadsky would write a good book (the Eurasianists had just commissioned him with *An Outline of Russian History*) and added that the Eurasianists were particularly lucky to have Vernadsky as collaborator because he was a "mature and talented scholar."[86]

But George Vernadsky, too, had likely viewed the beginning of his cooperation with the Eurasianist thinkers as a mutually beneficial relationship. The Eurasianist vision of Russia's former imperial space as a geographical, economic, and historical whole as well as the idea of overarching Eurasian nationalism, obviously appealed to him. These concepts appear to have neatly resolved—at least on a theoretical level—the Russian-Ukrainian dilemma that was troubling him. Within the Eurasianist paradigm, there could not be any such Russian-Ukrainian problem at all. Because Eurasia is indivisible from the geographic-historical point of view, Ukraine, being a component part of it (along with, for that matter, any other parts of this "special world") *objectively* belongs to the Eurasian space, whereas the cultivation of an overarching Eurasian nationalism (along with the nationalisms of the individual peoples residing in Eurasia) provides the Ukrainians, Tatars, or Georgians with a *subjective* feeling of belongingness in a "multiethnic nation." Thus for a Ukrainian, it is possible to retain local Ukrainian loyalty, see himself as part of the broader Russian (East-Slavic) unity and have affinity with a still larger Eurasian entity at one and the same time. This arrangement suited Vernadsky perfectly.

But for history writing, the concept of "Russia-Eurasia" clearly presented both advantages and problems. To be sure, the Eurasianist approach significantly broadened the geographical horizon of research and boldly shifted the perspective, challenging the well-established Eurocentric interpretation of Russian history that presented Russia as a "Europeanizing" country, undergoing the same evolutionary process as the other European nations but held back by Russian peculiarities. The originality and innovative character of the Eurasianist vision was quickly noticed by Mikhail Rostovtsev, a scholar of the older generation and outstanding historian, who wrote a courteous preface to Vernadsky's first American book, *A History of Russia*. Vernadsky, in the words of Rostovtsev, discarded the *Vulgata* of Russian nineteenth-century historiography that dwelled mostly on Russia's connection to Europe and pointed instead to the ties that Russia had from time immemorial with the East—in particular, to the fact that during the early centuries of Russia's history its territories were incorporated into the huge Iranian and Mongolian empires. True, Russia interacted intensively with Western and Central Europe, but it also expanded for thousands of kilometers to the east, actively engaging the numerous peoples of Siberia and Central Asia in the process of its colonization of the Eurasian hinterland. "No doubt Russia succeeded in partly absorbing, partly Europeanizing many Asiatic tribes," Rostovtsev noted. "However, the question arises, how large was the contribution of these tribes to the peculiar development of Russia?"[87] Vernadsky's studies over the next couple of decades would discuss this issue.

But the very term "Russia-Eurasia," although it widens the boundaries of historical exploration, has also obscured the object of research because in this category Russia and Eurasia found themselves inseparably merged, thus completely blurring the distinction between them. My brief analysis of methodological foundations of Vernadsky's historical writing demonstrates how he grappled with this problem, trying to both delineate Russian and Eurasian history and at the same time preserve the opaque situation in which they would remain virtually indistinguishable.

In his first major Eurasianist work, *An Outline of Russian History*, Vernadsky presents the Russian historical process as the expansion of the Russian state across the Eurasian landmass: "The history of the expansion of the Russian state is to a significant extent the history of the Russian people adapting to its *mestorazvitie*—Eurasia; it is also the history of the entire territory of Eurasia adapting to the historical-economic needs of the Russian people."[88]

Thus, the history of the Russian people was basically identified with the history of the state and included in the general history of Eurasia. In turn, the history of Eurasia was understood as a series of persistent attempts by various peoples to form a Eurasia-wide state—starting with the Scythians, Huns, and Mongols. The book seemed to imply, though, that as soon as the Russians completed their expansion across Eurasia and formed *their* pan-Eurasian state, the history of Russia and the history of Eurasia became identical.

Vernadsky tried to refine his thesis in several subsequent works and finally arrived at a formula that was included in a short memo titled "A Concise Exposition of the Eurasianist View on Russian History" (1938).[89] Of course, he again reasserted the Eurasianists' main credo that Eurasia as a whole constitutes the historical *mestorazvitie* of the Russian people.

But there was also one important nuance. "The history of the Russian people, however, does not incorporate in its narrative the histories of other Eurasian peoples that both cooperated and competed with the Russian people during a long period of time," noted Vernadsky. "Thus," he continued, "if Russian history is increasingly merging geographically with the history of Eurasia in its entirety as we approach the contemporary epoch, this does not exclude the other approach to the history of Eurasia [seen] as the history of all the peoples of Eurasia, including the Russian people." Remarkably, though, in this programmatic text he subsumed the histories of the East Slavs (the Great Russians, Ukrainians, and Belarusians) under the general rubric of "Russian history." Vernadsky's concluding passage reads as follows: "Russian history is, consequently, the history of the peoples of the entire East Slavic (Russian) family . . . seen against the backdrop of the history of their relations with other peoples of Eurasia and [developing] on the geographical basis of Eurasia in its entirety as the Russian historical *mestorazvitie*."

This formula was, no doubt, a big step forward because Vernadsky, for the first time in Russian historiographic tradition, fully appreciated the multi-ethnic character of "Eurasia" and its complex interaction with "Russia" that was steadily expanding "against the sun" and increasingly turning into "Russia-Eurasia."[90] But his approach still remains ambiguous because he begins to largely disregard the multiethnic factor when the merger between "Russia" and "Eurasia" reaches its peak. As the Russians in their eastward thrust reach the "end of the earth" on the Pacific, multiethnic Eurasia somehow dissolves into the pan-Eurasian Russian state. This state, Vernadsky asserts, is a "gigantic historical-cultural organism" and "a world power." The inclusion into this Russian state of the "individual regions and peoples gave them invaluable economic and cultural benefits" and made them "coparticipants in world history."[91]

All of his theoretical maneuverings notwithstanding, Vernadsky's ultimate reluctance to decouple "Russia" and "Eurasia" and to clearly distinguish Russian history from that of the Eurasian peoples is highly symptomatic because it reveals the Eurasianist agenda: to preserve the unity of the former imperial space at all costs.[92] This task presupposed the strategy of avoiding any descriptions of prerevolutionary Russia that might invite unwelcome comparisons with the European colonial empires. To write a truly comprehensive "Russian history" in its interrelation with the history of the peoples of Eurasia, one would have to pose the questions that Vernadsky paid little attention to or ignored: What methods were used to facilitate Russian expansion in Eurasia? What policies were employed to incorporate the territories with ethnically, religiously, and culturally diverse populations? How did the subjugated peoples and their elites react to the Russian advance? How did Russian rule affect the local government, social structure, economic life, and culture of the peoples that were drawn into the orbit of the Russian state? In discussing these issues, one would have to treat the borderland peoples not as the mere objects of government policies but as actors that to a large extent defined the course of history.

But to write such an analysis would mean to write the history of Russia as a multiethnic *empire*—an objective that Vernadsky definitely did not pursue. He and his Eurasianist friends had witnessed the power of ethnic nationalism and sincerely hoped that the new Eurasian identity that they fashioned in their bitter exile would help them to preserve the integrity of "historic Russia" (be it the pre-1917 Romanov Empire or the Soviet Union) in an age when empires appeared to be out of place. Their reasoning was indeed original if somewhat utopian: "if the Russian empire were a symphonic unity of people—more than that, if there were no Russian empire at all but only organic Eurasia—the issue of separatism would lose its meaning."[93]

However, George Vernadsky was not a mere ideologue, he was a serious scholar. Unlike all of his great nineteenth-century predecessors beginning with Karamzin and ending with his teachers Kliuchevsky and Platonov, who treated Russian history as a *national* history, Vernadsky clearly saw the Russian Empire's *multiethnicity* and tried to analyze the complex interplay between the "history of the Russian people" and the "history of the peoples of Eurasia." Vernadsky's Eurasianist approach toward Russian history appears to have been one possible way out of the tangled historiographical dilemma formulated by von Hagen—"the dilemma, which, on the one hand ignores the multinational character of the Russian Empire and the Soviet Union and chooses thereby to treat the Russian past as the history of a nation-state, or, on the other hand, highlights the multinational character of those two state formations only to condemn them, in the name of national liberation and nationalism, as anachronistic and thereby inevitably fated to collapse as such."[94] It is precisely this search for an alternative vision "between, or beyond, empire and nation-state"[95] that Vernadsky and his fellow Eurasianists referred to as their attempts to build a "true" theory of nationalism.[96]

Yet another aspect of Vernadsky's intellectual legacy merits attention here—namely, how his writings influenced studies of Russian history in North America and Europe. In this context, it would be interesting to compare his influence on the field with that of his close friend Mikhail Karpovich,[97] insofar as both émigré scholars began teaching courses in Russian history simultaneously, in 1927, in two prestigious American universities—Vernadsky at Yale and Karpovich at Harvard. "Though fast and lifelong friends," notes

Richard Pipes, who was enrolled in Karpovich's 1946 seminar, "Vernadsky and Karpovich differed in their views of Russia and its future."[98] Unlike his friend's unorthodox Eurasianist outlook, Karpovich's view on Russia's past and present was that of the classic Russian liberal and "Westerner." Specifically, on Russia's "national question," this view, so widespread among the former members of the Kadet party, tended to present Russia's history as one of the nation-state in the making, thus basically ignoring the multinational character of the Russian Empire. This "Kadet" and Eurocentric interpretation of the Russian historical process proved to be rather congenial to the younger generation of liberal-minded Russian historians in the West who have come to espouse what some contemporary scholars call the "Karpovich-shaped consensus."[99] But, as Pipes had to concede, Vernadsky's vision of Russia's historical development, including his acute sense of the country's non-European connections as well as its multiethnic nature, "proved closer to the truth."[100] Thus it is probably not accidental that Vernadsky's works as well as the studies of two other Russian émigrés—Boris Nolde[101] and Georg von Rauch[102]—published in the 1950s laid the scholarly foundation for the booming research on the Russian Empire and nationalism that started in the 1990s.[103]

SPATIALIZING THE SIGN

The Futurist Eurasianism of Roman Jakobson and Velimir Khlebnikov

Harsha Ram

And today! Modern phenomenology is exposing one linguistic fiction after another. It has skillfully demonstrated the prime importance of the distinction between the sign and designated object, between the meaning of a word and the content at which the meaning is directed. There is an analogous phenomenon in the sociopolitical field: the heated opposition to muddled, empty, harmfully abstract cant and phrase-mongering, the ideocratic struggle against "humbug words," to use the picturesque expression. . . . Finally, the poetry of the poetists and poets belonging to related schools gave a sound guarantee of the autonomy of the word.
—ROMAN JAKOBSON, "WHAT IS POETRY?" (PRAGUE, 1933–1934)

The thematics of time and space, so mysterious and head-spinning, opened up. For us there was no borderline between Xlebnikov the poet and Xlebnikov the mathematical mystic.
—ROMAN JAKOBSON, *MY FUTURIST YEARS*
(1977, RECALLING THE YEARS 1912–1914)

Here is an untapped mother lode of work for philosophers, journalists [*publitsistov*], poets, novelists, artists, musicians, scientists, and scholars of the most varied specializations. It is necessary to reexamine a number of scientific disciplines from the point of view of the unity of the multi-ethnic Eurasian nation, and to construct new scientific systems to replace old and antiquated ones. In particular, this perspective necessitates an entirely new construction of the history of the peoples of Eurasia, including the Russian people.
—N. S. TRUBETSKOI, "OBSHCHEEVRAZIISKII NATSIONALIZM" (1927)

IN his article "What Is Poetry?" published in Czech in 1933–1934 and quoted above, Roman Jakobson, a founding figure of Russian formalism and structural linguistics, made a striking set of analogies between politics, poetics, and the philosophy of language.[1] The autonomy of poetic language and the arbitrariness of the linguistic sign were to literature and theories of language what the *ideocratic* struggle against humbug" was to the "sociopolitical field." Jakobson's use of the term *ideocracy* is as striking as this analogy. A concept central to the Eurasianist movement that flourished in the Russian communities of Prague and other émigré centers of the 1920s and 1930s, "ideocracy" had been defined by the linguist and Eurasianist philosopher of culture N. S. Trubetskoi as a form of government in which the "ruling tier (*praviashchii sloi*) consists of people united by their worldview." Proper to ideocracy, Trubetskoi had argued, was a "maximalism of the state" (*gosudarstvennyi maksimalizm*), a "state ideological organization" that excluded multiparty democracy and embraced a doctrine that was "essentially universalist" in that it relied on "the well-being of the collective of peoples inhabiting a given specific autarchic world."[2] While Trubetskoi was careful to dismiss both Soviet Russia and fascist Italy as "pseudo-ideocracies,"[3] the general tendency of Eurasianist politics was decidedly illiberal. Rejecting the cultural legacy and scholarly traditions of western Europe, Eurasianism sought to discover in the putatively distinct historical and geographical patterns of the Russian-Eurasian landmass an inherent rationale for a prescriptive ideology of statist centralism and territorial integration that would ideologically justify the reconstitution of the Russian imperial state after tsarism's collapse.

A somewhat oblique reflection of Jakobson's encounter with Eurasianism during his Prague years, the article "What Is poetry?" sought to identify the specifically *political* elements of Eurasianist doctrine with the *linguistic* and *epistemological* ruptures that Jakobson had consistently associated with the Russian and Czech avant-garde as well as with the revolution in linguistic theory arising from structuralism and Husserlian phenomenology. Central to Jakobson's argument was the assumption that analogous tendencies could be discerned in distinct discursive realms. Thus "positivism and realism in philosophy" and "liberalism in politics" were equivalent to an "assuasive illusionism in literature and on the stage."[4] The coupling of literary modernism and political Eurasianism was conceived in opposition to these commensurable negative phenomena.

Jakobson's "futurist Eurasanism" thus involved more than the pervasive *thematic* presence of the Eurasian landmass in the texts of literary modernism. For Jakobson, it rested equally on the insistence, articulated by Russian futurists and formalists alike, on the autonomy of the sign and the specificity of poetic language. How precisely did Jakobson relate the problem of language and literary form to Eurasianism's larger historiosophical and geopolitical concerns? Answering this question requires a more differentiated account of modernist literary Eurasianism, one that distinguishes futurist redactions of the Eurasian question from earlier symbolist renderings of the same. Russian futurism in fact anticipated significantly the convergence between linguistic theory and the geographical determinism of the Eurasianists. Although Jakobson was a well-known champion and active theoretician of the futurist movement, his writings contain no specific reference to the tightly articulated nexus between space, time and linguistic signification to be found in the writings of the Russian futurist Velimir Khlebnikov. In this sense, the following pages explore a debt that was unacknowledged at the time and perhaps even actively disavowed.

Eurasianism's Literary Geographies

It is already something of a commonplace to speak of Russian literary modernism as an essential cultural antecedent of Eurasianist doctrine.[5] Yet most assessments of the question tend simply to name and accumulate the literary texts that would have influenced the Eurasianists, without differentiating their assumptions or suggesting which formulations were closest to Eurasianist doctrine.[6] Even more nuanced analyses have limited their accounts to the symbolist movement, without venturing more than gesturally to the post-symbolist avant-garde.[7] If we now turn to some of the founding literary texts of the period, it is in order to recapitulate their rhetorical moves, but also to distinguish them internally. Of particular relevance are the real differences that obtain between symbolist treatments of the Eurasian question and that of the futurist poet Velimir Khlebnikov (1885–1922), whom Jakobson had considered one of the "three geniuses" he had known personally (the other two being Trubetskoi and Claude Lévi-Strauss) and whom he championed as the "great renewer of the poetic word."[8]

Inaugurated for the modernist period by the poet-philosopher Vladimir Solov'ev's celebrated poem "Panmongolism" (written in 1894, first published in 1905), the Eurasian theme in Russian literature generated a historically charged and internally dynamic system of poetic symbols that read the ongoing crises of empire and revolution as part of a civilizational clash of East and West, whose meaning lay within a larger providential scheme of history. In Solov'ev's immensely influential formulation, the memory of past defeats inflicted on Christendom by the Turkic peoples was seen as the pattern of Russia's immediate future: "From the Malay waters to Altai, / Leaders from the Eastern islands / At the walls of flagging China / Have amassed their vast troops. . . . . / O Russia! Forget your former glory: / The two-headed eagle is smashed, / And the shreds of your banners have been given / To yellow children for their amusement."[9]

Solov'ev's vision, in itself not unnuanced (I have picked here his crudest lines), was easily simplified into a Russian variant of the Yellow Peril: a generic but racially colored Orient, whose threat appeared very real in the wake of the Russo-Japanese War of 1905, was mapped onto an eschatological scheme that collapsed the political present of Russian imperial policy into a remote past (the Tatar yoke or the defeat of Byzantium) and an impending future (the Apocalypse). A cluster of racial pathologies, class anxieties, and archaic historical traumas was thereby projected onto the immediate future as the chiliastic expectation of the end of history. Russia's own demise was here read as divine retribution for her act of political hubris in claiming great power status. For a generation of Russian symbolists, Solov'ev's panmongolian formula allowed Eurasia to be imagined as a geography of Ultimate Ends, within which ancient historical resentments, fears of racial miscegenation, messianic hopes for the spiritual realignment of the Christian world, and the political expectation of imperial collapse and social revolution could coexist in an anxious evaluation of Russia's own location between East and West.

Solov'ev's panmongolism was destined to reverberate through the works of writers such as Valery Briusov, Leonid Andreev, Maksimilian Voloshin, R. V. Ivanov-Razumnik (R. V. Ivanov), Andrei Bely, and Alexander Blok.[10] With Blok's poem "The Scythians" (1918), a crucial shift, already palpable in Briusov, occurs: the spatial thrust of Solov'evian millenarianism is deflected in its direction and meaning. The apocalypse, which for Solov'ev was an *external* threat to Christian Russia, is here internalized as Russia's own geographical and racial burden. The most enduring legacy of the Tatar yoke was to have transformed the Russians themselves into Asiatics: "Yes, we are Scythian!" Blok cries, "yes we are Asian, / with slanted and avaricious eyes!" In Andrei Bely's celebrated novel *Petersburg* (first published in full in 1916), the physiognomy of the racial hybrid becomes the incarnation of a broader civilizational dilemma—the confrontation between Western rationalism and the irrational East. Bely's "Eurasian" solution, however, was to suggest that just as "all Russians have Tatar blood," so too the forces of reason and unreason had become irretrievably contaminated in the hybrid body of Russian history. The significant innovation of Bely's novel, then, lay in his presenting apparent polarities as profoundly intertwined, a convergence that suggested the imminent end of St. Petersburg itself as the political center and cultural expression of Russia's Europeanized elite.

A consistent feature of symbolist treatments of the Eurasian theme, then, is to set up East and West as apparent racial or civilizational absolutes that are then forced from within to the point of collapse: East and West are *not* in fact dichotomies but perspectival thresholds through which Russia must contemplate its own identity in relation to its Eurasian neighbors, from the hinterlands of Central Asia to its imperial rivals in Europe and the Far East. Symbolist Eurasianism arranged Russia's cultural orientations as a series of shifting psychic identifications. Its hopes, fears, and uncertainties corresponded to geographical realignments, each of which involved complex incorporations and transformations of self and other. In the case of Blok's "the Scythians," for example, a former adversary (the Tatar-Mongol state) had first to be resisted and then *internalized* (in Pushkin's words to the philosopher Petr Chaadaev one century before, "c'est la Russie, c'est son immense étendue qui *a absorbé* la conquête Mogole"[11]), and the resulting composite self then contrasted to a new other, Europe, that figures both as erstwhile spiritual ally and as political rival. As Nicholas Riasanovsky has it, "terror turned into identification and exultation."[12]

Blok's apocalyptic identification of Russia with the Asiatic other has prompted critics such as Boris Gasparov to suggest that "eschatological 'Scythianism' unexpectedly *coincided* with positive Eurasian doctrine."[13] Yet this ignores a deeper difference between symbolism and postrevolutionary Eurasianism. "Scythianism," and Russian symbolist renderings of the Eurasian question in general, was characterized by a relatively consistent chronotope, or time-space. Given its eschatological expectation of an end to history, Scythianism can be read as a form of *temporal closure*. Spatially, however, Scythianism was typified by what might be called a *deterritorializing* effect: a shattering of boundaries, a rethinking of racial and civilizational limits, a decentering of space. Politically, Scythianism welcomed the collapse of borders; metaphysically, it extended this collapse to a critique of the founding opposition of East and West. Russia emerged less as a place than as a moving threshold, through which the spiritual and political destiny of humanity could be foreseen as a series of shifting spatial perspectives.

The point to be made here is this: whereas it provided a lively exploration of Russia's ambivalent relationship to Europe and Asia, Scythianism was in fact *chronotopically antithetical* to the basic vision of Trubetskoi and his colleagues. The Eurasianists had sought to discover a metaphysical or cultural truth, a geographical given, a historical precedent or pattern that would serve to guarantee the territorial unity of those far-flung regions that had constituted the Russian Empire. Even as they welcomed the ethnically diverse nature of the Soviet Union, to the point of attacking the Eurocentric biases of conventional accounts of its history, they urged the consolidation of the multiethnic Soviet nation under a new totalizing ideology. In Trubetskoi's words: "In the Eurasian brotherhood peoples are linked to each other not according to one or another one-sided set of attributes but according to the *sharedness of their historical destiny*. Eurasia is a geographical, economic, and historical whole. The destinies of the Eurasian peoples have become intertwined, firmly enjoined to make one huge ball that it would now be impossible to unwind."[14] Eurasianism thus involved reconceptualizing the Russian-Soviet state without calling its territorial integrity into question. In this sense Eurasianism was a *reversal* of the Scythian or symbolist premise, replacing its eschatological closure of time with a *spatial* closure necessary for the creation of a utopian state.

Khlebnikov and Eurasianism

A literary figure somewhat neglected in these discussions, but closer in spirit and doctrine to the Eurasianist writings of Jakobson and even Trubetskoi, is the futurist poet Velimir Khlebnikov.[15] Curiously, Khlebnikov's possible role as a literary and epistemological precursor to Eurasianism is hardly evident from Jakobson's own writings on the poet. This lacuna is best understood as the necessary by-product of the methodological assumptions of early formalism. In his classic treatise "Noveishaia russkaia poeziia" ("Recent Russian Poetry," 1919), Jakobson severed literary analysis from any considerations of content, a move he legitimated by invoking the revolutionary poetic premises of the futurist avant-garde itself. While all poetry was "indifferent to the object of utterance," Jakobson asserted, it was "precisely the futurists who founded the poetry of the 'self-sufficient, self-valuing word,' as material that has been laid bare and *canonized*. And so it is not surprising that Khlebnikov's poems sometimes deal with the depths of the Stone Age, sometimes with the Russo-Japanese War, sometimes with the days of Prince Vladimir or the campaign of Asparukh, and then again with the future of the world."[16] According to the early Jakobson, then, Khlebnikov's poetry was essentially a linguistic endeavor, whose meaning was distinct from the communicative function and from the varied objects and themes it depicted.

Jakobson's article, which founded the scholarly study of Khlebnikov's poetry, is in fact a forceful *misreading* of Khlebnikov as a poet of the unmotivated device or trope, and ignores the systematic ways in which Khlebnikov sought semantically, and chronotopically, to motivate the "self-sufficient word." If, in Khlebnikov's own words, the poet's "first relationship to language" had given rise to the "self-sufficient word outside of the everyday and its uses for life," then his "second relationship to language" involved the search for the "unity of all world languages," the "path to a universal transrational [*zaumnomu*] language."[17] Both conceptually and biographically, Khlebnikov's poetic and theoretical work evolved from the derealization of the verbal sign (the liberation of the signifier from its everyday referent) to its resemanticization and ontologization in the service a global utopian vision. By focusing chiefly on Khlebnikov's "first relationship to language," Jakobson effectively obscured the larger social and epistemological ambitions of the avant-garde. Even as he came to acknowledge these goals in the very different political and cultural context of interwar Prague, he did so without returning to Khlebnikov's poetics of time, space, and signification. It is only by elaborating what Jakobson did *not* say about Khlebnikov in 1919 that we can understand the poet's possible significance for subsequent attempts at constructing a "Eurasian linguistic alliance," a significant theoretical enterprise of the late 1920s and early 1930s pursued by Jakobson with Trubetskoi's support.

While symbolist Eurasianism was essentially predicated on Christian religious eschatology, Khlebnikov's vision, like that of the Eurasianists, was ultimately of a syncretic, scientifically constructed utopia. The "cold laws" of reason, claimed the poet, had replaced millenarian superstitions, with their "otherworldly gleam" and "hints of the Satanic."[18] Straddling the historical moment of revolution and civil war, Khlebnikov's legacy constitutes nothing less than a radical attempt at fusing literature, mathematics, geometry, and historiography into a unitary discourse. Khlebnikov was not content with effecting a radical innovation in poetic language, but sought in addition to discover the mathematical and linguistic laws that governed time and its relation to space. In the tract "Time Is the World's Measure" ("Vremia mera mira," 1916) the poet declared:

> If there are two twin concepts, then they are space and time. But what a different fate has befallen each of them. One has been studied, and only inaccuracy prevents us from deciding whether it is Greek, German, or Russian; while we know not a single truth about the other. If a, b, c are the laws of space, then everything located in space is subject to the action of these laws. If m, n, t are the laws of time, then all the citizens of time beginning with the soul and ending with the state [*gosudarstvom*] are subject to the laws m, n, t.[19]

The regularities of history, as yet only dimly understood, could be mapped with the same precision as the boundaries of political states.

Khlebnikov measured historical time by measuring the gaps between watershed events. According to a peculiar kind of numerological positivism, the dates designating such phenomena as war or the rise and fall of empires were declared not to be random, but related through consistent lapses of time whose iteration was governed by specific formulae. To quote a relevant example, Khlebnikov redefined the historic tensions between Slavs and Turks, between Russia, Central Asia, and the Far East in terms of a mathematical formula of 3^n, which governs the number of days separating victories and defeats in battle. Japan's crushing victory in the Russo-Japanese war of 1904–1905 was merely the historically predetermined reversal of Russia's own Siberian expansion. The symbolists' "Yellow Peril" was no longer the harbinger of universal destruction, but only the most recent manifestation of an ongoing arithmetical principle in which East and West are equal players, winning and losing in turn.[20]

Common to Khlebnikov's poetic works and his mathematical equations is a pervasive but sui generis Eurasianism, whereby history is seen to be dictated by a shifting East–West axis of which Russia finds itself to be the center. The unit of Khlebnikovian time was thus paradoxically geographical, more specifically, *territorial*, albeit in ways that ultimately exceeded the confines of the Russian Empire. The visionary core of his temporal unit was an Asiatic region slowly awakening to its historical destiny. In 1918, Khlebnikov authored a series of declarations that amounted to a sweeping act of global decolonization. These manifestos reveal cultural and political views that strikingly anticipate Trubetskoi's. In "Indo-Russo Union," for example, we read the following:

1.   The organization aims to defend the shores of Asia from sea pirates and to create a single maritime border.

2.   As we know, the bell that sounds for Russia's freedom will have no effect on European ears. . . .

5.   The great nations of the Continent of ASSU (China, India, Persia, Russia, Siam, Afghanistan) belong to the list of enslaved states. The islands are oppressors, the continents are enslaved. . . .

7.   A united Asia has arisen from the ashes of the Great War. . . .

9.   The will of Fate has ordained that this union be conceived in Astrakhan, a place that unites three worlds—the Aryan world, the Indian world, the world of the Caspian: the triangle of Christ, Buddha, Mohammad. . . .

11. May the citizens of our island pass from the Yellow Sea to the Baltic, from the White Sea to the Indian Ocean, without ever encountering a frontier. May the tattooed patterns of political boundaries be wiped from Asia's body by the will of Asiatics. The separate lands of Asia are united into an island.[21]

To a greater extent than any other Russian writer, Khlebnikov's writings reveal a geographical orientation and a set of epistemological principles and cultural sympathies that match those of the Eurasianists. Khlebnikov's hostility to European hegemony anticipates Trubetskoi's repeated denunciations of "Romano-Germanic" domination, and his call for the decolonization and unification of Asia is reminiscent of Trubetskoi's insistence that "in the great and difficult task of liberating the peoples of the world from the hypnosis of [European] 'civilization and its benefits,' . . . the intellectuals of all non-Romano-Germanic peoples . . . must act in friendly unison. The only true opposition is that of the Romano-Germans against all other peoples, *Europe and humanity*."[22] Both spoke against particularist nationalisms in favor of a broader anti-imperialist Eurasian cultural and political union, a "statist utopia"—the term is Nikolai Berdiaev's[23]—ruled by visionary creative artists in Khlebnikov's case, and "ideocrats" in the case of Trubetskoi. Divergences of view should also be noted. Certainly Khlebnikov's "pagan" universalism would have been alien to Trubetskoi, who believed in the irreducibility of cultural and religious forms and in the superiority of Christianity. Indeed, Trubetskoi acknowledged that given their numerical superiority and centuries-old tradition of statehood, the Russian people should "naturally play the primary role among all the peoples of the [Eurasian] state territory."[24] While Khlebnikov's theorizing was rooted in the Russian language and in Slavic philology, his vision was more generously universal, pan-Asian rather than Eurasian, ultimately related less to Russia's territorial integrity than to a global harmony in which the solidarity of all the Asiatic peoples would play a catalyzing role. If the past had been determined by bloody geopolitical conflict, then the future belonged to all of humanity. Yet Khlebnikov, Trubetskoi, and Jakobson all aspired, however differently, to create a synthetic discourse in which the imaginative projections of art and the calibrations of all the sciences would be reconciled, a totalizing vision that would reverse the centrifugal and disintegrative tendencies inherent in prerevolutionary artistic practice and philosophical speculation.

Eurasianism and Khlebnikov's Theory of Language

Clearly, Khlebnikov's views on the cultural kinship of Russia and Asia and the need for both to act in political unison was in broad consonance with Eurasianist doctrine. Yet we have left unexplored the one question with which we began, that of the relationship of Eurasianist doctrine to futurist theories of language. In a fascinating letter written in 1916 to two Japanese youths, Khlebnikov muses:

> Asia is not just a northern land populated by a multitude of nations, but is also a patchwork of written characters on which the word *I* must emerge [*no i kakoi-to klochok pis'men, na kotorom dolzhno vozniknut' slovo Ia*]. Perhaps it has yet to be posited; in that case shouldn't our shared destinies take up some kind of pen to write the next word? . . . So let us uproot a pinetree in

the forest, dip it in the inkwell of the sea and write this as our sign and banner: "I am of Asia [*Ia Azii*]." Asia has a will of her own.[25]

More than just a geographical orientation or a cultural sympathy, Khlebnikov's Eurasianism also involved an attempt at creating a new universal language. For Khlebnikov, Eurasia was, quite literally, a "patchwork of written characters," whose hidden meanings it was the poet's task to uncover. Khlebnikov achieved this in part by asserting that the initial consonantal sound of any word defined its deeper semantic import, determined by the abstract geometrical meaning that the sound inherently possessed. This meaning could be gleaned from lists of—generally Russian—words beginning with the same letter by discerning their putative connectedness and regularity: Providing a list of "l" words, "*l: lodka* [boat], *lyzhi* [skis], *lad'ia* [boat], *ladon'* [palm of the hand], *lapa* [paw]," and so forth, Khlebnikov concluded as follows:

> the meaning of *l* is the conversion of a body stretched along the axis of movement into a body stretched in two directions perpendicular to the axis of motion. . . . Let us consider a sailor in a boat: his weight is distributed over the broad surface of the bottom of the boat. The point where force is applied is spread out over a wide area, and the wider the area the less the weight. The sailor loses weight. For this reason we may define *l* as the decrease of a force at any given point brought about by an increase of the field of contact. A falling body comes to rest when it comes into contact with a large enough surface.

At this point Khlebnikov shifts from geometrical abstraction to political power: "An example of such a shift in the social order is the shift from tsarist Russia to Soviet Russia, since in the new order the weight of power was transferred onto an incomparably wider area of those bearing power: a sailor—the state—is supported by the boat [*lodka*] of broad popular sovereignty."[26] In Khlebnikov's hands the alliterative repetition of sound was no longer a mere poetic conceit: consonantal letters embodied a kind of *spatial inner form* with the capacity to affect the vicissitudes of history. This extraordinary leap, which Khlebnikov would repeatedly make both in his theoretical writings and in his poetic practice, rested on the intuition that spatial manipulation was the basis both of political history and the linguistic sign: "The simple bodies of language—the sounds of the alphabet—are the names of various kinds of space, the list of the occasions of its life. An alphabet shared by many nations is a short dictionary of the spatial world."[27] And elsewhere: "Power, the laws of nation-states are a closed body in space [*Vlast', zakony gosudarstv, zamknutoe telo v prostranstve*]. A spatial *yes* . . . we can seize them like lumps, like mountains of space-beasts, with a whole positive number."[28] According to Khlebnikovian epistemology, then, the dynamics of force was spatially registered in sounds, while its vicissitudes in time could be calculated by numbers.

How can we relate Khlebnikov's "alphabetization" of Eurasian geography to the linguistic insights of Jakobson? To be sure, I do not wish to equate the formulations of a giant of modern linguistics with the dubious scientificity of Khlebnikov's wildly speculative theories. And yet Jakobson was himself to freely admit that it was the art and poetry of the Russian avant-garde that, by "abolishing the represented or signified object, raised in the sharpest possible way the question of the nature and significance of those elements that carry the semantic function in spatial figures on the one hand and in language on the other." It was in a dialogue with Malevich, Filonov, Khlebnikov, and Kruchenykh that the young Jakobson had begun to "move away from meaningful words and focus on the elementary components of the word, the sounds of speech in and of themselves."[29]

Yet if Jakobson's early interest in the phoneme had been overtly stimulated by the futurist theory of transrational language or *zaum'*, might his most significant theoretical contribution to Eurasianist doctrine, the article "Toward a Characterization of the Eurasian Linguistic Alliance" (1931), have partly arisen from a more covert dialogue with the poet? The most vivid expression of Eurasianism as linguistic theory, the concept of linguistic alliance (*Sprachbund*, in Russian *iazykovoi soiuz*) had been proposed by Trubetskoi in 1923 as a means of studying systematic convergences between languages that were genetically unrelated but situated in close geographical proximity. It was Jakobson who first applied the term to the study of phonological patterns over the Eurasian landmass, in an article on which he worked for approximately three years. Over some fifty pages of argument Jakobson concluded that the Eurasian heartland was a "territorially compact group" characterized by the phonemic distinction between hard and soft consonants, as well as a by the absence of tonal range.[30] Languages of the same linguistic family were found to have different phonological traits depending on their geographical appurtenance to the Eurasian linguistic alliance. Thus while Tatar, Nogay, Kazakh, Kirghiz, and even Azeri, all spoken within the Soviet Union, were found to possess a "softening correlation of syllables," Anatolian Turkish was not.[31] Jakobson provided consistent examples of the phonological influence of the Great Russian heartland over the languages of the outlying regions, creating what Patrick Sériot has called "geometrical relations between the center and the periphery."[32] "The tendencies that characterize the Eurasian linguistic alliance," observed Jakobson, "have found their most complete expression in the phonological structure of Great Russian."[33]

Jakobson's article is a linguistic corollary to the attempts by Trubetskoi, Petr Savitskii, and other Eurasianists to find a natural—ethnic, geographical, climatic, or historical—basis for the centralized Russian state. It also recalls Khlebnikov's understanding of the relationship of sound to space. Like Khlebnikov, Jakobson here examines phonemes in terms of their areal distribution; like Khlebnikov he views cultural patterns and relations of force as the interaction of sounds that can be geometrically codified within an enclosed geographical terrain, or as a means of expressing relations of spatial contiguity. In Eurasianism, then, Jakobson, like Khlebnikov before him, was able to find a means to motivate the "self-sufficient" word. In principle, their essential premise did not wholly converge: Khlebnikov considered the initial letter to possess a meaning that was inherent and potentially universal, whereas Jakobson would maintain that the phoneme "participates in signification, yet has no meaning of its own," owing its significance to its *differential* function within a larger linguistic system.[34] Yet, as Sériot has observed, the principle of phonological correlation, once viewed as a kind of cultural and even psychological affinity linking contiguous Eurasian peoples, ceased to be a "structural phenomenon, but a *substance* . . . [leading to] an *ontologization* of a systemic trait."[35] Like Khlebnikov before him, Jakobson relied on a spatial determinism to ground his belief in the structural relatedness and inherent regularity of phenomena belonging to diverse planes of existence.

Whereas it would be an exaggeration to view Khlebnikov as a key influence on émigré Eurasianism as a whole, we can perhaps say this: if in the late teens Jakobson wrote as a militant formalist, then during the late twenties and early thirties Jakobson was able to politicize his formalist convictions through a conversion to Eurasianism. Where Khlebnikov had once been championed by Jakobson as a hypostasis of pure poetic expression, now he became an implicit precedent by which Jakobson could embrace and further elaborate the culturalist and linguistic tenets of Eurasianist doctrine. In doing so, Jakobson significantly reversed or distorted the legacy of Russian literary treatments of the Eurasian dilemma. For all their racial xenophobia, the Russian symbolists had insisted on a spatially decentered and culturally hybrid vision of East/West relations, while for Khlebnikov the political unity of Russia and Asia had merely been a preliminary stage in the construction of a planet-wide linguistic and social utopia. If Jakobson adopted and modified Khlebnikov's method of deploying linguistic abstraction as a tool for sketching a phonemically motivated and spatially determinist map of Eurasia, then he regrettably betrayed the Russian avant-garde's most universal aspirations, by reducing its generously global vision to the narrower confines of the Soviet Union. In a sense this betrayal mirrored a more general shift in the politics of

Eastern Europe, from the internationalism of the revolutionary years to the doctrine of "socialism in one country" promulgated by Stalin in 1926. While indifferent to Marxist doctrine, Jakobson's Eurasianism reflects his evolution from the vanguardist formalism of his youth to his complex entanglement with Soviet politics and the cultural left in Czechoslovakia during the turbulent interwar years.

EURASIANISM GOES JAPANESE

Toward a Global History of a
Russian Intellectual Movement

Hama Yukiko

IN 1920, Nikolai S. Trubetskoi criticized Japan in his book *Europe and Mankind* as having been voluntarily Europeanized and about to discard its uniqueness. This chapter considers how Trubetskoi's message was received in Japan and examines the relations between Russian émigré Eurasianism and Japan's pan-Asianism. This allows us to evaluate Eurasianism from a comparative perspective as one among several contemporary intellectual currents opposed to the international order dominated by the Western powers. The repercussions of Eurasianism should be studied in the context of international history. Whereas Eurasianism has been discussed mainly in the context of Russian intellectual history, its formation and development reflect the particular international situation in the interwar period. For example, as Trubetskoi indicated, Eurasianist "ideocracy" was inspired by the "crisis of democracy" in Europe in the 1920s, the outstanding example of which was the Weimar Republic.[1]

According to the classification of Kurt Sontheimer, intellectuals who influenced Eurasianism such as Oswald Spengler and Othmar Spann belonged to the "antidemocratic" group who were disappointed with and criticized parliamentary democracy.[2] Moreover, as Martin Beisswenger has demonstrated, Eurasianism had close relationships with the German "Conservative Revolution."[3] Both movements emerged out of the unstable situation after the First World War and the Russian Revolution. They both rejected "Western civilization" and the norms of older generations, and idealized instead a "harmonic" government ruled by a strong political party with particular ideas. Insofar as these movements were affected by Italian Fascism and the Bolshevik Revolution, a great deal of insight can be gained by considering the development of Eurasianism from the viewpoint of international history. This chapter sheds light on a little known reaction to Eurasianism from Asia and also demonstrates that such a historiography offers an approach to an emerging global history of Eurasianisms.

Published in Sofia, *Europe and Mankind* is often regarded as a forerunner of Eurasianism,[4] even if it was not a book on Eurasianism but an anticolonialist critique of Eurocentrism and Europeanization. Trubetskoi argued that European colonialism would subject increasing parts of the world to Europeanization and would ultimately destroy the world's cultural diversity as such, thereby leading to artificial homogeneity. Thus he called for the psychological transformation of non-European intellectuals to counter Europeanization. Among the non-European states subjected to the forceful march of Europeanization, Russia was foremost in Trubetskoi's mind. Trubetskoi thought that Russia's admiration for Europe throughout the eighteenth and nineteenth centuries led Russians to dismiss their traditional culture as obsolete, whereas the top-down process of Europeanization in Russia destroyed the social unity between the elite classes and the popular strata.

In this context, Trubetskoi referred to Japan for the first time in Eurasianist publications, stating that: "The same process is about to happen before our very eyes in Japan, which first wanted to borrow only military and naval technology from the Romano-Germans but gradually went much further in its imitative efforts, so that now a significant part of 'educated' society there has assimilated Romano-Germanic ways of thinking. To date Europeanization in Japan has been tempered by a healthy sense of national pride and respect for national traditions, but no one knows how long the Japanese will remain this way."[5]

Trubetskoi rightly pointed out that Japan had devoted itself to economic and military modernization as well as cultural Europeanization ever since opening itself up to the world and entering the Western state system in the mid-nineteenth century. Having faced the Western powers' overwhelming military force and technology, the Japanese government decided to learn from and even imitate them. In doing so, Japan sought to avoid being colonized, to maintain its independence, and indeed, to join the imperial powers as an equal.

Much like the Russian debate between the Westernizers and the Slavophiles, intellectual discourses about national identity emerged in Japan during the nineteenth century in response to modernization. Japanese intellectuals asked whether Japan was a part of the West or a part of Asia. Unlike the controversy in Russia, however, the arguments between "Westernizers" and "Asianists" were not inconclusive. Asianism in Japan was not powerful enough to influence government policy until the early twentieth century, when victories in the Russo-Japanese War and also in the Sino-Japanese War made Japan more confident as one of the Great Powers.

Pan-Asianism (Asianism) emerged in the late nineteenth century as an ideology aimed at uniting Asian peoples and countries against Western encroachment and was based on the belief that the Japanese share common physical traits, culture, and civilization with other Asian people.[6] At the moment of its appearance, Asianism was a romantic and vague sentiment as well as a representation of Japanese regional identity. Over time, pan-Asianism was developed by individual intellectuals and various political associations, both idealistic anticolonialists and aggressive ultranationalists. There were no coherent tenets. In the early days, part of the pan-Asianist association served as a network of students from several Asian countries who later became activists of independent movements. Consequently their activities were sometimes against the Japanese government's imperialist policy.

However, the colonialist rivalry with the Western states in the early twentieth century and the rise of anti-Asian racism increased criticism of Western Europe after the First World War, and the growing confidence of Japan as a Great Power made pan-Asianism more aggressive and gave it a stronger anti-Westernist character. At the same time, having faced anti-Japanese movements in Asian countries such as China and Korea, pan-Asianism began to play a role in ideologically justifying Japan's rule over these countries, stating that Japan had a mission as "a guardian of Asia against the West." It gradually penetrated into official ideology through political figures and military officers who joined pan-Asianist circles. As we shall see presently, Trubetskoi's book was introduced in Japan in this time of intellectual ferment by a proponent of pan-Asianism.

The Parallels between Eurasianism and Pan-Asianism

In spite of the different contexts in which they developed, Eurasianism and pan-Asianism had a number of elements in common. First, both movements held a critical view of the Western state system and the international order that originated in modern Western Europe. Eurasianists criticized Europeanization and the resulting homogeneity that it imposed. This was not simply a theoretical issue but also an attack on the interwar international order. Since Trubetskoi repeatedly criticized what he regarded as the mistaken notion of "self-determination" and the mobilization of culture for the new nation building,[7] his critique was derived partly from the contemporary situation in Europe, where Eurasianists lived and witnessed the emergence of nation-states modeled after West European states. At this very time, their homeland had faced dismemberment during the Allied intervention and the rise of separatism.[8] Therefore, they blamed "self-determination" for the aspirations on the part of the former subject peoples of the empire to become nation-states on the Western model, and they suggested that Russia overcome these separatist tendencies by fostering a sense of belonging to a broader region "Eurasia."[9] Russia, they argued, had been driven by historical necessity to modernize in order to face the threat of Europe.[10] For them, states such as Russia and Japan that voluntarily promoted Europeanization in order to survive in the Western state system seemed to be victims as well as enslaved colonized countries.

In Japan, which was threatened by the Western powers and had transformed itself into an imperial power, pan-Asianism attempted to offer a non-Western vision of the international order, based on the common race and culture of Asia. The rejection of the racial equality proposal at the Paris Peace Conference intensified these arguments.[11] Considering that Japan's pan-Asianism was antithetical to the modern nation-state system, there is no question that the movement shared with Eurasianism an inherent critique of the Western state system. On the other hand, however, by insisting that Japanese and Asian nations were racially and culturally connected closely and thus fundamentally different from the nations of the West, pan-Asianism rejected the principle of "self-determination" and the notion that its colonies be granted full independence. To the extent that Eurasianism also paid scant attention to the protest from those nations that it considered to be historically and geographically part of "Russia-Eurasia," both shared the same latent contradiction in their logic.

The second element that the two movements had in common was the diversity of the respective region that each addressed. Eurasianists recognized diversity as a counterconcept to Europeanization. Diversity was also an important concept in pan-Asianism. Japan's pan-Asianists imagined that a united Asia liberated from European oppression was similarly characterized by great ethnic diversity. However, there is a crucial geographical difference between Eurasianism and pan-Asianism. Whereas Eurasianists straightforwardly assumed that the territorial extent of "Eurasia" corresponded roughly to that of the Russian Empire, the "Asia" of pan-Asianism included several discrete states. Indeed, in the early stage "Asia" meant only East Asia (more precisely China, Korea, and Japan); subsequently pan-Asianism would expand its definition of "Asia" to include Southeast Asia and even South Asia.

As long as the precise geographical boundaries of a regional concept remain malleable, any readjustment of them has the potential to mutate into expansionism, depending on the specific context. In this case, it was pan-Asianism that took this path by broadening its definition of the region.

The third element that Eurasianism and pan-Asianism shared was a sense of mission to lead a regional union. Pan-Asianists set Japan as the center, while the Eurasianists assumed the central role of Russia. This nationalistic element kept them from simply being idealistic regionalist movements and it inevitably provoked objections from the nations who were to be included in the union.

Despite these common features, however, the two movements took very different courses. On one hand, Eurasianism fragmented and vanished into oblivion after the Second World War. In the USSR, Eurasianist texts were prohibited and the movement was denounced as "counterrevolutionary," and it attracted little attention in the West as well, at least until the USSR's collapse. Pan-Asianism, by contrast, was embraced by the Japanese government and the military, which invoked it ideologically to justify invading Asia. This difference derives from a difference in access to power. Whereas Eurasianism was an intellectual product of émigrés who had little political influence, pan-Asianism was promoted by intellectuals with close ties to politicians and the military.

Regardless of the different outcomes of these two intellectual movements in the interwar period, however, there was nonetheless contact and engagement between Eurasianism and pan-Asianism, brought about by the similarities they shared.

Eurasianism's Reception in Japan

Eurasianism was received in a variety of different ways. Its reception in Japan was unusual in that it had little to do with the context of the Russian Revolution and the disputes among Russian émigrés.

From the 1920s to the 1940s, several Eurasianist articles and books were translated into Japanese.[12] The first translation was Trubetskoi's *Europe and Mankind*. It was published in the form of a book in 1926,[13] however, the original manuscripts appeared in a monthly journal as early as 1925.[14] Translations of works by Nikolai N. Alekseev, the pamphlet *Eurasianism: Declaration, Formulation, Theses*,[15] Petr Savitskii's article, "Geopolitical Notes on Russian History,"[16] and E. Khara-Davan's books on Chingis Khan[17] followed. The translators had a variety of interests and aims, but aside from their scholarly appeal the translations can also be understood in terms of the political context.

Nakane Renji (?–1945), who translated Savitskii's article, paid attention to the latter's perception of Asia and his reevaluation of relations between Russia and Asia. He maintained that "relations between Russia and the Orient are neither as empty nor as meaningless as Russian historians have regarded up to now." Nakane was also interested in Savitskii's geopolitical perspective, considering it to be "a scientific view free from prejudice, which could replace the racism of the Slavophiles."[18] Unfortunately, there is little information about Nakane, except for the fact that he graduated from the Harupin Gakuin (a Japanese institute founded in Harbin for the purpose of training people to engage in business with Russia) in 1937, joined a political association, Manshūkoku Kyōwakai, that aimed at enlightening people for the nation building of Manchukuo, and then studied at the University of Tokyo. Mobilized in the Pacific War, Nakane was killed in battle in the Philippines.[19]

The rise of "Turanianism" (Turanism) in Japan encouraged the translation of Khara-Davan's books. Turanianism had been introduced into Japan before the Second World War. Although there were several different currents and interpretations, the main advocate of Turanianism was Imaoka Jūichirō (1888–1973), a pioneer of Hungarian studies in Japan, who regarded Turanianism as an ideological tool that justified Japan's advance from Manchuria into Central Asia and could be expected to induce the ideological rupture of the Soviet Union. Turanianism in Japan also had a close relationship with pan-Asianism in that it insisted on the solidarity of a certain imaginary group of nations, including Japan, to resist the Western powers. Judging from the two translations and the short prefaces to the books, it is reasonable to assume that the translations of Khara-Davan's books on the empire of Chingis Khan were inspired by Turanianism and subsequently connected with pan-Asianism.

The most outstanding figure among these translators was Shimano Saburō (1893–1982),[20] who translated *Europe and Mankind*, books by Alekseev, and the pamphlet *Eurasianism: Declaration, Formulation, Theses*. Shimano was employed at that time by the South Manchurian Railroad Company as a specialist in Russian affairs, and he had strong pan-Asianist sentiments. Although better known as the author of the first full-fledged Russian–Japanese dictionary, he was also responsible for introducing Eurasianism into Japan,

In order to understand the intention behind Shimano's translations, it is necessary to look at his life and activities. Shimano was born in Ishikawa prefecture on the coast of the Sea of Japan. Immediately after the war with Russia, the prefectural government began to provide scholarships to young students to train people who could engage in trade with the former adversary. As one of its recipients, Shimano studied in Vladivostok, Moscow, and St. Petersburg (Petrograd) from 1911 to 1918. In the imperial capital, he took courses with Semen Frank and Fedor Shcherbatskoi and witnessed the February Revolution.

On the train from Vladivostok to Moscow, Shimano met a Muslim. Their conversation made him aware of the antagonism between Muslims and the Russian Empire and subsequently led him to help an émigré Bashkir, Mukhammed G. Kurbangaliev—who had escaped to Japan by way of Manchuria in the 1920s—build the first mosque in Japan. Later, in 1940, Shimano suggested a plan to Matsuoka Yōsuke, Japan's minister of foreign affairs, to support the guerilla war of Muslims in Xinjiang, in order to damage the Soviet Union.[21] Although the proposal was not adopted, this episode demonstrates that Shimano was aware of the ethnic and religious tensions in Russia and its borderlands.

After completing his studies in Russia, Shimano began working in the South Manchurian Railroad Company and subsequently accompanied the Japanese military expedition as a translator during the Allied intervention. The confusion and tragedy he witnessed in Siberia in the aftermath of the Revolution and the Civil War induced him to consider a possible alternative to the Bolshevik regime. At the same time, the hardships of Siberia's peasants also led him to reconsider the proper state system of Japan, in which, just as in Russia, rapid modernization brought much suffering to peasants and workers.

Shimano's first employer, the South Manchurian Railroad Company, had been established in 1906 after the war with Russia, which relinquished its lease over the track to the victor. Japan established a quasi-governmental corporation to manage this railroad, but its true aim was to colonize Manchuria and to extend its influence into Inner Mongolia. With this aim in mind, the Research Department grew into "one of the largest research organizations in the world until 1945."[22] At first, the department's task was to study Chinese law and landownership in order to help manage the railroad. However, the political changes wrought by the First World War and the collapse of the Romanov dynasty heightened the importance of Russian (Soviet) studies. The company, which confronted Russia in Manchuria as the primary imaginary enemy, began to train Russian specialists.[23] Shimano was among them. This process shows that, much as in the United States during the Cold War half a century later, Russian (Soviet) studies in Japan developed as a "study of the enemy (*Tekikoku kenkyū*)" encouraged by the exigencies of geopolitical rivalry.

In 1919, Shimano joined the Yūzonsha, a political group that subsequently became the Kōchisha. This was the pan-Asianists organization, which included famous ideologues such as Kita Ikki, Ōkawa Shūmei, and Mitsukawa Kametarō,[24] all of whom later became leaders of the right-wing movement. Kita Ikki (1883–1937) was a leading national socialist in Japan. After an attempt to become involved in the Chinese Revolution in China, he returned to Japan and founded the Yūzonsha with Ōkawa. Kita advocated pan-Asianism, through which Japan would lead a united and free Asia against the Western powers. He also insisted on an authoritarian regime based on a direct relationship between the emperor and the people, and a socialist economy to benefit peasants and workers. Calling for violence to achieve political goals, Kita was eventually sentenced to death as a rebel in the so-called February 26 Incident in 1936.[25] The unique combination of nationalism and socialism based on anti-Westernism attracted and inspired some followers in that era.[26]

Ōkawa Shūmei (1886–1957), another influential leader of the right-wing movement, is also known for being charged as a class-A war criminal after the Second World War (although he escaped trial with a plea of insanity). Like Shimano, he worked for the South Manchurian Railroad Company, while continuing his political activities. He sympathized with Kita and they worked closely together until splitting in 1923. Ōkawa was willing to cooperate with bureaucratic and military elites in the interest of domestic reform, while Kita vigorously opposed such cooperation. Ōkawa was involved in several coups and conspiracies and was eventually arrested. His writings on pan-Asianism were read widely and spread the idea of the inevitability of a military clash between Japan and the West.[27]

The Yūzonsha called for a reorganization of Japan, a revival of patriotic spirit, and the emancipation of the Asian people. This political society is often referred to as the fount of Japanese fascism. Nevertheless, as Christopher Szpilman points out, its members had little in common with each other and the group's "vague" program only advocated domestic reform and Asian liberation.[28] Questions remain as to Yūzonsha's true nature, but it is clear that Shimano was close to Kita and sympathized with his ideas. It has also been suggested that when Shimano obtained some books written by the Eurasianist scholar Alekseev in Dairen, he translated them for the sake of Kita's underground tract, *Nihon kaizō hōan taikō* (The fundamental principles of the reorganization of Japan), thinking that they would be of help to provide a theoretical explanation of Kita's ideas.[29] When he also happened to find Trubetskoi's *Europe and Mankind* in Dairen on a business trip to the headquarters of the South Manchurian Railroad Company, he decided to translate it.

Kōchisha's decision to publish his translation in Tokyo suggests a certain linkage between Eurasianism and pan-Asianism in Japan. Moreover, in 1931, when Shimano was dispatched to Paris for two years to collect information on the Soviet Union from Russian émigrés, he came across the pamphlet *Eurasianism: Declaration, Formulation, Theses,* and contributed a translation to the pan-Asianist journal *Dai-Ajia* (Pan-Asia) two years later.[30] Shimano certainly had political motives for those translations. In other words, he hoped to connect Eurasianism with Japanese pan-Asianism and the pan-Asianists' scheme, as we will see later.

In 1936, a group of military officers attempted a coup in Tokyo, the "February 26 Incident." Kita's strong ideological influence on the rebellious officers led to his execution along with them. Because of Shimano's friendship with Kita and his circle of intellectuals, Shimano was imprisoned for some time and then banished to Paris from 1937 to 1939. Despite this punishment, he returned to his job in 1939, but found that there was no longer much work to be done. In the course of the war, the South Manchurian Railroad Company had come under the army's control and there was now little room for independent research. With Japan's defeat in the war, the research organization ceased to exist.

After Japan's defeat in 1945, men like Shimano, who had been a part of the right-wing prowar movement and had not completed any higher education in Japan had great difficulty in finding employment. Shimano himself spent the rest of his life teaching the Russian language in private schools and the police academy, writing a Russian textbook, and translating Russian books on philosophy that have never been published.

The Link of Eurasianism with Pan-Asianism

Shimano introduced Eurasianist ideas in Japan with the aim of incorporating them into pan-Asianism. His first attempt was *Europe and Mankind*. Judging from the "preface by the translator," the emphasis that Shimano put on the text, and Shimano's political activity, his intention seems clear. Shimano interpreted Trubetskoi's criticism of Eurocentrism arbitrarily and very much in the context of interwar Japan.

According to Shimano:

Professor Trubetskoi is an expert on history as well as an authority on the sociology of our time. As the fruit of research over ten years, he published this book, *Western Civilization and the Future of Mankind*, and presented it to the world. Although it is a brochure in the form of just one hundred pages or so, the content is a criticism of European civilization based on extraordinary insight, wide and profound learning, and detailed theoretical examination. It indicates the fundamental evil of European civilization and insists on overthrowing it. Reading this book, Europe may not be able to avoid shuddering with fear, but the rest of the world will be given formless spiritual fire and sword. Facing an obstinate and stubborn White Peril, . . . Japan is on an important mission to save all the colored races.

This book, which is based on unshakable historical facts and authoritative sociological theories, gives Japan an opportunity to realize this mission. Japan must regret and abandon its present attitude of negativism and passiveness. We, the whole nation, must unite all the colored races against Europe, and prepare to immediately vanquish it. Professor Trubetskoi was not allowed to remain in his homeland Russia and is now in Bulgaria. . . . He lectures history at Sofia University. He gained fame, won great reverence from all the students and faculties, and whenever he gives a lecture, the audience packs the auditorium.[31]

This preface contains several mistakes. To begin with, Trubetskoi did not teach history at Sofia University, nor was he particularly famous or popular. On the contrary, he lamented that there had been only three students in his linguistics class four times a week.[32] Still an unknown young linguist at that time, he was neither an "expert on history" nor an "authority on sociology" as Shimano claimed. Shimano also described Trubetskoi as "an old scholar with white hair, tall like a crane"; however, Trubetskoi was thirty years old when he emigrated, and a picture taken a decade later still shows a head of black hair. It is not certain whether these are just simple mistakes or overstatements with the aim of adding prestige to the book. Nevertheless, it is obvious that Trubetskoi's criticism of Europe attracted Shimano, who believed that Japan had a messianic mission to lead "all the colored races" to vanquish Europe.

Second, Shimano added emphases to the text that are not found in the Russian original. Thus he stressed Trubetskoi's warning to Japan quoted above and added a sentence, apparently without the author's permission. At the end of the paragraph, followed by the statement "but no one knows how long the Japanese will remain this way," is a sentence in Japanese stating, "no one knows how long the bastion of the Japanese spirit can endure Europeanization." Shimano's addition of this line shows that he felt a sense of crisis in the "Japanese spirit," as the contemporary right-wingers actively advocated. Shimano clearly saw a deeper meaning in Trubetskoi's remark than the author had intended.

Finally, Shimano's political activity in the Yūzonsha and the Kōchisha also explains his intentions. The Yūzonsha's founding declaration proclaims, "Because we really believe in the Japanese nation's destiny to be the great apostle of mankind's war of liberation, we want to begin with the liberation of Japan itself."[33] The statement also encouraged the revival of traditional values and a patriotic spirit, both of which were being lost by "aping" Europe.

Furthermore, it defined Japan as an Asian leader, whose duty was to liberate other Asian countries from Western imperialism. There is a clear parallel between this political society's claims and Shimano's preface in *Europe and Mankind*.

In his introduction to Trubetskoi's book, Shimano focused on a critique of Europeanization and its call for the psychological emancipation of non-European nations. The pan-Asianists read the work as a theoretical tool for their aggressive movement whose ideas later led to the notorious notion of the "Dai-Tōa Kyōeiken" (Greater East Asian Coprosperity Sphere) that justified Japanese imperial expansion. One of the characteristics of the right-wingers' ideas is that although they advocated "the emancipation of the Asian people," they did not promote communism or socialism. On the contrary, by identifying Japan as "the leader of Asia," they glorified Japan's special status, even justifying its rule over Asian countries. It can be said that this contradictory idea represented the germ of a quasi-revolutionary Japanese fascism that suppressed several national movements in Asian countries while proclaiming that the "emancipation of Asia" was Japan's duty.

At the same time, Shimano's incendiary preface reflected the contemporary political and social climate in Japan. Criticism of the Western powers escalated along with the rivalry with the United States and with European countries over China, conceit and self-confidence after the Russo-Japanese War, and anger against racism. In particular, his brief reference to race reveals that he was conscious of racism. For example, the term "White Peril" is a well-used phrase associated with the "Yellow Peril," and Shimano used the term "colored race" as a synonym for non-Western people. In the interwar period, racism was not only an ideological matter but also a reality for Japan. As is well known, the Quota Immigration Act, or the "Japanese Exclusion Act," was adopted in the United States in 1924 and subsequently in Australia, New Zealand, and South Africa. This legislation curtailed Japanese emigration abroad, placing the Japanese economy in a predicament. Prior to the act, at the Paris Peace Conference five years earlier, Japan's proposal to include a clause in the Charter of the League of Nations to abolish racism was rejected.

These developments disappointed Japanese intellectuals who believed that discrimination by the Western powers would disappear once Japan accomplished a certain level of civilization. The rise of anti-Japanese racism angered Japanese society, yet, at the same time, it functioned as a justification of pan-Asianism, supporting both fighting against the white race and ruling and leading the yellow races in Asia.[34] Shimano's references to race in his writing must be understood in this context.

In 1933, Shimano translated a Eurasianist tract, *Eurasianism: Declaration, Formulation, Theses*. However, the title and the words "Eurasianism" and "Eurasianists" were altered, and it is hard to tell that the text was originally a Eurasianist brochure. The title, *Nichiman kyōfukushugi*, means "The

Japan Manchukuo Co-Welfareism." Shimano changed not only the title and the keyword "Eurasianism" but also the brochure's content, even omitting some parts. He did not specify the original text, and moreover, misleadingly identified himself as the author.

By examining the differences between the translation and the original text, one can see that the translator thoroughly eliminated the Russian context from the text. For example, Shimano cut out the descriptions of the Orthodox Church, the location of Russia, the history of Russia, and the Russian Revolution. The words "Russian" and "the nations of Europe and Asia" were also removed. At times, "Russia-Eurasia" was replaced by "Asia" or "Japan-Manchukuo," or omitted altogether. The words "the Soviet Union," "Bolshevik," and "communism" remained only when they were criticized or compared with other political and economic models. In the section of the brochure "Theses," passages about nationality, religion, and ideology were largely skipped or replaced by a few inconsequential words. As a result, the text was turned into an article focused on a theory of the economic and political state system. There is no hint that the brochure was originally about an alternative to the Soviet regime that Russian émigrés regarded suitable for "Russia-Eurasia."

The original brochure was written against the background of a political split of the Eurasianist movement. It focused on the governmental and economic system, intentionally skipping the topics of nationalism, culture, and religion that Eurasianists had vigorously debated among themselves in the 1920s. *Eurasianism* did not even include the most distinctive definition of the movement, namely, the conceptualization of Russia as a unique entity that bridges Europe and Asia. Shimano must have read other Eurasianist texts when he was in Paris, but it was this tract that he chose to translate. He might have made such a choice because his object of interest was exclusively the political and economic state system. Shimano's objective in translating the brochure might seem unclear, but the new title he gave it could be a clue. One can guess that it contributed to the establishment in 1932 of Manchukuo, which had a planned economy as its basic economic policy, and that he made it overlap with the suggestion for domestic reform in Japan.

Considering the significant commitment of pan-Asianism to multinationalism in Manchukuo, it is unlikely that Shimano missed the concept of ethnic and cultural diversity in Eurasianism. Kasagi Yoshiaki (1892–1955), a colleague of Shimano's in the South Manchurian Railroad Company and also a member of the Yūzonsha and the Kōchisha, cooperated with the Japanese army in the nation-building movement of Manchukuo. Multinationalism in Manchuria, or more accurately the idea of concord of several nations (*minzoku kyōwa*), was at first advocated to counter the anti-Japanese movement in China and to protect the minority Japanese population who lived there. Later on, and in particular after the Manchuria Incident,[35] it served as an ideology for establishing and idealizing Manchukuo. The ideologues asserted that Japan should lead people in Manchuria to found a utopian anticolonial state in which several nations coexist and live in harmony. Kasagi was one of the believers in this idea and a zealous advocate.[36] Although pan-Asianism clearly influenced the ideology of Manchukuo, Shimano did not pay attention to the multiethnic aspects of Eurasianism in his translation. Rather, Shimano's focus seems to have been more on the domestic context of Japan and the importance of Eurasianism's political models.

Shimano introduced Eurasianism to Japan, replacing the term with "Ōa shugi" (Euro-Asianism) or "Shin Rosiya shugi" (New Russia-ism). Yet he was interested not in the core ideas of Eurasianism, in other words, Russia's identity and self-definition, but instead in its anti-European dimension and its vision of a domestic system. Shimano intentionally distorted Eurasianist messages and these translations were motivated by his political activity in the pan-Asianists' circles.

The Eurasianist Response

There is little evidence that Eurasianists in Europe knew how their ideas were received in Japan. However, there is a clue that they might have been aware that their works were translated into Japanese.

Among the one and a half to two million Russian émigrés who were scattered around the world,[37] Eurasianism had a network not only in Europe but also in Asia. The Asian portion of the émigré movements was centered in Harbin, Manchuria, which had a large Russian community. According to their records in archives and periodicals, Eurasianists had some correspondents and sympathizers there. Among such sympathizers, the best-known figure was the writer Vsevolod. N. Ivanov,[38] one of the very few intellectuals in Asia whose letters and reviews appeared in Eurasianist journals.

The correspondence between Ivanov and V. P. Nikitin, a specialist on Persia who joined the Eurasianist movement in the 1920s, appeared in a Eurasianist periodical in 1926.[39] In a letter, Ivanov wrote that not only Chinese and Japanese intellectuals were interested in Eurasianism, but also that people in Siberia and even the high-ranking Soviet diplomat Lev Karakhan bought Ivanov's book.[40] In the same letter, Ivanov also mentioned that a special department of the South Manchurian Railroad Company budgeted money for the translation of selected Eurasianist works. Regardless of whether or not Eurasianists believed Ivanov, this letter informed them of the fact that their works might have been translated into Japanese.

It should be noted that Eurasianists, at least those who were in Savitskii's group, did not approve of Ivanov as a member of the Eurasianist movement. In one instance in 1932, when Ivanov contributed a comment celebrating the establishment of Manchukuo to a Russian-language Japanese newspaper published in Harbin,[41] a Eurasianist protested in an article titled "Eurasianists on the Far Eastern Question," saying that Ivanov had no authority to speak on behalf of Eurasianism and had nothing to do with the movement.[42]

There was no direct link between Ivanov in Harbin and Shimano in Dairen. Although Eurasianists in Europe shared information about the translation via Ivanov's letter, and some of them even planned on translating their works into some other languages,[43] there is no evidence that Eurasianists obtained and read Shimano's translation. Thus, there was no feedback. Nevertheless, it would appear that they recognized the possibility that Eurasianism could be co-opted.

For example, whereas Eurasianists defined Russia as neither Europe nor Asia, Ivanov asserted that "Russia is for us not Europe but Asia."[44] Having mentioned the rise of the Asianist movement and its famous slogan "Asia for Asian people," Ivanov claimed that Eurasianists in Europe should look at Asia from the Asian perspective, and at the same time, Eurasianism should be actively involved in the real politics in Asia and stand up for it, because for him, Russia was Asia proper.[45] In response, Nikitin pointed out the danger of idealizing the situations of Asia. He maintained that the slogan "Asia for Asians" did not point the way to reclaiming "the magnificent cultural legacy" but instead merely signaled an "anti-European direction." In other words, he pointed out that the slogan could stir antagonism rather than encourage pride in Asian culture. He also criticized Ivanov's simple ideas about dividing the world into Europe and Asia. Nikitin argued that Eurasianists denied such an overly simplified dichotomy and Eurasianism must be understood in the context of Russia.[46] Nikitin's reply to Ivanov implies the possibility for Eurasianism to be confused with Asianism.

The article "On the Far Eastern Question" includes another example of Eurasianists' anxiety in a passage warning that Japan was trying to secure its interest in the continent by establishing Manchukuo as a "buffer state." This state would be "necessarily multinational, and Japan wants to rule it not by forceful colonial politics but by the power of the multinational inhabitants in the area." However, the sympathy of the inhabitants "would be gained if Japan . . . had a certain state ideology" and "thus naturally a question arises; isn't it possible to use Eurasianism for the purpose?"[47] Even though Shimano did not emphasize the concept of multinationalism, Eurasianists understood the potential danger that their ideas could be distorted and used improperly.

Beyond Time and Space

Eurasianism was born in Sofia and developed mainly in Prague, Paris, Berlin, and Vienna. It traveled to Dairen and Harbin, where it encountered Japanese proponents of pan-Asianism. Pan-Asianists introduced Eurasianism in Tokyo, where the ideas were received in a somewhat distorted form. This journey demonstrates the potential for Eurasianism to be transformed into an aggressive ideology, especially when it enjoyed access to power. For this reason, in a more recent context, many researchers have paid considerable attention to Eurasianism's renaissance in Russia, Kazakhstan, and Turkey in the 1990s, when leading politicians and intellectuals have invoked its ideology.[48] The discussion of this recurrence must be left for another time.

The legacy of Pan-Asianism simultaneously resurfaced in Japan in the 1990s, in the form of "New Asianism" or the "East Asian Community." These developments must be discussed not merely in their domestic contexts but also against the backdrop of post–Cold War international relations and growing regionalism, after the clear-cut worldview of the Cold War had disappeared, and the global reorganization of regions began to take place. The intellectual legacies of the Russian émigrés and Japanese ideologues from the interwar period have been rediscovered and reproduced in the context of this new transitional period, and they continue to provoke controversies today.

NARRATING KULIKOVO

Lev Gumilev, Russian Nationalists, and the Troubled Emergence of Neo-Eurasianism

Mark Bassin

ONE of the most striking features of identity debates in post-Soviet Russia has been the persistent appeal of the ideas of Eurasianism. Indeed, thanks to the efforts of enterprising and competent ideologues such as Aleksandr Dugin, what might be called "neo-Eurasianism" has now taken shape as a more or less discrete political-ideological camp, complete with its own manifestos, political parties, youth movements, and a highly effective presence on the Internet.[1] Since its emergence out of the turbulence of the early 1990s, neo-Eurasianism has cultivated a public image based on a number of implicit assumptions about its basic character. The most important of these, of course, is the claim that the principles and beliefs of Eurasianism correspond to those of Russian nationalism more generally. Indeed, neo-Eurasianism today offers itself as the most natural advocate for the nationalist sentiments and inclinations that are so powerfully manifested in post-Soviet Russia—a claim supported by the presence among its ranks of outspoken and visible nationalist representatives such as Aleksandr Prokhanov, Gennadii Ziuganov, Aleksandr Panarin, and Dugin himself. At the same time, neo-Eurasianism presents itself as the legitimate heir to the original Eurasianist project of the 1920s and 1930s, insisting that it remains faithful to the various theories and interpretations that were developed at that time. The importance of this latter claim to the historical legacy of classical Eurasianism should not be underestimated because it provides a fundamental enhancement for the doctrinal authority and indeed the legitimacy of neo-Eurasianism today.

But if neo-Eurasianism first began to attract broad support in the early 1990s, its initial manifestations can be traced back over the preceding two decades. And if one scrutinizes this earlier background, it quickly becomes apparent that both of the characterizations we have just noted are not only questionable but in fact highly tenuous. On the one hand, neo-Eurasianism from the outset displayed substantial differences from classical Eurasianism in regard to important questions of historical interpretation. At the same time, whereas this incipient neo-Eurasianist perspective did indeed attract the attention of Russian nationalist tendencies—quite well-developed already in the late Soviet period—the interest on the part of the nationalists before the advent of perestroika was not for the most part positive but rather skeptical or downright hostile.

This chapter considers the issues at the center of this controversy. They relate most immediately to the questions of historical interpretation just mentioned. Specifically, these involved the remote and traumatic period during which Russia was subjugated to the nomadic Tatar-Mongolian armies of the Golden Horde. This subjugation began in the 1220s, as the population of ancient Rus' was conquered in a series of devastating attacks by the warlord Batu, grandson of Chingis Khan. It lasted for more than two centuries, during which time the shattered remnants of Kievan Rus' lived as vassal subjects of the Golden Horde. The dominant Russian view, strongly reflected in Soviet historiography, was that this period of Tatar domination had been one of great suffering and sacrifice—a veritable "Mongol" or "Tatar yoke" in which the hapless Russo-Slavic population languished under the brutal domination of Asiatic occupiers. "This yoke was a terrible force," maintained one authoritative Soviet text from the 1960s, "which stood in the path of the development of the Russian people and the other nations of our country. It represented the greatest evil, which put a brake on all historical progress," above all the political "unification of the "Russian [*russkii*] people" within a single state structure.[2] The beginning of the end of Tatar domination was marked by the victory of Russian troops over Tatar armies at a battle on the Kulikovo fields in 1380. This early victory assumed great symbolic value and became one of the most important landmarks in Russian national memory, cherished as a dramatic catharsis that at once brought liberation from foreign domination, moral renewal, the rediscovery of a common national ethos, and the foundations of a new political structure that was to evolve into the mighty Russian state. The unquestionable power that the Kulikovo victory continued to exercise over the national imagination in the Soviet period was demonstrated on the occasion of its six-hundred-year anniversary in 1980, which developed into a major national celebration extending over several years.[3]

For the classical Eurasianists, the historical pattern of interactions between the ancient Russians and the Golden Horde had been a major preoccupation. Nikolai Trubetskoi and others offered a revisionist interpretation of this experience, which did not deny the dreadful realities of Mongol supremacy but pointed to the positive geopolitical "legacy" that Russia was eventually to inherit as it freed itself from the domination of the nomadic armies.[4] Thus it was not entirely surprising that the initial Eurasianist stirrings in post-Stalinist Russia should have taken the form of historical analyses devoted precisely to this period of ancient Russian history. These analyses were the work of Lev Nikolaevich Gumilev, the scholar son of Nikolai Gumilev and Anna Akhmatova, who languished for nearly fifteen years in Stalinist labor camps from the 1930s through the mid-1950s.[5] Gumilev was fascinated by the history of the nomadic peoples of the Eurasian steppes and their interactions with the Russians. He had a special interest in the role of the Khazars —a group occupying the lower Volga delta and the north Caspian steppes who in the eighth and ninth centuries converted to Judaism—and he wrote extensively about their interactions with Kievan Rus'.[6] Along with this, the relationship of ancient Rus' to the Golden Horde—and specifically the complex of circumstances and events surrounding the battle at Kulikovo—were at the very center of his attention. His historical account was heavily influenced by the teachings of the classical Eurasianists, and indeed was even more radically revisionist than theirs, completely contravening the popular interpretation just described. A close consideration of Gumilev's arguments, and the various reactions of contemporary Russian nationalists to them, will reveal the ambivalences and tensions that underlie neo-Eurasianism's relationship both to the legacy of classical Eurasianism and to late- and post-Soviet Russian nationalism.

Gumilev's Vision of Ancient Russian History

Until the late 1980s, Gumilev was probably best known not for his historical research at all but for his ideas about the nature of ethnicity and ethnic relations.[7] Insofar as certain elements of this "*etnos* theory" found their way into his reconstructions of ancient Russian history, however, they are significant for our purposes as well. Gumilev proposed a strongly essentialist and naturalistic vision of ethnic being, which he claimed was based on the principles of natural science. He characterized ethnicity as a biological phenomenon, and ethnic groupings, or *etnosy*, as natural organisms. Like all natural organisms, each *etnos* progressed through a process of what he called *etnogenez*, or ethnogenesis—a life cycle of birth, development, maturity, and decline. The main features of ethnogenesis were the same for all *etnosy*, and in all cases the process was set in motion by a *vzryv*, or dynamic eruption, of what Gumilev called *passionarnost'*. This was a massive charge of energy that formed within certain individuals, providing the impetus for the initial consolidation of the group and propelling it as it moved through the successive phases of the ethnogenetic cycle. Gumilev also developed a theory about the patterns of interaction between ethnic groups, which he argued were determined by the natural quality of *komplimentarnost'*, or complementarity, between the groups concerned. Complementarity between *etnosy* could be "negative" or "positive," the latter indicating that the groups concerned shared an innate sense of commonality and fraternity that allowed them to coexist and interact peacefully across centuries. Finally, a critical feature of Gumilev's theory was his belief that ethnicity was manifested in a hierarchy of generic ethnic units. In the middle of this hierarchy was the *etnos*. Below it were ranged subsidiary ethnic groupings called *subetnosy*, and above it were agglomerations of *etnosy* called *superetnosy*. The latter he referred to as "communities (*obshchnosti*) of historical destiny."

While Gumilev deployed elements of this *etnos* theory as conceptual building blocks for his Eurasianist perspective, the primary inspiration for his interpretative thrust came from classical Eurasianism.[8] He shared the Eurasianists' deep fascination with the history of the steppe peoples and their interaction with Russia, and his scholarly expertise on these subjects was at least a match for theirs. Like his predecessors, Gumilev was convinced of the primordial unity of the different Eurasian peoples and of the need to consolidate this unity in the form a single political entity.[9] Moreover, he shared their intense anti-Western bias and their insistence on the essential polycentricity of world history, which had moved geographically and chronologically through a succession of distinct civilizations. The classical Eurasianists had conceived of these civilizations in terms of Nikolai Danilevskii's "world-historical types" or Oswald Spengler's *Weltkulturen*, whereas Gumilev—who also appreciated the importance of the Spenglerian tradition—referred to them using his own neologism *superetnosy*. Testing the Soviet censorial boundaries, Gumilev openly cited their writings in his own publications, and he deployed their key concept of *mestorazvitie* in his own analyses.[10] At the end of his life he vigorously reaffirmed his commitment to the project of the classical Eurasianists, describing it as an "honor" that he was now often included among their ranks and declaring famously as the USSR broke apart that "if Russia is to be rescued, it can only be through Eurasianism."[11]

An examination of Gumilev's complicated and often confusing historical accounts, however, reveals that his arguments and conclusions in fact differed quite substantially from those of the classical Eurasianists. Gumilev himself appreciated this point, and spoke explicitly about the "divergences" (*raskhozhdeniia*) that set him apart from his interwar predecessors. But whereas Gumilev saw these divergences primarily in the fact that his own theories were based on natural science, there were more immediate differences in their respective understanding of the relationship between Ancient Russia and the Golden Horde and of the significance of this relationship for the evolution of the Russian nation.[12] To this extent, Gumilev's interpretation represents a revision not merely of the generally accepted and officially approved Soviet versions of these questions but also of the Eurasianist tradition itself—the very tradition that Gumilev is today credited with rescuing and resurrecting. The principal elements of Gumilev's revisionism relate to three fundamental historical questions: (a) the relationship between the Tatar-Turkic-Mongolian peoples of the Golden Horde and the ancient Russians, (b) the identity of Russia's genuine allies and opponents in the struggle at Kulikovo, and (c) the ethnogenetic origins of the modern Russian *etnos*.

The *Chernaia Legenda*

Gumilev rejected the argument that ancient Russian civilization had been destroyed by a rapacious Mongol conquest, and that the latter's ensuing domination represented a harsh yoke of oppression under which the hapless Russians languished for centuries. To the contrary, he insisted that accounts of Tatar predations were not merely exaggerated but historically incorrect. The thirty-thousand-strong nomad cavalry was simply too small to have wrought such damage on Kievan Rus', which itself could mobilize over one hundred thousand warriors. He described Batu's onslaught of the late 1230s, culminating in the fall of Kiev in 1241, as "nothing more than a big raid" (*nabeg*), the goal of which was not the conquest of Rus' at all but the extraction of revenge as part of a "steppe vendetta" with another nomadic people the Polovtsy.[13] Ultimately, the Golden Horde was only interested in securing its own boundaries between the Don and Volga rivers, and any notion of conquest of the indigenous population of Kievan Rus' was far from their minds. "They did not annex Russian lands and people to their own domains," he maintained, nor did they "attempt to subject the population of Kievan Rus'. They rather sought only to establish reliable boundaries that could provide security for their own country against the attacks of powerful and merciless enemies."[14]

> There can be no question of the conquest of Rus' by the Mongols. They did not leave their garrisons behind, and had no thought about establishing permanent control. At the end of his campaign Batu withdrew to the Volga, where he built his camp at the town of Sarai. In fact, he limited

himself to destroying only those towns that were on the path of his armies and that refused to make peace with the Mongols and instead offered armed resistance.[15]

To this general pattern Gumilev was prepared to concede only one exception. This was the wanton destruction of the town of Kozel'sk in 1238, the extremes of which were richly documented in the Russian Chronicles. Even in this case, however, Gumilev tried to justify the victors' behavior, arguing that the Slavic population of the town had themselves brutally murdered two envoys the nomads had dispatched into the town in a sincere attempt to negotiate terms of surrender. In so doing, he implied, the townspeople effectively invited the retribution they received.[16] Ancient Rus' was not "conquered" at all, he concluded, but submitted "voluntarily" (*dobrovol'no*) to Mongol authority.[17]

If there had been no vengeful conquest, then neither had the ensuing centuries witnessed the hostile domination of ancient Rus' by the Golden Horde. The notorious Tatar yoke, Gumilev maintained, was in fact a historical fiction, an elaborate myth constructed in later centuries by anti-Russian agents in the West. He gave his own name to the myth, calling it the *Chernaia Legenda* or "Black Legend," which he claimed was fabricated with the intention of setting the Turkic and Slavic peoples against each other in order to weaken the Russian state.[18] This false version of events was then unwittingly taken up in Russia itself and eventually embraced by most Russian historians, who based their entire understanding of early Russian history on it. In point of historical fact, however, the true pattern of relations between Rus' and the Mongols indicated precisely the opposite, namely, a strong positive complementarity between them. An important source of this interethnic amity, Gumilev argued, was the fact that many of the Mongols were converts to Nestorianism, a fifth-century Christian sect that had spread broadly across the Middle East and Central Asia. Nestorianism was particularly prevalent in the twelfth century, and Gumilev maintained that it provided an obvious source of affinity with Orthodox Rus'. When the Golden Horde eventually opted for Islam as its official religion of state in the fourteenth century, it did not seek to impose this foreign belief on the Slavic-Rus' population under its control, but rather allowed them to pursue their native beliefs. Indeed, the adoption of Islam actually served to strengthen the interconnection of the two groups because many Nestorians were unwilling to embrace the new faith and sought refuge among the Orthodox, becoming a part of early Russian society.[19]

Gumilev's insistence on the complementarity and "friendship" between the ancient Russians and the steppe nomads led him to challenge standard interpretations of one of the most important literary monuments in Russian history, the epic poem *The Song of Igor's Campaign*. Dating from the late twelfth century, the poem is generally understood as a description of an unsuccessful raid by the prince Igor Sviatoslavich in 1185 against the nomadic Polovtsians, who inhabited the southern part of the Don basin. Rejecting the scholarship of eminent authorities such as Dmitrii Likhachev, Gumilev refused to accept *The Song* as evidence of hostility on the part of Kievan Rus' toward the steppe peoples. In an essay tellingly titled "Overcoming Our Self-Deception" (*Opyt preodoleniia samoobmana*), he maintained that *The Song* was not a genuine and patriotic expression of national sentiment at all but the work of "pro-Western" agents, who deliberately crafted it to be misleading.[20] In effect, he suggested, this bogus manuscript fabricated an antagonism between the two groups in order better to manipulate and control both of them.

Gumilev referred to the experience of the great hero of early Russia Aleksandr Nevskii as conclusive evidence of the complementarity he had in mind. After his victory in 1242 against an invasion of the Teutonic Knights from the Baltic, Nevskii actively solicited the aid of Batu's forces in his "struggle against the pressure from the West—the *Drang nach Osten*—and to halt the advance of those Germans seeking to reduce the remnants of the ancient Russian population to serfdom."[21] In 1251 he traveled to meet Batu, and befriended the latter's son Sartaq, a Nestorian. Gumilev described how the two swore eternal brotherhood in an elaborate Mongol ritual, through which act Aleksandr became a stepson of the great Khan and was able to form an alliance with him against their common foe.[22] This alliance was maintained after Nevskii's death in 1263.[23] It brought enormous practical benefits, above all a "much-desired peace and a secure order" and enabled ancient Rus' to resist the encroachment of and eventual absorption by the forces of the West. This successful early resistance was then the key to Russia's later profile as a *velikaia derzhava*, or great power. "In the final analysis, Russia (*Rossiia*) emerged as a great power in those places where the Russian princes requested help from the Tatars."[24]

Kulikovo Was Really a Struggle against the West

The second dimension of Gumilev's revisionism involved a reinterpretation of the meaning of the Russian victory at Kulikovo. Here as well, he argued that the genuine challenge to Russia came not from the steppe nomads but from the perfidious forces of Western aggression and their traitorous agents among the Mongols. By the early 1300s, the unity of the far-flung Chingisid Empire was beginning to disintegrate, and the Golden Horde itself was increasingly divided between its western and eastern halves—the "Blue" and "White" hordes.[25] In 1312, Gumilev asserted, the warlord Uzbek unlawfully seized power in Sarai, proclaimed Islam as the state religion, and demanded that all of his subjects—mostly pagans and Nestorian Christians—convert.

In principle, Gumilev took a hostile view of Islam, characterizing it as a disruptive and pernicious belief system that opposed the legitimate interests of the Russians.[26] He argued that Uzbek's ascendance undermined the heretofore harmonious and fraternal relations between the Golden Horde and ancient Rus'.[27] This process of alienation was accelerated some decades later, when the powerful military commander Mamai seized control of the Blue Horde in the 1370s. Mamai was not a scion of the Chingisid line and thus had no legitimate pretensions to leadership. Alienated for this reason from the genuine Mongol-Tatar elite, he was compelled to rely upon alliances with external forces. As what Gumilev described as an "outspoken *zapadnik*," or Westernizer, he joined forces precisely with Russia's traditional enemies. These included wealthy Catholic merchants from Genoa, Catholic Lithuania, and Jewish merchants in Crimea.[28] Under Mamai's illegitimate control, Gumilev maintained, the natural kinship and affinity between the Mongols and the Russians was perverted into a hostile "negative" complementarity.[29] It was this situation that provided the immediate background for the confrontation at Kulikovo.

Gumilev also substantially revised the actual scenario of the Russian victory. He did not dispute the generally accepted account of the events themselves. In 1378, Mamai sent his warlord Murza Begich to enforce the obedience of the prince of Moscow. Murza was defeated by the forces of Dmitrii Ivanovich in battle near the river Vozha. Mamai then resolved to lead a second assault himself against Moscow two years later. He assembled a massive force of 150,000 soldiers, and reconfirmed his alliances with the Genoan merchants and the Lithuanians, who agreed to contribute reinforcements.[30] While Mamai was waiting for the latter at a camp near the Kulikovo field on the Don River in early September 1380, however, Dmitrii's forces attacked, and despite their inferior numbers were able once again to inflict a decisive defeat. There was, however, a hitherto unappreciated element to Dmitrii's victory, for Gumilev maintained that he had a vital ally, in the form of Mamai's chief opponent Tokhtamysh, the leader of the White Horde. Tokhtamysh was a genuine descendant of Chingis Khan, Gumilev explained, and thus unlike Mamai represented a legitimate contender for the leadership of the Golden Horde. In contrast to Mamai, moreover, he remained faithful to the traditionally friendly orientation of the Golden Horde toward the Russians. The Russians themselves recognized all this, Gumilev claimed, and thus supported him in his opposition to Mamai.[31] Tokhtamysh's intervention was critical, for Mamai's defeat at Kulikovo in 1380 did not put an end to the latter's hostile machinations. Already in the following year he was regrouping his forces and preparing for a further assault on Moscow. Before he was able to complete these preparations, however, he was preemptively attacked and now definitively routed in a battle on the Kalka River, not by the Russians but by Tokhtamysh himself. In defeat, Mamai fled to Crimea, where he was assassinated by his own Genoan allies. Thus it was the decisive intervention on the part of the Mongol White Horde, Gumilev asserted, that ultimately saved Moscow.

At this point, however, historical events took a turn that would appear to undermine Gumilev's interpretation. Having defeated Mamai, Tokhtamysh turned his attention back to Moscow and led an attack of his own on the city in 1282. His initial assault was beaten back, and so he laid siege to the city. When his forces finally gained access, they proceeded to slaughter the population, and tens of thousands perished. Here, it would seem, was incontrovertible evidence of the rapacious brutality of the Mongol *igo* that in reality had characterized relations with ancient Russia. Again, Gumilev did not deny the historical veracity of these events, but again he found a way to explain them that fit with his emphasis on the fundamental positive complementarity between the groups involved. The real culprits in this carnage, he explained, were not the Mongols but the Russian princes of Suzdal, who saw Moscow as a competitor and were particularly hostile to Dmitrii. They deliberately lied to Tokhtymash in saying that Dmitrii intended to betray him by forming an alliance with Lithuania, and the Mongol khan—generously described by Gumilev as a "good, simple, and uneducated man"—believed them. And this was not all. Gumilev argued further that the Russian inhabitants of Moscow themselves were culpable and bore responsibility for their awful fate in the Tatar pogrom. He described the following discouraging scenario.

> Tokhtamysh's raid would not have been brutal at all if not for the character of the city's population. . . . Just what did the townspeople want? To drink and carouse. For this reason, the besieged population of Moscow headed for the cellars of the boyars, broke open the locks, seized the barrels of honey, beer, and wine, and proceeded to get very drunk. In this state, to show just how "fearless" they were, they mounted the city walls, shouted profane epithets at the Tatars and made vulgar gestures. Now, the Tatars, especially those from Siberia, were easily offended, and they became extremely angry at the behavior of the Muscovites.[32]

Gumilev's clear implication was that the eventual Tatar excesses were not at all surprising—certainly they could not be seen as evidence of any elemental hostility toward the Slavic-Russian population. Dmitrii himself was apparently of this view, Gumilev suggested, for after the hostilities he reconfirmed the alliance with the Golden Horde, pledged loyalty to Tokhtamysh, and was duly appointed Grand Duke of Vladimir and the Mongols' principal tax collector among the Russians.

Thus Gumilev's Eurasianist reading of ancient Russian history completely contravened the broadly held view of Kulikovo as a victory secured at great odds against a cruel oppressor from the Asiatic steppes. It also contravened the view of the classical Eurasianists themselves, who despite their own radical revisionism never challenged the dominant view of the Mongol conquest as an extravagantly devastating and shattering experience for ancient Russia. For them, the *igo* image was an appropriate characterization of the experience, and they were entirely comfortable using it.[33] In arguing against this perspective, Gumilev maintained that the struggle at Kulikovo had not been "between 'forest' and 'steppe,' 'Europe' and 'Asia,' or 'Russians' and 'Tatars,'" but rather between the Russians and their steppe allies on the one hand and their mutual enemies in Western Europe, Islam and the Jews on the other.[34]

Russian Ethnogenesis as a Russo-Tatar Synthesis

There was, however, one very important point on which Gumilev concurred entirely with the standard interpretation. This was the identification of Kulikovo as a critical formative experience for Russia, a sort of national catharsis in which the disparate fragments of the nation that remained after the smashing of Kievan Rus' were roused for the first time to join forces, with the result that they were galvanized into a single mass that was to become the modern Russian nation. Through this cathartic experience, Gumilev observed, Ancient Rus' "was transformed into Great Russia."[35]

> I believe that at the Battle of Kulikovo the Russian (*russkii*) *etnos* was born. . . . The soldiers who fought there did not [identify their homeland] as Vladimir, Moscow, Suzdal, Tver, or Smolensk. They were not representatives of disconnected principalities, all struggling against each other, but rather were Russians (*russkie*), Great Russians (*velikorossy*), who set out entirely consciously to defend their world, their Fatherland, and their [shared] cultural-philosophical understanding of life.[36]

For Gumilev, this amounted to a new "Russian ethnic entity," which formed in the context of an existential and elemental struggle for its very existence.

But even in this regard, Gumilev's neo-Eurasianist argument followed a radically revisionist line. The ethnogenetic process that was initiated at this time was not limited to Russian populations that descended from Kievan Rus'. Rather, the Russian nation formed as a combination or confluence of three principal components: Slavic, Finno-Ugric, and Tatar (itself a mixture of Turkic and Mongolian elements).[37] Of the three, Gumilev maintained, the first and third were the most important. The ethnogenetic amalgamation of these two groups commenced already in the early thirteenth century, when as we have noted Uzbek's forced conversion of the Golden Horde to Islam caused numerous Nestorian Tatars to flee to Rus'. Here, Gumilev explained, they were offered generous refuge by Ivan I (1288–1340). Ivan actively supported their integration into the Russian society, the most effective means of which was intermarriage. The Tatar warrior-refugees "sought to marry Russian princesses, while young Tatar women converted to Orthodoxy in order to marry Russian boyars." Such conversions were widespread, and they played a critical role in the ethnogenetic process. As a result, Gumilev explained, "a mixed (*smeshannyi*) *etnos*" already began to take shape, which the experience of Kulikovo would further galvanize. "In the place of old Kievan Rus' emerged an entirely new Great Russian *etnos*—Muscovite Rus'—with its own ethnosocial system."[38]

Thus, in Gumilev's scheme the interaction between the Slavic Rus' and Tatars was not merely a fraternal alliance but actually amounted to a full ethnic fusion—a "*sliianie* of Orthodox and Nestorians" in which the two groups merged and then together were transformed into something entirely different.[39] Borrowing an expression from Nikolai Trubetskoi, he maintained that the real "legacy of Ghengis Khan" was not "the threatening *bunchuki* [an ornamental horsetail that served as a sign of authority] of the Mongol princes but rather the Christian crosses that they wore next to their bodies as they wed the young beauties of Rostov, Riazan, and Moscow."[40] In other words, this legacy was not the destruction of ancient Rus' but the co-creation of a modern Russian nation and *etnos*. In this way, Russia began its modern existence as a "Russian-Tatar country" (*russko-tatarskaia strana*), and has retained this character ever since.[41] Ultimately, Gumilev described the close relationship between ancient Rus' and the Golden Horde "not as the subjugation (*pokorenie*) of Rus' by the Golden Horde" but as an "ethnic symbiosis, a union between two major states that needed each other."[42]

Russian Nationalism in the Late Soviet Period

Until the late 1980s, Gumilev remained well outside the mainstream of Soviet scholarship, marginalized within the academic establishment, and indeed routinely condemned by it. As we have noted, only fragments and brief summaries of his historical accounts were available, and it is safe to say that his neo-Eurasianist retelling of Russia's ancient encounters with the Golden Horde remained largely unknown to the general public, even as the Kulikovo celebrations of the early 1980s focused unprecedented attention on the subject. There was one exception, however—a grouping that was not only aware of Gumilev's revisionist historiography but also had strong views of its own about it and offered highly spirited reactions. This interest came from a Russian nationalist tendency that had emerged in the 1960s and was eventually able to attract significant support among Russia's political and cultural elites.[43]

Sympathizers met regularly in so-called Russian clubs to discuss issues that they felt related especially to Russian ethnonational interests, and at least two influential journals—*Nash sovremennik* and *Molodaia gvardiia*—were broadly supportive of their concerns.[44] The Russian nationalist reception of Gumilev is quite revealing for what it says about the ideological tensions of the late Soviet period, but no less importantly for the fact that this Eurasianist "debate" among Russian nationalists in the early 1980s anticipated some of the important characteristics of neo-Eurasianism as it developed into a genuinely popular movement a decade later.

The nationalist reaction to Gumilev's historiography must be understood in the context of the tendency's more general perspectives and concerns. The movement had crystallized out of the ferment of the post-Stalinist period as a reaction to fundamental aspects of Soviet society and official policy that the nationalists believed to pose a direct threat to the welfare of ethnic Russia and its prospects for future development. On the one hand, these involved the "affirmative action" policies that had been pursued by the Soviet state since the 1920s on behalf of the country's non-Russian nationalities.[45] The nationalists were convinced that these policies not only benefited these nationalities disproportionately in terms of economic prosperity and political power, but that they did so at direct cost to ethnic Russians. This pervasive sense of ethnonational disadvantage and discrimination was exacerbated by demographic research in the 1970s that confirmed a far more robust rate of population growth among non-Russian nationalities (in particular in the Central Asian republics), and predicted that the proportion of Russians in the Soviet population would soon fall below 50 percent. With this, Russians would for the first time in their history become a minority group within the Russian state.[46]

Russian nationalists were also apprehensive about a new official line on nationality policy that was promulgated from the early 1960s. Under the conditions of ever-greater economic development and integration, the Communist Party authorities maintained, ethnonational differences between the Soviet peoples were beginning to fade, and within the foreseeable future would dissolve completely. This would lead to *sliianie*, that is, the merging and fusion of all these groups into a single inter- and supranational *sovetskii narod*, or "Soviet people," representing a "new historical, social, and international community (*obshchnost'*), possessing a single territory, economy, culture that is socialist in content, and a united all-national (*obshchenarodnoe*) state."[47] For the Russian nationalists, all of these factors combined to create an existential challenge, not only to ethnic Russia's traditionally dominant position in the Soviet polity but indeed to its very survival. The unprecedented perception of victimization and threat was expressed in the new concept of "Russophobia," coined by the dissident mathematician Igor Shafarevich, with the associated belief that fear or indeed hatred of ethnic Russians had become a dominant social and political attitude.[48] The nationalists of the late Soviet period demanded the reassertion of what one leading proponent called the "organic unity" and *monolitnost'* of Russia's traditional forms of *gosudarstvennost'*, or state life—a return, in other words, to the legacy of a powerful and highly centralized imperial state structure, which had been undermined by the increasing power and assertiveness of non-Russian nationalities.[49] Although this union should be voluntary and beneficial for all parties, it was imperative that ethnic Russia be accorded a special status and special role in it, a role that derived directly from Russia's historical function as leader of the state's formation. This legacy demonstrated the enduring "moral and political supremacy" of ethnic Russians and confirmed the legitimacy of the nationalist quest to reestablish Russia's traditional preeminence and role as national leader.[50] "In this state," declared a nationalist manifesto, "the Russian people must indeed become the ruling nation."[51]

Given these particular concerns, it can be readily appreciated that the nationalists were fully mobilized by the Kulikovo celebrations in the early 1980s. As Yitzhak Brudny's authoritative study indicates, the victory at Kulikovo had become one of Russian nationalism's principal cultural symbols in the late Soviet period—the occasion of its six-hundred-year anniversary even represented something of a defining moment for them.[52] The importance of the memorialization project can be measured among other things in the abundance of historical studies and popular commentaries they produced about Kulikovo, all of which repeated the same general line regarding its significance for the Russian nation. The domination by the Golden Horde had "brought countless misfortunes to the Russian people," interrupted the country's historical development for centuries, and left an indelible scar on its national psychology.[53] The eventual casting off of the Mongol yoke at Kulikovo represented a moment of intense national catharsis and a profound act of national redemption and liberation. It was animated by the selflessness of the Russian warriors, their fearless resistance to their Tatar oppressors, and their glorious assertion of national independence for the Russian people. The political formation that took shape after the decline of the Golden Horde—first consolidated around the principality of Muscovy and then growing into a great transcontinental empire—was dominated at all times by the Great Russian *etnos*. As Muscovy's "leading" nationality, ethnic Russia provided the creative impetus and initiative across the centuries and thus played the role of the "state-forming" (*gosudarstvennoobrazuiushchii*) element. The grand culmination of this process was plain for all to see in the present, for "the multinational Soviet people were welded together forever by *velikaia Rus'*," in other words ethnic Russia.[54] This, maintained Dmitrii Likhachev, was the symbolic value of Kulikovo for the Russian national memory: a *lieu de mémoire* "as holy to us as the field of Borodino or the land of Stalingrad."[55] And of course, this nationalist narrative about Kulikovo had everything to do with the present day. Under the foil offered by the extreme historical remoteness of the events in question, it provided an ideal discursive field upon which Russian nationalists could openly identify and denounce the pernicious challenges that they believed non-Russian nationalities posed to ethnic Russia's survival, as well as the natural historical role of the latter as creator and leader of the modern Russian state.

For the Russian nationalists, Lev Gumilev represented a profound enigma. On the one hand, they had a great deal of appreciation for certain aspects of his work, and he enjoyed the support of a number of influential figures within the nationalist ranks. His elaborate theories about ethnic groups as organic and biological entities were praised by many nationalists, who saw them as a "scientific" basis for their own strongly essentialist perspectives, and they seemed to confirm nationalist apprehensions about the future survival of the Russian ethnic organism. Lengthy extracts from his still-unpublished work on ethnogenesis circulated in samizdat form and stimulated considerable discussion in nationalist circles. Along with this, the nationalists were extremely interested in his reconstructions of ancient history, specifically his history of the Khazars and their interactions with Kievan Rus'. Gumilev had sought to demonstrate how the former had been subverted in the eighth century by an incursion of foreign Jewish merchantry, under whose pernicious influence an innocent steppe nation was corrupted into malignant ethnic deformity. Gumilev's historical reconstructions were important in that they once again provided the nationalists with what seemed to be a credible scientific-scholarly basis for the anti-Semitism that was a fundamental motivation for their movement.[56]

But if the nationalists welcomed Gumilev's Khazar historiography, they had a very different reaction to his interpretation of Kulikovo. His radical revisionism—in regard to both the actual facts of the historical record and their significance for the development of Russian nationhood—obviously contravened their own perspective and offended their nationalist sensibilities to the very core. On the one hand, in a stroke he dismissed the entire legacy of primordial struggle and heroic resistance to Asiatic oppressors that they cherished as the Russian nation's baptism in fire and one of its greatest historical accomplishments. At the same time, Gumilev's account did not offer any basis for prioritizing ethnic Russia as a preeminent nationality or first among equals. Indeed, the opposite was the case. For Gumilev, the historical collaboration of Russia's nationalities in a shared destiny was not the result of any one group's proactive leadership, but rather had been a natural and organic development based on mutually shared *komplimentarnost'*. To the present, Russians had coexisted peacefully with the steppe peoples, and indeed all other nationalities of the empire in a state of symbiosis—that is to say mutual understanding, affection, and support. Although Gumilev made little attempt to spell out the implications of his historical scenarios for the present day, it was clear that his ideal for Soviet society—or at least for its Slavic-Turkic axis—was a genuine fraternity of equally enfranchised *etnosy*, among whom there could be no "first among equals." All in all, as one of Gumilev's supporters later remembered, Gumilev was ultimately not accepted by the nationalists precisely because "he was a convinced Eurasianist."[57]

The considerable ideological stakes of these contending historical interpretations were confirmed by the harshness of the reactions to Gumilev. The displeasure of the nationalists became apparent well before the Kulikovo celebrations themselves, in an acerbic review by Boris Rybakov of Gumilev's book *Searches for an Imaginary Kingdom*. An eminent and politically powerful specialist on ancient Russia, Rybakov was the deputy dean of Moscow State University and director of the Academy of Sciences Institute of Russian History. He was an outspoken advocate of Russia's historical independence from Western influences and enjoyed considerable popularity and influence in nationalist circles.[58] Rybakov was scandalized by Gumilev's arguments. He rejected the assertion that relations between Rus' and the steppe peoples prior to the incursions of the Golden Horde had been cooperative, peaceful, and benign. All of the historical evidence offered by the Chronicles points precisely to the opposite conclusion, he insisted, namely, that the nomads had always been the scourge of ancient Russia and had brought it nothing but misfortune and ruin. Rybakov was particularly outraged by Gumilev's alternative interpretation of *The Song of Igor's Campaign* as the traitorous work of a thirteenth-century Russian turncoat in the service of the pro-Western camp, and he asserted his conclusions with striking ferocity. Gumilev's historical deductions were a "masquerade" presented "without proof, analysis, or evidence." He could elaborate them only through the "falsification of history," the "monstrous distortion" (*chudovishchnoe iskazhenie*) of historical sources and the "dishonest manipulation" (*nedobrosovestnaia podtasovka*) of historical facts.[59]

Rybakov's declamatory tirade was however merely a foretaste of what was to come during the Kulikovo celebrations themselves. In Brudny's estimation, Gumilev's historiographical heresies "provoked the most heated debate" of this entire period, as leading figures from the nationalist movement presented extensive condemnations of his views.[60] The most significant of these came from Vladimir Chivilikhin, an environmental activist and popular historian, and Apollon Kuz'min, an idiosyncratic historian and frequent contributor to nationalist publications who later in the decade would be an important supporter of the anti-Semitic organization Pamiat'.[61] Chivilikhin and Kuz'min were outraged by Gumilev's assertions, and both wrote major denunciations of his work.[62] Like Rybakov, the two historians objected most fundamentally to Gumilev's positive and benign characterization of relations between the Russians and the Golden Horde. In point of historical fact, they maintained, the tribulations of the Mongol conquest were comparable to those of the Second World War, and the Tatar domination that ensued was a "harsh regime of plunder and genocide (*genotsid*)." How would Russians who suffered through the battles for Stalingrad feel if they knew that, six hundred years from now, historians would write off their horrific experience in Gumilevian terms as "a couple of successful raids" by German fascists?[63]

Gumilev's critics also questioned his naturalist perspective on the nature of ethnicity, claiming that he attempted to explain history in terms of "vulgar-materialist" geographical determinism and denying outright that such a phenomenon as *passionarnost'* even existed. "Human communities are not hordes of lemmings," they mocked, and maintained that ancient Russian history was to be explained not in terms of "climatic cycles or the *passionarnost'* of the region" but in more familiar terms by "deep economic, social, and other objective historical processes."[64] They also flatly rejected Gumilev's assertion of a primal ethnogenetic symbiosis between Slavs and Turks, and were particularly scandalized by what they described as Gumilev's "Russophobic" assertion that the "redemptive (*spasitel'nyi*) Tatar invasion" served to "breathe new life into Rus'" by infusing it with new sources of *passionarnost'*.[65] The murder of Russian princes, the enslavement of the people, and the wholesale destruction of their cultural heritage, they wrote bitterly—"that's what the symbiosis of Rus' and the Golden Horde actually amounted to!"[66]

Kuz'min and Chivilikhin readily recognized the Eurasianist inspiration in Gumilev's thinking, and took the occasion to denounce the entire tradition of classical Eurasianism. They identified the classical Eurasianists as renegade White Guards (perhaps in part as a reminder for readers who might well never have heard of them), and maintained that they, like Gumilev, had similarly exaggerated the role of geography and natural law in their historical explanations. Like Gumilev, moreover, the classical Eurasianists sought to justify the Tatar yoke by identifying as virtuous historical actors, forces that in fact had been nothing more than "oppressors and hangmen." By drawing on national historiographies hostile to Russia—most notably the "anti-Russian tendency" of the Ukrainian nationalist historian M. S. Hrushevsky—the Eurasianist version of ancient Russian history actively betrayed ethnic Russia's genuine national interests. Simply put, like Gumilev himself, the Eurasianists expounded the "most vile form of *russofobiia*, much more dangerous than the notorious Norman theory" about the origins of Russia.[67] Indeed, in their view, Gumilev took this pernicious *russofobiia* yet one step further. Not content with spinning tendentious and flawed scholarly theories about Russia's ancient past, they accused him of actively siding in the present day with non-Russian nationalities in their struggle against ethnic Russia in the USSR. In the best traditions of Soviet conspiriology, Kuz'min darkly intimated that Gumilev had developed his "anti-Russian tendency" through his personal collusions with Tatar nationalist historians and also—quite remarkably, in view of Gumilev's own intense and very well-known anti-Semitism—with "Zionist agents." And in their own day, they pointed out, the Tatars were making active use of his incessant "juxtaposition of benevolent Mongols to Russian savages" to support their own arguments against the "myth" of a Mongol yoke.[68]

Nationalist Support for Eurasianism

Although Chivilikhin's and Kuz'min's critiques of Gumilev's historical scenario represented the dominant view of Russian nationalism, his alternative interpretation of ancient Russian history did receive some support from voices within the nationalist camp. One of these was Dmitrii Balashov, a folklorist and prolific writer of historical fiction. Balashov was a particular favorite in nationalist circles, a frequent contributor to the nationalist journals *Molodaia gvardiia* and *Nash sovremennik*, and a sought-after speaker at the Russian clubs.[69] From the 1970s to the early 1990s, Balashov published a series of novels that recounted the story of the formation of the Russian state and nation in the thirteenth and fourteenth centuries. To judge by their considerable sales success—Brudny estimates that nearly eight hundred thousand copies were sold in total[70]—Balashov's novels were extremely popular, and their historical veracity was confirmed by Likhachev himself, who wrote an introduction to one of them.[71]

It was however not from Likachev but from Gumilev himself that Balashov took his own interpretation of Russian history. He was a close associate and personal friend of Gumilev and—by his own admission—unquestioningly accepted the authority of his mentor's historical interpretation.[72] This is apparent, for example, in Balashov's 1977 novel *Mladshii syn* [The younger son] set in the time of ancient Rus'. Here the Gumilevian scenario is readily recognizable: the passionary decline of pre-Mongol Kievan Rus', the natural empathy and complementarity between the Slavs and the steppe nomads, and the option for an alliance with the latter against the Catholics of the West, described as "yet more terrifying than the Mongol Horde." Echoing Gumilev, Balashov maintained that the modern Russian nation was born out of an "eruption of spiritual energy of the people" in the crucible of Kulikovo, which gave rise to the Muscovite state and shaped the subsequent course of Russian history.[73] In an afterword, Balashov warmly acknowledged the extensive editorial input of Gumilev.[74]

Balashov himself seems not to have appreciated the contentiousness of his historical account for the nationalist narrative. The broad and apparently uncontroversial popularity of his work, moreover, suggests that the reading public as well did not readily pick up on the nuances of the Gumilevian perspective that inspired it—or at any rate did not find them particularly objectionable. This was not the case in regard to the engagement with Gumilev on the part of the noted literary historian and critic Vadim Kozhinov. Kozhinov was a visible and important participant in the Russian nationalist revival in the 1970s and 1980s. Like Gumilev a resident of Leningrad, he knew him personally, and although their relationship was not close he was influenced nonetheless by Gumilev's historical interpretations. As was the case with other nationalists, Kozhinov as well was interested most of all in Gumilev's highly charged arguments about the deleterious effects of the Jewish Khazars on ancient Russia, a subject to which Kozhinov himself devoted considerable attention.[75] Along with this, however, Kozhinov was beguiled by the Eurasianist account of relations between ancient Rus' and the Golden Horde. Kozhinov's reactions represent an important counterpoint to the nationalist critique of Gumilev we have just seen, for they provide the first suggestion that there could be a positive and constructive resonance between Eurasianism and mainstream Russian ethnonational sentiment. Kozhinov first formulated his ideas on the subject in an essay published in *Nash sovremennik* in 1981, and then returned to the subject in the following decade.[76]

Kozhinov's perspective, like Gumilev's, was founded on an intense antipathy to the West, and like Gumilev he viewed Russian history most fundamentally as a dramatic struggle of Russian national interests against Western influence. He referred approvingly to the work of classical Eurasianism in this regard, above all to the critique of Western cosmopolitanism developed by Nikolai Trubetskoi in his *Europe and Humankind*.[77] Kozhinov's explanation of the existential significance of this struggle for the evolution of the Russian nation, however, came directly from Gumilev. He accepted Gumilev's argument for the close interaction between ancient Rus' and the nomadic peoples of the steppe. It was the latter—and "not the Normans, or the Varangians or even Byzantium"—who had exercised the "most powerful influence" on the young Russian nation from the ninth to the eleventh centuries.[78] Referring directly to Gumilev's work, he argued that this fateful association found its grand culmination some three centuries later, on the Kulikovo field. Far from representing a conflict between Russians and their alleged Mongol-Tatar adversaries from the Asiatic steppes, Kulikovo actually witnessed an alliance of these two groups, united by their common opposition to enemies from the

West. He formulated his conclusion in terms that were unmistakably Gumilevian. "The struggle at Kulikovo, which [today] is understood by everyone exclusively as the turning back of a specifically 'Asiatic' attack by Russian forces, was actually a struggle of the Russian people above all with the aggression of global cosmopolitanism."[79]

Critically, however, Kozhinov did not accept Gumilev's ascription of an ethnogenetic significance to Russia's early interaction with the nomadic steppe forces and their shared struggle against the West. The events at Kulikovo did not initiate a process of ethnic formation, and they did not result in an ethnic union of any sort between the different national groups involved. While he praised Gumilev highly for "having done a great deal" to clarify the true nature of relations between the Russians and Tatar-Mongols, he criticized him for overemphasizing their "mutual interests," and flatly rejected the suggestion of a symbiosis between them as "unacceptable" (*nepriemlemyi*). Moreover, the fact that they shared a natural opposition to Western aggression did not mean that their own relationship was entirely free from strife. To the contrary, and in a substantial nod to the mainstream interpretation of these events, Kozhinov affirmed the essential hostility between the Russians and the Mongols. The latter had indeed been cruel conquerors, and it was true that their domination had caused great suffering to the Russian people.[80] Kozhinov's most important difference with Gumilev, however, related to the genesis of Russian *etnos* or nation. Rather than recognizing Kulikovo as a rupture with ancient Russian history and a new ethnogenetic Eurasian beginning, Kozhinov insisted that the unbroken primordial (*iznachal'nyi*) continuity of the Russian *etnos* dated back at least to the Nestorian Chronicles of the eleventh and twelfth centuries.[81] This meant that Russia's special ethnic qualities were already well-formed by the fourteenth century, and that Gumilev's interpretation was arranged backward. Gumilev maintained that an ethnic symbiosis between "Russians and Turks" had been consummated at Kulikovo, and that the Russian nation subsequently developed its fundamental ethnic qualities on the basis of this symbiotic interaction. While accepting that a positive rapprochement of some sort had taken place at Kulikovo, Kozhinov insisted that this combination was made possible by specifically Russian ethnic qualities that had developed long before any contact with the Golden Horde.[82] The Russian nation was not created in the 1380s, as Gumilev taught. Rather, the positive interethnic engagement at Kulikovo took place because of a singular Russian ethnic predisposition that had been formed in a much earlier period.

It was these primordial and exclusively Russian ethnic qualities that were most important for Kozhinov, and it was only in terms of them that Russia's Eurasian destiny could be understood. Among them, one quality in particular stood out—Russia's *vsechelovechnost'*, or its universalism and pan-humanism

—which gave Russian culture its unique capacity "for genuine fraternity with any nation." Since the time of Petr Chaadaev, Kozhinov maintained, Russian thinkers had argued that *vsechelovechnost'* represented the defining feature of Russian culture, setting it apart from all other cultures and at the same time providing it with an enduring world-historical mission. This mission was nothing less than the reconciliation of all humanity, in particular the bringing together of East and West. Russian culture represented "a sort of spiritual bridge between Europe and Asia" endowed with the immense power of its "universalist elementalism."[83] But in place of the grand projects of Chaadaev, Dostoevsky, and Vladimir Solov'ev, all of whom saw Russia at the center of pan-human reconciliation of genuinely universal dimensions, Kozhinov saw the ultimate fulfillment of Russia's *vsechelovechnost'* in a more limited, Eurasian framework. It consisted in the fostering of interethnic interaction with the steppe peoples and its subsequent empire building, which culminated grandly in the Soviet civilization of his own day. The creation of this civilization was not the result of a spontaneous historical-geographical intermingling among the groups occupying these vast continental spaces, as Gumilev taught, but rather was the entirely deliberate product of the national qualities and the dominating organizational initiative of ethnic Russia alone.

In effect, Kozhinov sought to bring Gumilev's Eurasianist perspective into line with the fundamental concerns of the Russian nationalist movement of his day. Specifically, he tried to mobilize certain aspects of Eurasianism in a manner that could support the two key nationalist concerns we have noted— the autonomy and exclusivity of ethnic Russia on the one hand, and its unique position of preeminence and authority among all Soviet nationalities on the other. This involved replacing Gumilev's picture of even-handed interethnic fraternity with an essentially instrumentalist and power-based understanding of Russia's relationship with other nationalities. For Kozhinov, the latter were significant above all by virtue of the opportunities they provided across history for Russians to demonstrate their own most positive ethnonational qualities, namely, the ability to create and maintain an imperial state capable of "civilizing" those who needed it and more generally providing security and welfare for all. And this civilizing activity, in turn, served to distinguish the humanity and justice of the ethnic Russian empire builders from the rapacity and reckless destructiveness of their imperial competitors in Western Europe and North America.[84] For Kozhinov, the universality of the Russian language among the Soviet peoples provided the ultimate demonstration of the natural fraternity of Russia's many different nations as well as the equally natural and legitimate preeminence of ethnic Russia over them. "All the nations of Russia are equal (*ravnopravnyi*) in their possession of Russian poetry, and of course Russian culture in general. . . . They all shared equally in the creation of an [ethnic] Russian state (*russkaia gosudarstvennost'*)."[85] It is in precisely these terms that Kozhinov understood the significance of *vsechelovechnost'*.

Ultimately, Kozhinov's entire Eurasianist vision was formulated based on an unrelenting sense of Russian ethnonational exclusivity. He spoke about a "Eurasian duality" (*dvoistvennost'*) that allowed the Russians to engage and interact with East and West, but understood this quality to be "precisely an ethnic Russian (*russkoe*) quality" that did not belong to any other Soviet nationality.[86] Genuine "Eurasians" were not, as Gumilev and the classical Eurasianists had taught, "ethnic Russians plus Turks, Finno-Ugric peoples and so on." On the contrary, it was really only ethnic Russia itself that could properly be called Eurasian: "It is *precisely and only* the ethnic Russian people (*russkii narod*) who are a Eurasian people." All of the other groups that make up the Russian state "are in their essence either European or Asiatic nations." They acquired whatever Eurasian features they may have "only in the 'magnetic field' (*magnitnoe pole*) of Russia," and once they have left this field they quickly revert back to their essential European or Asiatic type.[87] Indeed, in the early 1990s Kozhinov claimed that in the final analysis Russia's Eurasian essence would not be affected even if its links with these groups were dissolved.

> And for me personally, Eurasianism does not at all involve the fact that Russia (*Rossiia*) unites in itself Slavs on the one hand together with Turks, Mongols, and Islamic peoples on the other. In the final analysis, this is not so important. If a part of Russia were to be broken off in order to create a national ethnic-Russian state (*russkoe gosudarstvo*) . . . then this state would in no way cease to be Eurasian.[88]

Needless to say, such a vision was quite as heretical for Gumilev's Eurasianism as the latter's own Kulikovo historiography was for the likes of Chivilikhin and Kuz'min.

Over the course of the 1980s and early 1990s, Russian nationalism's evaluation of Eurasianism underwent a significant transformation. The skepticism and hostility documented in this chapter softened in many quarters into a more positive and receptive attitude, to the extent that eventually Eurasianism would become the dominating nationalist discourse described at the beginning of the chapter. A full account following this complex process into the post-Soviet period and down to the present day requires a separate examination. Here we may note that, as neo-Eurasianism gained ever broader support through the years of perestroika and finally emerged as a major political tendency after the collapse of the USSR, the original tensions with Russian nationalism that we have examined did not dissipate but continued to manifest themselves, albeit in a muted and nuanced form. A segment of nationalist opinion continued—and continues—to denounce Eurasianism in the spirit of Chivilikhin and Koz'min, denying the sort of symbiotic inter-ethnic connections that Gumilev and other Eurasianists identified and insisting on the need to maintain the autonomy and singularity of ethnic Russia at all costs.[89] But even among Russian nationalism's enthusiastic converts to Eurasianism, the tensions to which Kozhinov gave voice continue to characterize Eurasianist discourse. This relates above all to the specific position and role of ethnic Russia within the larger assembly of Eurasian peoples. Even a master ideologue such as Aleksandr Dugin cannot overcome an essential ambivalence on this question; indeed, he is yet more contradictory than Kozhinov. On the one hand, Dugin prioritizes the Great Russian *etnos* and accords it an entirely special significance in the creation and development of Eurasian civilization. Thus, ethnic Russia represented Eurasia's basic "civilizational constant" (*konstanta*), which across the ages has defined its essential political, social, and cultural forms. The development of the Russian state itself was a product of the special ethnic qualities of the Great Russians.[90] On the other hand, however, Dugin dismisses in a principled fashion the importance of ethnicity in the life of the state, which he insists is organized and ruled by geopolitical rather than ethnonational principles and imperatives. Ethnic Russia's leading civilizational role, in other words, does not necessarily translate into a position of special authority within the Eurasian state of the future.[91]

THE PARADOXICAL LEGACY OF EURASIANISM IN CONTEMPORARY EURASIA

Marlene Laruelle

READERS of this work will perhaps note above all Eurasianism's unsuspected diversity, a diversity that plays out in terms of intellectual lineages, scholarly orientations, and disciplinary methods, but also in terms of the individual trajectories of its main figures. This feeling is heightened upon encountering the multifaceted nature of the Eurasianist motif in the post-Soviet space and Eurasianism's paradoxical legacy in contemporary Russia.

Plural Neo-Eurasianisms

Are we, today, to speak of Eurasianism, or rather to define a specific category, that of neo-Eurasianism? Should we use the latter in the singular, neo-Eurasianism, or in the plural, neo-Eurasianisms? To respect intellectual lineages and historical contexts, here I define Eurasianism as the interwar movement, and speak about neo-Eurasianisms to describe the current movements that refer, one way or another, to this idea of Eurasia.

Eurasianism and neo-Eurasianisms have a complex relationship, and the impression at first glance of a direct continuity from the emigration to the post-Soviet period is debatable. Today's neo-Eurasianists have an ambivalent attitude toward the founding fathers. Lev Gumilev in his time, then more recently the Moscow State University philosophy professor Aleksandr Panarin

(1940–2003), and the fascist geopolitician Aleksandr Dugin (1962), as well as theorists of Turkic or Kazakhstani Eurasianism, often speak harshly of the original Eurasianists. Very few of them see themselves as disciples of the old masters, who they more often consider, at best, to have only partially antici-pated their own, much more accomplished ideas.

Conceptual differences between Eurasianism and neo-Eurasianisms are also important. First of all, Russian neo-Eurasianism does not share the ex-altation of the East so prominent among the original Eurasianists, who were strongly marked by Romantic Orientalism. Nor does it express any partic-ular sympathy for the cultures of Central Asia and Mongolia. Non-Russian neo-Eurasianists alone valorize their own cultures, branding them in a fash-ion similar to original Eurasianism by exalting both local ethnicities and their "symbiosis" with Russian culture. Neo-Eurasianism's views on history and geography are also less sophisticated than those of the founding fathers. No neo-Eurasianists have taken up Petr Savitskii's idea that the "rhythms of Russian history" govern the dialectic between forest and steppe. There have been no followers of his thinking about Russia's *spatiality* as the primordial justification of Eurasian unity, nor of his interest in the idea of a geographi-cal *symmetry* of empire and a *geometrical* rationality of Eurasian space. Neo-Eurasianisms have also radicalized the paradoxical determinism of interwar Eurasianism, upsetting the balance that the founding fathers had struck be-tween fatalism and liberty, between divine will and human choice.

Neo-Eurasianism*s* are diverse in space. The implosion of the Soviet Union also imploded narratives on the theme of Eurasia. They are to be found in present-day Russia but also in some of the other post-Soviet republics, in par-ticular Kazakhstan, where it functions as an official doctrine for a state that presents itself as an encounter between East and West, Europe and Asia, Rus-sia and the East, which places Kazakhs on a pedestal as the brilliant legacy of its location at the crossroads of worlds. Using the model of a *matrioshka* (Russian nesting doll), which served so well to describe the federal character of Russia, many neo-Eurasianisms are also present in the Russian space: in autonomous republics, some political figures and scholarly groups elaborate their own local versions of neo-Eurasianism. They inflect it with local topics and wield it as a tool that allows for claims of localism and of loyalty to the Russian state. Tatarstan has been at the forefront of this trend, followed by Yakutia-Sakha, and multiple local variations are taking shape in Bashkorto-stan, Buryatia, Tuva, Kalmykia, and so on.

Neo-Eurasianism*s* are also temporally diverse insofar as their narratives have evolved over the past two decades. At the start of the 1990s they were used primarily to compensate for the Soviet collapse because they offered a way of thinking about the suddenly fragmented post-Soviet space as a unity without using the reference to Communism. In the 2000s, the Kremlin's rehabilitation of the Soviet past as the key common dominator of Russian society, together with nostalgia for late-Soviet decades and its cultural classics, detracted from the specificity of neo-Eurasianisms. They made their return, however, with the emergence of the Eurasian Union project—an old scheme flagged by Kazakhstan's president Nursultan Nazarbayev in 1994, but updated to fit current tastes by Vladimir Putin in 2011. The establishing of the Russia–Belarus–Kazakhstan Customs Union, the first functional organization promoting post-Soviet reintegration, and the launching of the Eurasian Economic Union in January 2015, push neo-Eurasianist narratives to take on a more pragmatic color.

Neo-Eurasianisms are also diverse in terms of the figures that embody them. Lev Gumilev, who died in 1992, continues to enjoy unique posthumous prestige in Russia as well as in republics such as Kazakhstan. There, the national university of the new capital city, Astana, was named after him, but was somewhat overshadowed by the creation of the new university organized on the Anglo-Saxon model of a globalized campus, this time named after President Nazarbayev. Aleksandr Panarin, deceased in 2003, developed a form of neo-Eurasianism that is probably closest to that of the founding fathers in terms of its identity themes, its notion of Russia's relation to Europe and to Asia, and the religious philosophy underlying its geopolitical vision of Russia. However, the neo-Eurasianism field is dominated by one figure, namely, Aleksandr Dugin, in terms of both the academic interest in him in North America and Europe and his media influence in Russia. Dugin is a prolific writer, but his ideas are chameleon-like, and draw on multiple doctrinal sources, of which Eurasianism is only one possible orientation. While Dugin has contributed to spreading the term "Eurasia" and to rehabilitating classical geopolitics in the manner of Karl Haushofer—according to whom the world is structured by the opposition between civilizations of the sea (thalassocracies) and civilizations of the land (tellurocracies)—he also plays a key role in importing into Russia West European far-right ideologies, and in establishing contacts with its main representatives, mostly in France, Belgium, Italy, and Spain, but also in Hungary.

Lastly, and unsurprisingly, neo-Eurasianisms are diverse in their thematic foci. In many of the Russian Federation's autonomous republics, the Eurasianist motif is inflected by the theme of ethnicity; it is used to celebrated the unique character of the ethnos and its harmonious integration into a larger political ensemble. This gives a central place to the Gumilevian prism, and in this case, indigenous neo-Eurasianism is contrasted with ethnically Russian neo-Eurasianism, the latter often being judged too "chauvinistic" or purely "imperialist." In Dugin's neo-Eurasianism, Eurasia is seen as a

Russian-style formulation of the "Third Way." Like the German theories of Conservative Revolution that were contemporaneous with Eurasianism and inspired its founding fathers in the interwar period, this Third Way refutes both liberalism and communism, aiming to be a version of fascism "with clean hands," absolved of the crimes of World War Two or of the postfascist regimes that followed it in Europe or Latin America.

Just as its predecessor, neo-Eurasianisms zigzag between scholarly debates about identities and history, and political ideologies, and are characterized by blurry boundaries. An incredible incubator of ideas, the Eurasianist motif can be found in the most diverse forms: it can inspire literary writing, popular novels (the best-selling science fiction series *Etnogenez*), contemporary art (Eurasianism inspired the painter Aleksey Belyaev-Gintovt, a recipient of the Kandinsky Prize in 2008), and conspiracy theories as well as alternative history (for instance, Anatoly Fomenko's New Chronology, which attempts to demonstrate that Russia was at the origin of all the great ancient empires).

Do all of these neo-Eurasianisms and their derivatives share the same fundamental premises? Two can be indicated that constitute probably the only unchangeable core of an otherwise polymorphous ideology. The first one is that Russia is an empire, in the sense that the Russian nation and the Russian state do not totally overlap, which leaves open problematic interstices: part of what should be included in the nation (whatever its definition) is to be found outside the state, and some elements that are not always considered a part of the nation are inside state boundaries (internal others). The second premise is that Russia claims its right to the European legacy but refuses a status as epigone of Europe, which entails either that it exclude itself from Europe as a value, a political process, or geopolitical system, or else challenges it from the inside by affirming that it is an authentic Europe against a "false" one. This last element of the neo-Eurasianist discourse is at odds with the writings of classical, interwar Eurasianists.

Eurasia without Eurasianism?

However, the major development of the contemporary period is probably the unprecedented success of the term "Eurasia," whose influence on Eurasianism and neo-Eurasianisms as doctrine has been paradoxical.

The term "Eurasia" largely attained greater visibility for want of something better: it expresses conveniently, and in a rather intuitive way, the historical space of Russia and its "peripheries," and a certain geopolitical reality. The term contains a fundamental terminological ambiguity: Is it Europe *and* Asia, or *neither* Europe *nor* Asia? "Eurasia" was originally a geographical term used to designate countries located on the Euro-Asian tectonic plate, thus covering both Europe and Asia. Even in its restricted meaning of being neither Europe nor Asia, but a median space of Russia and its neighbors, however, the term does not inspire unanimity. It provoked debate on who did or did not in fact belong to it, and it is challenged as being Eurocentric (those standing at the doors of the European Union) or Russocentric (those that are part of the Russian orbit, whereas China would include Central Asia in its own neighborhood). The term has profitably replaced "post-Soviet" in many North American, European, and Asian academic institutions and international organizations, as a way to describe the post-Soviet space without referring openly to the Soviet legacy. Paradoxically, it is used to describe Russia *and* the new states as well as the new states *without* Russia. In this way, it is given adjectives ("Central Eurasia") to encompass all the "others" of Russia, both external others—Central Asia, South Caucasus, Mongolia—and internal ones—North Caucasian, Tatar, Bashkir, and Siberian cultures.

More striking still is the success of the term "Eurasia" within Russia, and consequently, among Russia's neighbors. In this instance, too, the term has found it easy to make a mark within a certain terminological vacuum, a situation in which it has offered a malleable enough notion enabling it to be adapted to shifting contexts and different realities. Under the label "Eurasia," it is in fact possible to express a geopolitical principle—that is, Russia's claim to be the "pivotal" state and "engine" of the post-Soviet world, and its right to oversee the strategic orientations of its neighbors. But the term can also be used to designate a philosophical principle—that is, Russia's status as the "other Europe," an already old notion expressed by the Slavophiles in the first half of the nineteenth century. In this latter case, Eurasia is above all a *mirror* of Europe and the West, a *response* to what is perceived as a challenge that would undermine Russianness, and an *alternative* to what is seen as the deadlock of liberalism as ideology and the West as a civilization. Lastly, the term "Eurasia" also points to a third dimension, that of memory, mourning, and commemoration. Through it Russian society can understand the imperial and Soviet experiences: it enables, in a complex and painful process, making peace with the lost past, closing these historical chapters, and at the same integrating them into a national grand narrative.

And it is probably the way that the term can inhabit the juncture of these different dimensions that explains its success and its instrumentalization by the Russian authorities. Indeed, when Vladimir Putin launched his Eurasian Union project, his speech articulated several dimensions. He proclaimed that reintegrating the post-Soviet space under its leadership is Russia's "natural" geopolitical destiny and that the country cannot be denied this vocation. He stated that the European Union (EU) has been a successful model to follow and that Russia should offer an "EU-like" construction to Eurasia, but also increasingly engage in a discourse criticizing liberal principles and call on Europe to remember its "true" (read: conservative) values. And, last but not least, he accelerated the previous trend of rehabilitating Russia's Soviet and, to a lesser extent, imperial past, in the hope that citizens' pride in their country and its legacy would be replicated as support for the regime.

Russia's actions in Ukraine in 2014 are part of this framework. Moscow clearly formulated what it would consider its red lines: Ukraine can be independent but only if "Finlandized"— that is, it must not adopt an anti-Russian profile. This red line has been crossed twice, both by discussing the association agreement with the EU and by succumbing to the Maidan revolution. The price to be paid is therefore twice as high: it had to lose part of its territory—Crimea—and to be destabilized by the creation of a new "frozen conflict" though secessionist movements in Donetsk and Lugansk. The significant support of the Russian population for the annexation of Crimea, which weakened even the liberal anti-Putin coalitions, marginal as they already were, again relies on this triple dimension of the Eurasia concept. In his annexation speech of March 18, 2014, Putin raised arguments that were geopolitical (Russia's legitimate role in Eurasia and its need to defend itself against possible NATO expansion), philosophical (Russia defending a universal right to self-determination coming from Europe), and memorial (Sevastopol as a symbol of Soviet and Russian imperial grandeur).

But what is the role of Eurasianisms in this Eurasia? Even if the founding fathers of Eurasianism have all been republished with large print runs at the beginning of the 1990s—as were all the great authors of the Russian Silver Age—and the interwar émigré culture was reintegrated into the national pantheon, they enjoy only success *de prestige*. In Kremlin circles, the preference is to refer to Nikolai Berdiaev, Konstantin Leont'ev, and Ivan Ilyin rather than Nikolai Trubetskoi or Petr Savitskii, who are not on Putin's communication gurus' list of "must-read" authors. In the autonomous republics and in Kazakhstan, the scholarly circles that celebrate Gumilev are much more interested in his concepts of ethnos and passionarity than in that of Eurasia, and they do not return to the founding fathers. Dugin borrows his entire repertoire from the German Conservative Revolution and from the French and Italian New Right far more than from the Eurasianist circles of the emigration. As for the high senior officials in charge of the Customs Union and Eurasian Union institutions, they derive inspiration from founding European texts such as Jean Monet's, or from Beijing's rhetoric of Chinese-style harmonious development, but not from Eurasianism.

Lastly, today's Eurasia is founded on a fundamental ambiguity—a nostalgia for empire *and* the fear of diversity. Russian society presents high rates of xenophobia—for close to a decade, all opinion surveys have confirmed that, irrespective of the question posed, about two-thirds of citizens would like to see a reduction in migration levels from the former Soviet southern republics. In this context, the notion, so important in classical Eurasianism, of Russia's inherent familiarity with Asia (although the ambiguities were several, including over which kind of Asia was decreed "compatible" with Russia's Eurasian destiny) disappeared from the majority of neo-Eurasianist repertoires. Central Asia, despite being a key piece in Russia's Eurasian Union project, is apprehended as a burden, not as a blessing, that Russia has to bear in order to protect itself against the West containment. The idea that Asia is calling Russia toward an "Eastern" destiny is built on a discourse that is entirely centered on arguments of a geopolitical (Russia's Pacific façade) and economic (the Asia-Pacific as the driver of world economy in the twenty-first century) nature; it is almost entirely devoid of any cultural rationale (such as the profound interaction between Slavic and some Asian populations through the centuries).

Hence the strange destiny of a movement that has contributed to shaping Russian intellectual life in the twentieth century—its many ramifications in the cultural and artistic domains and fertile interactions created with European host countries are still insufficiently understood—but is today both central and forgotten. The more "Eurasia" invades Russia's public space, popular culture, and state-produced narratives, the more forgetful of its Eurasianist founding fathers it seems to be.

NOTES

Introduction: What Was Eurasianism and Who Made It?

The editors would like to express their deep appreciation to the Baltic Sea Foundation (Stockholm), whose financial support helped make this publication possible.

1. Mark Bassin, "Russia and Asia," in *The Cambridge Companion to Modern Russian Culture*, ed. Nicholas Rzhevsky (Cambridge: Cambridge University Press, 1998), 57–84; Mark Bassin, "Russia between Europe and Asia: The Ideological Construction of Geographical Space," *Slavic Review* 50 (1991), 1–17.

2. Otto Böss, *Die Lehre der Eurasier: Eine Beitrage zur Russische Ideengeschichte des 20 Jahrhunderts* (Munich, 1962); Nicholas Riasanovsky, "Prince N. S. Trubetskoi's 'Europe and Mankind,'" *Jahrbücher für Geschichte Osteuropas* 13 (1964), 207–20; Nicholas Riasanovsky, "The Emergence of Eurasianism," *California Slavic Studies*, no. 4 (1967), 39–72; Nicholas Riasanovsky, "Asia through Russian Eyes," in *Russia and Asia: Essays on Russian Influence upon Asian Peoples*, ed. Wayne S. Vucinich (Stanford, CA: Hoover Institution Press, 1972), 3–29. For more recent studies, see Marlene Laruelle, *L'Idéologie Eurasianiste russe ou Comment penser l'empire* (Paris: L'Harmattan, 1999). Stefan Wiederkehr, *Die eurasische Bewegung* (Cologne: Böhlau, 2007). Sergei Glebov, *Evraziistvo mezhdu imperiei i modernom: Istoriia v dokumentakh* (Moscow: Novoe izdatel'stvo, 2009), 7–173. For a review of recent studies of Eurasianism, see Sergey Glebov, "Wither Eurasia? History of Ideas in an Imperial Situation," *Ab Imperio*, no. 2 (2008), 345–76.

3. On the history of the Russian political emigration, see Marc Raeff, *Russia Abroad: A Cultural History of Russian Emigration, 1919–1939* (New York: Oxford University Press, 1990).

4. See Sergey Glebov, "The Mongol–Bolshevik Revolution: Eurasianist Ideology in Search for an Ideal Past," *Journal of Eurasian Studies*, no. 2 (2011), 103–14. For a prosopography of the Eurasianist founders, see Glebov, *Evraziistvo mezhdu imperiei i modernom*, 20–45.

5. G. S. Smith, *D. S. Mirsky: A Russian–English Life, 1890–1939* (Oxford: Oxford University Press, 2000).

6. Erendzhen Khara-Davan, *Chingis-khan kak polkovodets i ego nasledie* (Belgrade, 1929).

7. See Iakov Bromberg, "O neobkhodimom peresmotre evreiskogo voprosa," in *Evraziiskii sbornik* (Prague: Evraziiskoe knigoizdatel'stvo, 1929), 43–48; Iakov Bromberg, "Evreiskoe vostochnichestvo v proshlom i budushchem," in *Tridtsatye gody* (Paris: Izdanie Evraziitsev, 1931), 191–211; Iakov Bromberg, *Zapad, Rossiia i evreistvo: Opyt peresmotra evreiskogo voprosa* (Prague: Izdatel'stvo evraziitsev, 1931).

8. See Sergey Glebov, "A Life with Imperial Dreams: Petr Nikolaevich Savitsky, Eurasianism, and the Invention of 'Structuralist' Geography," *Ab Imperio*, no. 3 (2005), 299–329.

9. This discussion relies on Glebov, *Evraziistvo mezhdu imperiei i modernom*, 41–45, 121–75.

10. The concept of "symphonic personality" was developed by the Eurasianists to link their theology (the concept was derived from the Augustinian comparison of God-given peace among peoples to a symphony of musicians) to their vision of hierarchical, multilayered societies (like Eurasia). According to the Eurasianists, the Church, the state, and the nation could all be described as "symphonic personalities." See *Evraziistvo: Opyt sistematicheskogo izlozheniia* (Paris: Izdatel'stvo evraziitsev, 1926).

11. See, for example, Richard Taruskin, *Stravinsky and the Russian Traditions: A Bibliography of Works through Mavra*, vol. 2 (Berkeley: University of California Press, 1996); and a less convincing Katerine Levidou, "The Artist-Genius in Petr Suvchinskii's Eurasianist Philosophy of History: The Case of Igor' Stravinskii," *Slavonic and East European Review* 89, no. 4 (October 2011), 601–29.

12. Mark Bassin, "Classical Eurasianism and the Geopolitics of Russian Identity," *Ab Imperio*, no. 2 (2003), 257–68.

13. Thorsten Botz-Bornstein, "European Transfigurations—Eurafrica and Eurasia: Coudenhove and Trubetzkoy Revisited," *European Legacy: Toward New Paradigms* 12, no. 5 (2007), 565–75.

14. Terry Martin, *Affirmative Action Empire: Nations and Nationalism in the Soviet Union, 1923–1939* (Ithaca, NY: Cornell University Press, 2001).

15. N. S. Trubetskoi, *Evropa i chelovechestvo* (Sofia: Rossiisko-Bolgarskoe knigoizdatel'stvo, 1920), 42–43.

16. Glebov, *Evraziistvo mezhdu imperiei i modernom*, 46–60; Glebov, "The Mongol–Bolshevik Revolution."

17. Georges Nivat, "Du 'Panmongolisme' au 'movement eurasien': Histoire d'une theme literaire," in *Annuaire de l'URSS. Droit—Economie—Sociologie—Politique—Culture* (Strasbourg, 1965).

18. David Schimmelpenninck van der Oye, *Toward the Rising Sun: Russian Ideologies of Empire and the Path to War with Japan* (DeKalb: Northern Illinois University Press, 2001).

19. Aleksandr Blok, "Krushenie gumanizma," in Aleksandr Blok, *Sochineniia* (Moscow: Izdatel'stvo khudozhestvennoi literatury, 1955), 2:305–26; Aleksandr Blok, "Intelligentsia i Revoliutsia," in Blok, *Sochineniia*, 2:218–28; Aleksandr Blok, "Iskusstvo i Revoliutsiia (Po povodu tvoreniia Rikharda Vagnera)," in Blok, *Sochineniia*, 2:229–33.

20. Patrick Sériot, *Structure et totalité: Les origines intellectuelles du structuralisme en Europe centrale et orientale* (Paris: PUF, 1999).

21. See N. S. Avtonomova and M. L. Gasparov, "Jakobson, Slavistics and the Eurasian Movement: Two Moments of Opportunity, 1929–1953," in Roman Jakobson, *Teksty, dokumenty, issledovaniia* (Moscow: RGGU, 1999), 334–40.

22. Böss, *Die Lehre der Eurasier*.

23. Riasanovsky, "The Emergence of Eurasianism"; Riasanovsky, "Prince Trubetskoy's 'Europe and Mankind'"; Charles Halperin, "George Vernadsky, Eurasianism, the Mongols and Russia," *Slavic Review* 41, no. 3 (1982), 477–93; Charles Halperin, "Russia and the Steppe," *Forschungen zur Osteuropäischen Geschichte* 36 (1985), 55–194.

24. Nikita Struve, *Soixante-dix ans d'émigration russe, 1919–1989* (Paris: Fayard, 1996); Georges Nivat, "Du panmongolisme au mouvement eurasien: Histoire d'un thème millénaire," *Cahiers du monde russe et soviétique* 7, no. 3 (1966), 460–78.

25. Emanuel Sarkisyanz, *Russland und der Messianismus des Orients, Sendungsbewusstsein und politischer Chiliasmus des Ostens* (Tübingen: J. C. B. Mohr, 1955).

26. Marlene Laruelle, *L'Idéologie eurasiste russe ou comment penser l'empire* (Paris: L'Harmattan, 1999); Anatoly Liberman, "N. S. Trubetzkoy and His Works on History and Politics," in N. S. Trubetzkoy, *The Legacy of Genghis Khan and Other Essays on Russia's Identity* (Ann Arbor: Michigan Slavic Publications, 1991), 295–375; Ryszard Paradowski, "The Eurasian Idea and Leo Gumilev's Scientific Ideology," *Canadian Slavonic Papers* 41, no. 1 (1999), 19–32; Dmitri Shlapentokh, ed., *Russia between East and West: Scholarly Debates on Eurasianism* (Leiden: Brill, 2006); Stefan Wiederkehr, *Die Eurasische Bewegung* (Cologne: Böhlau, Beiträge zur Geschichte Osteuropas, 2007).

27. Bassin, "Russia between Europe and Asia"; Bassin, "Classical Eurasianism and the Geopolitics of Russian Identity."

28. Sergei Glebov, "Granitsy imperii kak granitsy moderna: Antikolonial'naia ritorika i teoriia kult'urnykh tipov v evraziistve," *Ab Imperio*, no. 2 (2003), 267–92.

29. Leonid Liuks, "Evraziistvo i konservativnaia revoliutsiia: Soblazn antizapadnichestva v Rossii i Germanii," *Voprosy filosofii*, no. 6 (1996), 57–69; Leonid

Luks, "Die Ideologie der Eurasier im zeitgeschichtlichen Zusammenhang," *Jahrbücher für Geschichte Osteuropas* 34 (1986), 374–95; Leonid Luks, "Der 'Dritte Weg' der 'Neo-Eurasischen' Zeitschrift 'Elementy': Zurück ins Dritte Reich?" *Studies in East European Thought* 52 (2000), 49–71.

30. Boris Gasparov, "The Ideological Principles of Prague School Phonology," in *Language, Poetry and Poetics: The Generation of the 1890s: Jakobson, Trubetskoy, Majakovskij*, Proceedings of the first Roman Jakobson Colloquium, M.I.T. (Berlin: Mouton de Gruyter, 1987), 49–78; Sergei Glebov, "A Life with Imperial Dreams: Petr Nikolaevich Savitsky, Eurasianism, and the Invention of 'Structuralist' Geography," *Ab Imperio*, no. 3 (2005), 299–329; Sériot, *Structure et totalité*; Patrick Sériot, *Les langues ne sont pas des choses: Discours sur la langue et souffrance identitaire en Europe centrale et orientale* (Paris: Petra, 2010).

31. Martin Beisswenger, "Inventing Eurasia: The Life and Ideas of Petr Nikolaevich Savitskii (1895–1968)," PhD diss., University of Notre Dame, 2009.

32. George Nivat, *Russie-Europe, la fin du schisme* (Lausanne: L'Âge d'homme, 1993); Schimmelpenninck van der Oye, *Toward the Rising Sun*; Aldo Ferrari, *La foresta e la steppa: Il mito dell'Eurasia nella cultura russa* (Milan: Libri Scheiwiller, 2003).

33. Marlene Laruelle, *Mythe aryen et rêve impérial dans la Russie tsariste* (Paris: CNRS Editions, 2005).

Chapter 1: A Revolutionary and the Empire

1. Nathaniel Knight, "Grigor'ev in Orenburg, 1851–1862: Russian Orientalism in the Service of Empire?" *Slavic Review* 59, no. 1 (2000), 77–79; Nathaniel Knight, "On Russian Orientalism: A Response to Adeeb Khalid," *Kritika: Exploration of Russian and Eurasian History* 1, no. 4 (fall 2000), 701–15.

2. Vera Tolz, *Russia's Own Orient: The Politics of Identity and Oriental Studies in the Late Imperial and Early Soviet Periods* (Oxford: Oxford University Press, 2011).

3. Marlene Laruelle, "The Orient in Russian Thought at the Turn of the Century," in *Russia between East and West: Scholarly Debates on Eurasianism*, ed. D. Shlapentokh (Leiden: Brill, 2006), 9–38.

4. On Herzen's place as a profound contributor to the shaping of Russian cultural institutions, including the intelligentsia and its self-consciousness, see Irina Paperno, "Introduction: Intimacy and History. The Gercen Family Drama Reconsidered," *Russian Literature* 61, no. 1/2 (2007), 1–65; Irina Paperno, *Stories of the Soviet Experience* (Ithaca, NY: Cornell University Press, 2009), 9–15.

5. Susan Layton, *Russian Literature and Empire: Conquest of the Caucasus from Pushkin to Tolstoy* (Cambridge: Cambridge University Press, 1994), 81–132. See also Daniel R. Brower and Edward J. Lazzerini, eds., *Russia's Orient: Imperial Borderlands and Peoples, 1700–1917* (Bloomington: Indiana University Press,

1997); David Schimmelpenninck van der Oye, *Russian Orientalism: Asia in the Russian Mind from Peter the Great to the Emigration* (New Haven, CT: Yale University Press, 2010).

6. Chaadaev's Philosophical Letters are published in English in *The Philosophical Works of Peter Chaadaev*, ed. and trans. Raymond T. McNally and Richard Tempest (Dordrecht: Kluwer Academic, 1991).

7. V.G. Belinsky, "Rossiia do Petra Velikogo," in Belinsky, *Polnoe sobranie sochinenii*, vol. 5 (Moscow: Izdatel'stvo Akademii Nauk, 1954), 91–152.

8. This notion was refined by the historian S. M. Solov'ev and incorporated into schoolbooks in the latter half of the nineteenth century.

9. Nikolai Danilevskii's *Rossiia i Evropa* (1869) offered a classical articulation of this idea. For an English translation of the book, see Nikolai Iakovlevich Danilevskii, *Russia and Europe: The Slavic World's Political and Cultural Relations with the Germanic-Roman West*, trans. and annotated by Stephen M. Woodburn (Bloomington, IN: Slavica, 2013). Other writers popularized a belief in the characteristic Russian receptivity to foreign cultures and ability to adapt to different ethnic and cultural environments. This concept was most famously expressed in Dostoevsky's notion of the "universal responsiveness" (*vsemirnaia otzyvchivost'*) of the Russian people.

10. For a detailed discussion of how nineteenth-century Russians perceived Asia and how they defined themselves with regard to the East-West dichotomy, see Seymour Becker, "The Muslim East in Nineteenth-Century Russian Historiography," *Central Asian Survey* 5, nos. 3/4 (1986), 25–47; Seymour Becker, "Russia between East and West: The Intelligentsia, Russian National Identity and the Asia Borderlands," *Central Asian Survey* 10, no. 4 (1991), 47–64; Mark Bassin, *Imperial Visions: Nationalist Imagination and Geographical Expansion in the Russian Far East, 1840–1865* (Cambridge: Cambridge University Press, 1999).

11. This intellectual trajectory that Herzen traversed has been analyzed in Martin Malia's classic monograph, *Alexander Herzen and the Birth of Russian Socialism, 1812–1855* (Cambridge, MA: Harvard University Press, 1961). See also: Edward Acton, *Alexander Herzen and the Role of the Intellectual Revolutionary* (Cambridge: Cambridge University Press, 1979); Aileen Kelly, *Views from the Other Shore: Essays on Herzen, Chekhov, and Bakhtin* (New Haven, CT: Yale University Press, 1999).

12. For an analysis of Herzen's changing attitude toward the notion of progress, see Kelly, *Views from the Other Shore*. On the controversial issue of Herzen's philosophy of history and its evolution, see Ulrich Schmid, "The Family Drama as an Interpretive Pattern in Aleksandr Gercen's *Byloe i dumy*," *Russian Literature* 61, no. 1/2 (2007), 67–102; Ilya Kliger, "Auto-Historiography: Genre, Trope and Modes of Emplotment in Aleksandr and Natal'ja Gercen's Narratives of the Family Drama," *Russian Literature* 61, no. 1/2 (2007), 103–38.

13. A. I. Gertsen, *Sobranie sochinenii v tridtsati tomakh* (Moscow: Izdatel'stvo Akademii Nauk SSSR, 1957–1965), 11:75; Alexander Herzen, *My Past and Thoughts*, in *The Memoirs of Alexander Herzen*, trans. Constance Garnett (New York: Knopf, 1968), 3:1083. Here and throughout, Herzen's works are cited from A. I. Gertsen, *Sobranie sochinenii v tridtsati tomakh* (Moscow: Izdatel'stvo Akademii Nauk SSSR, 1954–1965). English translations of these citations are made with reference to published translations where such exist, but most were revised or newly translated by Rachel Harrell-Bilici, who did an invaluable job for me as translator.

14. Gertsen, *Sobranie sochinenii*, 11:75. Herzen, *The Memoirs of Alexander Herzen*, 3:1080–81.

15. Gertsen, *Sobranie sochinenii*, 11:74. Herzen, *The Memoirs of Alexander Herzen*, 3:1083.

16. For a comparison of their views on liberty, see Kelly, *Views from the Other Shore*, 114–38.

17. John Stuart Mill, *On Liberty*, ed. David Bromwich and George Kateb (New Haven, CT: Yale University Press, 2003), 130.

18. Mill, *On Liberty*, 134.

19. Kelly, *Views from the Other Shore*, 116.

20. Gertsen, *Sobranie sochinenii*, 11:77. Herzen, *The Memoirs of Alexander Herzen*, 3:1085.

21. Mill, *On Liberty*, 134–36.

22. Mill, *On Liberty*, 131–36.

23. Gertsen, *Sobranie sochinenii*, 11:73. Herzen, *The Memoirs of Alexander Herzen*, 3:1081.

24. Mill, *On Liberty*, 80–81.

25. Gertsen, *Sobranie sochinenii*, 11:73. Herzen, *The Memoirs of Alexander Herzen*, 3:1082.

26. Gertsen, *Sobranie sochinenii*, 11:73–75. Herzen, *The Memoirs of Alexander Herzen*, 3:1082–83.

27. Mill, *On Liberty*, 135.

28. Gertsen, *Sobranie sochinenii*, 11:72. Herzen, *The Memoirs of Alexander Herzen*, 3:1081.

29. Gertsen, *Sobranie sochinenii*, 11:76. Herzen, *The Memoirs of Alexander Herzen*, 3:1084.

30. For a discussion of the philosophical aspect of this shift in Herzen's views, see Kelly, *Views from the Other Shore*, 117–70. On the repercussions of this shift for the narration of *My Past and Thoughts*, see Schmid, "The Family Drama as an Interpretive Pattern in Aleksandr Gercen's *Byloe i dumy*."

31. Gertsen, "S togo berega," in Gertsen, *Sobranie sochinenii*, 6:30–31, 57–59, 68–69. Alexander Herzen, *From the Other Shore*, trans. Moura Budberg (London: Weidenfeld and Nicolson, 1956), 32, 66–67, 78.

32. Gertsen, *Sobranie sochinenii*, 6:58. Herzen, *From the Other Shore*, 66.

33. Gertsen, *Sobranie sochinenii*, 6:17. Herzen, *From the Other Shore*, 16.

34. Gertsen, *Sobranie sochinenii*, 6:68. Herzen, *From the Other Shore*, 78.

35. Gertsen,"O razvitii revoliutsionnykh idei v Rossii," in Gertsen, *Sobranie sochinenii*, 7:255.

36. Gertsen, "Rossiia i Pol'sha," *Sobranie sochinenii*, 14:31, 45, 51.

37. Uday Singh Mehta, *Liberalism and Empire: A Study in Nineteenth-Century British Liberal Thought* (Chicago: University of Chicago Press, 1999), 82.

38. Gertsen, "Rossiia i Pol'sha," *Sobranie sochinenii*, 14:56–57.

39. Gertsen, "Rossiia i Pol'sha," *Sobranie sochinenii*, 14:57.

40. Gertsen, "Rossiia i Pol'sha," *Sobranie sochinenii*, 14:53.

41. Though the famous proverb "scratch a Russian and you will find a Tartar" seems to suggest the opposite, in the nineteenth century most Russian intellectuals rebuffed any assumptions that the Asian components prevailed. It is telling that in *War and Peace* Tolstoy puts this proverb into the mouth of Napoleon expressly to demonstrate how little that "vain and narrow-minded" commander understood the country he had come to conquer.

42. In dividing all mankind into two major races—the Aryans (Indo-Europeans) and the Turanians (Finno-Ugrians, Mongols, Turks, Semites, Chinese)—Duchiński asserted the moral and intellectual superiority of the former over the latter. He claimed that the Poles (and indeed all the Slavs, including Ukrainians and Byelorussians) belonged to the Aryan group—except for the Russians (in the parlance of the day , the "Great Russians"), who were Turanians. For a detailed contextualization of his views, see Ivan L. Rudnytsy, "Franciszek Duchiński and His Impact on Ukrainian Political Thought," *Harvard Ukrainian Studies* 3 (1979), 690–705; Mikhail Dolbilov and Aleksey Miller, eds., *Zapadnye okrainy Rossiiskoi imperii* (Moscow: Novoe literaturnoe obozrenie, 2007), 113, 115, 141.

43. Among those who attacked this theory were people of varying political agendas—from the Ukrainian separatist Nikolai Kostomarov to the journalist Mikhail Katkov and the historian Mikhail Pogodin, who defended the integrity of the Romanov Empire. Later the famous linguist Ivan (Jan) Baudouin de Courtenay also voiced his criticism of Duchiński's theory (Baudouin de Courtenay was, in fact, of Polish origin but belonged to Russian academic circles).

44. Gertsen, "Rossiia i Pol'sha," *Sobranie sochinenii*, 14:44–45.

45. Gertsen, "Rossiia i Pol'sha," *Sobranie sochinenii*, 14:53.

46. Gertsen, "Rossiia i Pol'sha," *Sobranie sochinenii*, 14:54.

47. Gertsen, "Rossiia i Pol'sha," *Sobranie sochinenii*, 14:51.

48. Gertsen, "Rossiia i Pol'sha," *Sobranie sochinenii*, 14:46, In this context, it is not surprising that Herzen enthusiastically greeted Russia's advance into the Far East. For a discussion of his ambivalent attitude toward the Russian imperial project, see Bassin, *Imperial Visions*, 63–65, 163–67, 169–73, 181, 270–73.

49. Patrick Sériot, *Structure et totalité: Les origines intellectuelles du structuralisme en Europe centrale et orientale* (Paris: PUF, 1999); Sergei Glebov, *Evraziistvo mezhdu imperiei i modernom* (Moscow: Novoe izdatel'stvo, 2010).

50. Marlene Laruelle, *L'idéologie eurasiste russe, ou, Comment penser l'Empire* (Paris: L'Harmattan, 1999).

Chapter 2: The Eurasians and Liberal Scholarship of the Late Imperial Period

1. Mark Bassin, "Classical Eurasianism and the Geopolitics of Russian Identity," *Ab Imperio*, no. 2 (2003), 257–67.

2. V. Ia. Pashchenko, *Ideologiia evraziistva* (Moscow: Izdatel'stvo Moskovskogo universiteta, 2000), 224, 229–30; L. Liuks [Luks], "Evraziistvo i konservativnaia revoliutsiia," *Voprosy filosofii*, no. 3 (1996), 59; Nicholas Riasanovsky, "Asia through Russian Eyes," in *Russia and Asia: Essays on the Influence of Russia on the Asian Peoples*, ed. Wayne Vucinich (Stanford, CA: Hoover Institution Press, 1972), 27–28; B. Gasparov, "Evraziiskie korni fonologicheskoi teorii: Boduen de Courtene v Kazani," in *Kazan, Moskva, Peterburg: Rossiiskaia imperiia vzgliadom iz raznykh uglov*, ed. B. Gasparov, E. Evstukhov, A. Ospovat, and M. von Hagen (Moscow: OGI, 1997), 302–24; Marlene Laruelle, *Ideologiia russkogo evraziistva ili mysli o velichii imperii* (Moscow: Natalis, 2004), 21; on the relationship between Nikolai Marr's linguistic theories and those of Nikolai Trubetskoi and Roman Jacobson, see P. Sériot, *Struktura i tselostnost'* (Moscow: Iazyki slavianskoi kultury, 2001), 19; Stefan Wiederkehr, *Die eurasische Bewegung* (Cologne: Böhlau, 2007), 113.

3. See, for instance, Juliette Cadiot, *Le laboratoire imperial: Russie-URSS, 1860–1940* (Paris: CNRS, 2007); Charles Steinwedel, "To Make a Difference: The Category of Ethnicity in Late Imperial Russian Politics, 1861–1917," in *Russian Modernity: Politics, Knowledge, Practices*, ed. David Hoffman and Yanni Kotsonis (Houndmills: Macmillan, 2000), 70, 81; Francine Hirsch, *Empire of Nations: Ethnographic Knowledge and the Making of the Soviet Union* (Ithaca, NY: Cornell University Press, 2005), 21–61; Adeeb Khalid, *The Politics of Muslim Cultural Reform: Jadidism in Central Asia* (Berkeley: University of California Press, 1998); Daniel Beers, *Renovating Russia: The Human Sciences and the Fate of Liberal Modernity, 1880–1930* (Ithaca, NY: Cornell University Press, 2008).

4. Edward Said, *Orientalism* (London: Routledge, 1978).

5. Suzanne Marchand, *German Orientalism in the Age of Empire: Religion, Race, and Scholarship* (Cambridge: Cambridge University Press, 2009).

6. Marchand, *German Orientalism*, 496; Vera Tolz, *"Russia's Own Orient": The Politics of Identity and Russian Oriental Studies in the Late Imperial and Early Soviet Periods* (Oxford: Oxford University Press, 2011); and Ilya Gerasimov, Sergey Glebov, and Marina Mogilner, "The Postimperial Meets the Postcolonial: Russian Historical Experience and the Postcolonial Movement," *Ab Imperio*, no. 2 (2013), 97–135.

7. Suzanne Marchand, "German Orientalism and the Decline of the West," *Proceedings of the American Philosophical Society* 145, no. 4 (2001), 471. See also Marchand, *German Orientalism*, and her "The Rhetoric of Artifacts and the Decline of Classical Humanism: The Case of Josef Strzygowski," *History and Theory* 33, no. 4 (1994), 106–30.

8. Tolz, *"Russia's Own Orient."*

9. Marchand, "German Orientalism and the Decline of the West," 465.

10. Robert Nelson, "The Italian Appreciation and Appropriation of Illuminated Byzantine Manuscripts, ca. 1200–1450," *Dumbarton Oaks Papers* 49 (1995), 234.

11. M. I. Rostovtsev, "Nikodim Pavlovich Kondakov (k piatidesiatiletiiu nauchnoi deiatel'nosti)," reprinted in *Skifskii roman*, ed. G. M. Bongard-Levin (Moscow: ROSSPEN, 1997), 432–34. For a comprehensive overview of Kondakov's work, see I. L. Kyzlasova, ed., *Mir Kondakova* (Moscow: Russkii put', 2004). See also I. L. Kyzlasova, *Istoriia izucheniia vizantiiskogo i drevnerusskogo iskusstva v Rossii* (Moscow: Izdatel'stvo MGU, 1985), 74–155; and G. I. Vzdornov, *Istoriia otkrytiia i izucheniia russkoi srednevekovoi zhivopisi, XIX vek* (Moscow: Iskusstvo, 1986), 220–46.

12. Jane Ashton Sharp, *Russian Modernism between East and West: Natal'ia Goncharova and the Moscow Avant-Garde* (Cambridge: Cambridge University Press, 2006), 35, 37. On the influence of Kondakov's ideas on Mikhail Rostovtsev's works about Scythia as a crossroads between the Greek and Iranian cultures, see also Bongard-Levin, ed., *Skifskii roman*, 432. Kondakov's work also influenced the revisionist Austrian art historian, Josef Strzygowski (1862–1941), whose originality is sometimes overstated in regard to his explorations of the relationship between Oriental, Byzantine, and European art. See Marchand, "The Rhetoric of Artifacts and the Decline of Classical Humanism."

13. G. V. Vernadskii, *O znachenii nauchnoi deiatel'nosti N. P. Kondakova: K vosmidesiatiletiiu so dnia rozhdeniia* (Prague: Sine loco, 1924); N. V. Tunkina, "Akademik N. P. Kondakov: Prazhskie pisma na rodinu," in *Zarubezhnaia Rossiia, 1917–1939*, ed. V. Iu. Cherniaev (St. Petersburg: Evropeiskii dom, 2000), 232.

14. V. T. Pashuto, *Russkie istoriki emigratsii v Evrope* (Moscow: Nauka, 1992), 32–44; I. P. Savitskii, "Akademik N. P. Kondakov v Prage," in *Mir Kondakova*, ed. Kyzlasova, 197–204; Catherine Adreyev and Ivan Savicky, eds., *Russia Abroad: Prague and the Russian Diaspora, 1918–1938* (New Haven, CT: Yale University Press, 2004), 110–11.

15. N. I. Veselovskii, "Baron V. R. Rozen," *Zhurnal Ministerstva narodnogo prosveshcheniia*, ser. 14, no. 4, otd. 4 (1908), 170, 178, 186.

16. Vera Tolz, "European, National, and (Anti-)Imperial: The Formation of Academic Oriental Studies in Late Tsarist and Early Soviet Russia," *Kritika: Explorations in Russian and Eurasian History* 9, no. 1 (2008), 53–81.

17. N. Ia. Marr, "Baron V. R. Rozen i khristianskii Vostok," in *Pamiati Barona*

Viktora Romanovicha Rozena: Prilozhenie k XVIII tomu Zapisok Vostochnogo ot-
deleniia Imperatorskgogo Russkogo arkheologicheskogo obshchestva (St. Petersburg: Tipografiia Imperatorskoi Akademii nauk, 1909), 13.

18. Tolz, "European, National, and (Anti-)Imperial."

19. Contemporary scholars have noted the use of Bartol'd's works by the Eurasians. See, for instance, Pashchenko, *Ideologiia evraziistva*, 229–30; and Laruelle,
Ideologiia russkogo evraziistva, 77. Yet this acknowledgment is largely based on the
statements made in Savitskii's obituary of Bartol'd rather than on the reading of
Bartol'd's works and their comparison with the writings of the Eurasians.

20. P. Ia. Chaadaev, "Filosofskie pis'ma. Pis'mo pervoe," http://www.libs-web.ru
/philos/chaadaev/pisma1.html (accessed December 30, 2014).

21. E. V. Anichkov, "N. P. Kondakov (1844–1925)," *Slavica*, no. 7 (1928/1929), 49.

22. N. S. Trubetskoi, "Ob idee-pravitel'nitse ideokraticheskogo gosudarstva," in
N. S. Trubetskoi, *Istoriia, kultura, iazyk* (Moscow: Progress, 1995), 441. Translations are the author's unless otherwise indicated.

23. Sergei Glebov, "Granitsy imperii i granitsy moderna: Antikolonial'naia ritorika i teoriia kul'turnykh tipov v Evraziistve," *Ab Imperio*, no. 2 (2003), 282–83.

24. A debate about the "eastern" origins of Russian culture had already begun
among scholars in the 1860s with the publication in 1868 of Vladimir Stasov's
Proiskhozhdenie russkikh bylin.

25. Mark Bassin, "Russia between Europe and Asia: The Ideological Construction of Geographical Space," *Slavic Review* 50, no. 1 (1991), 13.

26. I. Tolstoi and N. Kondakov, *Russkie drevnosti v pamiatnikakh iskusstva*,
vol. 1 (St. Petersburg: Tipografiia Ministerstva putei soobshcheniia, 1889), iii.

27. Tolstoi and Kondakov, *Russkie drevnosti v pamiatnikakh iskusstva*, iii–iv.

28. Sharp, *Russian Modernism between East and West*, 30, 35, 37.

29. P. N. Savitskii, *Kontinent Evraziia* (Moscow: Agraf, 1997), 135. I am grateful to Martin Beisswenger for drawing my attention to the fact that Savitskii's
familiarity with Kondakov's work by 1921 was reflected in Savitskii's personal note-
books. (Slovanski knihovna, Prague, Savitskii papers, box 18, notebook 0 [1921].)

30. Marr, "Baron V. R. Rozen i khristianskii vostok"; and V. V. Bartol'd, "Baron
V. R. Rozen i russkii provintsial'nyi orientalism," both in *Pamiati Barona V. R.
Rozena* (St. Petersburg: Tipografiia Imperatorskoi akademii nauk, 1909), 12, 15,
17, 23, 31.

31. Martin Beisswenger, "Zhiznennyi put' i nauchnaia deiatel'nost N. P. Kondakova v emigratsii," *Zarubezhnye slaviane v proshlom i nastoiashchem*, ed. L. P.
Lapteva (Moscow: Dialog-MGU, 1999), 181–82.

32. P. N. Savitskii, "Step i osedlost'" (1922), reprinted in L. I. Novikova and I. N.
Sizemskaia, eds., *Rossiia mezhdu Evropoi i Aziei* (Moscow: Nauka, 1993), 123–30;
and P. N. Savitskii, "V. V. Bartol'd, kak istorik," *Seminarium kondakovianum*, no.
4 (1931), 261.

33. Savitskii, "Bartol'd, kak istorik," 267–68; and State Archive of the Russian Federation (hereafter, GARF), f. 5783, op. 1, d. 418, ll. 37 ob–38.

34. Glebov, "Granitsy imperii i granitsy moderna," 283–86.

35. Marchand, "German Orientalism and the Decline of the West."

36. Quoted in Rudi Paret, *The Study of Arabic and Islam at German Universities* (Wiesbaden: Franz Steiner, 1968), 12.

37. Marr, "Baron V. R. Rozen i khristianskii Vostok," 23.

38. N. Ia. Marr, "Kavkazovedenie i abkhazskii iazyk," *Zhurnal Ministerstva narodnogo prosveshcheniia* (ZhMNP), no. 5 (1916), reprinted in N. Ia. Marr, *Etapy razvitiia iafeticheskoi teorii* (Leningrad: Izdatelstvo GAIMK, 1933), 59–60, 64, 67. For recent excellent assessments of Marr's life and work, see N. I. Platonova, "Nikolai Iakovlevich Marr—arkheolog i organizator arkheologicheskoi nauki," *Arkheologicheskie vesti*, no. 5 (1998), 371–82; and Ia. V. Vasilkov, "Tragediia akademika Marra," *Khristianskii Vostok*, no. 2 (2001), 390–421.

39. Marr, "Kavkazovedenie i abkhazskii iazyk," 59–60.

40. V. V. Bartol'd, "Istoriia izucheniia Vostoka v Evrope i Rossii," in V. V. Bartol'd, *Sochineniia*, 9 vols. (Moscow: Nauka, 1977), 9:199–482.

41. Bartol'd, "Istoriia izucheniia Vostoka," ch. 3 and 5, esp. pp. 239–35, 310. See also the development of the same views in Bartol'd, "Kul'tura musul'manstva" (1918), in Bartol'd, *Sochineniia* (Moscow: Nauka, 1966), 6:143–45. Compare Bartol'd's arguments to Larry Wolff, *Inventing Eastern Europe: The Map of Civilization in the Mind of Enlightenment* (Stanford, CA: Stanford University Press, 1994).

42. "Ot redaktsii," *Mir Islama*, no. 1 (1912), 4. Reprinted in Bartol'd, *Sochineniia*, 6:366–71. See also Bartol'd, "Istoriia izucheniia Vostoka," 357–59; Bartol'd, "Istoricheskie i geograficheskie trudy V. P. Vasil'eva," in Bartol'd, *Sochineniia*, 9:621–22. See also Bartol'd's letter to Savitskii of October 14, 1927, GARF, f. 5783, op. 1, d. 418, l. 35. I am very grateful to Martin Beisswenger for passing on to me his transcripts of Vasilii Bartol'd's letters to Petr Savitskii, which are held in GARF, f. 5783, op. 1, d. 418, ll. 34–43.

43. Anna Ponomareva, "Andrei Belyi and Indian Culture: A Study of the Role of Indian Ideas in the Work of Andrei Belyi," MPhil thesis, University of Manchester, UK, September 2001, 14–16, 25, 33, 65, 113–16, 143; A. I. Andreev, *Khram Buddy v Severnoi stolitse* (St. Petersburg: Nartang, 2004), 17–18; Maria Carlson, *"No Religion Higher Than Truth": A History of the Theosophical Movement in Russia, 1875–1922* (Princeton, NJ: Princeton University Press, 1993), 193–94; Nikolai Rerikh, *Listy iz dnevnika*, 3 vols. (Moscow: Mezhdunarodnyi tsentr Rerikhov, 2002), 3:319, 321.

44. O. O. Rozenberg, "Ob izuchenii iaponskogo buddizma," in T. V. Ermakova, *Buddizm glazami rossiiskikh issledovatelei XIX–pervoi treti XX veka* (St. Petersburg: Nauka, 1998), 320.

45. "Ot redaktsii," *Mir Islama*, 368–71; and GARF, f. 5783, op. 1, d. 418, l. 37.

46. Savitskii, "Bartol'd, kak istorik," 266, 267–68.

47. P. N. Savitskii, "Migratsiia kul'tury," in *Iskhod k Vostoku* (Moscow: Dobrosvet, 1997), 119.

48. Savitskii, "Bartol'd, kak istorik," 264.

49. See, for instance, Charles J. Halperin, "George Vernadsky, Eurasianism, the Mongols, and Russia," *Slavic Review* no. 3 (1982), 479–80, 486; Slawomir Mazurek, "Russian Eurasianism: Historiography and Ideology," *Studies in East European Thought*, no. 1–2 (2002): 105–23.

50. Seymour Becker, "The Muslim East in Nineteenth-Century Russian Popular Historiography," *Central Asian Survey* 5, no. 3/4 (1986): 31–33, 36, 38.

51. See N. S. Trubetzkoy, "The Legacy of Genghis Khan: A Perspective on Russian History not from the West but from the East," in N. S. Trubetzkoy, *The Legacy of Genghis Khan and Other Essays on Russia's Identity* (Ann Arbor: Michigan Slavic Publications, 1991), 161–231; Halperin, "George Vernadsky, Eurasianism, the Mongols, and Russia."

52. V. V. Bartol'd, "Rech' pered zashchitoi dissertatsii," in *Sochineniia* (Moscow: Nauka, 1963), 1:606–8.

53. Bartol'd, "Istoriia izucheniia Vostoka," 364.

54. Bartol'd, "Istoriia izucheniia Vostoka," 363–64; see also Bartol'd, "Vostok i russkaia nauka," in Bartol'd, *Sochineniia*, 9:534–45.

55. G. V. Vernadskii, "Dvizhenie russkikh na Vostok," *Nauchnyi istoricheskii zhurnal*, no. 2 (1914), 52–61. For a reference to Bartol'd, see 55n2. In this article and in his later work, *Mongol'skoe igo v russkoi istorii*, Vernadsky failed to fully acknowledge his borrowing of Bartol'd's interpretations. This fact was noted by Bartol'd in one of his letters to Savitskii. GARF, f. 5783, op. 1, d. 418, l. 350b.

56. Savitskii, "V. V. Bartol'd, kak istorik," 266.

57. Glebov, "Granitsy imperii i granitsy moderna," 275.

58. David Chioni Moore, "Colonialism, Eurasianism, Orientalism: N. S. Trubetzkoy's Russian Vision," *Slavic and East European Journal* 41, no. 2 (1997), 323.

59. Moore, "Colonialism, Eurasianism, Orientalism," 323–24; see also Glebov, "Granitsy imperii i granitsy moderna," 275–76.

60. Bill Ashcroft and Pal Ahluwalia, *Edward Said and the Paradox of Identity* (London: Routledge, 1999), 87, 98.

61. Marchand, *German Orientalism*, 497.

62. Susan Gross Solomon, "Circulation of Knowledge and the Russian Locale," *Kritika* 9, no. 1 (2008), 21.

63. See, for instance, V. V. Grigor'ev, "V oproverzhenie nekotorykh mnenii, vyskazanykh v poslednee vremia o prepodavanii vostochnykh iazykov v Rossii i ob izuchenii u nas Vostoka voobshche," *Den'*, no. 18 (1865), 433.

64. Bartol'd, "Vostok i russkaia nauka," 534, 545.

65. Bartol'd, "Rech' pered zashchitoi dissertatsii," 610.

66. Marr, "Kavkazovedenie i abkhazskii iazyk," 67.

67. The quote is from Bartol'd, "Baron V. R. Rozen i russkii provintsial'nyi orientalizm," 589.

68. Bartol'd, *Istoriia izucheniia Vostoka*, 301.

69. "Ot redaktsii," *Mir Islama*, 374–75.

70. Yuri Slezkine noted the similarity of Marr's arguments of the 1920s and those of the Eurasians in his "N. Ia. Marr and the National Origins of Soviet Ethnogenetics," *Slavic Review* 55, no. 4 (1996), 833–34.

71. See GARF, f. 5783, op. 1, d. 359, l. 220 ob. (I am grateful to Martin Beisswenger for this reference.) For the argument that the Eurasians knew about Marr only as a "mad" linguist rather than as a sharp critic of European colonialism, see Sergei Glebov, "Postcolonial Empire? Russian Orientologists and the Politics of Knowledge in Late Imperial Russia," *Ab Imperio*, no. 3 (2011), 389.

72. Tolz, "European, National, and (Anti-)Imperial," 77–80.

73. S. F. Ol'denburg, "Sovetskoe vostokovedenie," *Front nauki i tekhniki*, nos. 7/8 (1931), 65.

74. S. F. Ol'denburg, "Chto dolzhno delat' sovetskoe vostokovedenie dlia izucheniia Turkestana" (1932), Petersburg Archives, Russian Academy of Sciences (hereafter, PF ARAN), f. 208, op. 1, d. 113, l. 5. See also the attacks on "old" Oriental Studies during the 1930 discussion, in "K polozheniiu na vostochnom fronte," PF ARAN, f. 208, op. 1, d. 122, l. 233.

75. S. F. Ol'denburg's report on the state of Soviet scholarship of 1927 is quoted in I. Iu. Krachkovskii, "S. F. Ol'denburg, kak istorik vostokovedeniia," in I. Iu. Krachkovskii, *Izbrannye sochineniia* (Moscow: Izdatel'stvo Akademii Nauk SSSR, 1958), 5:364; Ol'denburg, "Sovetskoe vostokovedenie," 65; Ol'denburg, "Vostokovedenie v Akademii Nauk na novykh putiakh," *Vestnik Akademii Nauk*, no. 2 (1931), 9–10. Similar arguments were developed in Ol'denburg's two unpublished articles, "Vostokovedenie i Oktiabr'" (1932), PF ARAN, f. 208, op. 1, d. 109; and "Chto dolzhno delat' sovetskoe vostokovedenie dlia izucheniia Turkestana."

76. Tolz, *"Russia's Own Orient,"* 100–101.

77. N. S. Trubetzkoy, "Pan-Eurasian Nationalism," in *The Legacy of Genghis Khan*, 233–44; Konstantin Chkhedize, "Natsional'naia problema," *Evraziiskaia khronika*, no. 4 (1926), 22–30.

78. Trubetzkoy, "Pan-Eurasian Nationalism," 241.

79. Trubetzkoy, "Pan-Eurasian Nationalism," 243.

80. Trubetzkoy, "The Ukrainian Problem," in *The Legacy of Genghis Khan*, 245–68.

81. See, for instance, Viktor Shnirelman, "The Fate of Empires and Eurasian Federalism: A Discussion between the Eurasianists and Their Opponents in the 1920s," *Inner Asia*, no. 3 (2001), 153–73; and Bassin, "Classical Eurasianism and the Geopolitics of Russian Identity."

82. Glebov, "Grantisky imperii i granitsy moderna," 278–79.

83. Bassin, "Classical Eurasianism and the Geopolitics of Russian Identity"; Igor Torbakov, "Understanding Classical Eurasianism," in *Sven Hedin and Eurasia: Knowledge, Adventure and Geopolitics*, ed. Ingmar Oldberg (Stockholm: Ostbulletinen, 2008), 35–45.

84. Aleksei Miller, *Imperiia Romanovykh i natsional'izm* (Moscow: NLO, 2006).

85. On the similarity of Ilminskii's ideas and those of Lenin, see Isabelle Kreindler, "A Neglected Source of Lenin's Nationalities Policy," *Slavic Review*, no. 1 (1977), 86–100.

86. Robert Geraci, *Window on the East: National and Imperial Identities in Late Tsarist Russia* (Ithaca, NY: Cornell University Press, 2001), 47–85.

87. Vera Tolz, "Orientalism, Nationalism and Ethnic Diversity in Late Imperial Russia," *Historical Journal*, no. 1 (2005), 137–45.

88. Tolz, *"Russia's Own Orient,"* 37–38. Such ideas resembled contemporary debates elsewhere in Europe regarding the relationship between national and regional or local identities. See, for instance, Celia Applegate, *A Nation of Provincials: The German Idea of Heimat* (Berkeley: University of California Press, 1990); and Alon Confino, *The Nation as a Local Metaphor* (Chapel Hill: University of North Carolina Press, 1997).

89. Yuri Slezkine, *Arctic Mirrors: Russia and the Small Peoples of the North* (Ithaca, NY: Cornell University Press, 1996), 114–19.

90. N. M. Iadrintsev, *Sibir', kak koloniia* (St. Petersburg: Tipografiia Stasiulevicha, 1882), 31.

91. N. Ia. Marr, "K voprosu o zadachakh armianovedeniia," *ZhMNP*, July 2/324 (1899), 244. See also Marr, "Kavkazskii kul'turnyi mir i Armeniia," *ZhMNP*, part 57 (June 1915), 329.

92. "Ot redaktsii," *Mir Islama*, 375; D. Klements, "Pessimizm na buriatskoi pochve," *Sibirskie voprosy*, no. 10 (1907), 22.

93. Tolz, *"Russia's Own Orient,"* ch. 5.

94. See Bartol'd's correspondence with the Ukrainian Arabist, A. E. Krymskii, in which Bartol'd demonstrated that he feared political separatism even in the instances where it did not exist. PF ARAN, f. 68, op. 2, d. 128, ll. 3–4. See also N. Ia. Marr, "Vserossiiskaia kul'turnaia problema" (written in the aftermath of the February Revolution of 1917), PF ARAN, f. 800, d. 2366, ll. 3–5, 9, and 11 ob.

95. Hirsch, *Empire of Nations*, 8, 11, 14, 44, 47, 59. Other scholars have mentioned a link between the emerging perceptions of ethnicity and nationality in the prerevolutionary period and the Bolshevik policies. Austin Jersild, "Faith, Custom, and Ritual in the Borderlands: Orthodoxy, Islam, and the 'Small People' of the Middle Volga and the North Caucasus," *Russian Review* 59, no. 4 (2000), 528; and Kreindler, "A Neglected Source of Lenin's Nationalities Policy"; Steinwedel, "To Make a Difference," 70. On the connection between the thinking of the Orientolo-

gists of the Rozen school and the Bolshevik nationalities policy, see Tolz, *"Russia's Own Orient,"* ch. 6.

96. Marchand, *German Orientalism*, 487.

97. In his letters to Savitskii, Bartol'd regularly emphasized his disagreements with the theories of the Eurasians. See GARF, f. 5783, op. 1, d. 418, ll. 34 ob., 35, and 37–38.

98. Marr, "Vserossiiskaia kul'turnaia problema."

99. Wolff, *Inventing Eastern Europe*.

100. This issue in relation to nineteenth-century Russian thought is discussed in Vera Tolz, "The West," in *The Cambridge History of Russian Thought*, ed. Derek Offord and William Leatherbarrow (Cambridge: Cambridge University Press, 2010), 197–216.

101. P. M. Bitsilli, "'Vostok' i 'Zapad' v istorii Starogo Sveta," in *Na putiakh* (Berlin: Gelikon, 1922), 317–40.

102. It was Kondakov who helped Bitsilli get an academic job in Bulgaria in 1924.

103. Bitsilli, "'Vostok' i 'Zapad' v istorii Starogo Sveta."

104. See Sergei Glebov, *Evraziistvo mezhdu imperiei i modernom* (Moscow: Novoe izdatel'stvo, 2010), 187.

105. See, in particular, N. S. Trubetzkoy, "On True and False Nationalism" (1921), in *The Legacy of Genghis Khan*, 65–79. For an analysis of this aspect of the legacy of the Eurasians, see Glebov, "Granitsky imperii i granitsy moderna."

106. N. I. Platonova, "Akademik Nikolai Iakovlevich Marr i Sankt-Peterburgskii Universitet," *Znamenitye universanty* (St. Petersburg: Izdatel'stvo SPbGU, 2002), 1:156–78.

107. Slezkine, "N. Ia. Marr and the National Origins of Soviet Ethnogenetics," 833–34.

108. Such an overdeterministic connection is articulated, for instance, in Beers, *Renovating Russia*.

109. For an excellent account of how a particular intellectual tradition can lead to an outcome that is very different from the perceptions of the tradition's founders, see Marina Mogilner, *Homo imperii: Istoriia fizicheskoi antropologii v Rossii* (Moscow: NLO, 2008).

Chapter 3: N. S. Trubetskoi's *Europe and Mankind* and Eurasianist Antievolutionism

1. Readers are referred to the Introduction to this volume for the general context of the Eurasianist movement, its main tenets and actors.

2. Sergei Glebov, "Granitsy imperii kak granitsy moderna: Antikolonial'naia ritorika i teoriia kul'turnykh tipov v evraziistve," *Ab Imperio*, no. 2 (2003), 267–92.

3. Edward W. Said, *Orientalism* (London: Routledge, 1978); Edward W. Said, *Culture and Imperialism* (New York: Knopf, 1993); William V. Spanos, *The Legacy*

of Edward W. Said (Urbana: University of Illinois Press, 2009). For a vivid discussion of "orientalism" in Russian history, see D. Brower and E. Lazzerini, eds., *Russia's Orient: Imperial Borderlands and Peoples, 1700–1917* (Bloomington: University of Indiana Press, 1997); C. Clay, "Russian Ethnographers in the Service of Empire, 1856–1862," *Slavic Review*, no. 1 (1995), 45–61; N. Knight, "Grigor'ev in Orenburg, 1851–1862: Russian Orientalism in the Service of Empire?" *Slavic Review* 59, no. 1 (2000), 74–100; Forum on Russian Orientalism: A. Khalid, "Russian History and the Debate over Orientalism; N. Knight, "On Russian Orientalism: A Response to Adeeb Khalid"; M. Todorova, "Does Russian Orientalism Have a Russian Soul? A Contribution on the Debate between Nathaniel Knight and Adeeb Khalid," *Kritika* 1, no. 4 (2000), 691–728; Forum on Russian Orientalism in *Ab Imperio:* D. Schimmelpenninck van der Oye, "A Subtle Matter: Orientalism"; A. Etkind, "The Saved Man's Burden, or the Inner Colonization of Russia"; N. Knight, "Was Russia Its Own Orient? Reflections on the Contributions of Etkind and Schimmelpenninck on the Debate on Orientalism"; E. Campbell, "On the Question of Orientalism in Russia (in the Second Half of the 19th–Early 20th Centuries)," *Ab Imperio* 3, no. 1 (2002), 239–311; see also Vera Tolz, *"Russia's Own Orient": The Politics of Identity and Oriental Studies in the Late Imperial and Early Soviet Periods* (Oxford: Oxford University Press, 2011).

4. Roman Jakobson, ed., *N. S. Trubetzkoy's Letters and Notes*, 2nd ed. (Amsterdam: Mouton, 1985), 443.

5. Anatoly Liberman, "Postscript," in N. S. Trubetzkoy, *The Legacy of Genghis Khan and Other Essays on Russia's Identity*, ed. Liberman (Ann Arbor: Michigan Slavic Publications, 1991), 297.

6. Tsentral'nyi Istoricheskii Arkhiv g. Moskvy (TsIAM), f. 418, op. 91, l. 4.

7. See *Trudy Moskovskoi dialektologicheskoi komissii (1908–1919)*, in particular, *Opyt dialektologicheskoi karty russkogo iazyka v Evrope s prilozheniem ocherka russkoi dialektologii*, ed. N. N. Durnovo, N. N. Sokolov, and N. N. Ushakov (Moscow, 1915).

8. G. Vinokur, "Moskovskii Lingvisticheskii Kruzhok," *Nauchnye Izvestiia Akademicheskogo Tsentra Narkomprosa*, vol. 2 (Moscow, 1922).

9. Roman Jakobson, Manuscript of "O knige N. S. Trubetskogo 'Evropa i chelovechestvo,'" MIT Archives, MC 72, Box 28, f 103, p. 2. Translations are by the author, unless otherwise indicated.

10. M. K. Azadovskii, *Istoriia russkoi fol'kloristiki*, vol. 2 (Moscow: Gos. uchebno-ped. izdatel'stvo, 1962), 296–306.

11. Michael G. Smith, *Language and Power in the Creation of the USSR, 1917–1953* (Berlin: Mouton de Gruyter, 1998) explores the role of linguists in the processes of "korenizatsiia." The latter was an effort by the Bolshevik rulers to promote national identities in the non-Russian republics, and support national cadres for as

long as these nationalizing tendencies did not threaten commitment to Soviet unity and socialism.

12. Jakobson, *N. S. Trubetzkoy's Letters and Notes*, 4.

13. Immediately following the events, the Baku Soviet tended to represent them as a "Muslim uprising against Soviet power," a view shared by the USSR historical profession. Publicists in the Russian emigration as well as Western scholars tended to emphasize the nationalist and ethnic component of these events and the clash of leading Armenian and Muslim parties, including the Dashnaktsutiun and the Musawat parties. See Ronald G. Suny, *The Baku Commune, 1917–1918: Class and Nationality in the Russian Revolution* (Princeton, NJ: Princeton University Press, 1972), 214–33.

14. N. S. Trubetskoi, *Evropa i chelovechestvo* (Sofia: Rossiisko-bolgarskoe knigoizdatel'stvo, 1920), 5.

15. Trubetskoi, *Evropa i chelovechestvo*, 1–3.

16. Trubetskoi, *Evropa i chelovechestvo*, 5, 6.

17. Trubetskoi, *Evropa i chelovechestvo*, 8–10.

18. Trubetskoi, *Evropa i chelovechestvo*, 21–24.

19. Trubetskoi, *Evropa i chelovechestvo*, 25–26.

20. Trubetskoi, *Evropa i chelovechestvo*, 17.

21. Trubetskoi, *Evropa i chelovechestvo*, 18–19.

22. Trubetskoi, *Evropa i chelovechestvo*, 21, 33–35.

23. Trubetskoi, *Evropa i chelovechestvo*, 27–30, 31, 22, 23.

24. Trubetskoi, *Evropa i chelovechestvo*, 39–40.

25. Trubetskoi, *Evropa i chelovechestvo*, 42.

26. Trubetskoi, *Evropa i chelovechestvo*, 42.

27. Trubetskoi, *Evropa i chelovechestvo*, 42–43.

28. See Gabriel de Tarde, *The Laws of Imitation* (New York: H. Holt, 1903); Gabriel de Tarde, *La Logique sociale* (Paris: G. Baillière, 1895); Gabriel de Tarde, *Interpsychologie infantile* (Paris: Rey, 1909). Gabriele de Tarde's sociology is currently being rediscovered and is assuming a central stage in contemporary sociological debates. See Robert Leroux, "Gabriel Tarde: Vie, Oeuvres, Concepts," in Robert Leroux, *Les Grands théoriciens: Sciences humaines* (Paris: Ellipses, 2011); Matei Candea, ed., *The Social after Gabriel Tarde: Debates and Assessments* (London: Routledge, 2010); Sergio Tonkonoff, "A New Social Physic: The Sociology of Gabriel Tarde and Its Legacy," *Current Sociology* 61, no. 3 (May 2013), 267–82; for a very interesting discussion of the political implications of Tarde's sociology, see Alberto Toscano, "Powers of Pacification: State and Empire in Gabriel Tarde," *Economy and Society* 36, no. 4 (November 2007), 597–613. Toscano's focus on Tarde's concern with "pacification" and avoidance of social conflict highlights the most sympathetic reading that Trubetskoi gave the French thinker.

29. Trubetskoi, *Evropa i chelovechestvo*, 45.

30. Trubetskoi, *Evropa i chelovechestvo*, 55.

31. Trubetskoi, *Evropa i chelovechestvo*, 58, 61–62.

32. Trubetskoi, *Evropa i chelovechestvo*, 62–64.

33. Trubetskoi, *Evropa i chelovechestvo*, 67–70.

34. Trubetskoi, *Evropa i chelovechestvo*, 71, 79, 82.

35. Trubetskoi, *Evropa i chelovechestvo*, 82.

36. Nicholas Riasanovsky, "Prince N. S. Trubetskoy's 'Europe And Mankind,'" in *Jahrbücher für Geschichte Osteuropas* 13 (1964), 212; see also Nicholas Riasanovsky, "The Emergence of Eurasianism," *California Slavic Studies* 4 (1967), 39–72; and his "Asia through Russian Eyes," in *Russia and Asia: Essays on Russian Influence upon Asian Peoples*, ed. Wayne S. Vuchinich (Stanford, CA: Hoover Institution Press, 1972), 3–29.

37. MIT Archives. MC 72, Box 28, f. 103. Po povodu knigi N. S. Trubetskogo "Evropa i Chelovechestvo" (manuscript).

38. Stefan Wiederkehr, "Der Eurasismus als Erbe N. Ja. Danilevskijs? Bemerkungen zu Einem Topos der Forschung," *Studies in East European Thought* 52, no. 1–2 (March 1, 2000), 119–50.

39. N. S. Trubetskoi to S. O. Jakobson, August 24, 1921, MIT Archives, Roman Jakobson Papers, MC 72, Box 28, Folder 109, ll. 3–4.

40. Leonid Luks, "Die Ideologie der Eurasier im zeitgeschichtlichen Zusammenhang," *Jahrbücher für Geschichte Osteuropas* 34 (1986), 374–95.

41. On the emergence of the conflict between *Zivilisation* and *Kultur* in the German context, where *Zivilisation* stood for the negative influence of modernity, see Jörg Fisch, "Zivilisation, Kultur," in *Geschichtliche Grundbegrife: Historisches Lexikon zur politisch-sozialen Sprache in Deutschland*, ed. Otto Brunner, Werner Conze, Reinhart Koselleck, vol. 7 (Stuttgart: Klett-Gotta, 1992), 679–774.

42. N. S. Trubetskoi, *Post-Scriptum zur deutschen Auflage* (manuscript dated February 14, 1922), in MIT Archives, Roman Jakobson Papers, MC 72, Box 28, Folder 109, ll. 1–2

43. Trubetskoi, *Evropa i chelovechestvo*, iv.

44. Trubetskoi, *Evropa i chelovechestvo*, iv

45. Nikolaus S. Trubetzkoy and Roman Jakobson, *N. S. Trubetzkoy's Letters and Notes* (The Hague: Walter de Gruyter, 1985), 22.

46. Trubetzkoy and Jakobson, *N. S. Trubetzkoy's Letters and Notes*, 12–13.

47. N. S. Trubetskoi, "Verkhi i nizy russkoi kul'tury (Etnicheskaia baza russkoi kul'tury)," and "Ob istinnom i lozhnom natsionalizme," in *Iskhod k Vostoku* (Sofia: Rossiisko-bolgarskoe knigoizdatel'stvo, 1921), 86–103, 71–85.

48. N. S. Trubetskoi, "Review of *Sbornik materialov dlia opisaniia mestnostei i plemen Kavkaza* (vyp. XXXVII, otd. 3, Tiflis, 1907)," *Etnograficheskoe obozrenie* 20, no. 3 (1908), 146–51; N. S. Trubetskoi, "Kavkazskie paralleli k frigiiskomu mifu o rozhdenii iz kamnia (-zemli)," *Etnograficheskoe obozrenie* 20, no. 3 (1908), 88–92;

N. S. Trubetskoi, "Rededia na Kavkaze," *Etnograficheskoe obozrenie* 23, no. 1–2 (1911), 229–38.

49. Vucinich, *Darwin in Russian Thought* (Berkeley: University of California Press, 1988), 236–37; D. N. Anuchin, "Pamiati Maksima Maksimovicha Kovalevskogo," *Etnograficheskoe obozrenie*, no. 102 (1916), 1–16; N. S. Timasheff, "The Sociological Theories of Maksim M. Kovalevskii," in *An Introduction to the History of Sociology*, ed. H. E. Barnes (Chicago: University of Chicago Press, 1948), 441–57; A. Walicki, *A History of Russian Thought from the Enlightenment to Marxism* (Stanford, CA: Stanford University Press, 1979), 367–80; E. Badredinov, "Problems of Modernization in Late Imperial Russia: Maksim M. Kovalevskii on Social and Economic Reform," PhD diss., Louisiana State University, 2006; A. Matieva, "M. M. Kovalevskii i ego sovremenniki," *Voprosy Istorii* 3 (2001), 135–43. See also the fascinating study by Karuna Mantena, *Alibis of Empire: Henry Maine and the Ends of Liberal Imperialism* (Princeton, NJ: Princeton University Press, 2010).

50. Maksim Kovalevskii, *Ocherk proiskhozhdeniia sem'i i sobstvennosti* (St. Petersburg: Iu. N. Erlikh, 1896).

51. M. Kovalevskii, "Le clan chez les tribus indigènes de la Russie," *Revue internationale de sociologie*, no. 2 (1905), 6–101.

52. Maksim Kovalevskii, *Zakon i obychai na Kavkaze*, 2 vols. (Moscow: A. I. Mamontov, 1890).

53. Marina Mogilner, "Russian Physical Anthropology in Search of 'Imperial Race': Liberalism and Modern Scientific Imagination in the Imperial Situation," *Ab Imperio* 8, no. 1 (2007), 213–14.

54. "Inorodtsy" was a legal category in imperial Russia, denoting some but not all non-Russian ethnic groups. Toward the end of the imperial period, the term acquired a generic meaning of "non-Russians." See John W. Slocum, "Who, and When, Were the Inorodtsy? The Evolution of the Category of 'Aliens' in Imperial Russia." *Russian Review* 57, no. 2 (1998), 173–90.

55. Maksim Kovalevskii, "Otnoshenie Rossii k okrainam," *Russkie Vedomosti* (1905), Sunday, October 9, 2. Cited from Mogilner, "Russian Physical Antropology," 213.

56. Mogilner, "Russian Physical Antropology," 214.

57. Gosudarstvennyi Arkhiv Rossiiskoi Federatsii (GARF), f. 5783, op. 1, d. 312, l. 62 ob. Letter of N. S. Trubetskoi to P. N. Savitskii, 1927, n.d.

58. Marc Raeff, "Patterns of Russian Imperial Policy toward the Nationalities," in *Soviet Nationality Problems*, ed. Edward Alwarth (New York: Columbia University Press, 1971), 23–42.

59. Karuna Mantena, *Alibis of Empire: Henry Sumner Maine and the Ends of Liberal Imperialism* (Princeton, NJ: Princeton University Press, 2010).

60. See, for example, Stephen Sanderson, *Social Evolutionism: A Critical History* (Cambridge: Blackwell, 1990).

61. Heinrich Fick, "Unterschiedliche unterthänigste Vorstellungen und Anmerckungen betreffende die Beförderung des Civil wesens und guten Ordnungen auch Ihre Keiserl. Mtt und Dehro Reichsinteresse. Beilage 5," in *Heinrich Fick: Ein Beitrag zur Russischen Geschichte des XVIII. Jahrhunderts*, ed. A. R. Cederberg (Tartu-Dorpat, 1930), 107–9.

62. Ilya Gerasimov, Sergey Glebov, and Marina Mogilner, "The Post-Imperial Meets the Postcolonial: Russian Historical Experience and the Postcolonial Moment," *Ab Imperio*, no. 2 (2013), 97–134.

63. For an overview of Kovalevskii's intellectual evolution, see M. M. Kovalevskii, *Moia zhizn'* (Moscow: ROSSPEN, 2005).

64. On the reception of Darwinism in Russia, see Alexander Vucinich, *Science in Russian Culture: 1861–1917* (Stanford, CA: Stanford University Press, 1970), 275–85; Alexander Vucinich, *Darwin in Russian Thought*.

65. N. Ia. Danilevskii, *Darvinizm: Kriticheskoe issledovanie*, vols. 1–3 (St. Petersburg, 1885, 1889).

66. L. S. Berg, "Nomogenez, ili evoliutsiia na osnove zakonomernostei," in *Trudy po teorii evoliutsii, 1922–1930* (Leningrad: Nauka, 1977). Berg's work was first published as *Nomogenez, ili evoliutsiia na osnove zakonomernostei*, Trudy Geograficheskogo Instituta, vol. 1 (Petrograd, 1922). Remarkably, in 1926 an English edition was published: Leo S. Berg, *Nomogenesis or Evolution Determined by Law* (London, 1926).

67. N. S. Trubetskoi to P. P. Suvchinskii, March 5, 1926. BNF. DdM. Not catalogued.

Chapter 4: Conceiving the Territory

1. Iu. Shirinskii-Shikhmatov, "Rossiiskii natsional-maksimalizm i evraziistvo," *Evraziiskii sbornik* 6 (1929), 28. Translations are the author's unless otherwise indicated.

2. On classic Eurasianism, see S. Glebov, "The Challenge of the Modern: The Eurasianist Ideology and Movement, 1920–29," PhD diss., Rutgers University, 2004; S. Wiederkehr, *Die eurasische Bewegung: Wissenschaft und Politik in der russischen Emigration und im postsowjetischen Russland* (Cologne: Beiträge zur Geschichte Osteuropas, 2007), 39; M. Laruelle, *L'Idéologie eurasiste russe ou comment penser l'empire* (Paris: L'Harmattan, 1999).

3. P. N. Savitskii, "Geograficheskie i geopoliticheskie osnovy evraziistva," in *Kontinent Evraziia* (Moscow: Agraf, 1997), 300.

4. Anonymous, "Evraziistvo: Opyt sistematicheskogo izlozheniia," in *Puti Evrazii: Russkaia intelligentsiia i sud'by Rossii* (Moscow: Russkaia kniga, 1992), 70.

5. P. N. Savitskii, "V. V. Bartol'd kak istorik," in *Sbornik statei po arkheologii i vizantinovedeniiu* (Prague, 1931), 12.

6. M. Bassin, "Russia between Europe and Asia: The Ideological Construction of Geographical Space," *Slavic Review* 50, no. 1 (1993), 1–17.

7. *Evraziistvo: Opyt sistematicheskogo izlozheniia* (Paris: Evraziiskoe knigoizdatel'stvo, 1926), 32.

8. G. V. Vernadskii, *Opyt istorii Evrazii* (Berlin: Izdanie Evraziitsev, 1934), 5.

9. Savitskii, "Edinstvo mirozdaniia," 134.

10. P. N. Savitskii, *Rossiia—osobyi geograficheskii mir* (Paris: Evraziiskoe knigoizdatel'stvo, 1927), 47.

11. P. N. Savitskii, "Evraziistvo," in *Evraziiskii vremennik* (Berlin: Evraziiskoe izdatel'stvo, 1925), 4:6.

12. Savitskii, "Geograficheskie i geopoliticheskie osnovy evraziistva," 299.

13. S. Lubenski (pseudonym of Savitskii), "L'eurasisme," *Le monde slave* (January–March 1931), 86.

14. P. N. Savitsky, "Les problèmes de la géographie linguistique du point de vue du géographe," *Travaux du cercle linguistique de Prague*, no. 1 (1929), 145–56. On this question, see P. Sériot, "La linguistique, le discours sur la langue et l'espace géo-anthropologique russe," in *Congrès des slavistes 1998* (Bern: Peter Lang, 1998).

15. G. Nicolas and P. Sériot, "La Russie-Eurasie d'après Savitsky," *Cahiers de géographie du Québec* 42, no. 115 (1998), 67–91.

16. Savitskii, *Rossiia—osobyi geograficheskii mir*, 33.

17. Savitskii, *Rossiia—osobyi geograficheskii mir*, 38.

18. G. V. Vernadskii, "Protiv solntsa: Rasprostranenie russkogo gosudarstva k Vostoku," *Russkaia mysl'*, no. 1 (1914), 4.

19. P. Sériot, "La clôture impossible (l'espace en géographie linguistique: La querelle du continu et du discontinu)," in *Géographie et langage(s): Interface, représentation, interdisciplinarité*, ed. G. Nicolas (Sion: Institut universitaire Kurt Bösch, 1999), 227–48.

20. S. Glebov, "Granitsy imperii kak granitsy moderna: Antikolonial'naia ritorika i teoriia kult'urnykh tipov v evraziistve," *Ab Imperio*, no. 2 (2003), 267–92.

21. Vernadskii, "Protiv solntsa," 22–23.

22. Letter from P. N. Savitskii to L. N. Gumilev, February 1959, Fonds P. N. Savitskii, Slavic Library, Prague.

23. V. Ivanov, *My: Kul'turno-istoricheskie osnovy rossiiskii gosudarstvennosti* (Harbin: n.p., n.d.).

24. E. Khara-Davan, *Chingis-Khan kak polkovodets i ego nasledie* (Belgrade, 1929), 53.

25. Letter from P. N. Savitskii to L. N. Gumilev, November 6, 1957, Fonds P. N. Savitsky, Slavic Library, Prague.

26. P. Sériot, "L'origine contradictoire de la notion de système: la genèse naturaliste du structuralisme pragois," *Cahiers de l'ILSL*, Lausanne, no. 5 (1994), 19–58.

27. V. Ivanov, "O novoi estetike," *Evraziia*, no. 9 (January 19, 1929), 6.

28. G. Gursdorf, *Le romantisme* (Paris: Payot, 1993).

29. Savitskii, "Geograficheskii obzor Rossii-Evrazii," 282.

30. N. S. Trubetzkoy, "Sur le problème de la connaissance de la Russie par elle-même," in *L'Europe et l'humanité: Ecrits linguistiques et para-linguistiques,* trans. Patrick Sériot (Liège: Mardaga, 1996), 179.

31. See M. Beisswenger in this volume.

32. Trubetzkoy, "Sur le problème de la connaissance de la Russie par elle-même," 178.

33. Trubetzkoy, "Sur le problème de la connaissance de la Russie par elle-même," 179.

34. Anonymous, "Edito," *Evraziia,* no. 6 (December 29, 1928), 1.

35. P. Sériot, "N. S. Trubetzkoy, linguiste ou historiosophe des totalités organiques?" in Trubetzkoy, *L'Europe et l'humanité,* 5–36; P. Sériot, "La double vie de N. S. Trubetzkoy ou la clôture des systèmes," *Le gré des langues,* no. 5 (1993), 88–115.

36. P. V. Logovikov, "Nauchnye zadachi evraziistva," *Tridtsatye gody* (1931), 62.

37. S. Glebov, "A Life with Imperial Dreams: Petr Nikolaevich Savitsky, Eurasianism, and the Invention of 'Structuralist' Geography," *Ab Imperio,* no. 3 (2005), 299–329.

38. Savitskii, *Rossiia—osobyi geograficheskii mir,* 58.

39. Savitskii, "Geograficheskii obzor Rossii-Evrazii," 288.

40. Savitskii, *Rossiia—osobyi geograficheskii mir,* 32.

41. P. Sériot, "Aux sources du structuralisme: Une controverse biologique en Russie," *Études de lettres,* Lausanne (1994), 89–104.

42. Trubetzkoy, "Sur le problème de la connaissance de la Russie par elle-même," 177.

43. The term "topogenesis" was proposed as a translation for *mestorazvitie* by J. Toman in "The Ecological Connection: A Note on Geography and the Prague School," *Lingua e Stile,* no. 16 (1981), 280.

44. Savitskii, *Rossiia—osobyi geograficheskii mir,* 29.

45. Letter from P. N. Savitskii to L. N. Gumilev, January 1, 1957, in L. N. Gumilev, *Ritmy Evrazii: Epokhi i tsivilizatsii* (Moscow: Progress, 1993), 205.

46. N. S. Trubetskoi, "Vavilonskaia bashnia i smeshenie iazykov," in Trubetskoi, *Istoriia, kul'tura, iazyk,* 334.

47. M. Bassin, "Classical Eurasianism and the Geopolitics of Russian Identity," *Ab Imperio,* no. 2 (2003), 257–68.

48. P. N. Savitskii, "Migratsiia kul'tury," in *Iskhod k Vostoku* (Sofia: Rossiisko-bolgarskoe izdatel'stvo, 1921), 40–51.

49. K. A. Chkheidze, "Iz oblasti russkoi geopolitiki," *Tridtsatye gody* (1931), 105–14.

50. "Evraziistvo: Opyt sistematicheskogo izlozheniia," 378.

51. Savitskii, *Rossiia—osobyi geograficheskii mir,* 23–24.

52. Savitskii, "V. V. Bartol'd kak istorik," 7.

53. N. S. Trubetskoi, "Mysli ob avtarkii," in Trubetskoi, *Istoriia, kul'tura, iazyk*, 436–37.

54. V. P. Nikitin, "Nash kontinentalizm," *Evraziia*, no. 17 (March 16, 1929), 3.

55. N. S. Trubetskoi, "Ob idee-pravitel'nitse ideokraticheskogo gosudarstva," *Evraziiskaia khronika* 11 (1935), 34.

56. P. N. Savitskii, "Step' i osedlost'," in *Rossiia mezhdu Evropoi i Aziei: Evraziiskii soblazn* (Moscow: Nauka, 1993), 129.

57. A. V. Usachev, "Gosudarstvenno-chastnaia sistema v sel'skom khoziaistve," in *Na putiakh k Rossii-Evrazii: Utverzhdenie evraziitsev* (Prague: Izd. Evraziitsev, 1931), 14.

58. Savitskii, "Geograficheskie i geopoliticheskie osnovy evraziistva," 301.

59. P. P. Suvchinskii, "K preodoleniiu revoliutsii," *Evraziiskii vremennik*, vol. 3 (Berlin: Evraziiskoe izdatel'stvo, 1923), 45.

60. Savitskii, *Rossiia—osobyi geograficheskii mir*, 57.

Chapter 5: Eurasianism as a Form of Popperian Historicism?

1. Patrick Sériot, *Structure et totalité: Les origines intellectuelles du structuralisme en Europe centrale et orientale* (Paris: PUF, 1999), 255–305; Stefan Wiederkehr, *Die eurasische Bewegung: Wissenschaft und Politik in der russischen Emigration der Zwischenkriegszeit und im postsowjetischen Russland* (Cologne: Böhlau, 2007), 69–109.

2. Michael Hagemeister, *Nikolaj Fedorov: Studien zu Leben, Werk und Wirkung* (Munich: Sagner, 1989), 417–57; Nikolai Fedorov, *Filosofiia obshchego dela*, 2 vols. (Moscow: Vernyi, 1906–13).

3. Karl Popper, *The Poverty of Historicism*, repr. (London: Routledge, 2004), 3. Another definition by Popper reads as follows: "The belief . . . that it is the task of the social sciences to lay bare the *law of evolution of society* in order to foretell its future . . . might be perhaps described as the central historicist doctrine" (105–6). See also Karl R. Popper, "Prediction and Prophecy in the Social Sciences," in *Conjectures and Refutations: The Growth of Scientific Knowledge*, 3rd rev. ed. (London: Routledge, 1969), 336–46; Karl R. Popper, *The Open Society and Its Enemies* (London: Routledge, 1945), 1:2–6.

4. Popper, *The Poverty of Historicism*, v.

5. Popper, *The Poverty of Historicism*, 128.

6. Popper, *The Poverty of Historicism*, 49. As to the historicists' "activism," Popper quotes Marx's eleventh Thesis on Feuerbach ("The philosophers have only *interpreted* the world in various ways; the point however is to *change it*") even twice in full (8, 52).

7. Popper, *The Open Society and Its Enemies*, 2:266; see also 1:4, 2:258–67. See also Karl R. Popper, "Utopia and Violence," in *Conjectures and Refutations*, 355–63.

8. Popper, *The Poverty of Historicism*, 17–19, 109–10.

9. On the history of Eurasianism, see Otto Böss, *Die Lehre der Eurasier: Ein Beitrag zur russischen Ideengeschichte des 20. Jahrhunderts* (Wiesbaden: Harrassowitz, 1961); Margarita G. Vandalkovskaia, *Istoricheskaia nauka rossiiskoi emigratsii: 'Evraziiskii soblazn'* (Moscow: Pamiatniki istoricheskoi mysli, 1997); Marlene Laruelle, *L'idéologie eurasiste russe ou comment penser l'empire* (Paris: Harmattan, 1999); Ryszard Paradowski, *Eurazjatyckie Imperium Rosji: Studium idei* (Toruń: UMK, 2001); Aldo Ferrari, *La Foresta e la Steppa: Il mito dell'Eurasia nella cultura russa* (Milan: Scheiwiller, 2003); Emil Voráček, *Eurasijství v ruském politickém myšleni: Osudy jednoho z porevolučních ideových směrů ruské meziválečné emigrace* (Prague: Set Out, 2004); Milan Subotić, *Put Rusije: Evroazijsko stanovište* (Belgrade: Plato, 2004); Nikolaj S. Trubetzkoy, *Russland—Europa—Eurasien: Ausgewählte Schriften zur Kulturwissenschaft*, ed. Fedor B. Poljakov (Vienna: Österreichische Akademie der Wissenschaften, 2005); Sergei Glebov, *Evraziistvo mezhdu imperiei i modernom: Istoriia v dokumentakh* (Moscow: Novoe izdatel'stvo, 2010); Wiederkehr, *Die eurasische Bewegung* (with an exhaustive bibliography).

10. Petr N. Savitskii, "Migratsiia kul'tury," in *Iskhod k Vostoku: Predchuvstvie i sverzheniia* (Sofia: Rossiisko-bolgarskoe knigoizdatel'stvo, 1921), 43–45.

11. The term "Eurasia" is used in the sense of Eurasianism, that is, as the name of a third continent between Europe and Asia, throughout this chapter.

12. Savitskii, "Migratsiia kul'tury," 46; in a slightly altered translation from Petr N. Savitsky, "The Migration of Culture," in *Exodus to the East: Forebodings and Events*, ed. Ilya Vinkovetsky and Charles Schlacks Jr. (Idyllwild, CA: Schlacks, 1996), 46–47.

13. The idea of *translatio studii* ("transfer of knowledge"), that is, the assumption that the cultural center of the world shifts from one geographical place to another, goes back to classical antiquity. It was especially popular among medieval authors and often went hand in hand with the idea of *translatio imperii* ("transfer of rule"). Jacques Verger, "Translatio studii," in *Lexikon des Mittelalters* (Stuttgart: Metzler, 1997), vol. 8, cols. 946–47.

14. Stefan Wiederkehr, "Der Eurasismus als Erbe N. Ja. Danilevskijs? Bemerkungen zu einem Topos der Forschung," *Studies in East European Thought* 52, no. 1–2 (2000), 119–50; Robert E. MacMaster, *Danilevsky: A Russian Totalitarian Philosopher* (Cambridge, MA: Harvard University Press, 1967); Stephen Lukashevich, *Konstantin Leontev (1831–1891): A Study in Russian "Heroic Vitalism"* (New York: Pageant Press, 1967).

15. Petr N. Savitskii, "Povorot k Vostoku," in *Iskhod k Vostoku*, 3; in a slightly altered translation from Savitsky, "A Turn to the East," in Vinkovetsky and Schlacks, *Exodus to the East*, 7. See also Georgii V. Florovskii, "O narodakh neistoricheskikh: Strana otsov i strana detei," in *Iskhod k Vostoku*, 63–66; Petr M.

Bitsilli, "'Vostok' i 'zapad' v istorii starogo sveta," in *Na putiakh* (Berlin: Gelikon, 1922), 338–40.

16. Oswald Spengler, *Der Untergang des Abendlandes: Umrisse einer Morphologie der Weltgeschichte*, repr. (Munich: dtv, 1993). On Spengler, see John Farrenkopf, *Prophet of Decline: Spengler on World History and Politics* (Baton Rouge: Louisiana State University Press, 2001). For example, Leonid Luks, "Die Ideologie der Eurasier im zeitgeschichtlichen Zusammenhang," *Jahrbücher für Geschichte Osteuropas* N. F. 34 (1986), 393; Sergei S. Khoruzhii, "Zhizn' i uchenie L'va Karsavina," in Lev P. Karsavin, *Religiozno-filosofskie sochineniia*, vol. 1 (Moscow: Renessans, 1992), xl.

17. In fact, Trubetskoi did without approaching Spengler when his translator Sergei O. Jakobson told him that he had successfully contacted Otto Hoetzsch, professor of Russian history at Berlin University, as the author of the preface. Nikolai S. Trubetskoi, Letter to Sergei O. Jakobson, August 24, 1921, in Kristina Pomorska, "N. S. Trubetskoi o perevode ego kniga *Evropa i chelovechestvo*," *Rossiia / Russia* 3 (1977), 235.

18. Petr N. Savitskii, "Evraziistvo," *Evraziiskii vremennik* 4 (1925), 11.

19. "Vstuplenie," in *Iskhod k Vostoku*, iv; Georgii V. Florovskii, "Razryvy i sviazi," in *Iskhod k Vostoku*, 11.

20. "The Russian Revolution attains a religious sense that it would be a sin not to understand." Petr P. Suvchinskii, Letter to Nikolai S. Trubetskoi, September 20, 1922, in "K istorii evraziistva: 1922–1924 gg.," comp. Elena Krivosheeva, *Rossiiskii arkhiv* 5 (1994), 476 (translations are by the author if not otherwise indicated). See also Georgii V. Florovskii, "O patriotizme pravednom i grekhovnom," in *Na putiakh*, 289.

21. Florovskii, "Razryvy i sviazi," 12–13. See also Florovskii, "O patriotizme pravednom i grekhovnom," 279; Petr P. Suvchinskii, "Sila slabych," in *Iskhod k Vostoku*, 8; Petr P. Suvchinskii, "K preodoleniiu revoliutsii," *Evraziiskii vremennik* 3 (1923), 37–38.

22. "Vstuplenie," in *Iskhod k Vostoku*, iii–v; in a slightly altered translation from the "Introduction" in Vinkovetsky and Schlacks, *Exodus to the East*, 1–2. See also *Evraziistvo i kommunizm* (n.p. [1930?]), 26.

23. Lev P. Karsavin, "Fenomenologiia revoliutsii," *Evraziiskii vremennik* 5 (1927), 28–74; Lev P. Karsavin, "K poznaniiu revoliutsii," *Evraziia* 11 (February 2, 1929), 2–3. See Julia Mehlich, "Lew Karsawin und die russische 'Einzigartigkeit'" (Cologne: BIOst, 1996), 31–32; Claire Hauchard, "L. P. Karsavin et le mouvement eurasien," *Revue des Études slaves* 68 (1996), 361–63.

24. On the Slavophiles, see Peter K. Christoff, *An Introduction to Nineteenth-Century Russian Slavophilism: A Study in Ideas*, 4 vols. ('s-Gravenhage: Mouton, 1961–1991); Andrzej Walicki, *The Slavophile Controversy: History of a Conservative Utopia in Nineteenth-Century Russian Thought* (Oxford: Clarendon, 1975); Su-

sanna Rabow-Edling, *The Intellectuals and the Idea of the Nation in Slavophile Thought* (Stockholm: University of Stockholm, 2001); Maja Soboleva, "Zur Typologie der 'russischen Idee': Kulturologische Konzeptionen im Rahmen des slavophilen Paradigmas," *Zeitschrift für Slawistik* 46 (2001), 157–84; Jekatherina Lebedewa, *Russische Träume: Die Slawophilen—ein Kulturphänomen* (Berlin: Frank und Timme, 2008).

25. "Vstuplenie," in *Iskhod k Vostoku*, vi; Petr P. Suvchinskii, "Epokha very: V. V. Gippiusu," in *Iskhod k Vostoku*, 14–27; Georgii V. Florovskii, "Khitrost' razuma," in *Iskhod k Vostoku*, 28–39; Petr N. Savitskii, "Dva mira," in *Na putiakh*, 9–26; Petr P. Suvchinskii, "Vechnyi ustoi," in *Na putiakh*, 127–28; Petr N. Savitskii, "Poddanstvo idei," *Evraziiskii vremennik* 3 (1923), 14; Petr N. Savitskii, "Evraziistvo," *Evraziiskii vremennik* 4 (1925), 5–23; Vladimir N. Il'in, "Evraziistvo i slavianofil'stvo," *Evraziiskaia khronika* 4 (1926), 1–21; "Evraziistvo: Opyt sistematicheskogo izlozheniia" [1926], in *Puti Evrazii: Russkaia intelligentsiia i sud'by Rossii*, ed. Igor' A. Isaev (Moscow: Russkaia kniga, 1992), 355–56.

26. Sériot, *Structure et totalité*, 255–70.

27. Nikolai S. Trubetskoi, "Ot avtora," in *K probleme russkogo samopoznaniia: Sobranie statei* (Paris: Evraziiskoe knigoizdatel'stvo, 1927), 4.

28. Petr N. Savitskii, "Geograficheskii obzor Rossii-Evrazii," in *Rossiia—osobyi geograficheskii mir* (Prague: Evraziiskoe knigoizdatel'stvo, 1927), 32; Petr N. Savitskii, Letter to Roman Jakobson, August 9, 1930, in *Letters and Other Materials from the Moscow and Prague Linguistic Circles, 1912–1945*, ed. Jindřich Toman (Ann Arbor: Michigan Slavic Publications, 1994), 131. On this, see also Patrik Serio [Patrick Sériot], "Lingvistika geografov i geografiia lingvistov: R. O. Jakobson i P. N. Savitskii," in *Roman Jakobson: Teksty, dokumenty, issledovaniia*, ed. Khenrik Baran and Sergei I. Gindin (Moscow: RGGU, 1999), 352–53.

29. P. V. Logovikov [pseudonym of Petr N. Savitskii], "Nauchnye zadachi evraziistva," in *Tridtsatye gody* (Paris: Izdanie evraziitsev, 1931), 56–57.

30. Petr N. Savitski, "'Pod"em' i 'depressiia' v drevne-russkoi istorii," *Evraziiskaia khronika* 11 (1935), 65. See also Georgii V. Vernadskii, *Nachertanie russkoi istorii*, part 1 (Prague: Evraziiskoe knigoizdatel'stvo, 1927), 5–23; Georgii V. Vernadskii, *Opyt istorii Evrazii s poloviny VI veka do nastoiashchego vremeni* (Berlin: Izdanie evraziitsev, 1934), 14–28.

31. Logovikov, "Nauchnye zadachi evraziistva," 58–59.

32. Sériot, *Structure et totalité*, 298–303.

33. Trubetskoi, "Ot avtora," 6.

34. Nikolai S. Trubetskoi, *Evropa i chelovechestvo* [1920], in *Istoriia. Kul'tura. Iazyk*, ed. Viktor M. Zhivov (Moscow: Progress, 1995), 56; in a slightly altered translation from Nikolai S. Trubetskoy, "Europe and Mankind," in *The Legacy of Genghis Khan and Other Essays on Russia's Identity*, ed. Anatoly Liberman (Ann Arbor: Michigan Slavic Publications, 1991), 3.

35. Savitskii, "Evraziistvo," 20.

36. Trubetskoi, "Ot avtora," 7.

37. Logovikov,"Nauchnye zadachi evraziistva," 57.

38. Nikolai S. Trubetskoi, "Obshcheevraziiskii natsionalizm," *Evraziiskaia khronika* 9 (1927), 30; in a slightly altered translation from Nikolai S. Trubetzkoy, "Pan-Eurasian Nationalism," in *The Legacy of Genghis Khan*, 242 (emphasis added). See also "Manifesto without Author and Title," *Evraziiskii sbornik* 6 (1929), 16.

39. Trubetskoi, "Obshcheevraziiskii natsionalizm," 28; translation from *The Legacy of Genghis Khan*, 239.

40. Savitskii, "Poddanstvo idei," 16–17.

41. Iakov D. Sadovskii, "Opponentam evraziistva," *Evraziiskii vremennik* 3 (1923), 170–71.

42. *Evraziistvo: Deklaratsiia, formulirovka, tezisy* (Prague: Izdanie evraziitsev, 1932), 3.

43. Nikolai S. Trubetskoi, "O gosudarstvennom stroe i forme pravleniia," *Evraziiskaia khronika* 8 (1927), 8.

44. Nikolaj S. Trubetskoi, "Ob idee-pravitel'nitse ideokraticheskogo gosudarstva," *Evraziiskaia khronika* 11 (1935), 29–30; in a slightly altered translation from Nikolai S. Trubetskoy, "On the Idea Governing the Ideocratic State," in *The Legacy of Genghis Khan*, 269. See also *Evraziistvo i kommunizm*, 29.

45. *Evraziistvo: Deklaraciia, formulirovka, tezisy*, 15. See also Trubetskoi, "Ob idee-pravitel'nitse ideokraticheskogo gosudarstva," 35.

46. Sofiia Bokhan, "K novoi epokhe," in *Novaia epokha: Ideokratiia. Politika— ekonomika. Obzory*, ed. Vladimir A. Peil' (Narva: Izdanie evraziitsev, 1933), 9–10. See also Lev P. Karsavin, "Osnovy politiki," *Evraziiskii vremennik* 5 (1927), 208–9.

47. P. V. Logovikov [pseudonym of Petr N. Savitskii], "Vlast' organizatsionnoi idei," in *Tridtsatye gody*, 134. Sometimes the expression is "sila organizatsionnoi idei" (Savitski, "'Pod"em' i 'depressiia' v drevne-russkoi istorii," 95). On the economic thinking of the Eurasianists, see Otto Böss, "Zur Wirtschaftskonzeption der 'Eurasier,'" in *Probleme des Industrialismus in Ost und West: Festschrift für Hans Raupach*, ed. Werner Gumpel and Dietmar Keese (Munich: Olzog, 1973), 481–92.

48. Vladimir A. Peil', "Za ideokratiiu i plan," in Peil', *Novaia epokha*, 3.

49. Bokhan, "K novoi epokhe," 9.

50. Trubetskoi, "Obshcheevraziiskii natsionalizm," 30; Petr N. Savitskii, *Mestorazvitie russkoi promyshlennosti* (Berlin: Izdanie evraziitsev, 1932).

51. Petr N. Savitskii, "Piatiletnii plan i khoziaistvennoe razvitie strany" [1932], in *Politicheskaia istoriia russkoi emigratsii, 1920–1940 gg.: Dokumenty i materialy*, ed. Aleksandr F. Kiselev (Moscow: Vlados, 1999), 283.

52. Savitskii, "Piatiletnii plan i khoziaistvennoe razvitie strany," 285.

53. "Evraziistvo: Formulirovka 1927 g.," in *Evraziiskaia khronika* 9 (1927), 14;

Nikolai L. Timofeev, "O sovetskoi promyshlennosti: Zametki evraziitsa," in *Evraziiskii sbornik* 6 (1929), 73; *Evraziistvo: Deklaraciia, formulirovka, tezisy*, 5, 21–22; Petr N. Savitskii, "Ocherednye voprosy ekonomiki Evrazii," in Peil', *Novaia epokha*, 13.

54. Savitski, "Dva mira," 23–25; *Evraziistvo i kommunizm*, 4–5.

55. *Evraziistvo: Deklaraciia, formulirovka, tezisy*, 17.

56. Luks, "Die Ideologie der Eurasier," 374–95; Leonid Luks, "'Eurasier' und 'Konservative Revolution': Zur antiwestlichen Versuchung in Russland und Deutschland," in *Deutschland und die russische Revolution 1917–1924*, ed. Gerd Koenen and Lew Kopelew (Munich: Fink, 1998), 219–39.

57. Bokhan, "K novoi epokhe," 10 (emphasis added).

58. Peil', "Za ideokratiiu i plan," 5. See also "Manifesto without Author and Title," 16; "Idet-li mir k ideokratii?" *Evrazijskaja Chronika* 11 (1935), 38–39.

59. Stefan Wiederkehr, "Eurasianism as a Reaction to Pan-Turkism," in *Russia between East and West: Scholarly Debates on Eurasianism*, ed. Dmitry Shlapentokh (Leiden: Brill, 2007), 39–60.

60. Nikolai S. Trubetskoi, "Russkaia problema," in *Na putiakh*, 296–300.

61. Trubetskoi, "Russkaia problema," 302, in a slightly altered translation from, Nikolai S. Trubetzkoy, "The Russian Problem," in *The Legacy of Genghis Khan*, 107. See also Trubetskoi, *Evropa i chelovechestvo*, 99–100.

62. Trubetskoi, *Evropa i chelovechestvo*, 104. See also Nikolai S. Trubetskoi, "My i drugie," *Evraziiskii vremennik* 4 (1925), 79–80. On Trubetskoi's *Evropa i chelovechestvo*, see Nicholas V. Riasanovsky, "Prince N. S. Trubetskoy's 'Europe and Mankind,'" *Jahrbücher für Geschichte Osteuropas* N. F. 12 (1964), 207–20.

63. Trubetskoi, "Russkaia problema," 304, 306.

64. Nikolai S. Trubetskoi, "Nash otvet" [1925], in *Istoriia. Kul'tura. Iazyk*, 344.

65. On Russian messianism, see Peter J. S. Duncan, *Russian Messianism: Third Rome, Revolution, Communism and After* (London: Routledge, 2000).

66. Karsavin, "Osnovy politiki," 188.

67. "Manifesto without Author and Title," 16.

68. Nikolai N. Alekseev, "Dukhovnye predposylki evraziiskoi kul'tury," *Evraziiskaia khronika* 11 (1935), 16.

69. Savitskii, "Poddanstvo idei," 15.

70. Alekseev, "Dukhovnye predposylki evraziiskoi kul'tury," 28.

71. Ivan V. Stepanov, *Belye, krasnye i evraziistvo* (Brussels: n.p., 1927), 1, 62–63; Georgii N. Polkovnikov, *Dialektika istorii* (Paris: Izdanie evraziitsev, 1931), 47, 155–56, 162–63.

72. *Evraziistvo i kommunizm*, 4. See also *Evraziistvo: deklaraciia, formulirovka, tezisy*, 19; Vladimir N. Il'in, "Pod znakom dialektiki: Progress tekhniki, krizis marksizma i problemy detsentralizatsii material'noi kul'tury,' in *Tridtsatye gody*, 142–45.

73. *Evraziistvo i kommunizm*, 31.

Chapter 6: Metaphysics of the Economy

I wish to thank Sergey Glebov, Gary M. Hamburg, and Liudmila G. Novikova for their valuable comments on this chapter.

1. Savitskii outlined his Eurasianist ideas first in early 1921, in P. N. Savitskii, "Evropa i Evraziia (Po povodu broshiury kn. N. S. Trubetskogo *Evropa i chelovechestvo*)," *Russkaia mysl'*, nos. 1–2 (1921), 119–38. On his biography and other writings, see Martin Beisswenger, ed., *Petr Nikolaevich Savitsky (1895–1968): A Bibliography of His Published Works* (Prague: Slavonic Library, 2008).

2. See, for example, G. Nicolas et al., "La Russie-Eurasie d'après Savitsky," *Cahiers de Géographie du Québec* 42, no. 115 (1998), 67–91; V. I. Durnovtsev, "Petr Nikolaevich Savitskii (1895–1968)," in *Istoriki Rossii: Biografii*, ed. A. A. Chernobaev (Moscow: ROSSPEN, 2001), 705–13; Serguei Glebov, "A Life with Imperial Dreams: Petr Nikolaevich Savitsky, Eurasianism, and the Invention of 'Structuralist' Geography," *Ab Imperio*, no. 3 (2005), 299–329; Stefan Wiederkehr, *Die eurasische Bewegung: Wissenschaft und Politik in der russischen Emigration der Zwischenkriegszeit und im postsowjetischen Russland* (Cologne: Böhlau, 2007), 75–84. Although V. Iu. Bystriukov pays some attention to Savitskii's economic views, he still claims that "Savitskii primarily studied the geographic characteristics of Eurasia." V. Iu. Bystriukov, *V poiskakh Evrazii: Obshchestvenno-politicheskaia i nauchnaia deiatel'nost' P. N. Savitskogo v gody emigratsii (1920–1938 gg.)* (Samara: Samarskoe knizhnoe izdatel'stvo, 2007), 164.

3. For instance, see, I. Rozental', "Savitskii, Petr Nikolaevich," in *Russkoe zarubezh'e: Zolotaia kniga emigratsii (pervaia tret' XX veka). Entsiklopedicheskii biograficheskii slovar'* (Moscow: ROSSPEN, 1997), 562–64; V. G. Makarov and A. M. Matveeva, "Geosofiia P. N. Savitskogo: Mezhdu ideologiei i naukoi," *Voprosy filosofii*, no. 2 (2007), 123–35.

4. Randall Poole, "The Neo-Idealist Reception of Kant in the Moscow Psychological Society," *Journal of the History of Ideas* 60, no. 2 (1999), 319–43. On the neoidealist tradition in Russian thought, see also Gary M. Hamburg and Randall A. Poole, eds., *A History of Russian Philosophy, 1830–1930: Faith, Reason and the Defense of Human Dignity* (Cambridge: Cambridge University Press, 2010).

5. On the *Problems of Idealism*, see Randall Poole, ed., *Problems of Idealism: Essays in Russian Social Philosophy* (New Haven, CT: Yale University Press, 2003). On the *Signposts* almanac, see Christopher Read, *Religion, Revolution and the Russian Intelligentsiia, 1900–1912: The Vekhi Debate and Its Intellectual Background* (London: Macmillan, 1979). The Silver Age has been characterized by Catherine Evtuhov, *The Cross and the Sickle: Sergei Bulgakov and the Fate of Russian Religious Philosophy* (Ithaca, NY: Cornell University Press, 1997), 1–17.

6. The term "revolt against positivism" appears to have been coined, albeit on

the basis of West European examples, by H. Stuart Hughes in *Consciousness and Society: The Reorientation of European Social Thought, 1890–1930* (New York: Knopf, 1958).

7. On this larger context, see Theodore H. von Laue, *Sergei Witte and the Industrialization of Russia* (New York: Columbia University Press, 1963); and Terence Emmons and Wayne S. Vucinich, eds., *The Zemstvo in Russia: An Experiment in Local Self-Government* (Cambridge: Cambridge University Press, 1982).

8. S. P. [Savitskii], "Ob ukrainskoi vyshivke XVIII veka i sovremennom ee vozrozhdenii," *Chernigovskaia zemskaia nedelia*, no. 20 (June 20, 1914), 4–5; S. P. [Savitskii], "Zamechaniia k programme klassicheskoi gimnazii," *Chernigovskaia zemskaia nedelia*, no. 25 (August 30, 1913), 1–3. Translations are the author's unless otherwise indicated.

9. P. B. Struve, "Velikaia Rossiia: Iz razmyshlenii o probleme russkogo mogushchestva," *Russkaia mysl'* 29, no. 1 (1908), 143–57.

10. P. N. Savitskii, "Bor'ba za imperiiu: Imperializm v politike i ekonomike," *Russkaia mysl'* 36, no. 1 (1915), 71.

11. Savitskii, "Bor'ba za imperiiu," 71, 73.

12. P. N. Savitskii, "K voprosu o razvitii proizvoditel'nykh sil," *Russkaia mysl'* 37, no. 3 (1916), 42–43.

13. "Metafizika khoziaistva i opytnoe ego poznanie" was written under P. B. Struve's supervision. There are two complete copies of this work: (a) a typescript version, kept at the Gosudarstvennyi archiv Rossiiskoi Federatsii [hereafter, GARF], f. 5783 [fond P. N. Savitskii], op. 1, ed. khr. 72 and ed. khr. 73, consisting of ten chapters and apparently completed in 1920; (b) a copy edited by Savitskii in the mid-1920s, kept at the Slovanská knihovna in Prague, P. N. Savitskii papers [hereafter, SKP], box 8, no. 176. There is no indication that Savitskii ever defended the thesis, which remained unpublished with the exception of a brief excerpt devoted to the critique of the economic views of Struve and Bulgakov. P. N. Savitskii, "Metafizika khoziaistva," in *Sbornik statei posviashchennykh Petru Berngardovichu Struve ko dniu tridtsatipiatiletiia ego nauchno-publitsisticheskoi deiatel'nosti* (Prague: n.p., 1925), 143–50.

14. Savitskii readily admitted this influence. GARF, f. 5765 [fond Russian Law Faculty in Prague], op. 2, ed. khr. 809, ll. 96–97, P. N. Savitskii, "Literatura k programme magisterskogo ispytaniia po politicheskoi ekonomii" [1922].

15. S. N. Bulgakov, *Filosofiia khoziaistva*, ed. V. V. Sapov (Moscow: Nauka, 1990). On Bulgakov's economic views, see in particular Evtuhov, *The Cross and the Sickle*, 158–86.

16. Savitskii, "Metafizika khoziaistva," SKP, box 8, no. 176, pp. 175, 180, 189–90.

17. P. B. Struve, *Khoziaistvo i tsena*, vol. 1: *Khoziaistvo i obshchestvo: Tsena i tsennost'* (St. Petersburg: V. P. Riabushinskii, 1913), 91.

18. On Struve's economic theory, see Richard Pipes, *Struve: Liberal on the Right* (Cambridge, MA: Harvard University Press, 1980), 115–68.

19. Savitskii, "Metafizika khoziaistva," SKP, box 8, no. 176, pp. 190, 193, 196.

20. Savitskii, "Metafizika khoziaistva," SKP, box 8, no. 176, p. 55.

21. Karl Marx, *Capital: A Critical Analysis of Capitalist Production* (Moscow: Foreign Languages Publishing House, 1954), 1:51.

22. Savitskii, "Metafizika khoziaistva," SKP, box 8, no. 176, pp. 61, 97, 62.

23. Savitskii, "Metafizika khoziaistva," SKP, box 8, no. 176, pp. 243–44, 282–83.

24. Savitskii was well aware of and interested in the Russian literary and religious context of the "Prekrasnaia Dama" as represented by the writings of Vladimir Solov'ev as well as Alexander Blok and Andrei Bely. See his sympathetic review of Bely's "Pervoe svidanie": Petronik [Savitskii], "'Pervoe svidanie': Poema Andreia Belogo," *Russkaia mysl'* 42, no. 8–9 (1921), 329–34.

25. Savitskii, "Metafizika khoziaistva," SKP, box 8, no. 176, pp. 249, 205.

26. GARF, f. 5783, op. 1, ed. khr. 403, l. 154, letter from Suvchinskii to Savitsky [mid-September 1923].

27. The precise emergence of the Eurasianist group is still largely unknown. In November 1920, Liven informed Savitskii about the presence in Sofia of the "Eurasianists" Suvchinskii and Trubetskoi, but Savitskii's personal acquaintance with them appears to have taken place only in January 1921: GARF, f. 5783, op. 1, ed. khr. 358, ll. 49–49 verso, letter from Liven to Savitskii [late November 1920]; published in M. Baissvenger [Beisswenger], "Chetyre pis'ma A. A. Livena k P. N. Savitskomu (1920–1922) i odno pis'mo P. N. Savitskogo k A. A. Livenu (1920)," *Transactions of the Association of Russian-American Scholars in the U.S.A.* 37 (2011–2012), 14–16.

28. GARF, f. 5783, op. 1, ed. khr. 357, l. 15, letter from Savitskii to "Dorogoi drug" [B. A. Nikol'skii] [late November 1921].

29. P. N. Savitskii, "Khoziaistvo i vera," *Rul'*, no. 295 (November 5, 1921), 2.

30. GARF, f. 5783, op. 1, ed. khr. 357, ll. 15–15 verso, letter from Savitskii to "Dorogoi drug" [B. A. Nikol'skii] [late November 1921].

31. GARF, letter from Savitskii to "Dorogoi drug" [B. A. Nikol'skii] [late November 1921].

32. P. N. Savitskii, "Poddanstvo idei," *Evraziiskii vremennik* 2 (1923), 13.

33. GARF, f. 5783, op. 1, ed. khr. 182, manuscript "Khoziaistvo blagoslovennoe" [late 1921/early 1922].

34. P. N. Savitskii, "K obosnovaniiu evraziistva," *Rul'*, no. 350 (January 11, 1922), 3.

35. P. N. Savitskii, "K voprosu ob ekonomicheskoi doktrine evraziistva," *Evraziiskaia khronika*, no. 6 (1926), 37.

36. P. N. Savitskii, "Dva mira," in *Na putiakh: Utverzhdenie evraziitsev* (Berlin: Gelikon, 1922), 25–26.

37. P. N. Savitskii, "Evraziistvo," *Evraziiskii vremennik* 4 (1925), 20.

38. P. N. Savitskii, "Khoziain i khoziaistvo," *Evraziiskii vremennik* 4 (1925), 406. The English translation of this term poses certain difficulties because the Russian term "khoziain" allows both for an explicitly secular, economic meaning as well as for a religious interpretation, as a "good Lord" or "steward." In a translated article in French that most probably received Savitskii's authorization, the term "khoziain" was rendered as "maître," which, in turn, suggests an English translation as "master." P. Vostokov [Savitskii], "L'U.R.S.S. en 1931," *Le Monde slave*, n.s., no. 9 (I) (1932), 270.

39. P. N. Savitskii, "Evraziistvo," 7.

40. GARF, f. 5783, op. 1, ed. khr. 325, l. 9, letter from Savitskii to A. G. Romanitskii, December 28, 1920; GARF, f. 5783, op. 1, ed. khr. 324, l. 12, letter from Savitskii to P. B. Struve, December 11, 1920; "Russkie s.-kh. kolonii," *Poslednie novosti*, no. 400 (August 6, 1921), 4. One *desiatina* is about 2.7 acres.

41. Savitskii, "Khoziain," 406, 408.

42. Savitskii, "Khoziain," 410–12, 424, 433–35.

43. Savitskii, "Khoziain," 425–26.

44. Savitskii, "Khoziain," 436–39. On discussions about the "person" in the Eurasianist movement more generally, see Martin Beisswenger, "Eurasianism: Affirming the Person in the 'Era of Faith,'" in *A History of Russian Philosophy, 1830–1930: Faith, Reason and the Defense of Human Dignity*, ed. Gary M. Hamburg and Randall A. Poole (Cambridge: Cambridge University Press, 2010), 363–80.

45. Savitskii, "K voprosu," 36.

46. P. N. Savitskii, *Geograficheskie osobennosti Rossii*, vol. 1: *Rastitel'nost' i pochvy* (Prague: Evraziiskoe knigoizdatel'stvo, 1927), 3.

47. P. N. Savitskii, *Mestorazvitie russkoi promyshlennosti* (Berlin: Izdanie evraziitsev, 1932), 10.

48. Savitskii, "K oboznovaniiu," 2.

49. Savitskii, "K oboznovaniiu," 3.

50. P. N. Savitskii, "Step' i osedlost'," in *Na putiakh*, 356.

51. P. V. Logovikov [Savitskii], "Nauchnye zadachi evraziistva," in *Tridtsatye Gody* ([Paris]: Izdanie evraziitsev, 1931), 53–54, 58–59.

52. Boris Gasparov, "The Ideological Principles of Prague School Phonology," in *Language, Poetry and Poetics: The Generation of the 1890s: Jakobson, Trubetzkoy, Majakovskij*, ed. Krystina Pomorska, Elżbieta Chodakowska, Hugh McLean, and Brent Vine (Berlin: Mouton de Gruyter, 1987), 72.

53. On Savitskii's contribution to the emergence of the Prague School's linguistic structuralism, see Nikolaj Savický, "O některých méně známých pramenech Tezí Pražského lingvistického kroužku," *Slovo a slovesnost* 52 (1991), 196–98; and Patrick Sériot, *Structure et totalité: Les origines intellectuelles du structuralisme en Europe centrale et orientale* (Paris: Presses Universitaires de France, 1999).

54. Glebov, "A Life with Imperial Dreams," 323–25; Roman Jakobson, "Über die heutigen Voraussetzungen der russischen Slavistik," *Slavische Rundschau* 1 (1929), 632–33, 642.

55. Gasparov uses this term to describe "cultural macro-organisms": Gasparov, "Ideological Principles," 74.

56. Savitskii, "Evraziistvo," 20.

57. GARF, f. 5783, op. 1, ed. khr. 414, ll. 231–231 verso, letter from Suvchinskii to Savitskii [mid-October 1926]; GARF, f. 5783, op. 1, ed. khr. 414, ll. 303–4, letter from Trubetskoi to Savitskii, October 14, 1926.

58. GARF, f. 5783, op. 1, ed. khr. 359, ll. 111–111 verso, letter from Suvchinskii to Trubetskoi, March 21, 1925.

59. Bibliothèque Nationale de France, Département de la Musique, collection P. Souvtchinsky, Rés. Vm. dos 92 (61), letter from Trubetskoi (with note by V. T. Trubetskaia) to Suvchinskii, April 11, 1925.

60. GARF, f. 5783, op. 1, ed. khr. 359, ll. 118–118 verso, letter from Suvchinskii to Trubetskoi, April 15, 1925.

61. The most detailed account of the "schism" from Savitskii's perspective can be found in Irina Shevelenko, "K istorii evraziiskogo raskola 1929 goda," *Stanford Slavic Studies* 8 (1994), 376–416.

62. GARF, f. 5783, op. 1, ed. khr. 359, l. 245 verso, letter from Suvchinskii to Trubetskoi, March 12, 1928.

63. "Khoziaistvo i lichnost'," *Dni*, no. 720, March 20, 1925; A. M. Melkikh, "K voprosu ob ekonomicheskoi doktrine evraziistva," *Evraziiskaia khronika*, no. 6 (1926), 31–34.

64. On the Orthodox tradition of stewardship, see, for example, Anthony Scott, ed., *Good and Faithful Servant: Stewardship in the Orthodox Church* (Crestwood, NY: St. Vladimir's Seminary Press, 2003).

65. Max Weber, "Die protestantische Ethik und der Geist des Kapitalismus," in *Gesammelte Aufsätze zur Religionssoziologie* (Tübingen: J. C. B. Mohr, 1920), 1:17–206.

66. GARF, f. 5765, op. 2, ed. khr. 809, l. 98 and l. 91, "Literatura (k programme magisterskogo ispytaniia po politicheskoi ekonomii)." Ernst Troeltsch, *Religion und Wirtschaft* (Leipzig: Teubner, 1913).

67. See Werner Sombart, *Der Bourgeois: Zur Geistesgeschichte des modernen Wirtschaftsmenschen* [1913] (Munich: Duncker und Humblot, 1920).

Chapter 7: Becoming Eurasian

1. Czeslaw Milosz, *Native Realm: A Search for Self-Definition* (London: Sidgwick and Jackson, 1981), 68.

2. Milosz, *Native Realm*, 23–24 (emphasis added).

3. See M. M. Bakhtin, *Tvorchestvo Fransua Rable i narodnaia kul'tura sred-*

nevekov'ia i Renessansa (Moscow: Khudozhestvennaia literatura, 1965); and Pam Morris, ed., *The Bakhtin Reader: Selected Writings of Bakhtin, Medvedev, and Voloshinov* (London: E. Arnold, 1994).

4. Mark von Hagen, in his stimulating article, "Writing the History of Russia as Empire: The Perspective of Federalism," in *Kazan, Moscow, St. Petersburg: Multiple Faces of the Russian Empire*, ed. Catherine Evtuhov et al. (Moscow: OGI, 1997), appears to be the first to have pointed to the intriguing intellectual parallels between Eurasianism and the ideas espoused by the Bakhtin Circle. For a thoughtful discussion of the interplay between Eurasianist concepts and those advanced by Mikhail Bakhtin, see Galin Tihanov, "Cultural Emancipation and the Novelistic: Trubetzkoy, Savitsky, Bakhtin," in *Bakhtin and the Nation*, ed. Barry Brown et al. (Lewisburg, PA: Bucknell University Press, 2000); Galin Tihanov, "When Eurasianism Met Formalism: An Episode from the History of Russian Intellectual Life in the 1920s," *Welt der Slaven* 48, no. 2 (2003). Bakhtin's position within the intellectual tradition of the early twentieth century is tackled in Galin Tihanov, *The Master and the Slave: Lukacs, Bakhtin, and the Ideas of Their Time* (Oxford: Oxford University Press, 2000).

5. The literature on Eurasianism is voluminous. For works written before 2000, see *O Evrazii i evraziitsakh (bibliograficheskii ukazatel')* (Petrozavodsk: Petrozavodskii gos. universitet, 2000). Among recent publications, the following are particularly useful: Sergei Glebov, *Evraziistvo mezhdu imperiei i modernom: Istoriia v dokumentakh* (Moscow: Novoe izdatel'stvo, 2010); Dmitry Shlapentokh, ed., *Russia between East and West: Scholarly Debates on Eurasianism* (Leiden: Brill, 2007); Marlene Laruelle, *Russian Eurasianism: An Ideology of Empire* (Baltimore: Johns Hopkins University Press, 2008); Marlene Laruelle, *Ideologiia russkogo evraziistva ili mylsi o velichii imperii* (Moscow: Natalis, 2004) (This work first appeared in French in 1999 as *L'ideologie eurasiste russe ou comment penser l'empire*); Stefan Wiederkehr, *Die Eurasische Bewegung: Wissenschaft und Politik in der Russischen Emigration der Zwischenkriegszeit und im postsowietischen Russland* (Cologne: Böhlau Verlag, 2007); Aleksandr Antoshchenko, *Evraziia ili 'Sviataia Rus'? Rossiiskie emigranty v poiskakh samosoznaniia na putiakh istorii* (Petrozavodsk: Petrozavodskii gos. universitet, 2003); Mark Bassin, "'Classical' Eurasianism and the Geopolitics of Russian Identity," *Ab Imperio*, no. 2 (2003), 257–66; Ilya Vinkovetsky, "Classical Eurasianism and Its Legacy," *Canadian-American Slavic Studies* 34, no. 2 (2000), 125–39; Leonid Liuks [Luks], "Evraziiskaia ideologiia v evropeiskom kontekste," *Forum noveishei vostochnoevropeiskoi istorii i kul'tury* 1 (2009), 39–56; V. G. Makarov, "'Pax Rossica': Istoriia evraziiskogo dvizheniia i sud'by evraziitsev," *Voprosy filosofii* 9 (2006), 102–17; V. M. Khachaturian, "Istoki i rozhdenie evraziiskoi idei," *Tsivilizatsii* 6 (2004), 187–201; I. N. Ionov, "Puti razvitiia tsivilizatsionnogo soznaniia v Evrazii i problema evraziistva," *Tsivilizatsii* 6 (2004), 158–87.

6. Mark von Hagen, "Empires, Borderlands, and Diasporas: Eurasia as Anti-

Paradigm for the Post-Soviet Era," *American Historical Review* 109 (April 2004), 445–68. For a critique of "Eurasia anti-paradigm," see Glennys Young, "Fetishizing the Soviet Collapse: Historical Rupture and the Historiography of (Early) Soviet Socialism," *Russian Review* 66 (January 2007), 95–122.

7. G. S. Smith, *D. S. Mirsky: A Russian-English Life, 1890–1939* (Oxford: Oxford University Press, 2000), 138.

8. Sergei Glebov, "Granitsy imperii kak granitsy moderna: Antikolonial'naia ritorika i teoriia kul'turnykh tipov v evraziistve," *Ab Imperio*, no. 2 (2003), 267–92; Leonid Liuks, "Zametki o 'revoliutsionno-traditsionalistskoi' kul'turnoi modeli 'evraziitsev,'" *Forum noveishei vostochnoevropeiskoi istorii i kul'tury* 2 (2004), 1–17; David Chioni Moore, "Colonialism, Eurasianism, Orientalism: N. S. Trubetzkoy's Russian Vision," *Slavic and East European Journal* 41, no. 2 (1997), 321–40; Sergei Averintsev, "Neskol'ko myslei o 'evraziistve' N. S. Trubetskogo," *Novy Mir* 2 (2003), http://magazines.russ.ru/novyi_mi/2003/2/aver.html.

9. For a useful discussion of Eurasianist views on the national question, see the exchange between V. Shnirel'man and V. Karlov: V. A. Shnirel'man, "Evraziiskaia ideia i teoriia kul'tury," *Etnograficheskoe obozrenie* 4 (1996), 3–16; V. V. Karlov, "Evraziiskaia ideia i russkii natsionalizm: Po povodu stat'i V. A. Shnirel'mana 'Evraziiskaia ideia i teoriia kul'tury,'" *Etnograficheskoe obozrenie* 1 (1997), 1–13; V. A. Shnirel'man, "Evraziistvo i natsional'nyi vopros: vmesto otveta V. V. Karlovu," *Etnograficheskoe obozrenie* 2 (1997), 112–25; V. V. Karlov, "O evraziistve, natsionalizme i priemakh nauchnoi polemiki," *Etnograficheskoe obozrenie* 2 (1997), 125–32. See also Viktor Shnirel'man, "The Fate of Empires and Eurasian Federalism: A Discussion between the Eurasianists and Their Opponents in the 1920s," *Inner Asia* 3 (2001), 153–73. Shnirel'man's main conclusion, however, is that Eurasianism did not have much that was original to offer and was basically an intellectual continuation of Russian imperial nationalism and "Great Power chauvinism." On Eurasianism as an ideological response to the concepts of pan-Turkism and pan-Turanism, see Stephan Wiederkehr, "Eurasianism as a Reaction to Pan-Turkism," in Shlapentokh, *Russia between East and West*, 39–60. The study by M. G. Vandalkovskaia, *Istoricheskaia nauka rossiiskoi emigratsii: "Evraziiskii soblazn"* (Moscow: Pamiatniki istoricheskoi musli, 1997), focuses mainly on the Russian émigré thinkers' critique of the Eurasianists' historical concept.

10. The works on Vernadsky published in the 1990s can be found in *O Evrazii i evraziitsakh*. For two biographical studies, see: Nikolai Bolkhovitinov, "Zhizn' i deiatel'nost' G. V. Vernadskogo (1887–1973) i ego arkhiv," *Slavic Research Center Occasional Papers* 82 (2002), 1–63; and Bolkhovitinov, *Russkie uchenye-emigranty (G. V. Vernadskii, M. M. Karpovich, M. T. Florinskii) i stanovlenie rusistiki v SShA* (Moscow: ROSSPEN, 2005). The short biographical essay by S. Rybakov, "Istorik-evraziets Georgii Vernadsky," *Voprosy istorii* 11 (2006), 157–64, is too descriptive and mainly restates well-known facts.

11. See Richard Pipes, "Review of *Russkie uchenye-emigranty (G. V. Vernadskii, M. M. Karpovich, M. T. Florinskii) i stanovlenie rusistiki v SShA*, and 'Garvardskii Proekt,'" *Kritika: Explorations in Russian and Eurasian History* 7, no 2 (Spring 2006), 386.

12. Bolkhovitinov, "Zhizn' i deiatel'nost' G. V. Vernadskogo," 47. Translations are the author's unless otherwise indicated.

13. The Harvard historian Serhii Plokhy, for example, bluntly calls Vernadsky "the scion of the Russian imperial historiographic school." Plokhy notes, though, that "In his Russian history courses Vernadsky paid unprecedented attention to the history of Ukraine." See Serhii Plokhy, *Unmaking Imperial Russia: Mykhailo Hrushevsky and the Writing of Ukrainian History* (Toronto: University of Toronto Press, 2005), 151.

14. Georgii Vernadskii, *Russkaia istoriografiia* (Moscow: AGRAF, 1998), 439.

15. On the relationship between Aleksandra Gol'shtein and the Vernadskys, see A. Sergeev and A. Tiurin, "Istoriia poluvekovoi druzhby," in *Minuvshee: Istoricheskii almanakh*, vol. 18 (St. Petersburg: Atheneum-Feniks, 1995), 353–425.

16. George Vernadsky's interest in Drahomanov was likely generated by his family ties—his father befriended Drahomanov in the late 1880s in Paris—as well as by the Eurasianists' interest in federalist theories.

17. Bakhmeteff Archive of Russian and East European History and Culture, Columbia University [hereafter, BAR], George Vernadsky Collection. The typescripts are in BAR, George Vernadsky Collection, Box 96. These two documents were published in *Ab Imperio*, no. 4 (2006).

18. See Charles J. Halperin, "Russia and the Steppe: George Vernadsky and Eurasianism," *Forschungen zur Osteuropaischen Geschichte* 36 (1985), 55–194.

19. Literary historians have demonstrated the fruitfulness of research that explores the links between discordant national identity and an author's creativity. In her study of Nikolai Gogol's internally contradictory (Ukrainian-Russian) identity, Edyta Bojanowska observes how the two different halves of Gogol's self evolved in his writing and she traces the relationship between them. See Edyta M. Bojanowska, *Nikolai Gogol: Between Ukrainian and Russian Nationalism* (Cambridge, MA: Harvard University Press, 2006).

20. See Bolkhovitinov, "Zhizn' i deiatel'nost' G. V. Vernadskogo."

21. N. Alevras, "G. V. Vernadskii and P. N. Savitskii: Istoki evraziiskoi kontseptsii," in *Rossiia i Vostok: Problemy vzaimodeistviia: Tezisy dokl. i soobshch. k mezhdunar. nauch. konf.* (Cheliabinsk: Cheliabinskii gos. univeritet, 1995), 1:121–24; N. Alevras, "Nachala evraziiskoi kontseptsii v rannem tvorchestve G. V. Vernadskogo i P. N. Savitskogo," *Vestnik Evrazii* 1 (1996), 5–17.

22. See G. V. Vernadskii, "O dvizhenii russkikh na vostok," *Nauchno-istoricheskii zhurnal*, no. 2 (1914); G. V. Vernadskii, "Protiv solntsa: Rasprostranenie russkogo gosudarstva k vostoku," *Russkaia mysl'*, no. 1 (1914), 56–79; G. V. Vernadskii, "Go-

sudarevy sluzhilye i promyshlennye liudi v Vostochnoi Sibiri XVII veka," *Zhurnal Ministerstva narodnogo prosveshcheniia*, no. 4 (1915); P. N. Savitskii, "Bor'ba za imperiiu: Imperializm v politike i ekonomike," *Russkaia mysl'*, no. 1–2 (1915).

23. True, before the Russian Revolution, Vernadsky displayed a keen interest in certain features of Russian colonialism and the empire's "eastern connection." However, as the two contemporary scholars argue—in my view, correctly—"even if some of the Eurasian ideas had their genesis before 1917, it was the experience of the Revolution and Civil War that caused these ideas to be taken up by the Russian émigrés." See Catherine Andreyev and Ivan Savicky, *Russia Abroad: Prague and the Russian Diaspora, 1918–1938* (New Haven, CT: Yale University Press, 2004), 141.

24. Charles J. Halperin, "George Vernadsky, Eurasianism, the Mongols, and Russia," *Slavic Review* 41, no. 3 (1982), 483. See also Charles J. Halperin, "Russia and the Steppe: George Vernadsky and Eurasianism," *Forschungen zur Osteuropaischen Geschichte* 36 (1985), 55–194.

25. Nicholas Riasanovsky, "The Emergence of Eurasianism," *California Slavic Studies* 4 (1967), 39–72.

26. Sergey Glebov briefly discusses the Ukrainian origin of the leading Eurasianists in Glebov, "Granitsy imperii kak granitsy moderna."

27. For information on Savitskii's life and work, see Sergey Glebov, "A Life with Imperial Dreams: Petr Nikolaevich Savitsky, Eurasiansim and the Invention of 'Structuralist' Geography," *Ab Imperio*, no. 3 (2005): 299–329; Vladimir Bystriukov, *V poiskakh Evrazii: Obshchestvenno-politicheskaia i nauchnaia deiatel'nost' P. N. Savitskogo v gody emigratsii (1920–1938 gg.)* (Samara: Samarskoe knizhnoe izdatel'stvo, 2007); V. G. Makarov and A. M. Matveeva, "Geosofiia P. N. Savitskogo: Mezhdu ideologiei i naukoi," *Voprosy filosofii* 2 (2007), 123–35.

28. See A. Bretanitskaia, ed., *Petr Suvchinskii i ego vremia* (Moscow: Kompozitor, 1999); John Malmstad, "K istorii 'evraziistva': M. Gor'kii and P. P. Suvchinskii," *Diaspora: Novye materialy* (Paris: Athenaeum-Feniks, 2001) 1:327–47.

29. Georgii Florovskii distanced himself from Eurasianism already in the mid-1920s. See his critique of the movement's cultural-philosophical tenets in "Evraziiskii soblazn," *Sovremennye zapiski* 34 (1928), 312–46.

30. See V. N. Toporov, "Nikolai Sergeevich Trubetskoi—ucheny, myslitel', chelovek," in *Pis'ma i zametki N. S. Trubetskogo* (Moscow: Iazyki slavianskoi kul'tury, 2004); N. I. Tolstoi, "N. S. Trubetskoi i evraziistvo," in N. S. Trubetskoi, *Istoriia. Kul'tura. Iazyk* (Moscow: Progress, 1995), 5–30; Anatoly Liberman, "N. S. Trubetzkoy and His Works on History and Culture," in Nikolai S. Trubetzkoy, *The Legacy of Genghis Khan*, ed. Liberman (Ann Arbor: Michigan Slavic Publications, 1991), 293–375.

31. George Vernadsky, "Kn. Trubetskoi i ukrainskii vopros," BAR, George Vernadsky Collection, Box 96.

32. On the Russian White movement and the Ukrainian question during the

Civil War, see Anna Procyk, *Russian Nationalism and Ukraine: The Nationality Policy of the Volunteer Army during the Civil War* (Edmonton: Canadian Institute of Ukrainian Studies Press, 1995). For a more general discussion of the nationality question within the Russian émigré communities in interwar Europe, see A. I. Doronchenkov, *Emigratsiia 'pervoi volny' o natsional'nykh problemakh i sud'be Rossii* (St. Petersburg: D. Bulanin, 2001). It is quite symptomatic that Pavel Milyukov, the Russian liberal politician who, arguably, was most sympathetic toward "national minorities," accepted the possibility of a "federal solution" only by the end of 1920, when it was obviously too late. At the same time, the views of the legal scholar and liberal imperial administrator, Baron Boris Nolde (who like Milyukov was a member of the Kadet party) appear to be quite representative of the prevailing perspective of Russian émigrés on the nationality question. "In Russia," Nolde asserted, "the nationality question will be decided either by the non-Russians [*inorodtsy*] cutting our throats, or us cutting theirs. . . . Once the revolutionary wave recedes, Russia will again become a unified state, so long as it does not break apart into its component parts and cease being Russia." Nolde specifically noted that there could be no compromise with the Ukrainians: "Either Ukraine will devour Great Russia, or we will uproot Ukrainian separatism." Nolde, however, greatly admired the way the Russian Empire was ruled for centuries before the "unfortunate" advent of the age of nationalism; specifically, he referred to the peculiar imperial system of informal "federalism" that would preserve local autonomies in the borderlands. For a detailed and thoughtful discussion of Nolde's views, see Peter Holquist, "Dilemmas of Progressive Administrator: Baron Boris Nolde," *Kritika: Explorations in Russian and Eurasian History* 7, no. 2 (spring 2006), 241–73. Nolde's quote is on p. 252.

33. Some important parts of his reminiscences, however—an account of his life in Athens in 1921–1922 and his description of the crucial Prague period, 1922–1927—remain unpublished.

34. George Vernadsky, "O rode Vernadskikh," BAR, George Vernadsky Collection, Box 98.

35. V. I. Vernadskii, *Dnevniki: 1917–1921, Oktiabr' 1917–ianvar' 1920* (Kyiv: Naukova dumka, 1994); V. I. Vernadskii, *Dnevniki: 1917–1921, Ianvar' 1920–mart 1921* (Kyiv: Naukova dumka, 1997); V. I. Vernadskii, *Dnevniki: Mart 1921–avgust 1925* (Moscow: Nauka, 1998); V. I. Vernadskii, *Dnevniki: 1926–1934* (Moscow: Nauka, 2001); V. I. Vernadskii, *Dnevniki: 1935–1941*, 2 vols. (Moscow: Nauka, 2006); V. I. Vernadskii, *Dnevniki: 1941–1943* (Moscow: ROSSPEN, 2010).

36. Geoffrey A. Hosking, "First through Kiev," *Times Literary Supplement*, June 1, 2007.

37. See a stimulating discussion on loyalties and identities in the Russian Empire in the forum held by the journal *Ab Imperio*: "Alfavit, iazyk i natsional'naia identichnost' v Rossiiskoi imperii," *Ab Imperio*, no. 2 (2005): 123–319, as well

as its continuation in *Ab Imperio*, no. 1 (2006). The Ukraine case is analyzed in Faith Hillis, *Children of Rus': Right-Bank Ukraine and the Invention of a Russian Nation* (Ithaca, NY: Cornell University Press, 2013); Olga Andriewsky, "The Russian-Ukrainian Discourse and the Failure of the 'Little Russian Solution,' 1782–1917," in *Culture, Nation, and Identity: The Ukrainian-Russian Encounter, 1600–1945*, ed. Andreas Kappeler, Zenon E. Kohut, Frank E. Sysyn, and Mark von Hagen (Edmonton: Canadian Institute of Ukrainian Studies Press, 2003), 182–214.

38. Aleksei Miller, *Imperiia Romanovykh i natsionalizm* (Moscow: NLO, 2006); Aleksei Miller, *"Ukrainskii vopros" v politike vlastei i russkom obshchestvennom mnenii* (vtoraia polovina XIX v.) (St. Petersburg: Aleteiia, 2000).

39. See a discussion of the issue of identities in prerevolutionary Ukraine in Aleksei Miller, "Dualizm identichnostei na Ukraine," *Otechestvennye zapiski* 1 (2007), 84–96.

40. Ernest Gyidel, "Ob 'ukrainofil'stve' Georgiia Vernadskogo, ili variatsiia na temu natsional'nykh i gosudarstvennykh loial'nostei," *Ab Imperio*, no. 4 (2006): 329–46.

41. In several diary entries dated from September 1924, Vladimir Vernadsky described this "Ukrainophile" atmosphere that was characteristic of his Kharkiv milieu. "Ukrainian tendencies," Vernadsky reminisced, "were undoubtedly strong in many families—not just in the families belonging to the ancient [Ukrainian] clans that took part in historical life during recent centuries, but also in families belonging to the local intelligentsia such as our family. . . . Deep in his heart, [my father] always remained a Ukrainian and sharply distinguished between Ukrainians and Russians. Both he and my mother had a very strong sense of Ukrainian nationality, and my father was conscious of the deep differences between the Ukrainian people [and the Russians]. . . . In my childhood years, I got a perspective from him on [Hetman] Mazepa different from the one that had been predominant within the Russian society. He held that Mazepa was right, not Peter [the Great]. From him I learned about Shevchenko; he told me that St. Petersburg had been built on the bones of the [Ukrainian] Cossacks. . . . In our household there were Ukrainian books but they were kept in a disorganized way. In Kharkov, due to hard times [in the 1870s, thanks to anti-Ukrainian imperial legislation] there were no Ukrainian books. My father received everything that could be subscribed to, through the Main Post Office, from Galicia. During my trip to foreign lands in 1873–1876, my father was telling me not only about the Slavs (Prague) but also about Lvov and Galicia and about the freedom that Ukrainian literature enjoyed there. . . . He tremendously loved Ukrainian songs and my mother sang them beautifully. At evening parties in Kharkov, in our big house—my father was the manager of the [State] bank's [Kharkov] branch—she would organize choirs: the windows would be opened and the Ukrainian songs would flow. . . . As if in a dream, I also remember Ukrainian plays and Ukrainian poems being discussed in Kharkov." See V. I. Vernadskii, *Dnevniki: Mart 1921–avgust 1925*, 176–77.

42. Before Vladimir Vernadsky decided to take a professorship at Moscow University he was thinking of settling down in Ukraine. On July 15, 1941, he reminisced in his diary that upon completion of his two-year research trip in Europe in 1890, he "returned from Paris . . . and was going to move to one of the Ukrainian universities—in Kyiv or in Kharkiv." See V. I. Vernadskii, *Dnevniki: 1935–1941*, 2:268.

43. See Kendall E. Bailes, *Science and Russian Culture in the Age of Revolutions: V. I. Vernadsky and His Scientific School, 1863–1945* (Bloomington: Indiana University Press, 1990). Bailes' is the only comprehensive biography of Vladimir Vernadsky in English. For an interesting analysis of Vernadsky's academic activities in postrevolutionary Ukraine, see Aleksandr Dmitriev, "Vladimir Vernadsky, 'akademicheskaia revoliutsiia' 1917–1918 godov i ukrainskaia emigratsiia," *Gefter*, May 19, 2014, http://gefter.ru/archive/12292/.

44. BAR, Aleksandra Gol'shtein Collection, Box 3.

45. BAR, George Vernadsky Collection, Box 97.

46. BAR, George Vernadsky Collection, Box 141.

47. See George Katkov, "Masaryk's Guests," in *The Other Russia*, ed. Michael Glenny and Norman Stone (London: Faber and Faber, 1990); Elena Chinyaeva, "Ruská emigrace v Československu: Vývoj ruské pomocné akce," *Slovanský přehled* 1 (1993); Zdenek Sladek, "Prag: Das 'russische Oxford,'" in *Der Grosse Exodus: Die russische Emigration und ihre Zentren 1917 bis 1941*, ed. Karl Schlogel (Munich: C. H. Beck, 1994), 218–33.

48. Vladimir Vernadsky's personal experiences in Ukraine during the turbulent times of the civil war—in particular, in his capacity as founder and first president of the Ukrainian Academy of Sciences in 1918–1919—appeared to confirm both his sense of Ukrainian identity and his understanding of how crucially important the "Ukrainian question" was. Upon his return from Crimea to Moscow in March 1921, according to his diary, he was "consciously raising the Ukrainian issue everywhere." He was dismayed at how "here [in Russia] its significance was so poorly understood: deep in their hearts many people believe that this is a kind of transitory phenomenon, which is destined to disappear quite soon!" See V. I. Vernadskii, *Dnevniki: Mart 1921–avgust 1925*, 15. On April 20, 1921, Vladimir Vernadsky wrote, in a letter to his friend, the Ukrainian academician N. P. Vasilenko: "You know how precious Ukraine is for me and how deeply the Ukrainian rebirth is penetrating my entire national and personal weltanschauung. . . . Russian culture should become a Russian-Ukrainian culture." See *Iz epistoliarnogo naslediia V. I. Vernadskogo: Pis'ma ukrainskim akademikam N. P. Vasilenko i A. A. Bogomol'tsu* (Kyiv: Naukova dumka, 1991), 13–14. On Vladimir Vernadsky's ties with Ukraine and Ukrainian scholars, see K. M. Sytnik, S. M. Stoiko, and E. M. Apanovich, *V. I. Vernadskii: Zhizn' i deiatel'nost' na Ukraine* (Kyiv: Naukova dumka, 1984).

49. BAR, George Vernadsky Collection, Box 103.

50. BAR, George Vernadsky Collection, Box 98.

51. BAR, George Vernadsky Collection, Box 98. Vladimir Vernadsky was acutely interested in the genealogical roots of the Vernadsky family. "In connection with the 'biological' studies of my own genealogy and that of my children," Vernadsky wrote in one of his diary entries, "I did research on the families" with which the Vernadskys were connected. This research gave Vernadsky a "strange impression: all were Ukrainians. . . . [There were] no Great Russians at all." See V. I. Vernadskii, *Dnevniki: 1935–1941*, 2:132.

52. V. I. Vernadskii, *Dnevniki: Mart 1921–avgust 1925*, 176.

53. BAR, George Vernadsky Collection, Box 50.

54. In a characteristic passage from an article titled "Ukrainian Question and Russian Society" (1916), Vladimir Vernadsky basically put Russian and Ukrainian ethnic nationalisms on equal footing in terms of how negatively both nationalisms affected the cause of the Russian-Ukrainian unity. "The government policy at that time [1870s–1880s]," noted Vernadsky, "was striving to achieve a certain goal— namely, to bring about the full merger of Ukrainians with the ruling [Russian] nationality and eliminate the awareness of national distinctiveness within the Ukrainian population perceived as being dangerous for the Great Russians. In essence, this policy of the Great Russian national centralism was, consequently, no less separatist than the Ukrainian movement that had always been suspected of separatism. Only the official separatism was Great Russian in nature and sought to transform the enormous multilingual and multicultural state into a country fashioned according to the Great Russian model. [Such a transformation would amount to turning] great Russia into *Velikorossiia* [the ethnic Russian state]." See V. I. Vernadskii, *Publitsisticheskie stat'i* (Moscow: Nauka, 1996), 214.

55. There is a growing literature on the Russian émigrés in Prague in general and on the Prague Eurasianist circle in particular. See Andreyev and Savicky, *Russia Abroad*; Ivan Savický, *Praga i zarubezhnaia Rossiia* (Prague: Izd-vo IDEG, 2002); Elena Chinyaeva, *Russians outside Russia: The Émigré Community in Czechoslovakia, 1918–1938* (Munich: R. Oldenbourg Verlag, 2001); Elena P. Serapionova, *Rossiiskaia emigratsiia v Chekhoslovatskoi Respublike (20–30-e gody)* (Moscow: Institut slavianovedeniia i balkanistiki RAN, 1995). Also useful is the conference symposium, *Russkaia, ukrainskaia i belorusskaia emigratsiia v Chekhoslovakii mezhdu dvumia mirovymi voinami: Rezul'taty i perspektivy issledovanii. Fondy Slavianskoi biblioteki i prazhskikh arkhivov* (Prague: Narodni knihovna CR, 1995).

56. N. S. Trubetzkoy, *N. S. Trubetzkoy's Letters and Notes,* ed. Roman Jakobson (The Hague: Mouton, 1975), 12. N. S. Trubetskoi, *Evropa i chelovechestvo* (Sofia: Rossiisko-bolgarskoe knigoizdatel'stvo, 1920).

57. Ladis K. D. Kristof, "The Russian Image of Russia: An Applied Study in

Geopolitical Methodology," in *Essays in Political Geography*, ed. Charles A. Fisher (London: Methuen, 1968), 374.

58. V. V. Zenkovsky, *Russian Thinkers and Europe* (Ann Arbor, MI: Published for the American Council of Learned Societies by J. W. Edwards, 1953), 106.

59. In his Parisian exile, when the senior contemporary of the Eurasianists, Pavel Nikolaevich Milyukov, turned to the systematic study of modern nationalism, he specifically stressed the "powerful impetus that the latest war [of 1914–1918] gave to the development of the national question." Having compared the state of Russia's "national problem" before and after the upheavals caused by the war and revolution, Milyukov came up with the following analysis. "Not long ago," he wrote in his learned essay, "Russia could be compared with the ethnographical museum where the remnants of the nationalities that took part in the historical process in the East European plain—they number around one hundred—were conserved, fully assimilated, or fading out. But now one can rather speak about the sociological laboratory where massive and systematic tests are being conducted using experimental methods that aim at reviving, resurrecting and waking up national consciousness even within the nationalities that were fading out—to say nothing of those in which the internal process of national self-awareness had already been developing." See P. N. Milyukov, *Natsional'nyi vopros (Proiskhozhdenie natsional'nosti i natsional'nye voprosy v Rossii)* (Moscow: Gosudarstvennaia publichnaia istoricheskaia biblioteka Rossii, [1925] 2005), 119. See also Eric Lohr, *Nationalizing the Russian Empire: The Campaign against Enemy Aliens during World War I* (Cambridge, MA: Harvard University Press, 2003).

60. Sergey Glebov, "A Life with Imperial Dreams: Petr Nikolaevich Savitsky, Eurasianism and the Invention of 'Structuralist' Geography," *Ab Imperio*, no. 3 (2005).

61. Trubetzkoy, *N. S. Trubetzkoy's Letters and Notes*, 3–4.

62. To be sure, the Eurasianists themselves dwelled at length on the "catastrophic nature" of events unleashed by the 1917 Russian Revolution. Already in their first collections of articles, *Exodus to the East*, they argued that the Russian people, including the Russian émigrés in Europe, had found themselves in the "midst of a cataclysm that could be compared with the greatest upheavals known in the human history." See *Iskhod k Vostoku* (Sofia: Balkan, 1921), iv.

63. N. S. Trubetskoi, *Evropa i chelovechestvo* (Sofia: Rossiisko-bolgarskoe knigoizdatel'stvo, 1920); P. N. Savitskii, "Evropa i Evraziia (Po povodu broshiury kn. N. S. Trubetskogo 'Evropa i chelovechestvo')," *Russkaia mysl'* 2 (1921).

64. Trubetzkoy, *N. S. Trubetzkoy's Letters and Notes*, 14. Some contemporary commentators quickly noticed that nationalist discourse lay at the very heart of Eurasianism. One reviewer for the Berlin-based émigré paper *Rul'*, while criticizing *Exodus to the East* for being too vague and general, admitted that Eurasianism was "one of the most interesting trends within Russian neo-nationalism." See Robert C.

Williams, *Culture in Exile: Russian Emigrés in Germany, 1881–1941* (Ithaca, NY: Cornell University Press), 260.

65. See Riasanovsky, "The Emergence of Eurasianism"; Sergei Glebov, "Mezhdu imperiiami: Iz perepiski uchastnikov evraziiskogo dvizheniia," *Ab Imperio*, no. 2 (2003), 293–304.

66. Sviatoslav Kaspe, "Imperial Political Culture and Modernization in the Second Half of the Nineteenth Century," in *Russian Empire: Space, People, Power, 1700–1930*, ed. Jane Burbank, Mark von Hagen, and Anatolyi Remnev (Bloomington: Indiana University Press, 2007), 455–93. For a comprehensive analysis of the Russian Empire's failure to create a multiethnic Russian nation by elaborating "an identity distinct from a religious (Orthodox), imperial, state or narrowly ethnic identity," see Ronald Grigor Suny, "The Empire Strikes Out: Imperial Russia, 'National' Identity, and Theories of Empire," in *A State of Nations: Empire and Nation-Making in the Age of Lenin and Stalin*, ed. Ronald Grigor Suny and Terry Martin (New York: Oxford University Press, 2001), 23–66.

67. See Miller, *Imperiia Romanovykh i natsionalizm*.

68. Peter A. Blitstein, "Nation and Empire in Soviet History, 1917–1953," *Ab Imperio*, no. 1 (2006), 208. On attempts to define the "imperial center," see Leonid Gorizontov, "The 'Great Circle' of Interior Russia: Representations of the Imperial Center in the Nineteenth and Earlier Twentieth Centuries," in Burbank, von Hagen, and Remnev, *Russian Empire*, 67–93.

69. BAR, George Vernadsky Collection, Box 8. Compare the contemporaneous debates within the Western and "Oriental" anticolonial milieu in Elleke Boehmer, *Empire, the National, and the Postcolonial 1890–1920: Resistance in Interaction* (Oxford: Oxford University Press, 2002).

70. For Trubetskoi, "'National self-determination' as it is understood by the former [U. S.] president [Woodrow] Wilson and various separatists—the Georgians, Estonians, Latvians, and so on—is a typical example of false nationalism." See Trubetzkoy, *N. S. Trubetzkoy's Letters and Notes*, 14. The influence of Wilsonianism on Eurasianist thinking is discussed in Bassin, "'Classical' Eurasianism and the Geopolitics of Russian Identity."

71. See Charlotte Alston, "'The Suggested Basis for a Russian Federal Republic': Britain, Anti-Bolshevik Russia and the Border States at the Paris Peace Conference, 1919," *History* 1 (2006), 24–44.

72. For a detailed analysis of how the victorious Bolsheviks addressed the imperial legacy, see Terry Martin, *The Affirmative Action Empire: Nations and Nationalism in the Soviet Union, 1923–1939* (Ithaca, NY: Cornell University Press, 2001).

73. G. V. Chicherin, "Rossiia i aziatskie narody," *Vestnik N.K.I.D.* 2 (August 13, 1919), 1–2 (emphasis added).

74. Nikolai Alekseev, the Paris-based Eurasianist and legal thinker, noted that the ethnoterritorial federation coupled with the principle of self-determination, hav-

ing gained wide currency, aroused "nationalist ghosts" inimical to the Soviet state and the proclaimed principle of internationalism. The Bolsheviks, wrote Alekseev, created "numerous national republics for peoples who never bothered to even think of any autonomy in the past." "It would seem," he continued, "that communist policy goes out of its way to make possible what now seems unthinkable—namely, the ruin of both Russia and internationalism by individual peoples currently contained within Russia." See Nikolai N. Alekseev, *Russkii narod i gosudarstvo* (Moscow: Agraf, 1998), 368.

75. For an excellent discussion of Savitskii's "structuralist" geography, see Glebov, "A Life with Imperial Dreams." It was none other than Roman Jakobson who, not long before his death, called Petr Savitskii "a highly gifted intellectual precursor of structuralist geography." See Roman Iakobson and Krystyna Pomorska, *Besedy* (Jerusalem: Izd-vo im. I.L. Magnesa, Evreiskii universitet, 1982), 68.

76. Petr N. Savitskii, *Rossiia—osobyi geograficheskii mir* (Prague: Evraziiskoe knigoizdatel'stvo, 1927). For a good analysis of the concept of *mestorazvitie*, see Mark Bassin, "Nationhood, Natural Region, Mestorazvitie: Environmentalist Discourses in Classical Eurasianism," in *Space, Place and Power in Modern Russia: Essays in the New Spatial History*, ed. Mark Bassin, Christopher Ely, and Melissa Stockdale (DeKalb: Northern Illinois University Press, 2010), 49–80.

77. It is noteworthy that Savitskii advanced the idea of Eurasia's cultural uniqueness very early on—even before the first formal Eurasianist collection of articles was published in 1922. Already in 1921, in his review of Trubetskoi's *Europe and Mankind*, Savitskii contended that the type of relations that existed between the Russian nation and other nations of Eurasia differed radically from those that "existed in the parts of the world involved in the sphere of European colonial policies." For him, Eurasia "is a region where there is certain equality and a certain amount of brotherhood between nations—phenomena that have no analogies in the international relations [within] the colonial empires." Furthermore, according to Savitskii, over the millennia of close and usually friendly interaction, the Eurasian peoples shaped what can be called a common culture: "One can posit the existence of a Eurasian culture, which, to a certain extent, is a common product and common asset of the peoples of Eurasia." See Savitskii, "Evropa i Evraziia," 135.

78. Trubetzkoy, *N. S. Trubetzkoy's Letters and Notes*, 22.

79. Igor S. Martynyuk, "Toward Understanding the Art of Modern Diasporic Ideology Making: The Eurasianist Mind-Mapping of the Imperial Homeland (1921–1934)," *Journal of the Interdisciplinary Crossroads* 3, no. 1 (April 2006), 106.

80. Nikolai S. Trubetskoi, "Obshcheevraziiskii natsionalizm," *Evraziiskaia khronika* 9 (1927), 24–31. An English translation of this article can be found in Trubetzkoy, *The Legacy of Genghis Khan*, 233–44.

81. Trubetzkoy, *The Legacy of Genghis Khan*, 239.

82. Trubetzkoy, *The Legacy of Genghis Khan*, 243.

83. On Ukrainian historian Mykhailo Hrushevsky's crucial role in nationaliz-ing the past of what was previously seen as part of a larger whole into a separate "Ukrainian history" and thereby "unmaking Imperial Russia," see Plokhy, *Un-making Imperial Russia*. In the 1920s, Ukrainian émigré intellectuals challenged Eurasianism's attempt to reconceptualize empire and nation. For a Ukrainian cri-tique, see D. I. Doroshenko, "'K ukrainskoi probleme': Po povodu stat'i kn. N. S. Trubetskogo," *Evraziiskaia khronika* 10 (Paris, 1928), 41–51; Oleksandr Mytsiuk, *Evraziistvo* (Prague, 1930).

84. BAR, George Vernadsky Collection, Box 51. Nikitin's letter from which the quotation is taken dates from 1952 but it neatly reflects the positions that the Eur-asianists firmly held back in the 1920s.

85. Trubetzkoy, *The Legacy of Genghis Khan*, 243 (emphasis added).

86. "Iz pisem N. S. Trubetskogo P. P. Suvchinskomu," in Glebov, *Evraziistvo*, 409–10. The correspondence between Trubetskoi and Suvchinskii, in particular the letters pertaining to Trubetskoi's 1925 essay "The Legacy of Genghis Khan," revealed just how badly the Eurasianists needed the solid expertise of a professional historian. When Trubetskoi was writing his reinterpretation of Russian history, he was perfectly aware that the scheme of Russian history he had advanced was not ex-actly a scientific one but rather one pursuing certain political aims. In a letter to Suv-chinskii of March 15, 1925, he was candidly self-critical: The way the study had been crafted, he wrote, might well result in a "certain propagandistic success, but could also seriously damage our cause. History is treated in it in a purposefully uncere-monious and tendentious manner—so for a serious historical critique it presents a rather convenient field and may become an easily vulnerable target" ("Iz pisem N. S. Trubetskogo P. P. Suvchinskomu," 297). In the other letter, from March 28, 1925, Trubetskoi returned to this issue and suggested that the essay be published under a pseudonym: "I am somewhat reluctant to put my name under this work, which is clearly demagogical and, from the scientific point of view, rather frivolous" ("Iz pisem N. S. Trubetskogo P. P. Suvchinskomu," 301). "The Legacy of Genghis Khan" was indeed printed under the pseudonym: I. R., *Nasledie Chingiskhana: Vzgliad na russkuiu istoriiu ne s Zapada, a s Vostoka* (Berlin: Evraziiskoe izdatel'stvo, 1925).

87. Michael Rostovtzeff, "Preface," in George Vernadsky, *A History of Russia* (New Haven, CT: Yale University Press, 1929), xi–xii. For his part, Vernadsky appeared to have been strongly influenced by Rostovtsev's seminal work *Irani-ans and Greeks in South Russia* (Oxford: Clarendon Press, 1922), which he mostly likely read in its first Russian edition—*Ellinstvo i iranstvo na iuge Rossii* (Petro-grad: Izd-vo Ogni, 1918). He highly appraised this study in the introduction to his multivolume magnum opus, *A History of Russia*. On the intriguing links between Rostovtsev's classical scholarship and early Eurasianism, see Caspar Meyer, "Ros-tovtzeff and the Classical Origins of Eurasianism," *Anabases* 9 (2009), 185–98.

88. G. V. Vernadskii, *Nachertanie russkoi istorii* (Prague: Evraziiskoe knigozdatel'stvo, 1927), 1:9.

89. See, for example, G. V. Vernadskii, *Opyt istorii Evrazii* (Berlin: Izdanie evraziitsev, 1934). For the memo, see Georgii Vernadskii, "Kratkoe izlozhenie evraziiskoi tochki zreniia na russkuiu istoriiu," BAR, George Vernadsky Collection, Box 96.

90. "Even now," Vernadsky noted, "the notion 'history of Eurasia' does not fully coincide with the notion 'Russian history' because today in Eurasia there live, besides the Russian people, also many other peoples whose (historic) development has been closely connected with the development of the Russian people but who are not identical with the Russians." See Vernadskii, *Opyt*, 5.

91. Vernadskii, *Nachertanie*, 231.

92. At one point Vernadsky would concede that a "separate," "national" history of the Russian people does have the right to exist. "Russian history," he wrote, "is [just] a subdivision of the [general] history of the Eurasian peoples." But, he immediately added, "Russian history had, nolens volens, to include in its field of vision geopolitically ever broader expanses because the Russian people, in its historical development, would increasingly spread over [its] Eurasian *mestorazvitie*." See Vernadskii, *Opyt*, 8.

93. Nicholas Riasanovsky, *Russian Identities: A Historical Survey* (Oxford: Oxford University Press, 2005), 234–35.

94. See von Hagen, "Writing the History of Russia as Empire," 397.

95. Von Hagen, "Writing the History of Russia as Empire," 397–98.

96. The left-wing Eurasianist Prince Dmitrii Sviatopolk-Mirsky praised Eurasianism because "despite inherent nationalist temptation, from the very outset it showed the way toward overcoming Russian nationalism [and] underscored the supranational character of its task by its very name." See Dmitrii Sviatopolk-Mirsky, "Natsional'nosti SSSR," *Evraziia* 22 (Paris, 1929) [pages not numbered].

97. On Karpovich's historical scholarship, see Alla Zeide, "Creating a 'Space of Freedom': Mikhail Mikhailovich Karpovich and Russian Historiography in America," *Ab Imperio*, no. 1 (2007), 241–76; Norman G. O. Pereira, "The Thought and Teachings of Michael Karpovich," *Russian History* 36, no. 2 (2009), 254–77; N. V. Iudaeva, "Mikhail Mikhailovich Karpovich: Russkii istorik v Amerike," *Vestnik Moskovskogo gosudarstvennogo oblastnogo universiteta*, Seriia "Istoriia i politicheskie nauki" 2 (2007), 52–58; Bolkhovitinov, *Russkie uchenye-emigranty*.

98. See *Kritika: Explorations in Russian and Eurasian History* 7, no. 2 (spring 2006), 387; G. V. Vernadskii, "M. M. Karpovich: Pamiati druga," *Novyi zhurnal* 58 (1959), 9–10.

99. Von Hagen, "Writing the History of Russia as Empire," 396, 397. For a general overview of Russian Studies in America, see Horace G. Lunt, "On the History of Slavic Studies in the United States," *Slavic Review* 46, no. 2 (1987), 294–301; Terence Emmons, "Russia Then and Now in the Pages of the *American Histori-*

cal Review and Elsewhere: A Few Centennial Notes," *American Historical Review* 100, no. 4 (1995), 1136–48; Martin Malia, "Clio in Tauris: American Historiography on Russia," in *Imagined Histories: American Historians Interpret the Past*, ed. Anthony Molho and Gordon S. Wood (Princeton, NJ: Princeton University Press, 1998), 415–33; A. Rieber, "Izuchenie istorii Rossii v SShA," *Istoricheskie zapiski* 3, no. 21 (2000), 65–105.

100. See *Kritika: Explorations in Russian and Eurasian History* 7, no. 2 (spring 2006), 387.

101. Boris Nolde, *La formation de l'Empire russe: Études, notes et documents*, vols. 1–2 (Paris: Institut d'études slaves, 1952–1953). The Russian translation of this magnum opus appeared only very recently: B. E. Nol'de, *Istoriia formirovaniia Rossiiskoi Imperii* (St. Petersburg: Dmitrii Bulanin, 2013). Nolde (b. 1876) was the Eurasianists' contemporary and fellow émigré who resided in Paris beginning in 1919. Remarkably, in his letter to Petr Suvchinskii of August 28, 1928, Nikolai Trubetskoi noted that Nolde's outlook was close to that of the Eurasianists. See Glebov, *Evraziistvo*, 533. Some contemporary Russian scholars, however, dispute Nolde's intellectual closeness to Eurasianism. They argue that in his scholarship Nolde never used specific Eurasianist terminology (such as *mestorazvitie*, the "state-continent," the "Romano-Germanic yoke," etc.), nor was he influenced by the geographic determinism that was so characteristic of the Eurasianists. See B. Aznabaev et al., "Imperiografiia Borisa Nol'de," in Nol'de, *Istoriia formirovaniia Rossiiskoi Imperii*, 22. Yet there was one important point of contact: like the Eurasianists, Nolde sought to "decenter" the Russian historical narrative because his ambition was to write not a history of Russia as a nation-state but a study that would explore —as he noted in a letter to Mikhail Vishniak—"the 'imperial' development of Russia." "No one," he added, "studied this imperial history in its entirety." See M. V. Vishniak, *'Sovremennye zapiski': Vospominaniia redaktora* (Bloomington: Indiana University Press, 1957), 152.

102. Georg von Rauch, *Rußland: Staatliche Einheit und nationale Vielfalt. Föderalistische Kräfte und Ideen in der russischen Geschichte* (Munich: Isar-Verlag, 1953).

103. It is noteworthy that Andreas Kappeler, who wrote a pioneering study *Russland als Vielvoelkerreich: Enstehung, Geschichte, Zerfall* (Munich: Beck, 1992), which was then translated into Russian, French, and English, acknowledges the important influence of George Vernadsky's research on his own understanding of Russian history. Kappeler also mentioned the importance of Nolde's and von Rauch's works.

Chapter 8: Spatializing the Sign

1. Roman Jakobson, "What Is Poetry?" (first published in Czech in 1933–1934), in *Language in Literature*, ed. Krystyna Pomorska and Stephen Rudy (Cambridge, MA: Belknap Press of Harvard University Press, 1987), 377.

2. N. S. Trubetskoi, from three articles, "O gosudarstvennom stroe i forme prav-leniia," "Ideokratiia i armiia," and "Ob idee-pravitel'nitse ideokraticheskogo gosu-darstva," in *Istoriia. Kul'tura. Iazyk*, ed. V. M. Zhivov (Moscow: Progress/Univers, [1927] 1995), 412, 433, 441. Translations are the author's unless otherwise indicated.

3. Trubetskoi, "O gosudarstvennom stroe i forme pravleniia," 413.

4. Jakobson, "What Is Poetry?" 377.

5. The literary context was acknowledged by Trubetskoi himself in a private letter dated July 28, 1921, to Roman Jakobson, where he speaks of Eurasianism as a "current that is part of the general atmosphere (*nositsia v vozdukhe*)" and is found in the "poetry of Voloshin, Blok, [and] Esenin." See "Iz pisem N. S. Trubetskogo k R. O. Iakobsonu o problemakh evraziistva," *Vestnik moskovskogo Universiteta*, Series 9: Filologiia 1 (1992), 63–64. The importance of literary culture to Eurasianism has frequently been acknowledged in scholarly reviews of Eurasian intellectual history. See Nicholas V. Riasanovsky, "Afterword: The Emergence of Eurasianism," first published in *California Slavic Studies*, 4 (Berkeley: University of California Press, 1967), 39–72, and republished in *Exodus to the East: Forebodings and Events. An Affirmation of the Eurasians*, trans. Ilya Vinkovetsky (Idyllwild, CA: Charles Schlacks, 1996), 115–42; see esp. 137; and Charles J. Halperin, "George Vernadsky, Eurasianism, the Mongols, and Russia," *Slavic Review* (fall 1982), 482.

6. Both Jindrich Toman and Patrick Sériot refer to symbolist Scythianism as Eurasianism's primary literary antecedent. See Jindrich Toman, *The Magic of a Common Language: Jakobson, Mathesius, Trubetzkoy, and the Prague Linguistic Circle* (Cambridge, MA: MIT Press, 1995), 198–99; and Patrick Sériot, *Structure et totalité: Les origines intellectuelles du structuralisme en Europe centrale et orientale* (Paris: Presses Universitaires de France, 1999), 71–73. Marlene Laruelle offers a more general list, "The 'Turanianism' of Belyi, the 'Asianism' of the Futurists, and the 'Scythianism' of the poetic avant-garde thus attempt, through this new termi-nology, to rename Russia precisely by differentiating it from Europe. They consti-tute the first culmination [*aboutissement*] of a tendency of thought that reflects on Russia's otherness with respect to Europe and reveals Russia's Asiatic elements. Eurasianism would be the second." See Marlene Laruelle, *L'idéologie eurasiste russe, ou comment penser l'empire* (Paris: L'Harmattan, 1999), 52.

7. For a literary genealogy of the Eurasian theme, from Vladimir Solov'ev's "panmongolism" to symbolism proper, see Ettore Lo Gatto, "*Panmongolismo* di V. Solov'ëv, *I venienti Unni* di V. Briusov e *Gli Sciti* di A. Blok," in *For Roman Jakob-son* (The Hague: Mouton, 1956), and for the remainder of the evolution, see Georges Nivat, "Du 'panmongolisme' au 'mouvement eurasien': Histoire d'un thème litté-raire," *Cahiers du Monde russe et soviétique* 3 (1966), 460–78. On Scythianism, see Elisabeth Dobringer, *Der Literaturkritiker R. V. Ivanov-Razumnik und seine Konzeption des Skythentums* (Munich: Verlag Otto Sagner, 1991).

8. For the statement on the "three geniuses," see Roman Jakobson, *My Futur-

ist Years, trans. and ed. Bengt Jangfeldt and Stephen Rudy (New York: Marsilio, 1997), 19.

9. V. S. Solov'ev, *Stikhotvoreniia*, 6th ed. (Moscow: I. N. Kushnere, 1915), 287–88. The poem was also used by Blok as an epigraph to his "Skify." It should be noted that Vladimir Solov'ev's celebrated "Kratkaia povest' ob Antikhriste" (published in 1900) has a more complex account of the same theme, in which the invasions of the Eurasian steppe are seen as a harbinger of the Antichrist. Panmongolism belongs to a preliminary period of chaos that prepares his coming. Temporally, then, panmongolism is a moment of interregnum, imminent but not final. Solov'ev's "Tri razgovora," *Izbrannoe* (Moscow: Sovetskaia Rossiia, 1990), 231–424, of which the story of the Antichrist is a part, is usefully read in the light of Solov'ev's ethicopolitical vision. In relation to the Orient, see his poem "Ex oriente lux" (1890), as well as the essays "Tri sily," in *Sochineniia v dvukh tomakh* (Moscow: Pravda, 1989), 1:19–31, "Mir Vostoka i Zapada," 2:602–5, and "Pis'mo o vostochnom voprose," 2:636–39.

10. Valery Briusov's "Griadushchie gunny" (The Future Hunns, 1904–1905) appeared as part of the collection *Stephanos* (1905), which is saturated with impressions of the 1905 Revolution. Leonid Andreev's fantasmagoria of the Russo-Japanese Warm "Krasnyi smekh" (Red Laughter, 1904) is also relevant. Maksimilian Voloshin's revolutionary poems are mainly in the cycle "Puti Rossii" (The Ways of Russia) written between 1905 and 1923. Blok's poem "Skify" (1918) appeared alongside an article by Ivanov-Razumnik in 1918; see Aleksandr Blok, *Sobranie sochinenii v shesti tomakh* (Leningrad: Khudozhestvennaia literatura, 1971), 2:253–55. The importance of Solov'ev's panmongolism for Russian modernism cannot be underestimated, although it was modified by each of those who felt its influence: see Andrei Bely, "Apokalipsis v russkoi poèzii," *Vesy* no. 4, (April 1905), 11–28 and his "Vladimir Solov'ev: Iz vospominanii," in *Arabeski* (Moscow: Musaget, 1911); the *Aleksandr Blok–Andrei Belyi perepiska*, ed. D. Orlov (Munich: Wilhelm Fink Verlag, 1969 [1940]), in particular the letters of 1911; and Blok's article "Narod i intelligentsia," where the Battle of Kulikovo is used as an allegory of the Russian intellectual's conflict with his *own* nation. A vivid interpretation of the Eurasian theme by a leading proponent of Scythianism is found in R. V. Ivanov-Razumnik's essay "Ispytanie v groze i bure," published in the volume *Ispytanie v groze i bure* (Berlin: Izdatel'stvo Skify, 1920), 7–44, as a preface to Blok's poems "Skify" and "Dvenadtsat'." Ivanov-Razumnik's essay is especially useful in providing the literary antecedents for Eurasianism in the "geopolitical" poetry of Pushkin, Tiutchev, and Khomiakov.

11. A. S. Pushkin, in his letter of October 19, 1836, to P. Ia. Chaadaev, *Perepiska A. S. Pushkina v dvukh tomakh* (Moscow: Khudozhestvennaia literatura, 1982), 2:287 (emphasis added). This letter is a locus classicus of the Eurasian debate in Russian literature.

12. Nicholas Riasanovsky, "Afterword: The Emergence of Eurasianism," 138.

13. Boris Gasparov, "The Ideological Principles of Prague School Phonology," in *Language, Poetry and Poetics: The Generation of the 1890's: Jakobson, Trubetzkoy, Majakovskij* (Berlin: Mouton de Gruyter, 1987), 54 (emphasis added).

14. Trubetskoi, "Obshcheevraziiskii natsionalizm," 425. In this context, see I. A. Isaev's very suggestive chapter, "Geopoliticheskaia utopiia evraziitsev," *Politiko-pravovaia utopiia v Rossii: Konets XIX–Nachalo XX vv.* (Moscow: Nauka, 1991), 206–7: "Spatial closure is the ideal condition for the formation of a utopian social model. . . . The isolation of a spatial milieu allows for the most fantastical and abstract constructions. The conservatism of Eurasianist geopolitical thinking was based above all on their extremely categorical appraisal of the spatial boundaries of Eurasia."

15. Nicholas Riasanovsky, in "Afterword: The Emergence of Eurasianism," 138, has observed that "Professor Roman Jakobson, a most important witness and indeed participant, attaches considerable significance to the Futurist roots of the Eurasian revolt." The latter observation was communicated by Jakobson to Riasanovsky in a private conversation that took place in the winter of 1961–1962.

16. Roman Jakobson, "Noveishaia russkaia poeziia. Nabrosok pervyi. Podstupy k Khlebnikovu," in *Raboty po poètike* (Moscow: Progress, 1987), 275, 274. On Jakobson's Khlebnikov article, see also Peter Steiner, *Russian Formalism: A Metapoetics* (Ithaca, NY: Cornell University Press, 1984), 199–241.

17. Velimir Khlebnikov, *Sobranie proizvedenii Velimira Khlebnikova*, ed. N. Stepanov (Leningrad: Izdatel'stvo pisatelei v Leningrade, 1929–1933), 1–2:9.

18. Velimir Khlebnikov, "V mire tsifr," in *Sobranie proizvedenii Velimira Khlebnikova*, 5:462.

19. Khlebnikov, "Vremia mera mira," in *Sobranie proizvedenii Velimira Khlebnikova*, 5:437.

20. See Khlebnikov's "supersaga" *Zangezi*, in *Sobranie proizvedenii Velimira Khlebnikova*, 3:350–51, or the more complex prose elaboration found in "Bitvy 1915–1917 gg.: Novoe uchenie o voine," 5:422–27.

21. For the full text of this manifesto, "Indo-Russian Union," and a more extensive treatment of Khlebnikov's theories of time, space, and language as a precocious and self-critical form of Eurasianism, see Harsha Ram, "The Poetics of Eurasia: Velimir Khlebnikov between Empire and Revolution," in *The Transformation of Russian Social Identities*, ed. Madhavan K. Palat (Basingstoke: Palgrave, 2001), 209–31.

22. N. S. Trubetskoi, "Evropa i chelovechestvo" (originally published in 1927), in *Istoriia. Kul'tura. Iazyk*, 104.

23. N. Berdiaev, "Utopicheskii etatizm evraziitsev" (1927), republished in the collection, *Rossiia mezhdu Evropoi i Aziei: Evraziiskii soblazn* (Moscow: Nauka, 1993), 305. Berdiaev effectively condemns the Eurasianists for betraying Solov'ev and Scythianism. See also Berdiaev's essay "Evraziitsy" (1925), in *Rossiia mezhdu Evropoi i Aziei*, 298.

24. Trubetskoi, "Obshcheevraziiskii natsionalizm," 417.

25. Khlebnikov, *Sobranie proizvedenii*, 5:155.

26. Khlebnikov, "Nasha osnova," in *Sobranie proizvedenii*, 5:237. A useful summary of Khlebnikov's linguistic theories can be found in Carla Solivetti's, "Lingvisticheskie prozreniia Velimira Khlebnikova," *Russian Literature* 55, nos. 1–3 (January–April 2004), 405–29.

27. Khlebnikov, "Khudozhniki mira!" in *Sobranie proizvedenii*, 5:219–20.

28. Khlebnikov, "Iz zapisnykh knizhek," in *Sobranie proizvedenii*, 5:268.

29. Roman Jakobson and K. Pomorska, *Besedy* (Jerusalem: Magnes Press, Hebrew University, 1982), 7, 8.

30. Roman Jakobson, "K kharakteristike evraziiskogo iazykovogo soiuza," in *Selected Writings* (The Hague: Mouton, 1971), 1:172–73. It is worth noting that Jakobson never renounced the article, and indeed defended its theses vigorously at the end of his life: see Roman Jakobson, "The Space Factor in Language (with Krystyna Pomorska)," (1980), in *On Language*, ed. Linda R. Waugh and Monique Monville-Burston (Cambridge, MA: Harvard University Press, 1990), 176–83.

31. Jakobson, "K kharakteristike evraziiskogo iazykovogo soiuza," 174–75.

32. Patrick Sériot, "Lingvistika geografov i geografiia lingvistov: R. O. Iakobson i P. N. Savitskii," in *Roman Iakobson: Tektsy, dokumenty, issledovaniia*, ed. Henryk Baran et al. (Moscow: Rossiiskii Gosudarstvennyi gumanitarnyi universitet, 1999), 350.

33. Jakobson, "K kharakteristike evraziiskogo iazykovogo soiuza," 190–91.

34. Jakobson, "Phonemic and Grammatical Aspects of Language," in *Selected Writings*, 2:105.

35. Sériot, *Structure et totalité*, 105–6.

Chapter 9: Eurasianism Goes Japanese

In this chapter, Japanese names (including the author's name) are given in the original order, namely, surname first and first name second.

1. Nikolai Trubetskoi, "O gosudarstvennom stroe i forme pravleniia," in *Nasledie Chingiskhana* (Moscow: Agraf, 2000), 482–87.

2. Kurt Sontheimer, *Antidemokratisches Denken in der Weimarer Republik: Die politischen Ideen des deutschen Nationalismus zwischen 1918 und 1933* (Munich: Nymphenburger Verlagshandlung, 1962); trans. Kawashima Sachio and Waki Keihei, *Waimaru kyōwakoku no seiji shisō: Doitsu nashonarizumu no hanminshushugi shisō* (Kyoto: Minerva Shobō, 1976), 148–56, 165–75.

3. Martin Baissvenger, "Konservativnaia revoliutsiia v Germanii i dvizhenie 'evraziitsev': Tochki soprikosnoveniia," in *Konservatizm v Rossii i mire* (Voronezh: Voronezhskii gosudarstvennyi universitet, 2004).

4. N. S. Trubetskoi, *Evropa i chelovechestvo* (Sofia: Rossiisko-bolgarskoe knigo-

izdatel'stvo, 1921); Nicholas Riasanovsky, "Prince N. S. Trubetskoy's 'Europe and Mankind,'" *Jahrbücher für Geschichte Osteuropas* 12 (1964), 212. About *Europe and Mankind* and Trubetskoi's ideas in Eurasianism, see also, Nicholas Riasanovsky, "The Emergence of Eurasianism," *California Slavic Studies*, no. 5 (1967); Marlen Lariuel' [Marlene Laruelle], *Ideologiia russkogo evraziistva ili mysli o velichii imperii* (Moscow: Natalis, 2004); Sergei Glebov, "Granitsy imperii i granitsy moderna: Antikolonial'naia ritorika i teoriia kul'turnykh tipov v evraziistve," *Ab Imperio*, no. 2 (2003).

5. N. S. Trubetskoi, "Evropa i chelovechestvo," in *Nasledie Chingiskhana*, 87; the English translation is from N. S. Trubetzkoy, "Europe and Mankind," in N. S. Trubetzkoy, *The Legacy of Genghis Khan and Other Essays on Russia's Identity*, trans. Kenneth Brostrom (Ann Arbor: Michigan Slavic Publications, 1991), 60–61.

6. Sven Saaler and J. Victor Koschmann, eds., *Pan-Asianism in Modern Japanese History* (London: Routledge, 2007). For a collection of materials, see Sven Saaler and Christopher W. A. Szpilman, eds., *Pan-Asianism: A Documentary History*, 2 vols. (Lanham, MD: Rowman and Littlefield, 2011).

7. N. S. Trubetskoi, "Ob istinnom i lozhnom natsionalizme," in *Iskhod k vostoku* (Sofia: Rossiisko-bolgarskoe knigoizdatel'stvo, 1921), 71–85; N. S. Trubetskoi, "K ukurainskoi probleme," *Evraziiskii vremennik*, no. 5 (1927), 165–84.

8. N. S. Trubetskoi, "Russkaia problema," *Na putiakh*, no. 2 (1922), 177–229. The leading Eurasianists, Trubetskoi and Savitskii, survived through the confusion of the Civil War and the Allied intervention. This experience may have caused them to retain a sense of crisis. *N. S. Trubetzkoy's Letters and Notes*, ed. Roman Jakobson with H. Baran, O. Ronen, and Martha Taylor (The Hague: Mouton, 1975), 4; Sergey Glebov, "A Life with Imperial Dreams: Petr Nikolaevich Savitsky, Eurasianism, and the Invention of 'Structuralist' Geography," *Ab Imperio*, no. 3 (2005), 302–3.

9. N. S. Trubetskoi, "Obscheevraziiskii natsionalizm," *Evrazaiiskaia khronika*, no. 9 (1927), 24–30.

10. N. S. Trubetskoi, *Nasledie Chingiskhana: Vzgliad na russkuiu istoriiu ne s zapada a s vostoka* (Berlin: Evraziiskii knigoizdatel'stvo, 1925).

11. Naoko Shimazu, *Japan, Race and Equality: The Racial Equality Proposal of 1919* (London: Routledge, 1998).

12. For translations of Eurasianists' works in Japan, see Fumiki Yoneshige, "Evraziistvo na dal'nem vostoke," *Japanese Slavic and East European Studies* 18 (1997), 11–32.

13. Torubekkoi, *Seiō bunmei to jinrui no shōrai* (Tokyo: Kōchisha shuppanbu, 1926).

14. Torubekkoi, "Seiō bunmei to jinrui no shōrai," *Gekkan Nippon*, no. 4 (1925), 32–40; no. 5 (1925), 35–39; no. 6 (1925), 29–38; no. 7 (1925), 24–32; no. 8 (1925), 40–47; no. 9 (1925), 45–54; no. 10 (1926), 36–45.

15. *Evraziistvo: Deklaratsiia, formulirovka, tezisy* (Prague: Izdanie evraziitsev, 1932); trans. Shimano Saburō, "Nichiman kyōfukushugi," *Dai-Ajia* (August 1933), 8–19; (September 1933), 6–17.

16. Petr N. Savitskii, "Geopoliticheskie zametki po russkoi istorii," in G. V. Vernadskii, *Nachertanie russkoi istorii* (Prague: Evraziiskoe knigoizdatel'stvo, 1927), 234–60; trans. Nakane Renji, "Roshiya-shi no chiseijigakuteki oboegaki," *Kokuritsu daigaku Harupin Gakuin ronsō*, no. 3 (1943), 1–61.

17. Hara-Dafun [*sic*], *Chingis-han: Ōa seifuku no eiyū*, trans. Wada Tarō (Tokyo: Ajia kenkyūkai, 1938); Erenjin Hara-Dawan, *Chingis-han den*, trans. Honma Shichirō (Tokyo: Asahi shinbunsha, 1938).

18. Nakane, "Roshiya-shi no chiseijigakuteki oboegaki," 13–15.

19. Yoneshige, "Evraziistvo na dal'nem vostoke," 11, 14.

20. Most of the information on Shimano's life is based on the following series of essays. Yoneshige Fumiki, "Seishin no tabibito: Shimano Saburō," *Mado*, nos. 92–104 (March 1995–March 1998); nos. 106–10 (September 1998–October 1999); see also a biography of Shimano. Mantetsukai (Shimano Saburō denki kankōkai), *Shimano Saburō: Mantetsu soren jōhōkatsudōka no shōgai* (Tokyo: Hara shobō, 1984). For additional information about Shimano's activities, see Yukiko Hama, "Russia from a Pan-Asianist View: Saburo Shimano and His Activities," *Ab Imperio*, no. 3 (2010).

21. Mantetsukai, *Shimano Saburō*, xii, 468.

22. Prasenjit Duara, *Sovereignty and Authenticity: Manchukuo and the East Asian Modern* (Lanham, MD: Rowman and Littlefield, 2004), 48.

23. John Young, *The Research Activities of the South Manchurian Railway Company, 1907–1945: A History and Bibliography* (New York: Columbia University Press, 1966), 3–34; Itō Takeo, *Life along the South Manchurian Railway: The Memoirs of Ito Takeo*, trans. Joshua Fogel (Armonk, NY: M. E. Sharpe, 1988).

24. Christopher W. A. Szpilman, "Between Pan-Asianism and Nationalism: Mitsukawa Kametarō and His Campaign to Reform Japan and Liberate Asia," in *Pan-Asianism in Modern Japanese History*, ed. Sven Saaler and J. Victor Koschmann (London: Routledge, 2007), 85–100.

25. On February 26, 1936, a group of young army officers leading about 1,400 troops attacked and assassinated several ministers and seized the center of Tokyo. They assumed that these acts against ministers and politicians would curtail political corruption and save the impoverished peasants. The officers hoped for the restoration of and absolute rule by the emperor. The rebellions were quickly suppressed and the leading officers were sentenced to death. This incident significantly influenced later relations between the army and politics in Japan as the country approached the war. *Kodansha Encyclopedia of Japan* (New York: Kodansha International, 1983), 249–50.

26. George M. Wilson, *Radical Nationalism in Japan: Kita Ikki, 1883–1937*

(Cambridge, MA: Harvard University Press, 1969); Brij Tankha, *Kita Ikki and the Making of Modern Japan: A Vision of Empire* (Kent, UK: Global Oriental, 2006).

27. Wilson, *Radical Nationalism in Japan*; Cemil Aydin, *The Politics of Anti-Westernism in Asia* (New York: Columbia University Press, 2007).

28. Szpilman, "Between Pan-Asianism and Nationalism," 89.

29. Yoneshige, "Seisin no tabibito," *Mado*, no. 103 (December 1997), 46–47.

30. Shimano, "Nichiman kyōfukushugi."

31. Shimano Saburō, "Yakusha jo," in Torubekkoi, *Seiō bunmei to jinrui no shōrai*.

32. *N. S. Trubetzkoy's Letters and Notes*, 3.

33. Wilson, *Radical Nationalism in Japan*, 98.

34. Yamamuro Shinichi, *Sisō kadai toshiteno Ajia* (Tokyo: Iwanami shoten, 2001).

35. On September 18–19, the Guandong Army, the Imperial Japanese Army's field command in Manchuria led by aggressive colonels, attacked the main Chinese garrison in Manchuria and succeeded in taking over and conquering Manchuria, where they established an autonomous state with some pliable Chinese leaders. Against the background of intensifying rivalry between Japan and China over Manchuria, the Guandong Army officers hoped to dominate the territory and resources of Manchuria. The plan for a sudden attack was conceived without the authorization of the headquarters and the civilian government in Tokyo. The foundation of Manchukuo, however, drove Japan into international isolation, especially as a consequence of the Lytton Commission's verdict, which led Japan to withdraw from the League of Nations. At the same time, this brought the rise of military tension with the Soviet Union in the Far East. *Kodansha Encyclopedia of Japan*, 5:97–99.

36. Yamamuro Shinichi, *Kimera: Manshūkoku no shōzō* (Tokyo: Chūō kōron shinsha, 2004), 92–108.

37. Mark Raeff, *Russia Abroad: A Cultural History of the Russian Emigration, 1919–1939* (New York: Oxford University Press, 1990), 23–24; Catherina Andreyev and Ivan Savicky, *Russia Abroad: Prague and the Russian Diaspora, 1919–1938* (New Haven, CT: Yale University Press, 2004), xi.

38. Vsevolod N. Ivanov (1888–1971) was a writer who worked for the Far Eastern Republic in 1920–1921, and emigrated to China in 1922. When he lived in Shanghai and Harbin, he published several novels and essays. In 1925, he started to cooperate with TASS and thus obtained a Soviet passport in 1931, returning eventually to Khabarovsk in 1945. His book *My* [We] (1925) affirmed the integration of East Asia with the Russian Far East and was sympathetic to Eurasianism. *Russkie pisateli 20 veka* (Moscow: Nauchnoe izdatel'stvo, Bol'shaia rossiiskaia entsiklopediia, 2000), 300–301.

39. "Perepiska s 'Aziatom' V. Ivanovym," *Evraziiskaia khronika*, no. 6 (1926), 6–13.

40. "Perepiska s 'Aziatom' V. Ivanovym," 10.

41. *Kharbinskoe vremia*, March 9, 1932.

42. "Evraziitsy o Dal'ne-Vostochnom voprose," Gosudarstvennyi Arkhiv Rossiiskoi Federatsii (GARF), fond. 5783, opis' 2, delo 26. This material does not show an author's name but indicates that it was written in the name of the caucus of the Eurasianism Organization.

43. "Iz perepiski evraziitsev," *Ab Imperio*, no. 2 (2003), 322, 332.

44. *Kharbinskoe vremia*, March 9, 1932.

45. "Perepiska s 'Aziatom' V. Ivanovym," 9–12.

46. "Perepiska s 'Aziatom' V. Ivanovym," 6–9.

47. "Evraziitsy o Dal'ne-Vostochnom voprose."

48. Marlene Laruelle, *Russian Eurasianism: An Ideology of Empire* (Washington, DC: Woodrow Wilson Center Press, 2008).

Chapter 10: Narrating Kulikovo

1. Marlene Laruelle, *Russian Eurasianism: An Ideology of Empire* (Washington, DC: Woodrow Wilson Center Press, 2008).

2. I. I. Smirnov, ed., *Kratkaia Istoriia SSSR: Chast' Pervaia* (Moscow-Leningrad: Iz-vo AN SSSR, 1963), 81; M. V. Nechkina and P. S. Leibengrub, eds., *Istoriia SSSR: Uchebnoe posobie dlia 7 klassa*, 5th ed. (Moscow: Izdatel'stvo Prosveshchenie, 1970), 74–77. On the Golden Horde in Soviet historiography, see Lowell Tillett, *The Great Friendship: Soviet Historians on the Non-Russian Nationalities* (Chapel Hill: University of North Carolina Press, 1969), 79, 89, 104. Translations are the author's unless otherwise indicated.

3. For a discussion of the Kulikovo celebrations, see Yitzhak M. Brudny, *Reinventing Russia: Russian Nationalism and the Soviet State, 1953–1991* (Cambridge, MA: Harvard University Press, 1998), 117, 136, 181–91.

4. Nikolai Sergeevich Trubetskoi, *Nasledie Chingiskhana: Vzgliad na russkuiu istoriiu ne s Zapada, a s Vostoka* (Berlin: Evraziiskoe Knigoizdatel'stvo, 1925); see also the discussion in Sergei Glebov, "The Mongol-Bolshevik Revolution: Eurasianist Ideology in Search of an Ideal Past," *Journal of Eurasian Studies* 2 (2011), 103–14.

5. S. S. Beliakov, *Gumilev syn Gumileva* (Moscow: Astrel', 2012); V. M. Demin, *Lev Gumilev*, 2nd ed. (Moscow: Molodaia gvardiia, 2008); S. B. Lavrov, *Lev Gumilev: Sud'ba i idei* (Moscow: Svarog i K, 2000); L. P. Karel'skaia, *L. N. Gumilev* (Moscow: MarT, 2005); E. M. Goncharova, ed., *Dni L. N. Gumileva v Bezhetske* (Bezhetsk: Ekopros, 1995).

6. L. N. Gumilev, *Otkrytie Khazarii: Istoriko-geograficheskii etiud* (Moscow: Nauka, 1966); L. N. Gumilev, "Gde ona, strana Khazariia?" *Nedelia* 24 (June 7–13,

1964); L. N. Gumilev, "Khazariia i Kaspii," *Vestnik Leningradskogo Universiteta: Seriia Geograficheskaia* 6, no. 1 (1964), 83–95.

7. L. N. Gumilev, *Etnogenez i biosfera zemli*, 2nd ed. (Leningrad: Izdatel'stvo Leningradskogo Universiteta, 1989); L. N. Gumilev, *Geografiia etnosa v istoricheskii period* (Leningrad: Nauka, 1990); L. N. Gumilev, *Etnosfera: Istoriia liudei i istoriia prirody* (Moscow: Ekopros, 1993); Mark Bassin, "Nurture *Is* Nature: Lev Gumilev and the Ecology of Ethnicity," *Slavic Review* 68, no. 4 (2009), 872–97.

8. Fragments of Gumilev's interpretation of ancient Russian history appeared elliptically in a 1970 monograph devoted to a different topic. L. N. Gumilev, *Poiski vymyshlennogo tsarstva: Legenda o "Gosudarstve 'presvitera Ioanna'"* (Moscow: Nauka, 1970). It was then presented rather more formally in two very short pieces that appeared during the Kulikovo commemorations themselves (L. N. Gumilev, "Epokha kulikovskoi bitvy," *Ogonek* 36 [1980], 16–17; L. N. Gumilev, "God rozhdeniia 1380," *Dekorativnoe iskusstvo* 12 [1980], 34–37), but the publication of his major study on the question had to await the liberalization of the late perestroika period. L. N. Gumilev, *Drevniaia Rus' i velikaia step'* (Moscow: Mysl', 1989). Moreover, he discussed these topics in great detail in the numerous interviews he gave in the years before his death in 1994. The analysis developed in this chapter draws on all of these sources.

9. L. N. Gumilev, "Etnos, istoriia, kul'tura," *Dekorativnoe iskusstvo SSSR* 5 (1989), 30.

10. Gumilev had personal links with two of the leading architects of the Eurasianist perspective—the geographer and economist Petr Savitskii, and George Vernadsky himself—and he corresponded with both. Remarkably, in 1966 he actually met Savitskii while attending an international conference in Prague. L. N. Gumilev, "Skazhu Vam po sekretu, chto esli Rossiia budet spasena, to tol'ko kak evraziiskaia derzhava . . ." in *Ritmy Evrazii: Epokhi i tsivilizatsii* (Moscow: Ekopros, 1993), 37. See also S. B. Lavrov, "Paradoksy L'va Gumileva," in *Vspominaia L. N. Gumileva. Vospominaniia. Publikatsii. Issledovaniia*, ed. V. N. Voronovich and M. G. Kozyreva (St. Petersburg: Rostok, 2003), 209–16. Excerpts from their correspondence are published in P. N. Savitskii, "Iz pisem P. N. Savitskogo L. N. Gumilevu," in L. N. Gumilev, *Chernaia legenda: Druz'ia i nedrugi Velikoi stepi* (Moscow: Ekopros, 1994), 164–66. See also Gumilev, *Etnogenez i biosfera zemli*, 38, 180; L. N. Gumilev, "On the Subject of the 'Unified Geography' (Landscape and Etnos, VI)," *Soviet Geography: Review and Translation* 9, no. 1 (1968), 42–43; L. N. Gumilev, "Letter to P. N. Savitskii, December 19, 1956" (personal archive of the author).

11. Gumilev, "Skazhu Vam po sekretu," 26; L. N. Gumilev, "'Menia nazyvaiut evraziitsem,'" *Nash sovremennik* 1 (1991), 132–41.

12. It happened to be the scientific work of George Vernadsky's father Vladimir on the biosphere concept that Gumilev drew most heavily on, and the latter specifically chided George for his "insufficient grasp of the ideas of his father." Gumilev,

"'Menia nazyvaiut evraziitsem,'" 132; Gumilev, "Skazhu Vam po sekretu," 26. For comparisons of Gumilev and the classical Eurasianists, see Marlene Laruelle, "Lev Nikolaevic Gumilev (1912–1992): Biologisme et eurasisme dans la penseé russe," *Revue des études slaves*, no. 1–2 (2000), 163–89; S. A. Ivanov, "Vzaimootnosheniia Rusi i Stepi v kontseptsiiakh evraziitsev i L'va Gumileva," *Slaviane i ikh sosedi: Slaviane i kochevoi mir* 10 (2001), 213–18; V. A. Shnirel'man and S. A. Panarin, "Lev Nikolaevich Gumilev: Osnovatel' etnologii?" *Vestnik Evrazii* 3, no. 10 (2000), 5–37; R. R. Vakhitov, "Reabilitatsiia kul'tur kochevnikov russkimi evraziitsami 20-kh–30-kh gg," http://nevmenandr.net/vaxitov/mongol.php (accessed March 6, 2014); A. V. Samokhin, "Istoricheskii put' evraziistva kak ideino-politicheskogo techeniia (ch. 2)," *Al'manakh 'Vostok'* 3, no. 15 (2004), http://www.situation.ru/app /j_art_317.htm (accessed June 16, 2014).

13. Gumilev, "'Menia nazyvaiut evraziitsem,'" 134.

14. L. N. Gumilev, "Istoriko-filosofskie trudy kniazia N. S. Trubetskogo (zametki poslednego evraziitsa)," in N. S. Trubetskoi, *Istoriia. Kul'tura. Iazyk* (Moscow: Progress-Univers, 1995), 31–54, 38–39.

15. L. N. Gumilev, *Ot rusi do rossii: Ocherki etnicheskoi istorii* (Moscow: Airis-Press, 2000), 121.

16. Gumilev, "'Menia nazyvaiut evraziitsem,'" 134.

17. Gumilev, "'Menia nazyvaiut evraziitsem,'" 136.

18. L. N. Gumilev, "Chernaia Legenda," in Gumilev, *Chernaia Legenda*, 42–147.

19. L. N. Gumilev, *Poiski vymyshlennogo tsarstva* (St. Petersburg: Arbis, 1994), 369; Gumilev, "Istoriko-filosofskie trudy," 41; Gumilev, "'Menia nazyvaiut evraziitsem,'"136. On Gumilev's idiosyncratic emphasis on the importance of Nestorianism, see Laruelle, "Lev Nikolaevic Gumilev," 182n; David O. Morgan, "Review of L. N. Gumilev, *Searches for an Imaginary Kingdom*," *Journal of the Royal Asiatic Society* 1 (1989), 161–62.

20. L. N. Gumilev, "Opyt preodoleniia samoobmama," in Gumilev, *Poiski vymyshlennogo tsarstva*, 294–95.

21. L. N. Gumilev and Dmitrii Balashov, "V kakoe vremia my zhivem?" in L. N. Gumilev, *Ritmy Evrazii: Epokhi i tsvilizatsiia* (Moscow: Ekopros, 1993), 145; Gumilev, *Poiski vymyshlennogo tsarstva*, 173–74, 295–96.

22. L. N. Gumilev, *Konets i vnov' nachalo: Populiarnye lektsii po narodovedeniiu* (Moscow: Rol'f, 2001), 124–25; Gumilev, *Poiski vymyshlennogo tsarstva*, 133; Gumilev, "'Menia nazyvaiut evraziitsem,'" 135; Gumilev, *Etnogenez i biosfera zemli*, 357.

23. Gumilev, *Ot rusi do rossii*, 130–31; Gumilev, "'Menia nazyvaiut evraziitsem,'" 134–35; Gumilev, "Epokha kulikovskoi bitvy," 16.

24. Gumilev and Balashov, "V kakoe vremia my zhivem?" 145; Gumilev, "Istoriko-filosofskie trudy," 42–43; Gumilev, *Ot rusi do rossii*, 129–31.

25. Gumilev, "God rozhdeniia 1380."

26. L. N. Gumilev and K. P. Ivanov, "Etnicheskie protsessy: Dva podkhoda k

izucheniiu," *Sotsiologicheskie issledovaniia* 1 (1992), 56. L. N. Gumilev, *Drevniaia Rus' i velikaia step'* (Moscow: Airis, 2004), 332; Loren R. Graham, *Science, Philosophy, and Human Behavior in the Soviet Union* (New York: Columbia University Press, 1987), 225; Laruelle, "Lev Nikolaevic Gumilev," 185.

27. Gumilev, *Ot rusi do rossii*, 137–38. Gumilev, "'Menia nazyvaiut evraziitsem,'" 135.

28. Gumilev, *Ot rusi do rossii*, 158; Gumilev, "God rozhdeniia 1380," 34–35; Gumilev, "'Menia nazyvaiut evraziitsem,'" 137; L. N. Gumilev, "'Ia, russkii chelovek, vsiu zhizn' zashchishchaiu tatar ot klevety," in *Chernaia legenda*, 311.

29. Gumilev, "God rozhdeniia 1380," 35.

30. Gumilev, *Drevniaia Rus' i velikaia step'*, 529, 535, 538–41, 579–87; Gumilev, "'Menia nazyvaiut evraziitsem,'" 137.

31. Gumilev, "God rozhdeniia 1380," 34; Gumilev, "'Menia nazyvaiut evraziitsem,'" 137.

32. Gumilev, *Ot rusi do rossii*, 161.

33. The "Legacy of Genghis Khan" that Nikolai Trubetskoi embraced so enthusiastically referred only to the principle of geopolitical and cultural-historical unity of the spaces of Eurasia first established by the Golden Horde. It was not intended to suggest that Tatar domination over Rus' was anything other than a painful and agonizing experience. Trubetskoi, *Nasledie Chingiskhana*. For the *igo* image in classical Eurasianism, see "Evraziistvo: Opyt sistematicheskogo izlozheniia," in *Mir Rossii-Evrazii: Antologiia*, ed. L. I. Novikova and I. N. Sizemskaia (Moscow: Vysshaia shkola, 1995 [1926]), 256–57; Ivanov, "Vzaimootnosheniia Rusi i Stepi," 215.

34. Gumilev, "God rozhdeniia 1380," 35.

35. Gumilev, "'Ia, russkii chelovek," 286.

36. Gumilev, "God rozhdeniia 1380," 34.

37. Gumilev, "'Menia nazyvaiut evraziitsem.'" On the complicated ethnic composition of the *velikorossy*, see Gumilev, *Etnogenez i biosfera zemli*, 143.

38. Gumilev, *Ot rusi do rossii*, 144–45.

39. Gumilev, "'Ia, russkii chelovek," 307.

40. Gumilev, "Istoriko-filosofskie trudy," 41.

41. Gumilev and Balashov, "V kakoe vremia my zhivem?" 156.

42. Gumilev, "'Menia nazyvaiut evraziitsem,'" 135; Gumilev, "Epokha kulikovskoi bitvy," 17.

43. On Russian nationalism in the late Soviet period, see Brudny, *Reinventing Russia*; John Dunlop, *The Rise of Russia and the Fall of the Soviet Empire* (Princeton, NJ: Princeton University Press, 1993); Nikolai Mitrokhin, *Russkaia partiia* (Moscow: NLO, 2003); Hildegard Kochanek, *Die russisch-nationale Rechte von 1968 bis zum Ende der Sowjetunion: Eine Diskursanalyse* (Stuttgart: Franz Steiner, 1999); Edward Allworth, ed., *Ethnic Russia in the USSR: The Dilemma*

of Dominance (New York: Pergamon, 1980); Alexander Yanov, *The Russian New Right: Right-Wing Ideologies in the Contemporary USSR* (Berkeley: Institute of International Studies, University of California, 1978); Frederick C. Barghoorn, *Soviet Russian Nationalism* (New York: Oxford University Press, 1956).

44. S. N. Semanov, "Russkii klub," *Moskva* 3 (1997), 177–82.

45. Terry Martin, *The Affirmative Action Empire: Nations and Nationalism in the Soviet Union, 1923–1939* (Ithaca, NY: Cornell University Press, 2001).

46. Victor Shnirelman and Galina Komarova, "Majority as a Minority: The Russian Ethno-Nationalism and Its Ideology in the 1970s–1990s," in *Rethinking Nationalism and Ethnicity: The Struggle for Meaning and Order in Europe*, ed. Hans-Rudolf Wicker (Oxford: Berg, 1997), 211–13.

47. S. T. Kaltakhchian, "Sovetskii narod," in *Bol'shaia Sovetskaia Entsiklopediia* (Moscow: Sovetskaia Entsliklopediia, 1976), 25; Iu. Iu. Veingol'd, *Sovetskii narod: Novaia internatsional'naia obshchnost' liudei. Sotsiologicheskii ocherk* (Frunze: Kyrgyzstan, 1973); M. P. Kim, *Sovetskii narod: Novaia istoricheskaia obshchnost' liudei* (Moscow: Nauka, 1975); Ronald J. Hill, "The 'All-People's State' and 'Developed Socialism,'" in *The State in Socialist Society*, ed. Neil Harding (Albany: State University of New York Press, 1984), 109; Terry L. Thompson, *Ideology and Policy: The Political Uses of Doctrine in the Soviet Union* (Boulder, CO: Westview, 1989), 66–72; Kaija Heikkinen, "Ethnicity and Nationalism in Contemporary Russian Ethnography," in *The Fall of an Empire, the Birth of a Nation: National Identities in Russia*, ed. Chris J. Chulos and Timo Piirainen (Aldershot: Ashgate, 2000), 101–2.

48. I. R. Shafarevich, *Rusofobiia: Dve dorogi k odnomu obryvu* (Moscow: Tovarishchestvo russkikh khudozhnikov, 1991).

49. S. N. Semanov, "O tsennostiakh otnositel'nykh i vechnykh," *Molodaia gvardiia* 8 (1970), 317; Brudny, *Reinventing Russia*, 184–85.

50. Yanov, *The Russian New Right*, 72; G. M. Shimanov, "Kak ponimat' nashu istoriiu i k chemu v nei stremit'sia," June 2, 1974, http://chri-soc.narod.ru/sh_kak _ponimat_nashu_istoriu.htm (accessed June 16, 2014).

51. "A Word to the Nation," *Survey* 17, no. 3 (1971), 195–96.

52. Brudny, *Reinventing Russia*, 181.

53. Ruslan Skrynnikov, "Kulikovskaia bitva," *Zvezda* 9 (1980), 9; Smirnov, *Kratkaia istoriia SSSR*, 81; Nechkina and Leibengrub, *Istoriia SSSR*, 74–77.

54. Mark Liubomudrov, "Sila edinstva," *Ogonek* 4 (1981), 17.

55. Cited in Kochanek, *Die russisch-nationale Rechte*, 247. See also Skrynnikov, "Kulikovskaia bitva," 81. For a full discussion of Russian nationalist views of Kulikovo, see Brudny, *Reinventing Russia*, 181–85.

56. For analyses of Gumilev's influential historiography on Khazaria, see Victor A. Shnirelman, *The Myth of the Khazars and Intellectual Antisemitism in Russia, 1970s–1990s* (Jerusalem: Vidal Sassoon International Center for the Study of An-

tisemitism, Hebrew University, 2002); Vadim Rossman, "Lev Gumilev, Eurasianism and Khazaria," *East European Jewish Affairs* 32, no. 1 (2002), 30–51.

57. A. I. Baigushev, *Russkii orden vnutri KPSS: Pomoshchnik M. A. Suslova vsopominaet . . .* (Moscow: Algoritm, 2006), 253. This was another point on which Gumilev diverged from the arguments of the classical Eurasianists, who were much more prepared to acknowledge Russia's special historical role in leading the Eurasian peoples. Glebov, "The Mongol-Bolshevik Revolution."

58. Semanov, "Russkii klub," 181; Baigushev, *Russkii orden*, 243–44.

59. B. A. Rybakov, "O preodolenii samoobmana," *Voprosy istorii* 3 (1971), 153–59, http://gumilevica.kulichki.net/debate/Article34.htm (accessed March 24, 2014); Brudny, *Reinventing Russia*, 187.

60. Brudny, *Reinventing Russia*, 187.

61. Kochanek, *Die russisch-nationale Rechte*, 85, 251–54, 257, 255–58; Walter Laqueur, *Black Hundred: The Rise of the Extreme Right in Russia* (New York: HarperCollins, 1993), 114, 246; Brudny, *Reinventing Russia*, 55–56, 70, 105, 122, 131, 173, 184–85; Douglas R. Weiner, *A Little Corner of Freedom: Russian Nature Protection from Stalin to Gorbachev* (Berkeley: University of California Press, 1999), 334–37; Nikolai Mitrokhin, "'Russkaia partiia': Fragmenty issledovaniia," *NLO* 48 (2001), http://magazines.russ.ru/nlo/2001/48/mitr.html (accessed April 2, 2014).

62. S. B. Lavrov, *Lev Gumilev: Sud'ba i idei* (Moscow: Airis-Press, 2003), 314–17, 364. On Chivilikhin's and Kuz'min's "obsessive" hostility to Gumilev, see Semanov, "Russkii klub," S. G. Liubkin, "A. Kuz'min i L. Gumilev," *Duel'* 24, no. 472 (June 13, 2006), http://www.duel.ru/200624/?24_6_2 (accessed April 3, 2014).

63. V. A. Chivilikhin, "Pamiat'," *Nash sovremennik* 12 (1980), 118–19, 111, 102, 107–8.

64. Chivilikhin, "Pamiat'," 103–4, 106; Apollon Kuz'min, "Sviashchennye kamni pamiati," *Molodaia gvardiia* 1 (1982), 257.

65. Kuz'min, "Sviashchennye kamni pamiati," 258–62; Apollon Kuz'min, "Propeller passionarnosti. . . ." *Molodaia gvardiia* 9 (1991), 262.

66. Chivilikhin, "Pamiat'," 113–14, 118–19.

67. Chivilikhin, "Pamiat'," 125; Kuz'min, "Sviashchennye kamni pamiati," 256; Kuz'min, "Propeller passionarnosti," 257–58; Apollon Kuz'min, "Otvety ili navety," *Molodaia gvardiia* 11–12 (1993), 276–80.

68. Liubkin, "A. Kuz'min i L. Gumilev"; Kuz'min, "Propeller passionarnosti," 256, 263; Kuz'min, "Otvety ili navety," 276. On accusations by Russian "patriots" that Gumilev sided with Tatars and Kazakhs against ethnic Russia, see Myrzatai Zholdasbekov and Abai Kairzhanov, *Evraziiskaia teoriia L. N. Gumileva* (Astana: n.p., 2002), 8. Gumilev published some limited responses to his critics, but a major rebuttal he planned for the journal *Kommunist* was blocked by the authorities. L. N. Gumilev, "Chto-to s pamiat'iu . . ." *Den'* 1, no. 29 (December 29, 1991), 5; Lavrov, *Lev Gumilev*, 314–15.

69. Baigushev, *Russkii orden*, 252–53; see also Semanov, "Russkii klub," 181–82; Brudny, *Reinventing Russia*, 70–71.

70. Brudny, *Reinventing Russia*, 106, 313n.

71. Dmitrii Balashov, *Simeon Gordyi* (Moscow: AST, 2006 [1984]).

72. On Balashov and Gumilev, see Valdislav Krasnov, *Russia beyond Communism: A Chronicle of National Rebirth* (Boulder, CO: Westview, 1991), 158–62.

73. D. M. Balashov, *Mladshii syn* (Moscow: Sovremennik, 1986), 14, 22–23, 37–38, 40, 449.

74. Balashov, *Mladshii syn*, 591. For Gumilev's appreciation of Balashov, see L. N. Gumilev, "Bremia talanta," in D. M. Balashov, *Sobranie sochinenii* (Moscow: Khudozhestvennaia literatura, 1991), http://gumilevica.kulichki.net/articles /Article55.htm (accessed April 5, 2014).

75. For example, see V. V. Kozhinov, *Istoriia Rusi i russkogo slova* (Moscow: Moskovskii uchebnik-2000, 1997).

76. V. V. Kozhinov, "'I nazovet menia vsiak sushchii v nei iazyk'", *Nash sovremennik* 11 (1981), 153–76; "Evraziistvo i sovremennost': Kruglyi stol," *Liki Rossii: Al'manakh* 2 (1993), http://www.patriotica.ru/actual/stol_eurasia.html (accessed June 16, 2014). For discussions of Kozhinov's essay, see Brudny, *Reinventing Russia*, 119–20, 189–90; Mikhail Agursky, "The Prospects of National Bolshevism," in *The Last Empire: Nationality and the Soviet Future*, ed. Robert Conquest (Palo Alto, CA: Hoover Institution Press, 1986), 87–108, 103–5; Kochanek, *Die russisch-nationale Rechte*, 259–64.

77. N. S. Trubetskoi, *Evropa i chelovechestvo* (Sofia: Rossiisko-Bolgarskoe knigoizdatel'stvo, 1921); Kozhinov, "'I nazovet menia," 162–63; V. V. Kozhinov, "O evraziiskoi kontseptsii russkogo puti," in *O russkom natsional'nom soznanii* (Moscow: Algoritm, 2000), 226–29; Samokhin, "Istoricheskii put' evraziistva."

78. "Evraziistvo i sovremennost'."

79. Kozhinov, "'I nazovet menia," 173–74; Brudny, *Reinventing Russia*, 189.

80. Kozhinov, "'I nazovet menia," 174, 172; V. V. Kozhinov, "Poiski budushchego," *Nash sovremennik* 3 (1991), 127–28.

81. Kozhinov, "'I nazovet menia," 158.

82. Kozhinov, "O evraziiskoi kontseptsii russkogo puti," 224.

83. Kozhinov, "'I nazovet menia," 175.

84. Kozhinov, "'I nazovet menia," 171, 171n, 174–75.

85. Kozhinov, "'I nazovet menia," 158.

86. "Evraziistvo i sovremennost'."

87. Kozhinov, "O evraziiskoi kontseptsii russkogo puti," 233; see also Aleksei Malashenko, "Russkii natsionalizm i islam," *Vestnik Evrazii* 2, no. 3 (1996), 101.

88. "Evraziistvo i sovremennost'."

89. Kseniia Mialo, "Est' li v Evrazii mesto dlia russkikh?" *Nash sovremennik* 9 (1992), 102–5; N. R. Guseva, "Vyzyvaiut nedoumenie: Vzgliady L. N. gumileva na

razvitie russkoi natsii," *Russkii vestnik* 27 (November 19, 1991), 10; Sh. Rusakov, "Ot rusofobii k evraziistvu (kuda vedet gumilevshchina?)," *Molodaia gvardiia* 3 (1993), 127–43. For a critique of Eurasianism (and Gumilev) in contemporary Russian nationalist thinking, see V. B. Avdeev, "Snachala Evraziia, teper' Aziopa," in *Metafizicheskaia antropologiia* (Moscow: Belye al'vy, 2002), 43–67, http://rusograd .xpomo.com/avd_metaph/avd_asiopa.html (accessed June 16, 2014).

90. Aleksandr Dugin, *Osnovy geopolitiki: Geopoliticheskoe budushchee Rossii. Myslit' prostranstvom*, 2nd ed. (Moscow: Arktogeia-tsentr, 2000), 188–89, 256.

91. Dugin, *Osnovy geopolitiki*, 197, 216, 255, 258. For a discussion of these ambivalences in Dugin's thinking, see Laruelle, *Russian Eurasiansim*, 107–44.

CONTRIBUTORS

Mark Bassin is research professor of the history of ideas, in the Center for Baltic and East European Studies at Södertörn University in Stockholm. His research focuses on problems of space, ideology, and identity in Russia and Germany. He is the author of *Imperial Visions: Nationalist Imagination and Geographical Expansion in the Russian Far East, 1840–1865* (Cambridge, 1999) and has coedited the collections *Soviet and Post-Soviet Identities* (Cambridge, 2012); *Space, Place, and Power in Modern Russia: Essays in the New Spatial History* (Northern Illinois University Press, 2010); and *Geografiya i Identichnost' v Postsovetskoy Rossii* (St. Petersburg, 2003). Mark is currently directing the research project *The Vision of Eurasia*, financed by the Baltic Sea Foundation (2013–2016).

Martin Beisswenger is an assistant professor in history at the National Research University—Higher School of Economics in Moscow. His fields of interest are the history of Eurasianism, the history of Russian and European thought, and the intellectual history of European unification. He is the author of articles and book chapters on Eurasianism and other aspects of the intellectual history of the postrevolutionary Russian emigration as well as of a bibliography of P. N. Savitskii's published works. He is currently revising his doctoral dissertation, an intellectual biography of P. N. Savitskii, for publication.

Sergey Glebov is assistant professor of Russian history at Smith College and Amherst College. He holds an MA degree in nationalism studies from the Central European University in Budapest and a PhD in history from Rutgers University. His publications includes a documentary history of the Eurasianist movement (*Evraziistvo mezhdu imperiei i modernom*, Moscow, 2009). Glebov is also a founding editor of *Ab Imperio: Studies in Nationalism and New Imperial History in the Post-Soviet Space*.

Hama Yukiko is a research fellow at the Institute of International and Cultural Studies, Tsuda College, Tokyo. Her fields of specialization are international history and ideologies in Russia. She is currently working on a comparative studies of *pan*-movements during the interwar period. She has published a monograph, *What Is Eurasianism?* (Seibunsha, 2010), based on her PhD dissertation, and has written articles and book chapters on Eurasianism, as well as some comparative studies of Eurasianism and Japan's Pan-Asianism.

Marlene Laruelle is the director of the Central Asia Program and a research professor of international affairs at the Institute for European, Russian, and Eurasian Studies (IERES), Elliott School of International Affairs, the George Washington University, Washington, DC. She has been working on identity politics and Russian nationalism since the 1990s and has published on Eurasianism in French and Russian. In English she has authored *Russian Eurasianism: An Ideology of Empire* (Johns Hopkins University Press, 2008), *In the Name of the Nation: Nationalism and Politics in Contemporary Russia* (Palgrave, 2009), and *Russia's Strategies in the Arctic and the Future of the Far North* (M. E. Sharpe, 2013). She is currently working on a study of Russian nationalism.

Olga Maiorova is associate professor of Russian literature and history at the University of Michigan. She specializes on the Russian empire-nation problem and the intersections between literature, intellectual history, and representations of nationality, especially in the context of Imperial Russia. Her book *From the Shadow of Empire: Defining the Russian Nation through Cultural Mythology, 1855–1870* (Wisconsin University Press, 2010) examines how Russian writers, journalists, and scholars from across the political spectrum embarked on a major project of rendering the multiethnic empire in increasingly nationalistic, Russian terms. Her current project, "Ambiguous Encounter: Russia's National Self-Perception and the Cultural Appropriation of Central Asia," examines fictional and non-fictional accounts focused on Central Asia, which came under the Romanovs' complete control by the late nineteenth century.

Harsha Ram is associate professor of Slavic languages and literatures and comparative literature at the University of California, Berkeley. He is the author of *The Imperial Sublime: A Russian Poetics of Empire* (University of Wisconsin Press, 2003) and is currently working on a monograph-length study of Russian-Georgian cultural relations during the imperial and early Soviet periods. Other articles by him on the Eurasian problematic include "The Poetics of Eurasia: Velimir Khlebnikov between Empire and Revolution," in *Social Identities in Revolutionary Russia*, edited by Madhavan K. Palat (Palgrave, 2001), and "Imagining Eurasia: The Poetics and Ideology of Olzhas Suleimenov's *AZ i IA*," *Slavic Review* 60, no. 2 (summer 2001).

Vera Tolz is Sir William Mather Professor of Russian Studies at the University of Manchester. She has published widely on various aspects of Russian nationalism and identity politics past and present and on the relationship between intellectuals and the state in the imperial and Soviet periods. Her books include *"Russia's Own Orient": The Politics of Identity and Oriental Studies in the Late Imperial and Early Soviet Periods* (2011); (coeditor) *Gender and Nation in Contemporary Europe* (2005); *Russia: Inventing the Nation* (2001); (coeditor) *European Democratization since 1800* (2000); and *Russian Academicians and the Revolution* (1997). Together with Professor Stephen Hutchings, she recently completed a three-year project on Russian television representation of interethnic cohesion issues, which was funded by the UK's Arts and Humanities Research Council. Their coauthored book *Nation, Ethnicity and Race on Russian Television* will be published by Routledge in 2015.

Igor Torbakov is a senior fellow at the Center for Russian and Eurasian Studies at Uppsala University and at the Center for Baltic and East European Studies at Södertörn University in Stockholm, Sweden. A trained historian, he specializes in Russian and Eurasian history and politics. He was a research scholar at the Institute of Russian History, Russian Academy of Sciences in Moscow; a visiting scholar at the Kennan Institute (Woodrow Wilson International Center for Scholars) in Washington, DC; a Fulbright scholar at Columbia University; a visiting fellow at Harvard University; a fellow at the Swedish Collegium for Advanced Study; senior fellow at the Finnish Institute of International Affairs in Helsinki; and a visiting fellow at the German Council on Foreign Relations in Berlin. He holds an MA in history from Moscow State University and a PhD from the Ukrainian Academy of Sciences. His recent publications discussed the history of Russian nationalism, the linkages between Russia's domestic politics and foreign policy, Russian-Ukrainian relations, and the politics of history and memory wars in Eastern Europe.

Stefan Wiederkehr is the head of Collections and Archives at the ETH-Bibliothek in Zurich, Switzerland. Before, he held research positions at the German Historical Institute Warsaw, Poland, and the Berlin-Brandenburg Academy of Sciences and Humanities, Germany. His publications include *Die* *eurasische Bewegung: Wissenschaft und Politik in der russischen Emigration der Zwischenkriegszeit und im postsowjetischen Russland* (2007); *Lithuania and Ruthenia: Studies of a Transcultural Communication Zone (15th–18th Centuries)* (coeditor, 2007); *Sport zwischen Ost und West: Beiträge zur Sportgeschichte Osteuropas im 19. und 20. Jahrhundert* (coeditor, 2007); *Expert Cultures in Central Eastern Europe: The Internationalization of Knowledge and the Transformation of Nation States since World War I* (co-editor, 2010); and numerous articles on Russian intellectual history.

INDEX

Tufan, 107
Turan, 22, 23, 24, 25, 60
Turkestan, 37, 64, 70, 81, 131
Turkey, 9, 164
Turkic peoples, 23, 139, 169, 170, 174, 179
Turkmen, 13
Turks, 53, 143, 180, 183, 185, 201n42
Tuva, 188
Tver, 174

Ukraine, 3, 81, 115–21, 123–26, 131–32, 192, 230n13, 231n32, 234nn42–43, 234n48
Ukrainians, 41, 115, 118–21, 123, 124, 132, 134, 201n42, 232n32, 233n41, 235n51, 235n54
United States of America, 2, 3, 6, 21, 38, 73, 81, 116, 122, 156, 160
Ural Mountains, 69, 81
Uyghurs, 74
Uzbek, khan, 171–172, 174

Vernadskaia, Nina Petrovna, 122
Vernadskii, Ivan Vasil'evich, 123
Vernadsky, Georgii Vladimirovich (George), 3, 5, 9, 10, 11, 30, 33, 36, 37, 69, 71, 72, 73, 113–19, 121–24, 131, 134–36, 206n55, 229n10, 230n13, 230nn15–16, 231n23, 233n41, 240n92, 241n103, 250n10, 250n12
Vernadsky, Vladimir Ivanovich, 3, 69, 115, 119, 121, 122, 123, 124, 233n41, 234nn42–43, 234n48, 235n51, 235n54, 250n12

Versty, journal, 4, 8
Vienna, 51, 164
Vilnius, 113
Vipper, Robert Yur'evich, 50
Vladimir, city of, 173–74
Vladimir, Grand Prince of Kiev, 142, 173
Vladivostok, 73, 155–56
Volga, 42, 167, 169
Voloshin, Maksimilian Aleksandrovich, 140, 242n5
Volynia, 73
Vozha, river, 172

Weber, Max, 111
Weimar Republic, 1, 158
Westernizers, 15–16, 151–52
White Sea, 70, 144
Wilson, Woodrow, 5, 38, 128, 237n70
Wrangell, Petr Nikolaevich, Baron, 3, 4, 65, 121

Xinjiang, 156

Yalta, 51
Yarkand, 107
Yellow Sea, 144
Yenisei, 71
Yugoslavia, 3

Zaitsev, Arsenii Aleksandrovich, 4
Zenkovsky, Vasilii Vasil'evich, 125
Ziuganov, Gennadii Andreevich, 165